PostgreSQL 8
for Windows

RICHARD BLUM

New York Chicago San Francisco
Lisbon London Madrid Mexico City
Milan New Delhi San Juan
Seoul Singapore Sydney Toronto

Library of Congress Cataloging-in-Publication Data

Blum, Richard.
  PostgreSQL 8 for Windows / Richard Blum.
    p. cm.
  ISBN 0-07-148562-7 (alk. paper)
  1. Database management. 2. PostgreSQL. I. Title.
  QA76.9.D3B583 2007
  005.74--dc22

                                        2007007201

McGraw-Hill books are available at special quantity discounts to use as premiums and sales promotions, or for use in corporate training programs. For more information, please write to the Director of Special Sales, Professional Publishing, McGraw-Hill, Two Penn Plaza, New York, NY 10121-2298. Or contact your local bookstore.

PostgreSQL 8 for Windows

1234567890 FGR FGR 01987

ISBN-13:   978-0-07-148562-3
ISBN-10:   0-07-148562-7

Sponsoring Editor
  Lisa McClain
Editorial Supervisor
  Jody McKenzie
Project Manager
  Vasundhara Sawhney
Acquisitions Coordinator
  Mandy Canales
Technical Editor
  Michael Wessler

Copy Editor
  Bill McManus
Proofreader
  Malvika Shyam
Indexer
  Kevin Broccoli
Production Supervisor
  Jean Bodeaux
Composition
  International Typesetting
  and Composition

Illustration
  International Typesetting
  and Composition
Art Director, Cover
  Jeff Weeks
Cover Designer
  Jeff Weeks

To Tony Amico. Not only was I fortunate enough to have
a knowledgeable mentor in my chosen profession, but to have the same
mentor guide me through yet another profession was truly a blessing.
Thanks Tony for all your help and guidance in both my system
administration and writing careers. Enjoy retirement. "For the LORD gives
wisdom, and from his mouth come knowledge and understanding."
Proverbs 2:6 (NIV)

ABOUT THE AUTHOR

Richard Blum has worked for more than 18 years for a large U.S. government organization as a network and systems administrator. During this time he has administered Unix, Linux, Novell, and Microsoft servers and has helped to design and maintain a 3500-user network utilizing Cisco switches and routers.

Rich has a BS in Electrical Engineering and an MS in Management, specializing in Management Information Systems, from Purdue University. He is the author of several books, including *sendmail for Linux* (Sams Publishing, 2000), *Running qmail* (Sams Publishing, 2000), *Postfix* (Sams Publishing, 2001), *Open Source E-mail Security* (Sams Publishing, 2001), *C# Network Programming* (Sybex, 2002), *Network Performance Open Source Toolkit* (John Wiley & Sons, 2003), and *Professional Assembly Language Programming* (Wrox, 2005).

When he is not being a computer nerd, Rich plays electric bass for the church worship and praise band and enjoys spending time with his wife Barbara and daughters Katie Jane, and Jessica.

About the Technical Editor

Michael Wessler received his BS in Computer Technology from Purdue University. He is an Oracle Certified Database Administrator for 8 and 8*i*, an Oracle Certified Web Administrator for 9*i*AS, and a 10*g* Database Technician. He has administered Oracle on Windows and various flavors of Unix and Linux, including clustered Oracle Parallel Server (OPS) environments. Currently his focus is managing Oracle Web Application Server environments for various government and private-sector organizations. Michael can be reached at mwessler@yahoo.com.

CONTENTS

Part I
Installation and Administration

Part II

Using PostgreSQL in Windows

Part III

Windows Programming with PostgreSQL

ACKNOWLEDGMENTS

First, all glory and praise go to God, who through His Son makes all things possible, and gives us the gift of eternal life.

Many thanks go to the great team of people at McGraw-Hill for their outstanding work on this project. Thanks to Lisa McClain, Sponsoring Editor, for offering me the opportunity to write this book. Also thanks to Alex McDonald, the original Acquisitions Coordinator for the book, and to Mandy Canales, who took over from Alex during the production of this book, for keeping things on track and helping make this book presentable. I am forever indebted to Mike Wessler, the Technical Editor, for his database expertise and guidance. Thanks Mike for catching my goofs, and making suggestions for improvements throughout the book. Any leftover mistakes are completely my fault. I would also like to thank Carole McClendon at Waterside Productions, Inc. for arranging this opportunity for me, and for helping out in my writing career.

Finally, I would like to thank my parents, Mike and Joyce Blum, for their dedication and support while raising me, and to my wife Barbara and daughters Katie Jane, and Jessica for their love, patience, and understanding, especially while I was writing this book.

INTRODUCTION

D atabases have become a necessity for almost any application. The ability to store and quickly retrieve information is a hallmark of the personal computer revolution. Everything from store inventories to bowling league scores is kept in databases, often on personal computers.

For most Windows users, the word *database* is synonymous with the Microsoft Access product. Microsoft Access provides a simple graphical interface for creating data tables, and the reports necessary to view the data. However, Access has its limitations, especially in a multi-user environment. This book shows how to overcome these limitations by using the PostgreSQL Open Source database software.

OVERVIEW

While a mainstay in the Linux world, Open Source software is slowly starting to make inroads into the Microsoft Windows world. Windows users and developers can now download and install many Open Source applications compiled specifically for the Windows environment. Starting with version 8.0, the PostgreSQL database server package includes an easy-to-install Windows version. Now any Windows user and developer can incorporate PostgreSQL's commercial-quality database features at no cost.

This book describes the PostgreSQL database server, and how to use it in a Windows environment. If this is your first time using a large-scale database server, you will be amazed at how easy it is to create and manage your own database server. You will quickly see the benefits of moving your databases from an Access database to a PostgreSQL database server. You can even keep your Access applications while utilizing the PostgreSQL database server to control your data.

If you are a seasoned Windows database administrator, you may be pleasantly surprised at the features and resources available in PostgreSQL. PostgreSQL provides both commercial-quality database features, such as transactions, triggers, and stored procedures, and programming interfaces for all of the common programming languages used in the Windows environment. This book shows detailed examples of how to create programs in several common Windows programming languages that can access a PostgreSQL database server.

HOW THIS BOOK IS ORGANIZED

This book is organized into three sections. The first section, "Installation and Administration," guides you through installing a basic PostgreSQL server and learning how to manage databases, schemas, and tables within the server.

Chapter 1, "What is PostgreSQL?" compares PostgreSQL to other Open Source and commercial database packages. The basic ideas behind why you would switch to PostgreSQL are presented, allowing you to decide for yourself if PostgreSQL is right for you.

Chapter 2, "Installing PostgreSQL on Windows," walks you through the steps required to get a PostgreSQL server installed and running on your Windows platform.

Chapter 3, "The PostgreSQL Files and Programs," describes the file and folder structure PostgreSQL uses on the Windows platform for storing database data, utilities, and library files. The various command-prompt PostgreSQL utilities installed with the server software are also discussed.

Chapter 4, "Managing PostgreSQL on Windows," shows how to use the pgAdmin III graphical administration tool to create new databases, schemas, tables, and user accounts. Knowing how to use pgAdmin III makes administering a PostgreSQL database server easy, and can save you lots of time because you do not have to use SQL commands to create these items.

The second section, "Using PostgreSQL in Windows," demonstrates how to use the `psql` command-line program to manually execute SQL commands on the PostgreSQL server. This section also discusses the basic and advanced SQL features supported by PostgreSQL.

Chapter 5, "The psql Program," describes the command-line `psql` program and demonstrates how to use it to get PostgreSQL server information and execute SQL commands.

Chapter 6, "Using Basic SQL," provides a primer for novice database users on how to use SQL commands to create tables and login accounts, and then insert, delete, and query data within the tables.

Chapter 7, "Using Advanced SQL," shows how views and transactions can be used to help simplify SQL queries and to ensure data integrity within the database.

Chapter 8, "PostgreSQL Functions," walks through the built-in functions available in PostgreSQL, as well as demonstrates how to create your own functions that can be used by database users.

Chapter 9, "Stored Procedures and Triggers," dives into the complicated world of creating functions that automatically execute based on database events, such as inserting or deleting data from a table.

Chapter 10, "Security," covers the important aspects of protecting your database data and tracking user access to your data.

Chapter 11, "Performance," closes out the section by providing some information and tips on how to monitor and possibly increase the performance of your PostgreSQL server.

The last section of the book, "Windows Programming with PostgreSQL," is intended to show developers how to access and use a PostgreSQL database server in various Windows programming environments.

Chapter 12, "Microsoft Access and PostgreSQL," provides detailed instructions on how to access a PostgreSQL database from a Microsoft Access application. Instructions are also provided on how to covert an existing Access database application to a PostgreSQL server, and how to use an existing Access application with a PostgreSQL database.

Chapter 13, "Microsoft .NET Framework," demonstrates how to create .NET applications using Visual Basic .NET and C# that can access data on a PostgreSQL server. Details on how to install and use the PostgreSQL Npgsql library are shown.

Chapter 14, "Visual C++," helps more advanced programmers who are comfortable with the Microsoft Visual C++ product to interface their programs with a PostgreSQL server. The PostgreSQL libpq library is presented, showing how to install and use the library with Visual C++ programs.

Chapter 15, "Java," walks Java programmers through the steps required to use the PostgreSQL JDBC driver to access a PostgreSQL server from a Java application. Both the Java command-line interface and the Java NetBeans graphical development environment are demonstrated.

WHO SHOULD READ THIS BOOK

This book is primarily intended for Windows users who are searching for a simple, full-featured database for their applications. Now that PostgreSQL fully supports the Windows environment, incorporating a PostgreSQL server into Windows applications is an easy process. The goal of the book is to help both novice and professional Windows database developers become familiar with the PostgreSQL database, and demonstrate how to convert existing Windows database applications to a PostgreSQL database.

The book can also be used by experienced PostgreSQL database administrators who are interested in porting existing PostgreSQL applications into the Windows environment. With the popularity of the Windows workstation platform, being able to write Windows applications that can access your PostgreSQL database server (running either on a Windows platform or a Unix/Linux platform) can greatly increase your customer base.

PART I

Installation and
Administration

CHAPTER 1

What Is PostgreSQL?

There have always been a handful of different commercial database systems available for Microsoft Windows users and developers to choose from. The choices vary widely, from simple user database systems such as Microsoft's Access or FoxPro to more advanced systems such as Microsoft's SQL Server, IBM's DB2, or the Oracle suite of database software packages. However, now there's yet another player in the Microsoft database world.

If you are new to Open Source software, you may not have ever heard of the PostgreSQL database system. It has been around in the Unix and Linux worlds for quite some time, gathering quite a following of users and developers. Unfortunately, in earlier versions of PostgreSQL you had to be pretty knowledgeable and computer-savvy to get PostgreSQL to work on a Windows platform. This left PostgreSQL as an unknown for most Windows database users. However, as of PostgreSQL version 8, installing and running PostgreSQL in Windows is a snap. Now any Windows developer and common user can create professional databases using the high-quality, free PostgreSQL package.

This chapter introduces PostgreSQL, and explains the myriad of features available that make it a great choice for both Windows application developers and normal Windows users when creating database applications. You will see that just because a software package is free doesn't mean that it cannot compete with high-quality, expensive commercial products.

THE OPEN SOURCE MOVEMENT

Usually Windows developers and users reach for commercial products as the first solution to provide software for projects. The term "free software" conjures up memories from the old days of sloppily written freeware, packages with pop-up advertisements in them, or limited shareware applications. The Open Source movement cannot be farther from that concept. Open Source projects are written by teams of both amateur and professional programmers working to produce commercial-quality applications, mostly for the love of programming.

One of the first misconceptions of Windows users when starting out with Open Source software is the definition of the term *free*. The free part of Open Source is more related to sharing than price. Under Open Source software rules, a company or organization is allowed to charge a price for distributing Open Source software (although many do not). The free part comes from the program source code being freely sharable to anyone who wants to view and modify it.

Since sharing is the cornerstone of Open Source, any modifications made to Open Source code must also be shared. This process encourages improvements and feature enhancements from both developers and users. Many programmers feel this is the main reason Open Source software has enjoyed the popularity it has. This method of sharing new ideas quickly propels simple software ideas into mainstream applications.

There are many different types of licenses that Open Source software is released under. The most popular is the GNU General Public License (GPL). The GNU organization (www.gnu.org) supports Open Source software projects, and has published the GPL as a guide for how Open Source projects should be licensed to the public. If you have had any dealings with the popular Linux operating system, no doubt you have heard of the GPL. The GPL stipulates that any changes made to an Open Source project's code must be publicly published and available at no cost. While this is great for hobbyists and academics, it can cause problems for commercial organizations wanting to use Open Source code.

The developers of PostgreSQL have decided to release PostgreSQL under a slightly different Open Source license. PostgreSQL uses the BSD license, developed at the University of California (UC), Berkeley for public projects. This license is less restrictive than the GPL. It allows organizations to modify the code for internal use without being bound to publicly release the changes. This allows corporations (and private users as well) to use PostgreSQL however they want. This has provided a catalyst for many companies to use the PostgreSQL database as an internal database engine for many different commercial applications, as well as using PostgreSQL as the back-end database for some web sites.

Under the BSD license, the developers of PostgreSQL are able to provide PostgreSQL free of charge at the same time that a few companies provide their versions of PostgreSQL as a for-profit commercial product. If you want to use PostgreSQL as-is on your own, you are free to download it and use it for whatever purposes you want. If you want to use PostgreSQL for a high-visibility production application that requires 24-hour support, you are able to purchase it from a company that provides such services. This is the best of both worlds.

THE HISTORY OF POSTGRESQL

To fully appreciate PostgreSQL, it helps to know where it came from. PostgreSQL started life as an academic database project at UC Berkeley. Professor Michael Stonebraker is credited as the father of PostgreSQL. In 1986 he started a project (then called Postgres) as a follow-up to another popular database packaged called Ingres. Ingres started out as an academic project to prove theoretical database concepts about relational database structures. In relational database theory, data is arranged in tables. Tables of data can be connected together by related data. This was a radical idea, compared to the existing types of database models at the time.

A classic example of a relational database is a typical store computer system. This database must contain information on the store's customers, the products it carries, and the current inventory. It must also keep track of orders made by customers. In the past, all of this data would be jumbled together in multiple data files, often duplicating information between the files.

In relational database theory, data is divided into separate groups, called tables. Customer information is stored in the Customer table. The Customer table contains data pertinent to a customer, such as the customer name, address, and billing information. Each customer is assigned a unique ID in the Customer table, with each customer record

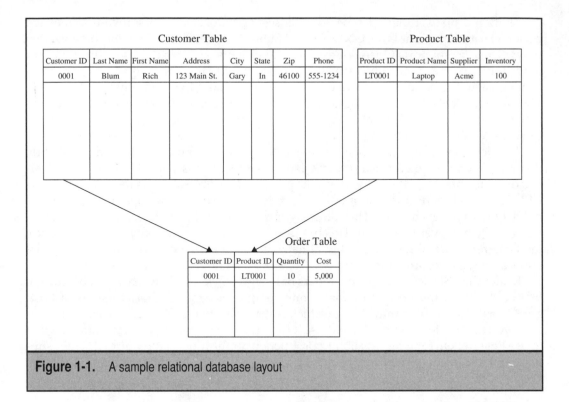

Customer Table

Customer ID	Last Name	First Name	Address	City	State	Zip	Phone
0001	Blum	Rich	123 Main St.	Gary	In	46100	555-1234

Product Table

Product ID	Product Name	Supplier	Inventory
LT0001	Laptop	Acme	100

Order Table

Customer ID	Product ID	Quantity	Cost
0001	LT0001	10	5,000

Figure 1-1.   A sample relational database layout

being a separate row in the Customer table. Similarly, product data is stored in a separate Product table. The Product table contains detailed information about each product, including a unique product ID, with each product being a separate row of data in the Product table. This is demonstrated in Figure 1-1.

As shown in Figure 1-1, to track orders, database programmers create a separate Order table using the unique IDs from the Customer and Product tables. The Order table relates a customer to the products that are bought. This relationship shows that a single customer can be related to multiple product orders, but each product order belongs to a single customer.

Ingres was one of the first database products available to handle these types of data relationships. With its success, Ingres quickly became a commercial product, and Dr. Stonebraker started working on another database system. Postgres was started in a similar manner as Ingres, attempting to prove the academic theory of object-relational databases.

Object-relational databases take relational databases one step further. In object-oriented programming, data can inherit properties from other data, called a *parent*. The object-oriented principle of inheritance is applied in object-relational databases. Tables can inherit fields from base tables (also called parent tables). For example, a database table of cars can inherit properties (fields) from a parent table of vehicles. This is demonstrated in Figure 1-2.

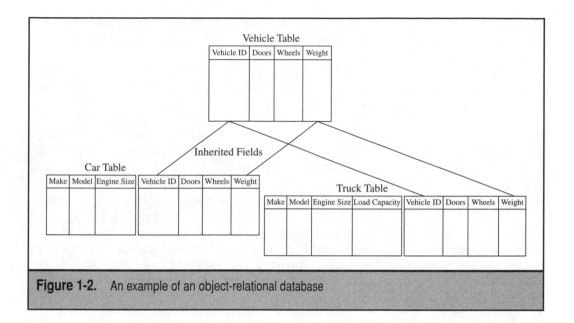

Figure 1-2. An example of an object-relational database

Since cars are a type of vehicle, they inherit the properties (or in this case database fields) of their parent, the Vehicle table. When inserting data into the Car table, you can also specify values from the Vehicle table. Querying the Car table will return fields from both the Vehicle and Car tables. However, querying the Vehicle table only returns fields from that table, not the Car table.

After several years of development work on Postgres, the database package came upon a major change. A couple of Dr. Stonebraker's students modified Postgres by adding the Structured Query Language (SQL) interface (early versions of Postgres used their own data query language). In 1995 this package was re-released as Postgres95. Due to the rising popularity of SQL, the Postgres95 release helped Postgres migrate into the mainstream of database products.

It was clear that they had another hit product on their hands. Instead of going commercial, in 1996 the Postgres95 project team broke off from UC Berkeley and started life as an Open Source project, open to the world to modify. At the same time, to emphasize its newfound SQL capabilities, Postgres95 was renamed PostgreSQL (pronounced post-gres-Q-L). Also, to emphasize its past history, the first Open Source version of PostgreSQL was labeled as version 6.0.

Vast improvements have been made to PostgreSQL since its first release in 1996. Many modern database features have been added to make each release of PostgreSQL faster, more robust, and more user-friendly. For Windows users, the biggest PostgreSQL feature appeared in 2005 with the release of version 8.0.

Prior to version 8.0, PostgreSQL lived its life primarily in the Unix world. Developers wanting to experiment with PostgreSQL on a Windows platform had to perform some amazing feats of code compilation to get it to even work halfway. This prevented most ordinary Windows users from being able to utilize PostgreSQL's advanced features. This all changed in version 8.0.

Starting with version 8.0, PostgreSQL has incorporated a complete version for Windows, including an easy installation program. Suddenly, installing PostgreSQL on a Windows workstation or server is as easy as installing any other Windows software package.

Since its release to the Windows platform, PostgreSQL has been bundled with several Windows-based GUI administration and utility tools to help Windows developers work with PostgreSQL. The pgAdmin program provides a fully graphical environment for database administration. An administrator can create databases, tables, and users simply with mouse clicks. Similarly, the pSQL program provides a command-line interface (CLI) for users and administrators to enter SQL commands to databases, and view results.

Also, not to forget Windows developers, the PostgreSQL community has provided programming interfaces to access PostgreSQL databases from common Windows programming languages. Developers have produced an Open Database Connectivity (ODBC) driver for PostgreSQL, which provides a common interface for all applications that utilize ODBC database connectivity. Similarly, application program interfaces (APIs) for the .NET and Java programming environments were developed to allow .NET and Java programmers direct access to the PostgreSQL server. These features provide a wealth of possibilities for Windows programmers wanting to work with PostgreSQL.

COMPARING POSTGRESQL

As mentioned earlier, the Windows user has a vast selection of database products to choose from. You may be asking why you should choose PostgreSQL over any of the other products. This section helps clarify where PostgreSQL fits into the Windows database product world. Hopefully you will see how PostgreSQL competes against all of the other Windows database products, and choose to use PostgreSQL in your next Windows database project.

PostgreSQL Versus Microsoft Access

Microsoft Access is by far the most popular end-user database tool developed for Windows. Many Windows users, from professional accountants to bowling league secretaries, use Access to track data. It provides an easy, intuitive user interface, allowing novice computer users to quickly produce queries and reports with little effort.

However, despite its user-friendliness, Access has its limitations. To fully understand how PostgreSQL differs from Access, you must first understand how database systems are organized.

There is more to a database than just a bunch of data files. Most databases incorporate several layers of files, programs, and utilities, which all interact to provide the database experience. The whole package is referred to as a *database management system (DBMS)*.

While there are different types of DBMS packages, they all basically contain the following parts:

▼ A database engine

■ One or more database files

■ An internal data dictionary

▲ A query language interface

The database engine is the heart and brains of the DBMS. It controls all access to the data, which is stored in the database files. Any application (including the DBMS itself) that requires access to data must go through the database engine. This is shown in Figure 1-3.

As shown in Figure 1-3, queries and reports talk to the database engine to retrieve data from the database files. The database engine is responsible for reading the query, interpreting the query, checking the database file based on the query, and producing the results of the query. These actions are all accomplished within the program code of the database engine. The interaction between the database engine and database files is crucial.

The internal data dictionary is used by the database engine to define how the database operates, the type of data that can be stored in the database files, and the structure of the database. It basically defines the rules used for the DBMS. Each DBMS has its own data dictionary.

If you are a user running a simple database on Access, you probably don't even realize you are using a database engine. Access keeps much of the DBMS work under the hood and away from users. When you start Access, the database engine starts, and when you stop Access, the database engine stops.

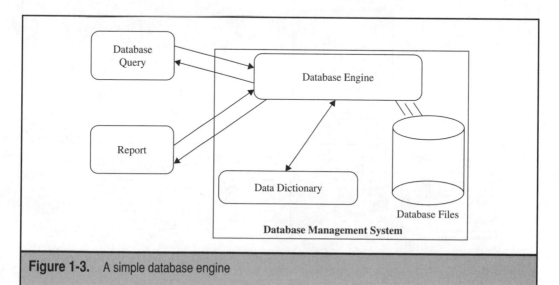

Figure 1-3. A simple database engine

In PostgreSQL, the database engine runs as a service that is always running in the background. Users run separate application programs that interface with the database engine while it's running. Each application can send queries to the database engine, and process the results returned. When the application stops, the PostgreSQL database engine continues to run in the background, waiting for the next application to access it.

Both Access and PostgreSQL require one or more database files to be present to hold data. If you work with Access, no doubt you have seen the .mdb database files. These files contain the data defined in tables created in the Access database. Each database has its own data file. Copying a database is as easy as copying the .mdb file to another location. Things are a little different in PostgreSQL.

In PostgreSQL the database files are tied into the database engine, and are never handled by users. All of the database work is done behind the database engine, so separating data files from the database engine is not recommended. To copy a PostgreSQL database, you must perform a special action (called an *export*) to export the database data to another database.

This shows a major philosophical difference between Access and PostgreSQL. The difference between the two products becomes even more evident when you want to share your data between multiple users.

In the Access environment, if two or more people want to share a database, the database .mdb file must be located on a shared network drive available to all users. Each user has a copy of the Access program running on the local workstation, which points to the common database file. This is shown in Figure 1-4.

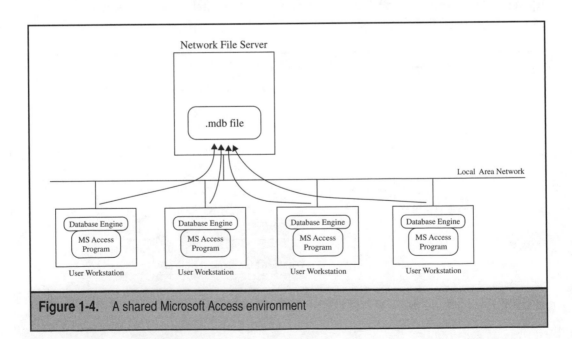

Figure 1-4.   A shared Microsoft Access environment

Where this model falls apart is how queries or reports are run from the separate workstations. Since the Access database engine is part of the Access program, each user is running a separate database engine, pointing to the same data file. This can have disastrous effects, especially on the Local Area Network (LAN).

Each query and report requires the database engine to search through the database files looking for the appropriate data. When this action occurs on a local workstation, it's not too big of a deal. When this action occurs across a LAN, large amounts of data are continually passed between the database engine and database files through the network. This can quickly clog even the most robust network configurations, especially when ten or more users are actively querying a database, and even more so as Access databases become large (remember, the database engine must check lots of records for the query result, even if the query matches only one record).

In the PostgreSQL model, the database engine and database files are always on the same computer. Queries and reports are run from a separate application program, which may or may not be located on the same computer as the database engine. A multiuser PostgreSQL environment is demonstrated in Figure 1-5.

Here, the PostgreSQL database engine accepts data requests from multiple users across the network. All of the database access is still performed on the local computer running the PostgreSQL database engine. The query and report code transmitted across the LAN is minimal. Of course, for large data queries the results sent back across the network can be large, but still not nearly as large as in the Access environment.

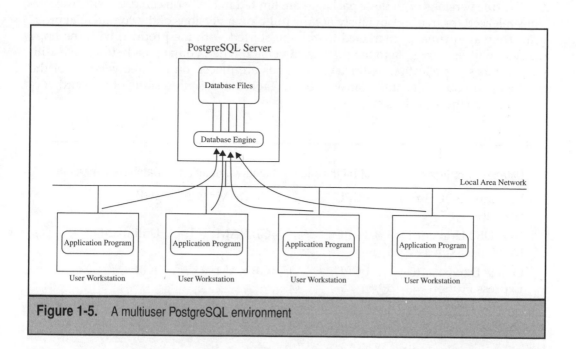

Figure 1-5.   A multiuser PostgreSQL environment

If you are using Access in a multiuser environment, it should be easy to see that Access will not perform as well as PostgreSQL when you get more users. You can scale PostgreSQL to however many users you need to support. Since PostgreSQL can run on many different platforms, you can even build your database using PostgreSQL on a Windows workstation, then easily migrate it to use PostgreSQL running on a powerful Unix server. The PostgreSQL databases will migrate from one server to another with minimal effort. This allows you greater flexibility when expanding office applications.

This feature alone makes PostgreSQL a better database choice in a multiuser database environment. However, with its advanced object-relational database features, PostgreSQL can also outperform Microsoft Access even in simple single-user database projects. If you are considering a multiuser database application, I would strongly encourage you to give PostgreSQL a try. If you are just toying around with a single-user database project, you can still test out PostgreSQL and see if its features can help you out.

PostgreSQL Versus Commercial DBMS Products

Since the availability of free Open Source database packages for Windows platforms, the owners of some popular commercial Windows database packages have changed their worldview. In the past, companies such as Microsoft, IBM, and Oracle made you pay a premium to purchase their database products. Now you can install special versions of the popular Microsoft SQL Server, IBM DB2, and even the Oracle database server free of charge. However, there are some limitations.

The free versions of all these packages are limited in how you can use them. The versions released for free are obviously not the full-blown versions of the commercial products. They are primarily marketed to get you started with the product, with the hope that you will then migrate to the purchased version when you are ready to go live with your database application. Artificial limitations are placed on the free versions of the products, so you can't get too far with them. Table 1-1 describes some of the hardware limitations of these packages.

Database Product	CPU Limitation	Memory Limitation	Database Limitation
Microsoft SQL Server Express	1 CPU	1GB RAM	4GB
IBM DB2 Universal Database Express-C	2 CPUs	4GB RAM	Unlimited
Oracle Database 10*g* Express Edition	1 CPU	1GB RAM	4GB

Table 1-1.   Free Commercial Database Limitations

Besides the hardware limitations, some of these packages put limitations on the software features available in the free version. For example, Microsoft SQL Server Express does not allow you to import or export data from the database. This limitation alone prevents it from being used as a serious production database.

In contrast, with PostgreSQL you get the complete package for free. There are no limitations to how many CPUs, the amount of memory, or the database size you can use. You may be thinking that there must be some catch. Perhaps the full versions of the Open Source packages can't compete with the free versions of the commercial packages. That is not true.

The PostgreSQL database product has most of the same features as the commercial products. Most users and developers won't be able to tell the difference. In fact, PostgreSQL has some features that the commercial packages don't include. The next section describes these features.

POSTGRESQL FEATURES

If you go to the PostgreSQL web site (www.postgresql.org), you will see a list of all the database features supported by PostgreSQL. To the normal computer user, this list can look like a course list for an advanced programming degree. This section walks through some of the advanced features PostgreSQL supports, and explains just exactly what each one means for the common database user.

Transaction Support

All DBMS packages allow users to enter database commands to query and manipulate data. What separates good DBMS packages from bad ones is the way they handle commands.

The DBMS database engine processes commands as a single unit, called a *transaction.* A transaction represents a single data operation on the database. Most simplistic DBMS packages treat each command received, such as adding a new record to a table or modifying an existing record in a table, as a separate transaction. Groups of commands create groups of transactions. However, some DBMS packages (including PostgreSQL) allow for more complicated transactions to be performed.

In some instances, it is necessary for an application to perform multiple commands as a result of a single action. Remember, in relational databases tables can be related to one another. This means that one table can contain data that is related (or tied) to the data in another table. In the store example earlier, the Order table relied on data in both the Customer and Product tables. While this makes organizing data easier, it makes managing transactions more difficult. A single action may require the DBMS to update several data values in several different tables.

In our store example, if a new customer comes into the store and purchases a laptop computer, the DBMS must modify three tables. First, the Customer table must be updated with the information of the new customer. Second, the Order table must be modified to reflect the new order for the laptop. Finally, the Product table must be modified to show that there is now one less laptop in the store inventory. In an advanced DBMS package (such as PostgreSQL), all of these steps can be combined into a single database transaction, which represents the activity of a customer purchasing a laptop.

Of course, with a multistep transaction there are more opportunities for things to go wrong. The trick for any DBMS is to know how to properly handle transactions. This is where the database ACID test comes in.

ACID Compliant

Over the years, database experts have devised rules for how databases should handle transactions. The benchmark of all professional database systems is the ACID test. The ACID test is actually an acronym for a set of database features defining how a professional-quality database should support transactions. These features are as follows:

▼ Atomicity

■ Consistency

■ Isolation

▲ Durability

The ACID tests define a set of standards for ensuring that data is protected in all circumstances. It is crucial for databases to protect data at all cost. Invalid or lost data can render a database useless. The following sections describe each of the features of the ACID test.

Atomicity

The atomicity feature states that for a transaction to be considered successful, all steps within the transaction must complete successfully. For a single command transaction, this is no big deal. The trick comes when handling transactions that contain multiple commands.

In atomicity, either all of the database modification commands within the transaction should be applied to the database, or none of them should. A transaction should not be allowed to complete part-way.

In our store example, it would be a huge problem if the Order table is updated to reflect a purchase without the Product table inventory field being updated to reflect the number of items purchased. The store would have one less laptop in inventory than what the database thought was there.

To support atomicity, PostgreSQL uses a system called commit and rollback. Database modifications are only temporarily performed during a transaction. When it appears that all of the modifications in a transaction would complete successfully, the transaction is committed (all of the data in the affected tables is modified per the transaction commands). If it appears that any of the modifications in the transaction would fail (such as an item not being in the Product table), the transaction is rolled back (any previous steps that were successful are reversed). This ensures that the transaction is completed as a whole.

PostgreSQL uses the two-phase commit approach to committing transactions. The two-phase commit performs the transaction using two steps (or phases):

1. A prepare phase where a transaction is analyzed to determine if the database is able to commit the entire transaction.
2. A commit phase, where the transaction is physically committed to the database.

The two-phase commit approach allows PostgreSQL to test all transaction commands during the prepare phase without having to modify any data in the actual tables. Table data is not changed until the commit phase is complete.

Consistency

The concept of consistency is a little more difficult than atomicity. The consistency feature states that every transaction should leave the database in a valid state. The tricky part here is what is considered a "valid state." For most simple databases, this is not an issue. Transactions that update or modify simple tables are usually not a problem.

Often this feature is used when advanced rules or triggers are present in a database for defining how data is stored (we will talk more about these in the "Rules" and "Triggers" sections later in this chapter). For now, it is sufficient to know that rules and triggers are internal database functions that occur based on a specific activity on data in a table.

Developers create triggers to ensure that data is entered into the database correctly, such as ensuring that each record in the Customer table contains a valid phone number. If a customer record is added to the Customer table without a phone number entry, a trigger can cause the record to be rejected by the DBMS.

Consistency states that all rules and triggers are applied properly to a transaction. If any rule or trigger fails, the transaction is not committed to the database. For our example, if a store clerk attempts to add a new customer record without a phone number, the trigger would prevent the record from being added, causing the transaction to fail, thus preserving the integrity of the customer record.

Consistency can also be applied to multiple tables. For example, a developer can create a rule for the Order table that automatically updates a Billing table with the cost of a customer's order. What would happen if an order was inserted into the Order table, but the database system crashed before the rule could update the Billing table? Free products are good for customers, but a bad way to do business for the store.

To meet the ACID consistency test, an entry into the Order table should not be made until it is certain that the database rule creating an entry in the Billing table was completed. This ensures that the data in the two tables remains consistent.

Isolation

The isolation feature is required for multiuser databases. When there is more than one person modifying data in a database, odd things can happen. If two people attempt to modify the same data value at the same time, who is to say which value is the final value?

When more than one person attempts to access the same data, the DBMS must act as a traffic cop, directing who gets access to the data first. Isolation ensures that each transaction in progress is invisible to any other transaction that is in progress. The DBMS must allow each transaction to complete, and then decide which transaction value is the final value for the data. This is accomplished by a technique called *locking*.

Locking does what it says; it locks data while a transaction is being committed to the database. While the data is locked, other users are not able to access the data, not even for queries. This prevents multiple users from querying or modifying the data while it is in a locked mode. There are two basic levels of locking that can be performed on table data:

▼ Table-level locking

▲ Record-level locking

Early DBMS implementations used table-level locking. Any time a user required a modification to a record in a table, the entire table was locked, preventing other users from even viewing data in the table. In some database implementations the lock produces an error event, while in others, the database engine just waits its turn in line to access the data. It's not hard to see that this method has its limitations. In a multiuser environment, it would be frustrating to be continually locked out of your database table while updates were being made by other users.

To help solve the table-level locking problem, most modern DBMS packages use record-level locking. This method allows access to most of the table; only the record that contains the value being modified is locked. The rest of the table is available for other users to view and even modify.

Although using record-level locking helps, it still does not solve the problem of when two users want to modify the same data at the same time. PostgreSQL, however, takes record locking a step further. PostgreSQL uses a technique called Multiversion Concurrency Control (MVCC).

MVCC uses a sophisticated locking system that, to the user, does not appear to lock records at all. To accomplish this, PostgreSQL maintains multiple versions of records that are being updated. If an update is made to a record that is currently in use, PostgreSQL keeps the new (updated) version of the record on hold, allowing queries to use the current version of the record. When the record becomes available, PostgreSQL applies the new version to the record, updating the table. If multiple updates are being made on a record, PostgreSQL keeps each version on hold, and applies the latest version to the record. To users and application programs, at least some version of the record is always available.

This feature in itself allows for other features to be included in PostgreSQL. Since no records are ever locked, a backup copy of any table can be made without stopping the DBMS. This technique is called *online backups* (also called *hot backups*). It ensures that every database backup contains a copy of every record in the table, even the ones currently in use. Not having to take a database down for backups is a great feature for high-demand production environments that do business 24 hours a day.

Durability

The durability feature is a must for a modern-day DBMS. It states that once a transaction is committed to the database, it must not be lost. While this sounds like a simple concept, in reality durability is often harder to ensure than it sounds.

Durability means being able to withstand both hardware and software failures. A database is useless if a power outage or server crash compromises the data stored in the database.

The basic feature for durability is obviously good database backups. As was mentioned in the "Isolation" section, PostgreSQL allows administrators to back up databases at any time without affecting users.

However, databases are usually only backed up once a day, so what about protecting transactions that occur during the day? If a customer comes into the store in the morning to order a new laptop, you wouldn't want to lose that information if the database server crashes that afternoon before the evening backup.

While it is impossible to account for every type of disaster, PostgreSQL does its best to prepare for them. To solve this situation, every transaction that operates on the database is placed into a separate log file as the database engine processes it. This is demonstrated in Figure 1-6.

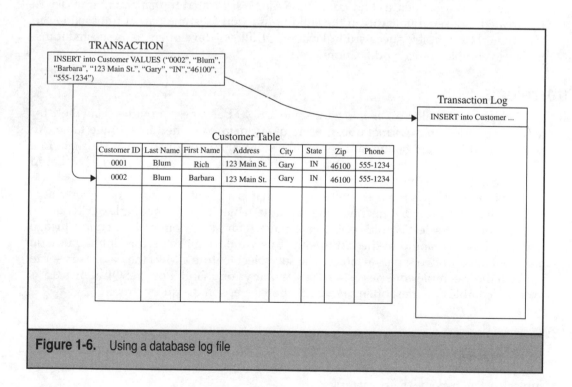

Figure 1-6. Using a database log file

The log file only contains transactions made to the database since the last database backup. If for some reason the database becomes corrupted before a new backup, the administrator can restore the previous backup copy, and then apply the transactions stored in the log file to bring the database back to where it was before the crash. When a new backup is complete, the database engine clears the log file and starts adding any new transactions. As the log file fills up, a new log file is started, as long as there is available disk space on the hard drive.

Nested Transactions

Nested transactions are an advanced database concept that can further help isolate problems in transactions. While the example transactions shown so far are pretty simplistic, in real-life databases transactions can become quite complicated. It is not uncommon to run across applications where a single transaction must update dozens of tables.

Sometimes in these larger environments a single transaction will spawn child transactions that update tables separate from the parent transaction. The child transactions are separate from the main parent transaction, but nonetheless are part of an overall transaction plan. In these cases the overall result of the parent transaction is not dependant on the result of the child transaction. If a child transaction fails, the parent transaction can continue operating.

In nested transactions, a child transaction can be separated from a parent transaction and treated as a separate entity. If the child transaction fails, the parent transaction can still attempt to complete successfully. PostgreSQL allows developers to use nested transactions in complex table modifications.

Sub-selects

A *sub-select*, also called a *sub-query* by some DBMS packages, provides a method for chaining queries. In a normal query, users query data contained in a single table. An example of this would be to search for all the store customers that live in Chicago. In a simple query, the user requests data from a table that matches a specific criterion based on data contained in the same table.

A sub-select allows the user to query data that is a result of another query on a separate table. This provides for querying multiple tables based on complex criteria. An example of a sub-select would be to create a query for all customers located in Chicago who purchased a laptop in the last month. This would require performing a query on data contained in two separate tables. The sub-select feature allows the database user to perform these complex queries using a single query command. PostgreSQL allows users to create complex queries, often saving additional steps in the query process.

Views

As we saw in the preceding section, developers can create complex queries to extract data from multiple tables. However, for queries that span more than a couple of tables, a sub-select can become overly complex.

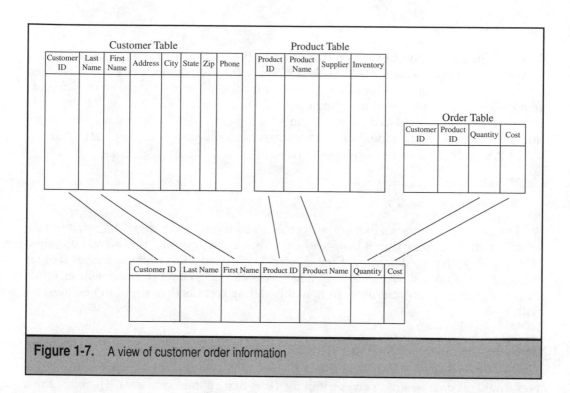

Figure 1-7. A view of customer order information

To help simplify complex query statements, some DBMS packages (including PostgreSQL) allow administrators to create views. A *view* allows users to see (or view) data contained in separate database tables as if it were in a single table. Instead of having to write a sub-select query to grab data from multiple places, all of the data is available in a single table.

To a query, a view looks like any other database table; however, it only contains fields from existing tables. The DBMS can query views just like normal tables. A view does not use any disk space in the database, as the data in the view is generated "on-the-fly" by the DBMS when it is used. When the query is complete, the data disappears. Figure 1-7 shows a sample view that could be created from the store database example.

The view in Figure 1-7 incorporates some of the customer data from the Customer table, product data from the Product table, and order data from the Order table into the single virtual table. Queries can access all of the fields in the view as if they belonged to a single table. In many DBMS products (including PostgreSQL), views are read-only, that is, users cannot alter data in a view. This makes sense, in that the database engine artificially generates the data contained in the view. Some more-complex DBMS products, such as Oracle, do allow data in views to be directly modified. While PostgreSQL does not support this, it does include a method of using rules to get around this limitation.

Rules

PostgreSQL allows you to use complex rules in the database structure. As mentioned earlier, under the consistency test, a rule performs a function on one or more tables based on an event occurring in a table. Developers use rules when they need to modify data in more than one table based on a single action. The example of updating a Billing table based on adding a record to the Order table is a good example. The rule is responsible for adding the record to the Billing table whenever a record is added to the Order table.

In PostgreSQL there are two types of rules:

▼   Do rules

▲   Do instead rules

Do rules are commands that are performed in addition to the original command submitted by the database user. Do instead rules replace the original command submitted by the user with a predetermined set of rules. Do instead rules provide a great tool for the database administrator to control what users can do to data in the database. Often rules are created to prevent users from manipulating records they shouldn't be messing with.

Triggers

Besides rules, PostgreSQL also supports triggers. A *trigger* is a set of instructions that is preformed on data based on an event in the table that contains the data. There are three types of table events that can cause a trigger to activate:

▼   Inserting a new row in a table

■   Updating one or more rows in a table

▲   Deleting one or more rows in a table

A trigger differs from a rule in that it can only modify data contained in the same table that is being accessed. Triggers are most often used to check or modify data that is being entered into a table, such as the earlier example of ensuring each customer record contains a phone number.

Support for Binary Large Objects (BLOBs)

Most database users are familiar with the common types of data that can be stored in databases. These include integers, Boolean values, fixed-length character strings, and variable-length character strings. However, in the modern programming world, support for lots of other data types is necessary. It is not uncommon to see applications that are used to store and index pictures, audio clips, and even short video clips. This type of data storage has forced most professional database systems to devise a plan to store different types of data.

PostgreSQL uses a special data type called the Binary Large Object (BLOB) to store multimedia data. A BLOB can be entered into a table the same as any other data type. This allows developers to include support for multimedia storage within applications. Caution should be taken, though, when using BLOBs, as they can quickly fill a database disk space as the BLOB images are stored in the table.

User-Defined Types

If BLOBs don't get you what you want, PostgreSQL also allows you to roll your own data types. Creating your own data types is not for the faint of heart. It requires creating C language subroutines defining how PostgreSQL handles the user-defined data type.

Functions must be created for defining how data is both input into the system by the user, and output by the system. The output function must be able to display the user-defined data type as a string. The input function accepts string characters from the user and converts them into the user-defined data type.

The most common example used for a user-defined data type is complex numbers. A complex number consists of a pair of floating-point numbers, representing the X and Y value (such as the value (3.25, 4.00)). The C language input function converts the string representation of the value into the appropriate floating-point values. Likewise, the output function converts the floating-point values into the string representation.

Roles

Of course, a huge factor in any DBMS package is security. Different tables often require different access levels for users. Data in a DBMS is protected by requiring each user to log into the DBMS using a specific userid. The DBMS data dictionary maintains a list of userids, tables, and access levels. Access to data in individual tables is controlled by the security list. As many database administrators will attest, in an organization with lots of people coming and going, trying to maintain database security can be a full-time job.

To help database administrators perform this function, PostgreSQL uses a concept called *roles*. Roles allow the database administrator to assign access privileges to a generic entity instead of assigning table rights directly to userids. The database administrator can create separate roles for different types of access to different tables, as shown in Figure 1-8.

In Figure 1-8, separate roles are defined for each type of access required for the tables. The Salesperson role allows read access only to the Customer and Product tables. The Accountants role allows read access to the Product table, plus write access to the Customer and Billing tables. Once the roles are created, a database administrator can assign individual user accounts to the appropriate role, depending on the access required by the user. If user Fred is an accountant, he is added to the Accountant role. If user Barney is a salesperson, he is added to the Salesperson role. If Barney takes night classes, then transfers to become an accountant, rather than have to figure out what access rights should be added or deleted, all the database administrator needs to do is move Barney's user account from the Salesperson role to the Accountant role. Barney automatically has the appropriate accesses he needs to be an accountant. This feature makes life much easier for database administrators.

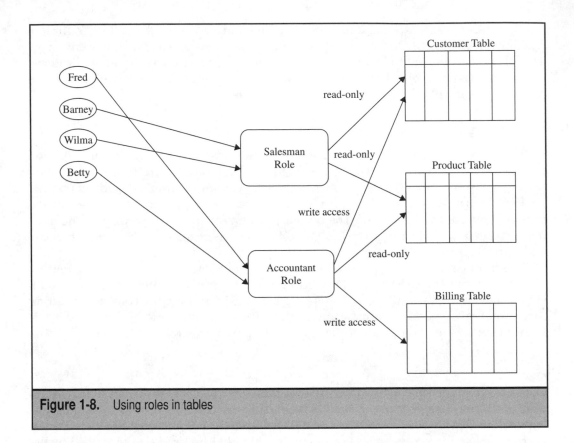

Figure 1-8. Using roles in tables

Table Partitioning

Table partitioning is a relatively new database concept that not all databases support. It allows a database administrator to split a single large table into multiple smaller tables. The database engine still treats the smaller tables as a single logical table, but directs queries and updates to the appropriate smaller table that contains the pertinent data. This allows queries to be performed quicker, since they can be performed in parallel on several small tables, rather than having to trudge through a single large table searching for data.

It is common to partition data based on a physical attribute of the data, such as dates. All data for a specific time period, such as a fiscal quarter, is stored in the same partition. Queries requesting data for a specific quarter then only need to search the appropriate partition instead of the entire table.

Another benefit to table partitioning is table access speeds. Once the logical table is divided into smaller physical tables, the database engine can store each table piece in a separate location on the server. This allows the database engine to migrate sections of the table that are not used much to slower disk resources, while keeping more active sections of the table on quicker disk resources. This is shown in Figure 1-9.

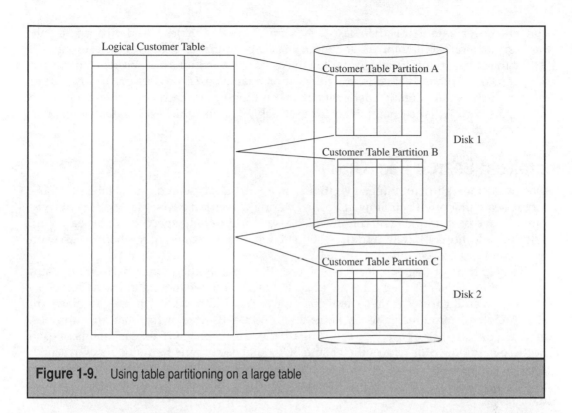

Figure 1-9.   Using table partitioning on a large table

Partitions can also be migrated off of disk storage as the data on them is no longer needed. It is common to have a rotation system where older partitions are moved to tape for long-term storage.

Of course, creating table partitions does produce some overhead. The point at which using a table partition outweighs the overhead is a hotly debated topic in the database world. The rule of thumb is to partition a table when its size becomes larger than the amount of memory available to the DBMS. At this point the DBMS can no longer load the entire table into memory to perform operations, and must swap pieces out to the hard disk while it works.

PostgreSQL uses the object-relational property of table inheritance to implement table partitioning. It does this by creating child tables as table partitions of a single parent table. The parent table contains all of the required fields for the table, but no data. Each child table contains the same fields as the parent table, but contains a different data set. There are two methods to partition data between the child tables:

▼   Range partitioning

▲   List partitioning

With range partitioning, data is divided into separate ranges based on a key value in the table. Each range of data is stored in a separate child table (partition). This is extremely convenient for data that is date based. By setting up child tables based on specific date ranges, partitions containing older data can easily be migrated to slower disk storage.

With list partitioning, data is divided into separate partitions not based on any order. This can come in handy if you want to partition a table based on data groups instead of ranges, such as partitioning customers based on their cities. Each city can have its own table partition. A list is maintained for each table listing which key values appear in which partition.

Generalized Search Tree (GiST)

One of the most difficult things to optimize in a database is searching. As tables become larger, searching often gets slowed down, creating frustrated users. Many different techniques have been implemented in the database world to help speed up data searching. With the addition of BLOBs and user-defined data types, searching has become an even more complicated procedure.

To help speed things up, PostgreSQL uses the GiST method when performing database queries. The GiST method is an advanced method for searching indexes that incorporates several features from several common search methods. If you are familiar with search methods, you may already know about B-tree, B+-tree, R-tree, partial sum trees, and various other trees used for speeding up data searches. GiST uses elements of each of these methods, plus allows the PostgreSQL database engine to define its own search methods. This technique provides for speedier search times for most PostgreSQL applications. Chapter 6 covers how to create indexes for your tables to help speed up your data access.

SUMMARY

While relatively new to the Microsoft Windows world, PostgreSQL has made quite a name for itself in the Unix world as a robust, professional-quality database system. Now with version 8.0, PostgreSQL has native support for the Windows platform, allowing Windows users and developers to take advantage of its unique features. PostgreSQL differs significantly from the popular Microsoft Access database system. PostgreSQL provides many features not found in Microsoft Access, such as table partitioning. PostgreSQL also provides an easy migration path, allowing you to easily migrate your database from a Windows workstation to a Unix server. Of course, one of the best features about PostgreSQL is that it is Open Source software and available for free.

The next chapter discusses what type of hardware you will need to run a PostgreSQL database, as well as show how to download and install the latest version from the PostgreSQL web site.

CHAPTER 2

Installing PostgreSQL on Windows

Now that you have made the decision to use PostgreSQL, you will need to get it running on your Windows system. PostgreSQL 8 supports many different Windows platforms and hardware configurations. Your job is to determine which platform and configuration is best for you.

This chapter walks through the decisions that you must make before installing PostgreSQL. If you only have one Windows system available to run PostgreSQL on, you don't have much of a choice (other than knowing if your system can support PostgreSQL). However, if you are in the market for purchasing a new system to run PostgreSQL on, there are a few things you should consider before making your purchase.

After going through the system requirements for PostgreSQL, the chapter next demonstrates the process of downloading and installing the PostgreSQL software package. If you have never installed Open Source software before and are expecting the worse, you will be pleasantly surprised at how easy it is to get your PostgreSQL system going.

SYSTEM REQUIREMENTS

Obviously, if you are reading this book, you are interested in installing PostgreSQL on a Windows platform. You many not, however, have decided exactly which Windows platform to use. This section describes the different Windows platforms, and the requirements for running PostgreSQL on each.

Back in the early days of Windows (such as versions 3.0 and 3.1) there was only one Windows version released by Microsoft at a time. Software developers had a relatively easy task of knowing what platform to develop software for. Now, however, there are multiple types and versions of Windows platforms available in the marketplace, not to mention all of the older Windows versions that some people still have lying around (and of course still want to use).

Each platform has its own set of items for you to think about before starting the PostgreSQL software installation. This section breaks down the PostgreSQL Windows platform requirements into two categories:

▼ Windows workstation platforms

▲ Windows server platforms

Your PostgreSQL installation will go smoothly if you do a little work ahead of time. Here are some tips to help you out.

Windows Workstations

One of the great features of PostgreSQL is that it is just as comfortable running on a Windows workstation as it is on a Windows server system. However, there are a few requirements you need to know about before starting PostgreSQL on your workstation.

The Windows release of PostgreSQL version 8 attempts to be as Windows friendly as possible, making few requests of the system. Basically, if your workstation is powerful enough to run Windows, it should be able to run a basic PostgreSQL database. In a database environment, having as much RAM as possible is always helpful, but not a necessity for PostgreSQL to run. Just don't expect to be able to support a large database project off of your laptop.

There is one hardware point that can be a problem for some Windows workstation users. Reparse points are a feature of the Windows New Technology File System (NTFS) version 5.0 format that were introduced by Microsoft starting with the Windows 2000 line of operating systems. Without getting too technical, *reparse points* allow programs to set tags for files and directories. When the operating system attempts to access the file or directory, the tag redirects the access request to an alternative application registered in the system. PostgreSQL uses reparse points to help speed up data access in the database files. While this helps the performance of PostgreSQL, it limits the types of Windows systems you can use to support a PostgreSQL database.

Because of this requirement, PostgreSQL won't run on Windows workstations released before Windows 2000. This means you cannot run PostgreSQL on Windows 95, 98, 98SE, ME, or even NT workstation systems. With all of these versions of Windows eliminated, that currently leaves us with four versions that can support PostgreSQL:

▼ Windows 2000 Workstation

■ Windows XP Home Edition

■ Windows XP Professional Edition

▲ Windows Vista

Of course, any future versions of Windows will also support PostgreSQL just fine. There is another point to consider here, though. Since reparse points are only available on NTFS-formatted hard drives, PostgreSQL will only run on workstations that have an NTFS-formatted disk partition available. Unfortunately, when Windows 2000 first came out, many people were still using the older File Allocation Table 32 (FAT32) hard drive format, and even today I have seen a few Windows XP workstations formatted using the FAT32 format, although most new systems use the NTFS format by default. If you are not sure how your workstation hard disks are formatted, you can use the Windows Disk Management tool to find out.

To start the Disk Management tool, right-click the My Computer icon that is located either on your desktop or in the Start menu. From the context menu that appears, select Manage. The Computer Management window appears, providing lots of options for you to manage your workstation. Click the Disk Management item to start the Disk Management tool, shown in Figure 2-1.

The Disk Management tool displays each of the hard drives installed in your workstation, plus any removable media types, such as CD-ROMs, USB memory sticks, or external drives. Each detected drive is shown as a separate text line item in the top-right frame, as well as a separate graphical item in the lower-right frame.

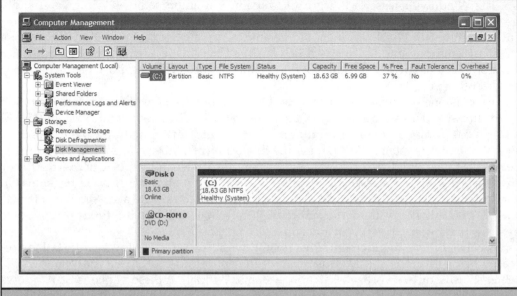

Figure 2-1. Windows Disk Management tool

In both the text and graphical representations, the drive type and file system format are shown. If you have a disk installed with an NTFS file system partition available, you will be fine. If you don't, you can easily convert an existing FAT32-formatted file system into NTFS format by using the built-in Windows convert utility.

The `convert.exe` program is used to convert FAT- and FAT32-formatted file systems into NTFS format. All data on the disk will be preserved, but any time you mess with your hard drive, it is always a good idea to make a clean backup copy of any important data before starting the conversion.

To run `convert.exe` you must be at a command prompt. To start a command prompt, click Start | Run. The Windows Run window appears. In the textbox, type **cmd** and click OK.

In the command prompt window, type **convert.exe**, followed by the drive letter assigned to the drive you want to convert, followed by the option **/fs:ntfs.** The final entry should look like this (though your drive letter may differ):

```
convert.exe d: /fs:ntfs
```

The convert program will start the conversion process. Please do not try to do anything on your system while the hard drive is being converted. When it is done, you will have an NTFS-formatted hard drive available to install PostgreSQL on.

Windows Servers

Windows servers present another type of problem. If you are planning on building a PostgreSQL server to support multiple users, you have lots more things to worry about than just whether your hard drive file system is formatted as NTFS.

At the time of this writing, there are currently four platform choices in the Windows server environment:

- ▼ Windows 2000 Server
- ■ Windows 2000 Advanced Server
- ■ Windows 2003 Standard Server
- ▲ Windows 2003 Enterprise Server

Each of these server platforms fully supports PostgreSQL and is more than capable of being built to handle a multiuser PostgreSQL database. For servers, the hard drive file system formatting should not be a problem. Since the NTFS disk format provides for securing data by user accounts, for security reasons all Windows servers should have their hard drives formatted as NTFS.

Performance is usually the biggest problem in a multiuser database server environment. Customers always want faster query times for their applications. In the Windows server environment, there are basically three items that can affect the performance of the PostgreSQL database:

- ▼ The Central Processing Unit (CPU) speed
- ■ The amount of Random Access Memory (RAM) installed
- ▲ The type of hard disk drives used

Obviously, obtaining the fastest CPU, largest amount of RAM, and fastest hard drives is the optimal solution. However, in the real world of people on limited budgets, it is not always possible to obtain such a server configuration.

Sometimes things must be compromised in the server configuration. There is a pecking order for determining how much to spend on the CPU, RAM, and hard disks. When you have limited funds, a small improvement in just one area can help increase the overall performance of the server.

For a database server, the main item you should attempt to maximize is the disk access speed. Applications that perform lots of queries on stored data can benefit from disk configurations with quick read speeds. Alternatively, applications that perform lots of data inserts and deletes can benefit from disk configurations with quick write speeds.

After maximizing your disk configuration, the next item you should consider is the amount of RAM in the system. PostgreSQL requires lots of memory to perform its functions. Although it will attempt to work given whatever amount of memory you provide it, obviously more memory will increase performance. Finally, you should look at the CPU and how it affects your overall database system.

The following sections break these features down and give some advice to help you decide how you can build your PostgreSQL server.

Hard Drive Performance

The first feature to consider is the type of hard drive to use. A slow hard drive will bring a busy database system to its knees, no matter how much memory or how fast the processor.

There are a few different types of hard drives available in the Windows server market. The most common types you will run across on server hardware are the following:

▼   Enhanced Integrated Drive Electronics (EIDE)

▲   Small Computer Systems Interface (SCSI)

Figure 2-2 demonstrates how the EIDE and SCSI technologies handle hard drives.

As shown in Figure 2-2, EIDE technology provides for two hard drives per channel, and most EIDE computer systems only have two channels, allowing for a maximum of four hard drives. As you will see shortly, this can be a limitation for larger systems. SCSI allows up to seven hard drives per channel, with most systems capable of using multiple channels. The downside to SCSI technology is that a separate controller card is required

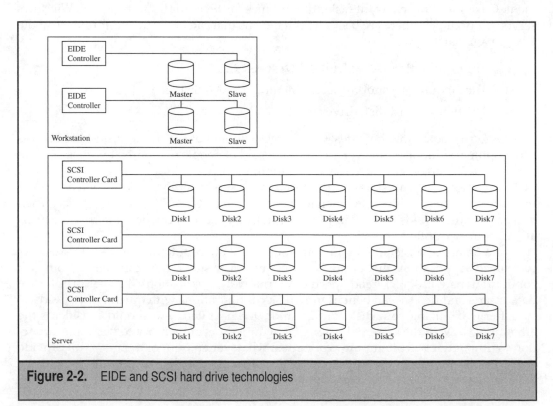

Figure 2-2.   EIDE and SCSI hard drive technologies

for each channel. The upside to this, though, is that you can often put three or four SCSI controller cards in a single server, allowing for lots of hard drives.

Most workstation systems use EIDE disk technology. While this is a relatively inexpensive disk controller technology, EIDE technology is not the fastest disk access technology available. Unfortunately, some low-end server systems also use EIDE disk technology. Most high-end server systems use SCSI disk technology.

As a whole, SCSI disks outperform EIDE disks when it comes to disk access speeds. However, newer EIDE technology is improving the data access speeds to approach those of SCSI drives. In a high-performance database server, though, SCSI disks are almost always preferred. The ability to easily add multiple hard drives is a necessity when considering the second feature required for a good server hard drive system, discussed next.

The second hard drive feature is the type of fault tolerance used on the hard drive system. On a workstation system, there is often just one disk drive with no fault tolerance. This is fine, until something goes wrong with the disk drive. A drive failure can mean catastrophic results for your database (remember from Chapter 1, durability is a key feature of an ACID-compliant system). If a hard drive crashes, the transaction log file is lost, along with all of the transactions made to the database since the last backup.

To help lessen the impact of disk problems, administrators have resorted to using a technology called Redundant Array of Inexpensive Disks (RAID). RAID technology provides for several different techniques to safeguard stored data. Each of these techniques requires using multiple hard drives. Because of this requirement, almost all RAID configurations are implemented using SCSI technology, which easily accommodates large numbers of disk drives.

In a RAID disk configuration, one disk in a multi-disk configuration can fail without losing data. This is possible using a logical disk volume structure. Although there are multiple disks on the system, the operating system (Windows) treats them as a single logical disk. Data is put on the multiple disks in such a manner that the data contained on a single failed drive can be recovered based on the data placed on the other active drives.

There are multiple levels of RAID technology available. Each one configures the multiple disks in a slightly different manner, providing different levels of data security. Table 2-1 shows the levels of RAID that are commonly available in modern-day Windows servers.

The trick for database administrators is to pick the RAID level that gives the best performance and the most data security. In each of these standard RAID levels, performance is traded for data redundancy. In the RAID 0 method, data write speeds are improved as the data is spread out over multiple disks, minimizing the amount of time the disk write heads must travel. Read speeds are also increased, as the disk head travels a shorter distance to pick up each piece of data. While RAID 0 systems improve disk access speeds, they do not have fault tolerance. If one of the striped disks goes bad, you lose all of the data on the system.

The RAID 1 approach solves the fault-tolerance problem, as a complete duplicate hard drive is available at all times. However, this comes at the cost of disk access times. Since both disks must always be in sync, data must always be written twice, once on each disk.

RAID Level	Name	Description
RAID 0	Striped set	Data is split (striped) evenly between two or more disks. Each block of data is stored on a different disk.
RAID 1	Mirror	Data is duplicated on two separate disks. Each disk is a complete duplicate of the other.
RAID 5	Striped set with parity	Data is split evenly between multiple disks using striping. However, an additional bit is added to the end of each written data block, called the *parity bit*. The parity bit is used to rebuild any of the other data disks if they fail.
RAID 0+1	Striped mirrored set	Data is split between a mirrored set of two or more striped disks.

Table 2-1.   Common Server RAID Levels

The RAID 5 level attempts to lessen the impact by writing a parity bit for each block of data striped across the disks. The thing that slows RAID 5 down is that the parity bit must be computed for each data write, but it is still faster than RAID 1.

RAID 0+1 attempts to take the best of both the RAID 0 and RAID 1 worlds. By using the RAID 0 striping of data across multiple disks, read and write speeds are improved. By using RAID 1 mirroring of the striped disks, if one disk goes bad, you still have the mirrored set to recover from. The increased speed of the RAID 0 system helps offset the RAID 1 slowness.

RAID 5 is the most common fault-tolerance method implemented by server manufactures. In RAID 5 systems having fewer than six disks, the overhead in writing the parity bit becomes a larger factor. It has been shown that this overhead is lessened in systems that have six or more disks.

In most tests, the RAID 1+0 level has proven to be the most efficient method for database servers. This level provides basic data security, while providing minimal delays in data reading and writing.

As a final warning, be careful about how the RAID technology is implemented on your server. Most RAID configurations are built into the SCSI disk controllers themselves. The RAID functions are performed at a hardware level, providing minimal overhead for disk operations. Unfortunately, the Windows Disk Management tool allows you to emulate RAID technology within the operating system software itself, using standard hard drives (even using EIDE drives). Although Windows allows you to create RAID configurations on standard disks, this provides a huge overhead for accessing data on the disk. Avoid this feature, especially for large servers where you expect lots of database traffic.

RAM Performance

PostgreSQL attempts to use as much memory as possible when processing data transactions. PostgreSQL loads as much of a data table into memory as possible when processing transactions. If you have your data divided into lots of small tables, PostgreSQL must swap tables in and out of memory for each transaction. This requires fast memory speeds to keep up with the transactions. If you have your data placed in large tables, PostgreSQL will attempt to load as much of the table into memory as possible to speed up transactions. This is where having lots of RAM available helps out.

The bottom line is that the more data you expect to have in your tables, the more memory you should try to install on your server. PostgreSQL will operate to the best of its ability with the amount of RAM you have installed on your system. You can just help it along if possible.

CPU Performance

PostgreSQL is not too picky about CPU speeds and types. At the time of this writing, the only CPU requirements PostgreSQL has are that the processor must be at least a Pentium III or later Intel processor (or equivalent) and that the processor must be a 32-bit series bus.

PostgreSQL has not been fully tested on 64-bit CPUs. That does not mean that it will not run on a 64-bit system, just that the PostgreSQL developers have not fully tested and certified it on 64-bit systems. If you are running a standard 32-bit CPU Windows system, you should not have any trouble getting PostgreSQL to run on your system.

DOWNLOADING POSTGRESQL

One of the best features of Open Source software is that it is freely available on the Internet. You don't have to worry about registering your name and address with a company to receive a complimentary CD in the mail (along with an endless supply of junk mail). For most Open Source packages, all you need is an Internet connection and a web browser.

Instead of distributing software on a CD, Open Source packages are distributed by combining all of the necessary files into a single distribution package file. For Windows systems, this is a zipped file that contains all of the files required for the installation. To be able to install PostgreSQL on a Windows platform, you must have an unzip utility handy. Fortunately, in Windows XP and 2003, this utility is built into the operating system (called Compressed Folders). If you are using a Windows 2000 platform, you will have to obtain a third-party unzip program.

When you are ready to download PostgreSQL, you will probably want to use a high-speed Internet connection. The PostgreSQL download is fairly large (about 23MB at the time of this writing), so you would not want to download it using a dial-up modem. If you don't have access to a high-speed Internet connection, there are commercial versions of PostgreSQL you can purchase. There are also some companies on the Internet that will burn Open Source software onto a CD for you for a small fee (usually $5 per CD). Just do some searching on the Internet and you will find them.

If you are ready to download PostgreSQL yourself, go to the PostgreSQL home page, located at www.postgresql.org. On the home page, there is a list of the current versions still supported by the PostgreSQL development community under the Latest Releases section. You will see a few different versions listed in this section. Now is a good time to explain the PostgreSQL version numbers.

Unlike other software packages, PostgreSQL does not force you to upgrade from one version to another. The developers of PostgreSQL realize that often users run production databases and do not need to upgrade to the latest major version (using the "if it ain't broke, don't fix it" theory). Currently, there are two major releases that are supported: 7 and 8 (signified by the first digit in the release number).

Within each major release are several update releases. Each update release adds new minor features to the major release that you may or may not need to implement in your database system. The update release is signified by the second digit in the release number. The PostgreSQL 8 series is currently on update release 2 (8.2), although update releases 0 and 1 are still available. The PostgreSQL 7 series also supports two update releases, versions 7.3 and 7.4.

Within update releases, there are patches that are released to fix bugs and security problems. These patches are released more often than update releases, and do not add any new functionality to the software. While you do not necessarily have to upgrade your PostgreSQL system to the latest and greatest major or update release level, it is recommended that you should at least keep up with the patches released for the version you have installed.

At the time of this writing, there are five releases available for download on the PostgreSQL home page:

▼ 8.2.0 (original release of the 8.2 update release)

■ 8.1.5 (patch 5 for the 8.1 update release)

■ 8.0.9 (patch 9 for the 8.0 update release)

■ 7.4.14 (patch 14 for the 7.4 update release)

▲ 7.3.16 (patch 16 for the 7.3 update release)

Another thing to notice in the Latest Releases section on the PostgreSQL home page is that each release has two links. The first link (associated with the release name) points to a source code download area. The second link (associated with the word *Binary* next to the release name) points to the binary application download area. While the source code release allows you to view and modify the official PostgreSQL source code, for most Windows users, all you will want to download is the binary version of the latest release.

This package provides everything you need to get PostgreSQL running on your Windows system.

After clicking the binary link of the release you want to use, you are taken to a directory that contains two links. The first link, linux, points to the Linux repository, and the second link, win32, points to the Windows repository. Click the win32 link to get to the PostgreSQL install packages.

The Win32 repository contains several downloads for different types of install packages. You will want to download the complete package, which includes the PostgreSQL software and the Windows install routines. At the time of this writing, this link is called *postgresql-8.2.0-1.zip*.

When you click the link, you are directed to a list of the available servers from which to download the package. When you click a server link, the download starts. Save the file to a convenient place on your local hard drive. When the download completes, you are ready to start the installation process.

INSTALLING POSTGRESQL

After you have the PostgreSQL Win32 zip package on your PC, you can start the installation process. The first thing to do is unzip the distribution package. If you have a Windows XP, Vista, or 2003 system, this is easy, as the Windows operating system includes support for zipped files. Just click the distribution file in Windows Explorer and extract the files to a temporary directory. It is important that you extract the files to a temporary directory. The installation program will not work properly if you attempt to run it directly from the zipped file. Also, remember if you are using a Windows 2000 workstation or server, you will have to obtain an unzip program if you don't already have one. There are plenty of free and commercial zip packages available.

After unzipping the distribution package into a working directory, you should see a few different files. Don't be concerned about the name of the installation files. The files only contain the update version names and not the complete patch names. This is to simplify the install scripts for each version.

There is also a batch file available to automatically update an existing installation. This batch file can only be used to install a new patch version of the same update version (such as going from version 8.1.3 to 8.1.4). It cannot be used to install a new update version (such as going from version 8.0 to 8.1). To upgrade to a new update version, you must export all of your data, reinstall PostgreSQL, then import your data back (this is covered in Chapter 4).

The installation package divides the PostgreSQL packages into two `.msi` files, a base file called `postgresql-x.y.msi`, and an additional installation file called `postgresql-x.y-int.msi`, where *x* is the major release number, and *y* is the update release number. For a new installation, double-click the base `.msi` file (currently called `postgresql-8.2.msi`) to start the installation.

There are several windows that appear throughout the PostgreSQL Windows installation. The first window allows you to select the language used in the installation process (this selection does not set the language used by the PostgreSQL system; that selection comes later in the installation process). Also, don't neglect the little check box at the bottom of this window. It is a good idea to allow the installer to create a log file showing the installation progress in case anything goes wrong. Click Next to go to the next window in the installation.

The rest of the installation process can be as simple or as complicated as you want to make it. If all you are interested in is getting a basic PostgreSQL installation, you can take the default values for all of the prompts and quickly get through the installation process. If you want to customize your PostgreSQL installation later, you can rerun the installation program and just select the items you need to install. Just remember that you should deselect the Data Dictionary option if you want to keep the existing data dictionary files. If you reinstall the Data Dictionary option, the installer will overwrite the existing database files, so any databases or tables you created will be lost.

If you want to customize your PostgreSQL installation now, you can choose to select or deselect the desired options during the initial installation. The following sections describe the choices that are available to you during the installation process.

Installation Options Window

The Installation Options window presents you with some choices on how and where you want PostgreSQL installed. Figure 2-3 shows the Installation Options window.

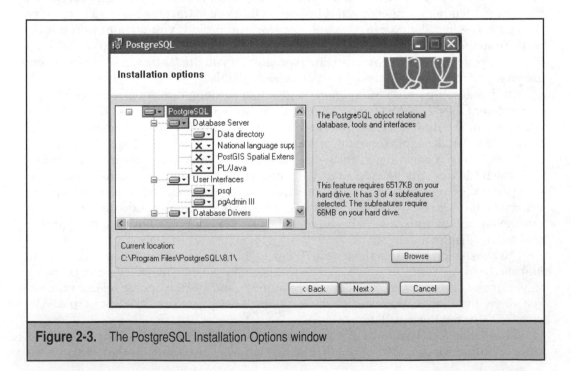

Figure 2-3. The PostgreSQL Installation Options window

The Installation Options window shows each component of the installation package and allows you to choose whether or not to install it and, if so, where to install it on your system. Each component is shown as a separate box in the window.

The top-level item is the main PostgreSQL package. Clicking the package icon activates the Browse button near the bottom of the window and displays the current location where the PostgreSQL package will be installed. You can change the installation location on your system by clicking the Browse button and choosing a different location. This changes the location where all of the PostgreSQL files will be stored. The default location is `C:\Program Files\PostgreSQL\8.2` (for the 8.2 update version release).

The main installation package also has four separate icons for each of the packages included in the installation package:

▼ Database Server
■ User Interfaces
■ Database Drivers
▲ Development

You can choose to install or skip each of these packages. The following sections describe the packages to help you decide if you need them.

Database Server

The Database Server is the database engine portion of the PostgreSQL package. It includes four modules that can be installed:

▼ The Data Dictionary
■ National language support
■ PostGIS spatial extensions
▲ PL/Java

The Data Dictionary is required if you plan to access data from your PostgreSQL server. It is the module that controls all interaction with the databases maintained by the server. When you click the Data Dictionary icon, the Browse button appears, as well as the path where data files are stored.

In a workstation environment, you probably can keep the default location of the Data Dictionary. The only time you will need to move it on a workstation is if you only have one NTFS-formatted hard drive file system and it is not the `C:` drive. Remember, the Data Dictionary must be placed on an NTFS formatted file system. In a server installation, you may want to consider changing the default location.

The Data Dictionary maintains all of the data files for PostgreSQL. Here is where you need to worry about data durability. For a server, it is best to place the Data Dictionary on a hard drive that has better performance and durability, such as a RAID drive. To relocate the Data Dictionary, click the Browse button and choose the proper location on your system.

National language support allows PostgreSQL to provide messages in several different languages. If you want your PostgreSQL system to only display messages in English, the National language support module is not necessary.

The PostGIS spatial extensions module installs support for geographic objects for the PostgreSQL database. This feature allows PostgreSQL to handle data from Geographic Information Systems (GIS). If you are not planning on using this type of data in your database, you can accept the default of not installing PostGIS.

The PL/Java module allows you to use the Java programming language for stored procedures, triggers, and functions within the PostgreSQL database. By default, PostgreSQL only supports the internal PL/pgSQL language for these objects. If you are interested in writing Java code within your database, install this module.

User Interfaces

The User Interfaces package includes two separate packages you can install:

▼ psql

▲ pgAdmin III

Both packages are selected to be installed by default. The `psql` program provides a simple command-line interface for running ad hoc SQL commands in your database. It is extremely handy to have around when working on your database.

The pgAdmin III package provides a fancy Windows GUI program for administering your PostgreSQL databases. It makes administering a PostgreSQL database almost easy. Both of these packages are covered later in this book. pgAdmin III is covered in Chapter 4 and `psql` is covered in Chapter 5. I strongly recommend installing both packages to make your PostgreSQL experience much easier.

Database Drivers

If you are creating your PostgreSQL database in a production environment, most likely you will need to interface it with application programs. Different application development environments require different methods to interface with the PostgreSQL database. PostgreSQL provides a few drivers to support the following interfaces:

▼ JDBC

■ Npgsql

■ ODBC

▲ OLEDB

If you plan to work in a Java development environment, the Java Database Connectivity (JDBC) driver allows your Java applications to connect to the PostgreSQL database and perform database transactions. Similarly, the Npgsql driver allows applications created in Microsoft's .NET environment to connect to PostgreSQL. The ODBC and Object Linking and Embedding Database (OLEDB) drivers interface legacy Microsoft applications, including Microsoft Access, with the PostgreSQL database.

Part III, "Windows Programming with PostgreSQL," demonstrates how to use each of these drivers in their respective development environments. If you plan to follow along in this section, you need to install these drivers if they are not already installed. All of these drivers are installed by default. If you decide you do not want to use any of these drivers, you can choose not to install them. They can be individually installed later on if you need them.

Development

The development install packages include libraries and header files for use with various development environments. If you plan on developing C or C++ applications for PostgreSQL (as covered in Chapter 13), you need to include the development packages in your installation. If you choose not to install any of the features during the initial installation process, you can always rerun the PostgreSQL installer and select just the options you did not install the first time.

Service Configuration Window

After selecting the appropriate installation pieces, click Next to continue with the installation. The Service Configuration window allows you to configure how PostgreSQL is started on your Windows system. Figure 2-4 shows how the window appears.

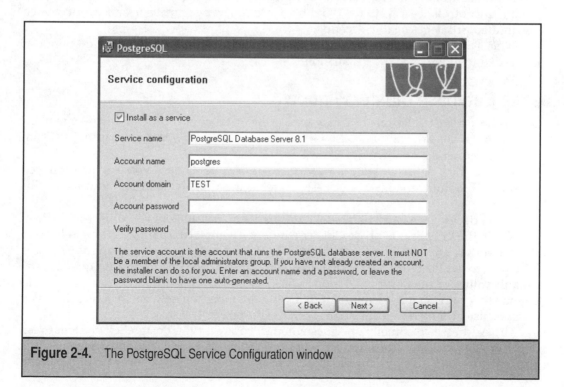

Figure 2-4.   The PostgreSQL Service Configuration window

There are two methods you can use to run PostgreSQL on your Windows system:

▼   As a background service

▲   As a normal program

The PostgreSQL installation process provides an easy way for you to create a PostgreSQL background service on your Windows system. Checking the Install as a Service check box allows the PostgreSQL installer to create the necessary service objects on the Windows system. This method allows PostgreSQL to automatically start when the system is booted. This is almost always the preferred method of running PostgreSQL on servers. It also comes in handy if you are doing development work on your workstation. If you are just playing around with PostgreSQL on your workstation, you might not want it to load every time you turn on your system. In that case, choose to not install PostgreSQL as a service (clear the check box).

The Service Configuration window allows you to customize the way the service runs. You can specify the name of the service, as well as the user account used to run the service. If the user account does not exist on the system, the installer will attempt to create it. The default account PostgreSQL will create is called `postgres`.

There is one word of caution if you run PostgreSQL as a service. To support strict security requirements, PostgreSQL will not allow itself to be started by a user account that has administrator privileges. This blocks hackers from utilizing the PostgreSQL program to gain uncontrolled access to the Windows system. The `postgres` user account created has limited privileges on the system.

When you have completed your selections for the Services Configuration window, click Next to move on in the installation.

Initialise Database Cluster Window

If you chose to install PostgreSQL as a service, the installer next provides an easy method for you to create a default database for your system. This is done in the Initialise Database Cluster window, shown in Figure 2-5.

This section makes creating a new database simple. Unless you are an advanced PostgreSQL administrator, it is easiest to create the default database now using this window.

If you decide to create a database, there are a few parameters you must set for PostgreSQL in the Initialise Database Cluster window. The first two parameters are related to the network connectivity for the database. The Port Number parameter assigns a specific TCP port to the PostgreSQL server so that applications can connect to send queries. The default value for the PostgreSQL port is 5432, as shown in Figure 2-5. You can elect to change this value, but it is important that you remember the new value you assign, as it must be used for all communications with the PostgreSQL system.

The Addresses parameter specifies whether you want the PostgreSQL system to accept connections only from applications running on the local Windows system. This prevents network access to the database. Checking the check box allows PostgreSQL to

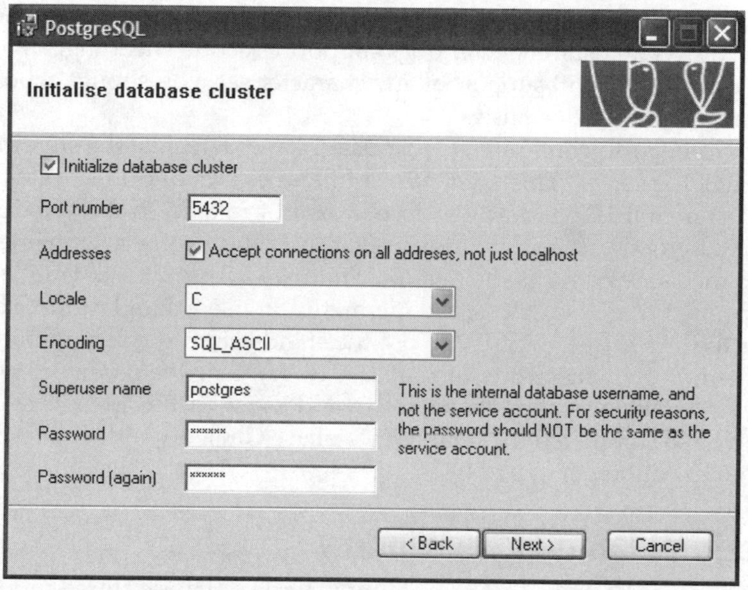

Figure 2-5.   The PostgreSQL Initialise Database Cluster window

accept network connections from all network interfaces on the Windows system. Even with this check box checked, by default, PostgreSQL will not accept connections from external network clients. You will see in Chapter 3 that there is an additional configuration item you need to make to allow remote clients to access your database.

The Locale parameter is where you configure the language used on the PostgreSQL system. There are lots of values that this parameter can be set to. If you select a non-English Locale, you must have the national language support module selected in the Installation Options window shown earlier in Figure 2-3.

You will notice that the default value of Locale is not set to a language. Instead, it is set to the value *C*. The *C* stands for the ISO C standard, which allows PostgreSQL to obtain the locale information from the host system. Theoretically, this should not be a problem; however, some host systems do not follow the ISO C standards properly, thus creating a problem for PostgreSQL. Fortunately for us, this is not a problem on Windows systems, so you can leave this default value alone.

The Encoding parameter determines how data is stored in the database. This parameter depends on how the host system stores values. The default value is SQL_ASCII for Windows systems. This encoding stores data in standard ASCII format in the database. While ASCII encoding works great for English characters, it is extremely limited for many other language character sets.

Windows uses Unicode encoding to support multinational language sets. Unfortunately this encoding was not available in PostgreSQL version 8.0, thus the default of SQL_ASCII. However, PostgreSQL 8.1 does support Unicode encoding, although it calls it by the name UTF8. For full support of any character set, you should choose the UTF8 encoding scheme for your database.

The last parameter to configure is Superuser Name, which is the superuser account for the PostgreSQL system. This account has full access to all of the system tables and features in PostgreSQL. Note that this account is not related to the Windows account used to start PostgreSQL. It just so happens that the default superuser name used in the installation is the same name as the default Windows account used. Unlike some other database systems, PostgreSQL does not automatically use a standard user account and password for the superuser. Even if you use the standard `postgres` account, you must come up with your own password for it. Please do not lose the password you select for this step. If you do, you won't be able to log in and use your PostgreSQL system.

When you have completed the Initialise Database Cluster window, click Next for the next set of configuration parameters.

Enable Procedural Languages Window

One of the features of PostgreSQL is the ability to write database stored procedures, triggers, and functions in a variety of languages. The Enable Procedural Languages window, shown in Figure 2-6, allows you to define which procedural languages you want to use in your system.

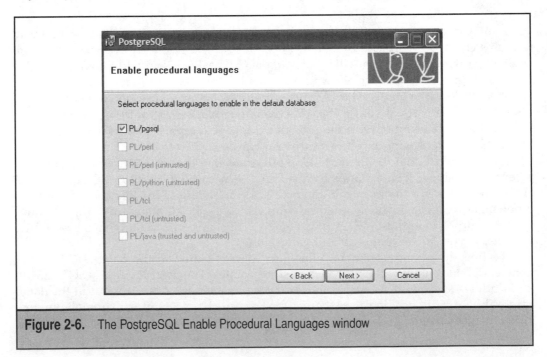

Figure 2-6. The PostgreSQL Enable Procedural Languages window

Procedural Language	Web Address
Perl	www.activestate.com
Python	www.python.org
Tcl	www.activestate.com
Java	java.sun.com

Table 2-2.   Finding Alternative PostgreSQL Procedural Languages

As you can see from Figure 2-6, you have a few different choices of what programming languages to use within your PostgreSQL system. However, you may also notice that most of the choices are grayed out and not available.

By default, PostgreSQL supports only its own pgsql procedural language. If you have the Sun Java runtime installed on your system, and its location is specified in the Windows PATH environment variable, PostgreSQL will also allow you to select PL/Java as a procedural language. The other procedural languages require you to install additional third-party software packages.

If you are familiar with the Unix world, you may have heard about the other procedural language options available in PostgreSQL. The Perl, Python, and Tcl languages are popular Unix scripting languages that are supported by most Unix and Linux platforms. Unfortunately, Windows does not support these languages without additional software. There are both commercial and free Windows versions of these scripting languages. Table 2-2 lists as an example one of several web addresses where a Windows version of each language package can be found.

In order to have these procedural language options available, you must install the appropriate package before starting the PostgreSQL installation. If the procedural language is installed, PostgreSQL will allow you to select the language to install in the PostgreSQL system. Remember, you can always rerun the PostgreSQL installer program again after the initial installation to install just these additional components.

Enable Contrib Modules Window

The final choice you have to make is if you want to enable any of the extra contrib modules included with PostgreSQL. Figure 2-7 shows what this installation window looks like.

The contrib modules are not specifically supported by PostgreSQL, but created by other developers for use in PostgreSQL systems. Each of the contrib modules creates special functions within the PostgreSQL Data Dictionary that you can use in your SQL code.

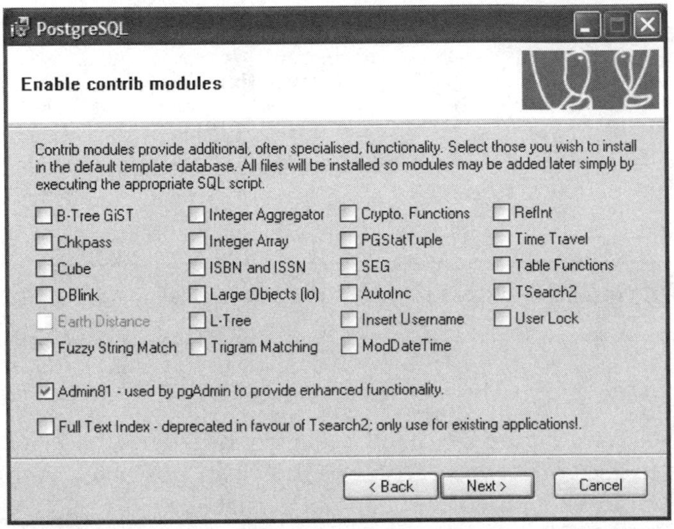

Figure 2-7. The PostgreSQL Enable Contrib Modules window

The functions created by the contrib modules are not the same as the internal PostgreSQL functions, like the ones that are covered in Chapter 8. Instead, these are specialized functions created by running the contrib module SQL scripts in the database. Table 2-3 describes the functions available in the PostgreSQL installation at the time of this writing.

You may notice that the Admin81 contrib module is already selected by default. This contrib module is required if you are using the pgAdmin III application to administer the PostgreSQL system. If you do not plan on using pgAdmin III, you can unselect this item.

Don't worry if you cannot decide whether you want a contrib module installed. This step only installs the contrib modules into the database. The SQL code used to create the contrib modules is automatically stored in the PostgreSQL installation directory on your system. You can always go back and run the SQL code to manually install the contrib module at a later time.

Finish the Install

After the contrib module section, the installer continues the installation by installing the files into the directory you requested, creating the PostgreSQL service and user account (if you selected that option), and creating and initializing the default PostgreSQL database (also if you selected that option).

When the installation is complete, the final installation window offers you the opportunity to subscribe your e-mail address to the PostgreSQL announcements news list. This allows you to stay up-to-date with the latest releases and news about PostgreSQL. At this point the PostgreSQL installation is complete. The next step is to test it out.

Contrib Module	Description
B-Tree GiST	Emulates B-tree indexing using the PostgreSQL GiST functions
Chkpass	A password data type for storing and comparing encrypted passwords
Cube	A data type for multidimensional cubes
DBlink	Returns results from a remote database
Fuzzy String Match	Functions for fuzzy string comparisons
Integer Aggregator	Functions to collect sets of integers from input arrays
Integer Array	Index functions for one-dimensional arrays of integers
ISBN and ISSN	A data type for book ISBNs and serial ISSNs
Large Objects (lo)	A data type for handling large objects in the database
L-Tree	Data types, indexed access methods, and queries for data organized in tree-like structures
Trigram Matching	Functions for determining the similarity of text based on groups of three consecutive string characters
Crypto Functions	Provides encrypting and decrypting functions
PGStatTuple	Function to return the percentage of dead lists (tuples) in a table
SEG	Data type representing floating-point intervals used in laboratory measurements
AutoInc	Functions to automatically increment an integer field
Insert Username	Functions for checking username validity
ModDateTime	Specialized functions for handling dates and times
RefInt	Functions to create table keys that enforce referential integrity (also called foreign keys) using triggers
Time Travel	Functions to create tables with no overwrite storage that keep old versions of rows
Table Functions	Functions to return scalar and composite results from sets
TSearch2	Full text search support functions
User Lock	Implements user-level long-term locks on data
Admin81	Provides functions for extended administration capabilities, used by pgAdmin III
Full Text Index	Implements full text indexing using triggers

Table 2-3. PostgreSQL 8.2 Contrib Modules

RUNNING POSTGRESQL

Now that you have PostgreSQL installed, it's time to either see if it's running (if you chose to install it as a background service) or get it running (if you did not choose to start it automatically). The following sections describe both of these two methods for running PostgreSQL on your Windows system.

Service Method

If you chose to run PostgreSQL as a background service, it should now be running on your system. You can use the Windows Task Manager to check for yourself. The Task Manager allows you to see what services are currently running on your system. You must be logged in with a user account that has administrator privileges to see system services.

The easiest way to start the Task Manager is to right-click on an empty place on the system taskbar and select Task Manager from the menu that appears. Figure 2-8 shows the Task Manager in action.

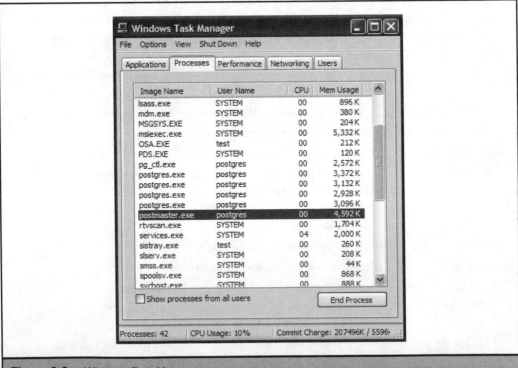

Figure 2-8. Windows Task Manager

In the Task Manager window, click the Processes tab. This shows a list of all the services running on the system. You can click the Image Name column heading to sort the processes by their names. If you scroll down to the *P* section, you should see several processes related to PostgreSQL.

The main PostgreSQL process is called `postmaster`. This process controls the PostgreSQL system and database engine. You should also see several other `postgres` processes, which handle queries to the database engine. These processes control connectivity to the PostgreSQL system. The number of `postgres` processes created is controlled by an entry in the PostgreSQL configuration file (discussed in Chapter 3).

Manual Method

If you do not want the PostgreSQL system running all the time on your Windows system, you have to manually create the default database, and start and stop the program. This is done using a couple of the programs included with PostgreSQL.

To be able to start PostgreSQL, it must have the Data Dictionary area created. To manually create this, you must use the `initdb` program. The `initdb` program uses command-line parameters to define where the Data Dictionary should be created, and what type of encoding to use:

```
initdb -D datapath -E encoding
```

By default, the Data Dictionary is located in the `data` directory within the PostgreSQL installation directory. The *datapath* must exist, and the user account used to run PostgreSQL must have write access to it.

The `initdb` program must be run by the Windows user account that controls PostgreSQL. This cannot be a user account with administrator privileges. To run the `initdb` program as the user account, you can either log in using that account or use the Windows `runas` command to start the program as the user. The easiest way to do this is to start a command-prompt session as the PostgreSQL user account:

```
runas /user:postgres cmd
```

After prompting you for the `postgres` password, Windows starts a command-prompt session as that user. By default, the `initdb` program is located in the PostgreSQL `bin` directory. You can change to that directory and run the program as follows:

```
cd \program files\postgresql\8.2\bin
initdb -D "c:\program files\postgresql\8.2\data"
```

Note that you must enclose the *datapath* value in double quotes if it includes spaces.

After the Data Dictionary is created, you can start PostgreSQL. This is done using the `pg_ctl` program. Again, to run the `pg_ctl` program you must be logged in as a nonadministrator user account, or use the `runas` command as you did with the `initdb` program.

There are several functions you can perform with the `pg_ctl` program. The format of the `pg_ctl` command for controlling the PostgreSQL server is

```
pg_ctl command -D datadir
```

The *command* parameter can be one of five basic options: start, stop, restart, reload, and status. The *datadir* parameter points to the location of the Data Dictionary. If the pathname includes spaces (such as in the default directory location) you must enclose the pathname in double quotes. Thus, to start PostgreSQL using the default Data Directory location, you would use the following command:

```
pg_ctl start -D "c:\program files\postgresql\8.2\data"
```

Remember, you cannot start the PostgreSQL server from a user account that has administrator privileges. If the PostgreSQL server starts, you will be able to see the `postmaster` and `postgres` processes running in the Task Manager.

SUMMARY

This chapter discussed how to get PostgreSQL running on your Windows workstation or server. There are a few things that need to be addressed before starting the software installation. PostgreSQL is robust enough to work well even on a Windows workstation platform. For workstations, you must ensure that you have an NTFS version 5.0 partition available to install PostgreSQL on. For a multiuser server environment, there are few additional things to worry about. The most important feature for a PostgreSQL server is the disk access speeds. The quicker the disk access speed the better the database performance. Servers using EIDE disk technology are poor choices for database servers. The SCSI disk technology provides for faster data transfer speeds, as well as providing for more disk drives to be added to the system. Servers using SCSI disk systems can also implement RAID technology to provide a fault-tolerant disk environment for the database. Next to fast disk speeds, PostgreSQL also prefers to have as much RAM available as possible.

When you have your workstation or server ready for PostgreSQL, you can download the Windows binary distribution package directly from the PostgreSQL web site. The PostgreSQL developers support several versions of PostgreSQL at the same time. For a new database implementation, you will want to download the latest version available. New patches are releases often to fix bugs and security problems. Updates to releases are released less often, and major releases are released even less often.

After downloading the distribution package, you must unzip it and store it in a temporary location. The PostgreSQL installation program is started by double-clicking the `.msi` installer file. The installer program starts by asking a few questions regarding the type of installation you want, as well as the features you desire for your PostgreSQL setup. After answering the questions, the PostgreSQL software loads.

After PostgreSQL is installed, it's time to start exploring. The next chapter walks through the various utilities and configuration files found in the PostgreSQL package.

CHAPTER 3

The PostgreSQL Files and Programs

Now that you have PostgreSQL installed on your system, we can take a walk through the various pieces of it. There are lots of files associated with the PostgreSQL install. Most of them work behind the scenes with the database engine. The two main types of files you will have to worry about are configuration files and utilities. This chapter shows where PostgreSQL keeps all of these files, then explains how to customize your PostgreSQL system using the configuration files. Finally, the chapter presents a rundown of the various PostgreSQL utilities you have available to use on your PostgreSQL system.

THE POSTGRESQL DIRECTORY

After you get PostgreSQL installed on your system, it is a good idea to become familiar with the general PostgreSQL directory layout. There are lots of utilities and configuration files installed for you to play with. There are often times when you have to go hunting for a specific utility, or need to locate a specific configuration file to help troubleshoot a problem.

If you accepted the default installation values during the PostgreSQL installation (see Chapter 2), the main PostgreSQL directory is located at

```
C:\Program Files\PostgreSQL
```

Under this directory is a directory named after the update version you installed. At the time of this writing, that directory is called 8.2. If you install additional patch releases for the update, the files remain in the same directory. If you upgrade to a new update release, for example version 8.3, the PostgreSQL installer will create a new directory for the new files. Patch releases are kept in the same directory as the original update release.

If you accepted all of the default locations during installation, all of the PostgreSQL files are located beneath the update release directory. Table 3-1 outlines the directories you should see using a default installation.

The data directory is especially important in that it contains files and directories specific to the operation of the database engine. As mentioned in Chapter 2, you can choose to relocate this directory during the installation phase to a separate place on the system.

The data directory is referred to as the *database cluster,* as this is where all of the database files are located. The PostgreSQL system must have at least one database cluster to operate. The next section takes a closer look at the database cluster directory structure.

DATABASE CLUSTER DIRECTORY

There is a wide assortment of files and directories that are stored in the database cluster directory. Table 3-2 describes the directories located in the database cluster directory.

Directory	Description
bin	The PostgreSQL main programs, utilities, and library files
data	PostgreSQL Data Dictionary, log files, and the transaction log
doc	Documentation on contrib modules, PgOleDb, and psqlODBC
include	C program header files for developing C programs for PostgreSQL (if the Development package was installed)
jdbc	Java JDBC library files for developing Java programs for PostgreSQL (if the JDBC package was installed)
lib	PostgreSQL library files for the executable programs
npgsql	Microsoft .NET library files for developing .NET programs for PostgreSQL (if the npgsql package was installed)
PgAdmin III	The pgAdmin III program documentation
share	Contrib modules and timezone information for PostgreSQL

Table 3-1.   PostgreSQL Directories

Directory	Description
base	Contains a directory for each database
global	Contains system tables for the Data Dictionary
pg_clog	Contains status files on transaction commits
pg_log	Contains PostgreSQL system log files
pg_multixact	Contains multitransaction status information used for row locking
pg_subtrans	Contains subtransaction status information
pg_tblspc	Contains links to database tables
pg_twophase	Contains phase files for the two-phase transaction commit process
pg_xlog	Contains the transaction log files

Table 3-2.   The PostgreSQL Database Cluster Directories

The base directory contains subdirectories for each database created on the PostgreSQL system (creating databases is described in Chapter 4). PostgreSQL names the directory after the object ID (OID) assigned to the database in the PostgreSQL Data Dictionary. As a normal PostgreSQL user, you will not have to worry about these files, because PostgreSQL takes care of them behind the scenes.

As a PostgreSQL administrator, one area you should become familiar with is the pg_log directory. This is the place where the PostgreSQL system maintains system log files. These log files track events that occur in the database using text messages stored in the log file. As the administrator, it is your job to watch these log files for any problems that appear.

Each time the PostgreSQL system is started, a new log file is created. The default format of the log filename is

```
postgresl-year-month-day-time.log
```

You can change the filename format using features in the postgresql.conf file (discussed in "The postgresql.conf File" section later in this chapter).

Each major event that happens in the PostgreSQL system is logged in the system log file. The default format shows a timestamp and the event that occurred. Some sample entries from a log file are given here:

```
2006-06-29 20:13:45 FATAL:   database "test" does not exist
2006-06-29 20:24:01 LOG:    transaction ID wrap limit is 2147484148,
                             limited by database "postgres"
2006-06-29 20:25:05 LOG:    autovacuum: processing database "Test"
2006-06-29 20:26:05 LOG:    autovacuum: processing database "template1"
2006-06-29 20:27:05 LOG:    autovacuum: processing database "postgres"
2006-06-29 20:28:18 NOTICE:  ALTER TABLE / ADD PRIMARY KEY will create
                             implicit index "ItemID" for table "test"
2006-06-29 20:28:46 ERROR:   syntax error at or near "connect" at character 1
2006-06-29 20:30:35 LOG:    autovacuum: processing database "postgres"
2006-06-29 20:31:35 LOG:    autovacuum: processing database "Test"
2006-06-29 20:32:35 LOG:    autovacuum: processing database "template1"
2006-06-29 20:33:18 ERROR:   duplicate key violates unique constraint "ItemID"
2006-06-29 20:33:52 ERROR:   column "itemid" does not exist
2006-06-29 20:34:34 LOG:    autovacuum: processing database "postgres"
2006-06-29 20:35:34 LOG:    autovacuum: processing database "Test"
2006-06-29 20:35:40 ERROR:   syntax error at or near "1" at character 36
```

You can change the format of the log file entries (this is also discussed in "The postgresql.conf File" section). You may notice that after the timestamp on each line is a keyword, which describes the severity of the event, followed by a short description of the event. There are a few different levels of information logged in the system log file, each one signified by a special keyword. Table 3-3 describes the different information levels stored in the log in order of severity.

Message Severity	Description
DEBUG	Program information for developers
INFO	Information requested by a database user from a database command
NOTICE	Information that may be useful to the database user regarding a submitted command
WARNING	Information about possible problems in a user session
ERROR	A minor error that caused a user command to abort
LOG	Information of interest for the administrator related to the PostgreSQL system
FATAL	A major error that caused a user session to abort
PANIC	A major error that caused the PostgreSQL system to abort

Table 3-3.   PostgreSQL Log Message Levels

As you can see from the example entries above, there are lots of events that are logged in the log file. On a busy system, it does not take long for the log file to get rather large. You can configure how PostgreSQL handles system logging using the PostgreSQL configuration file (discussed in the next section). You have lots of options of how to handle log files, such as setting the level at which PostgreSQL logs messages (the NOTICE level is the default), and setting the log file to automatically roll over to a new file if it gets past a preset size. This helps you to sift through the log file looking for problems among the normal messages.

It is always a good idea to keep an eye on the PostgreSQL log files. If you let them go on for too long, they will consume the entire available disk space on your system, and cause the PostgreSQL server to stop. Most database administrators institute a policy on when to delete old log files, and whether or not to save them before deletion.

CONFIGURATION FILES

How PostgreSQL behaves on your system is controlled by three separate configuration files. While the PostgreSQL install process creates standard configuration file values for the system to operate, knowing how to fine-tune your PostgreSQL configuration values can be a necessity for large installations. There are plenty of advanced features that you can turn on or off via the configuration files.

The PostgreSQL configuration files are standard text files, located in the database cluster directory, described earlier. Since they are standard text files, you can use the Windows Notepad application to view and modify them. On a Windows PostgreSQL installation, there is an easy way for you to edit the configuration files. The PostgreSQL menu area on the Windows Start | Programs menu (called PostgreSQL 8.2 on my installation) contains links to edit each of the three configuration files:

▼   postgresql.conf

■   pg_hba.conf

▲   pg_ident.conf

All you need to do is click the appropriate link to bring the configuration file up in a standard Windows Notepad session.

You can change configuration file values at any time while the system is running. However, the new changes will not take effect until either the system is restarted or you use the reload feature located on the PostgreSQL menu (or manually use the pg_ctl reload command, discussed later in this chapter).

When working with the configuration files, there are a few things to keep in mind. Each entry in the configuration files is on a separate line. Lines that start with a hash mark (#) are comments and not processed by the PostgreSQL system (a hash mark can be added at the end of an entry to add a comment on the entry line). If a configuration line is commented out, PostgreSQL uses the default value for that entry. You can change the default value to another value by removing the comment symbol from the line and reloading or restarting the PostgreSQL system.

However, if you want to revert to the default value for an entry, you cannot just put the comment symbol back and reload the PostgreSQL system. You must stop and restart the PostgreSQL system for the default value to take effect. This is a big "gotcha" for many novice PostgreSQL administrators.

The following sections describe the entries in the three configuration files and walk through the settings that can be controlled within the configuration files.

The postgresql.conf File

The postgresql.conf file is the main configuration file for PostgreSQL. It controls how each of the features of PostgreSQL behaves on your system. The configuration file consists of records that define each PostgreSQL feature. The format of a feature record is

```
featurename = value
```

While this is the formal definition of a feature record, in reality, the equal sign (=) is optional. As long as the *value* item is separated from the *featurename* item using white space (either one or more spaces or tabs), PostgreSQL will understand what you mean. Comments are preceded by a pound sign (#), which can be either at the start of a line to comment the entire line, or after a valid feature definition to add a comment to a feature line.

When you view the `postgres.conf` file, you will see that there are lots of feature entries that are commented out. When a feature is commented out from the configuration file, PostgreSQL assumes the default value for the feature. The configuration file shows the default value within the commented line.

In the sample `postgresql.conf` file created by the PostgreSQL installer, similar features are grouped together into sections, but this is not a requirement. Feature records can be placed anywhere in the configuration file.

You can view and modify the contents of the `postgresql.conf` file by choosing Start | Programs | PostgreSQL 8.2 | Configuration Files | Edit postgresql.conf. The configuration file contains entries for all of the features available to modify, along with their default values. The following sections describe the different configuration file sections and the features that can be modified. In each section, the feature entries are shown with their default values, followed by a description of what the feature is used for.

File Locations Section

The first section in the `postgresql.conf` configuration file is the File Locations section. This section contains features that define where the Data Dictionary and other PostgreSQL configuration files are located.

```
data_directory = 'ConfigDir'
```

The `data_directory` feature value is somewhat misleading. On the surface, it appears to point to the location where the PostgreSQL `data` directory is located. However, the location of the database cluster directory that PostgreSQL uses is specified on the command line when the PostgreSQL system starts. This location is automatically placed in the `ConfigDir` variable when the PostgreSQL system starts, which is then used in the configuration file. You cannot just enter the location of the `data` directory in this feature value and expect PostgreSQL to be able to find the file to read it.

```
hba_file = 'ConfigDir/pg_hba.conf'
```

This feature is used to reference the location of the `pg_hba.conf` configuration file. By default, it is located in the database cluster directory. You can elect to move the file to an alternative location on your system.

```
ident_file = 'ConfigDir/pg_ident.conf'
```

Similarly, this feature allows you to relocate the `pg_ident.conf` configuration file.

```
external_pid_file = '(none)'
```

By default, PostgreSQL maintains a file that contains the system process ID (PID) of the currently running PostgreSQL system. This file is used by PostgreSQL utilities to track the current PostgreSQL running process. You can define an additional copy of that file by using the `external_pid_file` feature. The default location is always kept for internal PostgreSQL use.

Connections and Authentication Section

The Connections and Authentication section contains several features that define how the PostgreSQL system interacts with clients across the network. The first group contains features that handle how the PostgreSQL system allows remote clients to connect to the server:

```
listen_addresses = 'localhost'
```

The `listen_addresses` option defines what network interfaces PostgreSQL will accept connections on. The keyword *localhost* specifies that PostgreSQL will accept connections only from applications running on the same system as the server. If you checked the Listen on All Addresses box during the installation, you will see an asterisk (*) value here. This specifies that PostgreSQL will accept connections from all network interfaces on the system. You can also specify individual network connections by their IP addresses. If there is more than one network interface on the system, you can determine which network interfaces PostgreSQL will accept connections on by placing their IP addresses in a comma-separated list.

```
port = 5432
```

The `port` feature allows you to set the TCP port that PostgreSQL listens for client connections on. If you change this value, you will have to use the new value in the client configurations.

```
max_connections = 100
```

The `max_connections` feature allows you to limit the number of clients that can connect to your PostgreSQL system simultaneously. Be careful with this value, as each connection defined consumes additional memory on your system, even when no clients are connected.

```
superuser_reserved_connections = 2
```

The `superuser_reserved_connections` feature is important if you are working in a multiuser environment. It reserves a set number of connections from the `max_connections` pool (two by default) that are reserved only for the PostgreSQL superuser (the `postgres` account by default). This ensures that there will always be a connection available for the superuser to connect, even if all of the other connections are in use.

The next group of features handles internal connections on the PostgreSQL system:

```
unix_socket_directory = ''
unix_socket_group = ''
unix_socket_permissions = 0777
```

On Windows and Unix systems, internal system communications can occur via temporary socket files created by applications. By default, PostgreSQL creates the temporary socket connections in the directory defined by the TEMP Windows environment variable. You can elect to use a different directory on your system by using this feature value. By default, the owner of the socket files is the group of the current user. You can change the group permission for these files, although it is not recommended. The 0777 permission is a Unix octal format that allows anyone to connect to PostgreSQL using the internal connection. This is not needed in the Windows PostgreSQL installation.

```
bonjour_name = ''
```

The Bonjour server is a method for network servers to advertise their DNS names on the network for servers and clients to recognize. By default, the Bonjour name of the PostgreSQL is the same as the Windows computer name. You can change the value by entering a text value in the bonjour_name feature.

The security and authentication group of features allows you to configure the user authentication features of your PostgreSQL system:

```
authentication_timeout = 60
```

This value sets the maximum amount of time (in seconds) that a client has to authenticate with the PostgreSQL server. If authentication is not complete, the connection is terminated.

```
ssl = off
```

Determines if Secure Sockets Layer (SSL)-encrypted network sessions can be used with the PostgreSQL server. The SSL feature allows clients to communicate with the PostgreSQL server using encrypted sessions.

```
password_encryption = on
```

Determines if passwords used when creating or altering PostgreSQL user accounts are encrypted by default. These passwords are stored in the PostgreSQL Data Dictionary files, which may be hacked on the local system. It is best to leave them encrypted if possible.

```
db_user_namespace = off
```

When enabled, this feature allows separate PostgreSQL user accounts to be created for each created database. As you will see in Chapter 4, by default, each PostgreSQL user account can be used to access any database on the system (limited by permission restrictions created by the administrator). By enabling this feature, you can restrict user accounts to only a single database.

Kerberos servers are popular in the Unix environment for client authentication. Most Windows administrators do not need to work with Kerberos servers, as Windows provides its own authentication method using Active Directory. If you do use Kerberos servers in your network, the following features can be used to define your environment:

▼ `krb_server_keyfile = ''` Determines the directory where Kerberos key files are located on your system

■ `krb_srvname = 'postgres'` Sets the Kerberos service name on your system

■ `krb_server_hostname = ''` Sets the Kerberos hostname for the service

▲ `krb_caseins_users = off` Determines if Kerberos usernames are case sensitive

The final group of features in this section defines advanced TCP control behavior. These features define advanced TCP parameters for fine-tuning the PostgreSQL network connectivity. For most normal situations, you should not have to worry about messing with these values.

▼ `tcp_keepalives_idle = 0` Sets the number of seconds between sending TCP keepalive packets on an idle remote client connection. The value of 0 indicates for PostgreSQL to use the Windows operating system default.

■ `tcp_keepalives_interval = 0` Specifies how long to wait for a response to a keepalive before retransmitting. The default value of 0 indicates for PostgreSQL to use the Windows operating system default.

▲ `tcp_keepalives_count = 0` Specifies how many keepalive packets can be lost before the client connection is considered dead. Again, the default value of 0 allows PostgreSQL to use the Windows operating system default.

Be careful when changing the TCP features. If you are interested in changing any of these values, please consult a TCP/IP networking book.

Resource Usage Section

The Resource Usage section of the configuration file defines how PostgreSQL handles memory usage on your system. As mentioned in Chapter 2, PostgreSQL will attempt to use as much memory as you give it. The feature values in this section help control exactly how much memory in your system PostgreSQL attempts to take for its internal processes.

```
shared_buffers = 1000
```

The `shared_buffers` value determines the amount of overall memory PostgreSQL will consume. Each shared buffer is 8124 bytes. Unfortunately, there are no hard rules for setting this value. One rule of thumb is that it should be at least double the number you define in the `max_connections` feature value. Obviously, the larger the value the more memory PostgreSQL will use, and the faster the PostgreSQL system will operate.

Most PostgreSQL administrators recommend using a value of at least 2000, and working up or down from there, depending on the performance of your particular system. For a standard Windows workstation installation, the default value of 1000 should be fine.

```
temp_buffers = 1000
```

This feature determines the maximum number 8124 byte temporary memory buffers used by each database session. As individual sessions access tables, temporary memory buffers are created to store information. You can limit the amount of memory each session is allowed to consume using this value. Again, this is a performance feature that can be experimented with in your specific PostgreSQL environment.

```
max_prepared_transactions = 5
```

The `max_prepared_transactions` feature value determines the number of simultaneous transactions that are in the PREPARE TRANSACTION process before the two-phase transaction commit process is run (transactions are discussed in Chapter 7). Processing a transaction uses memory resources, so allowing parallel transaction processing, while helpful in increasing database performance, can be a drain on system memory. If your applications do not use this feature, you can set this value to zero. If you are in a multiuser environment, this value should be at least as large as the `max_connections` feature value, so each client has the ability to have transactions processed simultaneously.

```
work_mem = 1024
```

This feature limits the amount of memory used by internal sort and hashing functions in the entire PostgreSQL system. This value is in kilobytes, so the default value of 1024 kilobytes is 1MB of memory space. If a sort or hash function exceeds this limit, data is swapped out to temporary files to complete the process. This is extremely costly to database performance, and is a crucial element in performance tuning (see Chapter 10).

```
maintenance_work_mem = 16384
```

Sets the amount of memory (in kilobytes) allowed for internal PostgreSQL database maintenance operations. These functions include creating table indexes, removing deleted records, and altering existing tables. This value is in kilobytes, so the default value is 16MB.

```
max_stack_depth = 2048
```

This feature sets the size of the PostgreSQL server's execution stack level. This limits the number of processes that can wait for execution. The value is in kilobytes, so the default value is 2MB.

```
max_fsm_pages = 20000
max_fsm_relations = 1000
```

The `max_fsm_relations` value should be set to the maximum number of tables and indexes you plan on having in your database. The `max_fsm_pages` value defines the number of disk pages for which free space will be tracked. This value should be at least 16 times the value in the `max_fsm_relations` value.

```
max_files_per_process = 1000
```

The `max_files_per_process` feature limits the number of open files a single PostgreSQL process can have.

```
preload_libraries = ''
```

This feature specifies a list of libraries that are preloaded into the PostgreSQL server at startup. The default is not to load any libraries.

The next group of features in the Resource Usage section deals with database vacuuming. The PostgreSQL system utilizes a feature called *vacuuming* to remove deleted records. Vacuuming the database is described in detail a little later in the "Autovacuum Parameters" section. When the PostgreSQL system initiates a vacuum process, the system tracks how many system resources are consumed by the vacuum. You can control how many resources the system allows the vacuum process to take before limiting the process by using these feature values:

▼ `vacuum_cost_delay = 0` The length of time in milliseconds that the vacuum process will sleep if it exceeds its process limits. The default value of 0 disables this feature.

■ `vacuum_cost_page_hit = 1` The estimated cost for vacuuming a buffer found in the shared buffer cache.

■ `vacuum_cost_page_miss = 10` The estimated cost for vacuuming a buffer that has to be read from disk.

■ `vacuum_cost_page_dirty = 20` The estimated cost for modifying a block that was previously clean.

▲ `vacuum_cost_limit = 200` The total cost that will cause a vacuum process to sleep.

The PostgreSQL *background writer* process ensures that memory buffers containing transaction data are written to the hard disks as soon as possible. This group of feature values can be fine-tuned by advanced administrators to determine exactly how often the memory buffers are written.

▼ `bgwriter_delay = 200` Specifies the delay in milliseconds between background writer process runs.

■ `bgwriter_lru_percent = 1.0` The percentage of buffers examined in one background writer process.

- `bgwriter_lru_maxpages = 5`   The maximum number of buffers that can be written in one background writer process. Left over buffers are saved for the next background writer process run.

- `bgwriter_all_percent = 0.333`   The percentage of the entire buffer pool examined in one background writer process. This value states that one-third of the buffer pool will be examined during each background writer process, so the entire pool will be examined every three runs.

▲ `bgwriter_all_maxpages = 5`   The maximum number of buffers from the entire buffer pool that can be examined in one background writer process.

Write Ahead Log Section

The Write Ahead Log (WAL) feature allows PostgreSQL to submit transactions to the transaction log before they are processed in the database. This provides for a more stable environment where all transactions are recoverable in case of a database crash. The transaction log is guaranteed to contain the transactions performed on the database data, even if the database crashes before a transaction is committed to the database. The transaction logs are created as files (called segments) that are stored in the `pg_xlog` directory of the database cluster area.

`fsync = on`

This feature ensures that each individual transaction is written to disk immediately instead of being stored in the WAL. Keeping this feature enabled results in decreased database performance, but ensures data durability and security. Disabling this feature allows multiple transactions to accumulate in the WAL transaction log files before being written to disk.

`wal_sync_method = fsync`

This value determines the method PostgreSQL uses to write data to disk. This value is set by the PostgreSQL installer and is optimized for the operating system that PostgreSQL is installed on. The other values listed under this feature in the configuration file are used for other operating systems that PostgreSQL can run on. You do not need to change these values for a Windows environment.

`full_page_writes = on`

Determines if PostgreSQL writes data to the WAL transaction log files based on a single database record or an entire page of records.

`wal_buffers = 8`

The number of 8124-byte disk page buffers allocated in shared memory for the WAL.

`commit_delay = 0`

The delay in microseconds between when PostgreSQL writes a committed record to the WAL and when it writes the WAL log files to the database. If the value is larger than 0, PostgreSQL can write multiple transactions that occur during that timeframe to disk in one process.

```
commit_siblings = 5
```

The minimum number of open concurrent transactions before starting the `commit_delay` timer.

```
checkpoint_segments = 3
```

The maximum number of 16MB log file segments between writing the WAL log files to the database. *Checkpoints* are points in the transaction process when PostgreSQL stores all of the data in the WAL to disk. After the checkpoint, it is guaranteed that the data in the WAL is safely in the database files. This value means that for every three segments (48MB) of data, PostgreSQL will force the WAL to be saved to disk.

```
checkpoint_timeout = 300
```

The time in seconds between writing the WAL to the database. If the `checkpoint_segment` value hasn't been met within this timeframe, the WAL is written to disk.

```
checkpoint_warning = 30
```

PostgreSQL writes a message to the system log file if the WAL segment files get filled within the defined value (in seconds).

```
archive_command = ''
```

The `archive_command` feature allows you to define a system command to copy (archive) WAL files to another location on the server for additional backup. In a high-availability production environment, you can configure PostgreSQL to copy the WAL files to an alternative location (usually on a separate physical disk). This is covered in more detail in Chapter 10.

Query Tuning Section

PostgreSQL allows you to fine-tune how it handles database queries. PostgreSQL attempts to optimize all database queries. You can control the methods PostgreSQL uses to optimize queries using these features. Query performance is discussed in detail in Chapter 10, but nonetheless, here are the features associated with this function:

```
enable_bitmapscan = on
enable_hashagg = on
enable_hashjoin = on
enable_indexscan = on
```

```
enable_mergejoin = on
enable_nestloop = on
enable_seqscan = on
enable_sort = on
enable_tidscan = on
effective_cache_size = 1000
random_page_cost = 4
cpu_tuple_cost = 0.01
cpu_index_tuple_cost = 0.001
cpu_operator_cost = 0.0025
geqo = on
geqo_threshold = 12
geqo_effort = 5
geqo_pool_size = 0
geqo_generations = 0
geqo_selection_bias = 2.0
default_statistics_target = 10
constraint_exclusion = off
from_collapse_limit = 8
join_collapse_limit = 8
```

Error Reporting and Logging Section

The Error Reporting and Logging section allows you to define how PostgreSQL logs errors and informational messages generated by the system. You can configure PostgreSQL to be as verbose or as quiet as you need in your environment.

```
log_destination = 'stderr'
```

This value sets the location to which PostgreSQL sends log messages. The possible entries for this value can only be the standard error file (stderr), the standard log (syslog) file, or in the case of Windows, the system eventlog. The Windows eventlog can be viewed from the Windows Computer Manager window (discussed in Chapter 2).

```
redirect_stderr = on
```

Enabling this feature allows you to redirect log messages sent to stderr to an alternative location, such as a log file. This feature is enabled by default, to create a separate log file for PostgreSQL.

```
log_directory = 'pg_log'
```

The directory where the redirected log files will be written.

```
log_filename = 'postgresql-%Y-%m-%d_%H%M%S.log'
```

The filename the log file will be redirected to. The filename can use wildcard characters to use the current year (`%Y`), month (`%m`), day (`%d`), hour (`%H`), minute (`%M`), and section (`%S`).

```
log_truncate_on_rotation = off
```

When this feature is enabled, PostgreSQL will overwrite an existing log file using the same log filename when PostgreSQL is restarted. When disabled, existing log files will be appended with the new log messages.

```
log_rotation_age = 1440
```

Sets the time (in minutes) when a new log file will automatically be started. Depending on the `log_filename` feature, the new log file may be a separate file (such as if the filename uses a timestamp). If the new log filename is the same name, depending on the `log_truncate_on_rotation` feature, it may or may not overwrite the existing log file.

```
log_rotation_size = 10240
```

Sets the size (in kilobytes) when a new log file will be started.

```
syslog_facility = 'LOCAL0'
```

Defines the system facility used for logging log files. The `LOCAL0` value instructs PostgreSQL to use the syslog (or Windows eventlog) feature.

```
syslog_ident = 'postgres'
```

Identifies the username used when logging messages to the syslog (or the Windows eventlog).

```
client_min_messages = notice
```

Sets the minimum level of log messages logged by client connections. All messages with this severity or higher (see Table 3-3) are logged.

```
log_min_messages = notice
```

Sets the minimum level of log messages logged by the PostgreSQL server. All messages with this severity or higher (see Table 3-3) are logged.

```
log_error_verbosity = default
```

Sets the amount of detail logged to the system log for each message. The other values are `terse`, for shortened messages, and `verbose`, for longer messages.

```
log_min_error_statement = panic
```

Sets the severity of errors in SQL statements that are logged. The hierarchy of error messages was shown earlier in Table 3-3.

```
log_min_duration_statement = -1
```

Logs the SQL statement that produced the error and its duration to the log file. If set to 0, all SQL statements are logged. If set to -1, no SQL statements are logged.

```
silent_mode = off
```

If enabled, this feature allows the PostgreSQL server to run as a background process with no standard output or error connections. All messages sent to the logging facilities are ignored.

```
debug_print_parse = off
debug_print_rewritten = off
debug_print_plan = off
debug_pretty_print = off
```

The debug family of features determines how debugging output is handled. These features, described in Chapter 10, are used by developers.

```
log_connections = off
```

This feature enables PostgreSQL to log each client connection made to the system.

```
log_disconnections = off
```

This feature logs each time a client disconnects from the system.

```
log_duration = off
```

Logs the duration of each client session with the system.

```
log_line_prefix = '%t '
```

Sets the first identifier on the log line. The default value (%t) uses the timestamp of the message as the first identifier on the log line. Other options that you can use are username (%u), database name (%d), remote hostname or IP address and port (%r), remote hostname or IP address only(%h), the process ID (%p), timestamp with milliseconds (%m), command tag (%i), session ID (%c), log line number (%l), session start timestamp (%s), transaction ID (%x), and no identifier (%q). Any combination of these values can be used.

```
log_statement = 'none'
```

Determines what SQL statements are logged in the system log file. The default is to log no SQL statements. You can also use ddl to log data definition SQL statements, such as CREATE, ALTER, and DROP, mod to log data definition SQL statements and data modification SQL statements such as INSERT, UPDATE, DELETE, and TRUNCATE, and all, which logs all SQL statements.

```
log_hostname = off
```

This feature allows you to record the hostname of all client connections in the system log file.

Runtime Statistics Section

The Runtime Statistics section allows you to configure PostgreSQL to log database performance statistics. These features allow you to view internal PostgreSQL statistics. These features are discussed in more detail in Chapter 10.

```
log_parser_stats = off
log_planner_stats = off
log_executor_stats = off
log_statement_stats = off
stats_start_collector = on
stats_command_string = off
stats_block_level = off
stats_row_level = on
stats_reset_on_server_start = off
```

Autovacuum Parameters Section

In a DBMS, deleted records are not really removed from the database at the time you execute a delete command. Instead, deleted records are just marked for deletion and kept in the database. This feature enables you to restore any deleted records if you (or your customers) change your mind.

The downside to this feature is that deleted records take up space in the database. Depending on the amount of updates and deletes performed on data, over time this extra space can add up and have a negative impact on database performance. To accommodate this problem, PostgreSQL allows you to remove database records marked for deletion. This process is called *vacuuming*.

Besides manually vacuuming a database, you can allow PostgreSQL to automatically vacuum the database at preset times. The autovacuum feature in PostgreSQL is controlled by this section.

```
autovacuum = on
```

This value enables or disables (off) the database autovacuum feature within PostgreSQL.

```
autovacuum_naptime = 60
```

This value sets the amount of time (in seconds) that PostgreSQL will run the autovacuum feature.

```
autovacuum_vacuum_threshold = 1000
autovacuum_analyze_threshold = 500
autovacuum_vacuum_scale_factor = 0.4
autovacuum_analyze_scale_factor = 0.2
autovacuum_vacuum_cost_delay = -1
autovacuum_vacuum_cost_limit = -1
```

Once the `autovacuum` feature is enabled, these features control when tables are autovacuumed, based on the number of transactions (vacuum threshold), or when tables are analyzed, based on the number of transactions (analyze threshold). If any of these parameters are met before the configured `autovacuum_naptime` value, the autovacuum is performed.

Client Connection Defaults Section

This section allows you to specify special parameters for how data is handled in client connections.

```
search_path = '$user,public'
```

Defines the default order in which database schemas (described in Chapter 4) are searched when an object is referenced without a schema. By default, the user's own schema is searched first, followed by the public schema.

```
default_tablespace = ''
```

This value specifies the default tablespace (described in Chapter 4) where PostgreSQL creates objects. The default value is for PostgreSQL to use the tablespace where the database is located.

```
check_function_bodies = on
```

This value instructs PostgreSQL to check new functions as they are created by users to ensure the functions will work within the database tables.

```
default_transaction_isolation = 'read committed'
```

This value defines the default isolation level used by PostgreSQL for transactions (described in Chapter 7).

```
default_transaction_read_only = off
```

This value, when enabled, prevents transactions from altering tables.

```
statement_timeout = 0
```

This value provides the time, in milliseconds, that PostgreSQL allows an SQL statement to run. The default value of 0 disables this feature, which allows SQL statements to take as long as they need to process.

The next group of features defines how times, dates, and characters are formatted within PostgreSQL.

```
datestyle = 'iso, mdy'
```

This value specifies the format used to display dates. The default value displays dates using the ISO format, using the month/day/year style. Other styles available are DMY and YMD.

```
timezone = unknown
```

This value sets the default time zone for displaying times. The default of unknown forces PostgreSQL to use the system settings.

```
australian_timezones = off
```

When enabled, PostgreSQL interprets the ACST, CST, EST, and SAT time zones as Australian instead of North American.

```
extra_float_digits = 0
```

This value specifies the number of extra digits displayed for floating-point numbers.

```
client_encoding = sql_ascii
```

This value specifies the client-side data encoding method used by the PostgreSQL client. The default value is the database encoding.

```
lc_messages = 'C'
lc_monetary = 'C'
lc_numeric = 'C'
lc_time = 'C'
```

These features set the language locale used for messages, money values, number formatting, and time formatting. The default is set in the PostgreSQL installer program (see Chapter 2). The C value formats all values using the ISO C format, which assumes that the local operating system controls language formatting.

Lock Management Section

Lock management defines how PostgreSQL handles record lock situations.

```
deadlock_timeout = 1000
```

This feature defines the time in milliseconds for PostgreSQL to wait for a record lock before checking for a deadlock situation (when two or more processes attempt to access the same record at the same time). If a deadlock situation occurs, PostgreSQL initiates the Multiversion Concurrency Control (MVCC) feature to resolve the deadlock. Implementing this feature too early can negatively impact database performance.

```
max_locks_per_transaction = 64
```

This value sets the number of locked records allowed per transaction per client.

Version/Platform Compatibility Section

The Version/Platform Compatibility section defines how the currently installed PostgreSQL version behaves with previous versions of the software, as well as when working on different platforms.

```
add_missing_from = off
```

When this value is enabled, tables referenced by a query are automatically added to the FROM SQL clause if not already present. While this behavior is not standard SQL, this feature was present in previous PostgreSQL versions.

```
backslash_quote = safe_encoding
```

This value controls how the PostgreSQL server handles backslashes in client connections. This feature was recently modified due to a security exploit. When the feature is disabled (off), statements with backslashes are always rejected. When the feature is enabled (on), statements with backslashes are always allowed. The default value of safe_encoding allows backslashes if the client also supports an encoding that allows backslashes.

```
default_with_oids = off
```

This value controls whether a CREATE TABLE or CREATE TABLE AS statement includes an object ID (OID) column by default. In PostgreSQL versions previous to 8.1, this was enabled by default. If you reference a table field as a foreign key in another table (see Chapter 4), the referenced table must be created with an OID. However, not all tables need to be created with an OID column.

```
escape_string_warning = off
```

When this value is enabled, PostgreSQL writes a warning message to the system log file when a SQL statement contains a backslash character.

```
regex_flavor = advanced
sql_inheritance = on
```

These two features control the behavior of the PostgreSQL system to match previous versions. The regex feature changed in PostgreSQL 7.4. If you need to run applications from a previous version of PostgreSQL, you may need to set this value to either `basic` or `extended`. The table inheritance feature of PostgreSQL (discussed in Chapter 1) changed significantly in version 7.4. If you need to run applications created in a previous version of PostgreSQL, you will have to disable this feature.

```
transform_null_equals = off
```

This feature is extremely important if you are accessing your PostgreSQL database from Microsoft Access (see Chapter 12). Microsoft Access uses the `NULL` value in queries somewhat differently than the standard SQL specifications. If you are building queries using Access, you will need to enable this feature.

Customized Options Section

Finally, as a catchall, PostgreSQL allows you to define your own internal variable classes:

```
custom_variable_classes = ''
```

This feature allows you to define new variables for special classes within PostgreSQL. A comma-separated list of the new classes must be provided to this feature. Variables within the class are identified as *classname.variable*. This is an advanced feature that is not normally used by PostgreSQL users.

The pg_hba.conf File

You can restrict how clients connect to your PostgreSQL system by editing the host-based authentication configuration file, named `pg_hba.conf`. There are four things you can restrict from this configuration file:

- ▼ Which network hosts are allowed to connect to PostgreSQL
- ■ Which PostgreSQL usernames can be used to connect from the network
- ■ What authentication method users must use to log into the system
- ▲ Which PostgreSQL databases an authenticated client can connect to

Each line in the `pg_hba.conf` file contains a separate definition (record) controlling access to the system. Multiple records can be created to define different access types and categories to the system. For a remote client to gain access to the PostgreSQL system, the conditions of at least one record must be met. If multiple records match a specific client, only the first matching record in the configuration file is used for authentication.

The format of a `pg_hba.conf` record is

```
connection-type  database  user  network-address  login-method  options
```

The following sections describe each of these fields.

Connection-type Field

The *connection-type* field defines the method used by the client to connect to the PostgreSQL system. There are four types of connections that are supported by PostgreSQL:

▼ `local`   Uses a local Unix-domain style socket on the system

■ `host`   Uses a plain or SSL-encrypted TCP/IP socket

■ `hostssl`   Uses an SSL-encrypted TCP/IP socket

▲ `hostnossl`   Uses a plain TCP/IP socket

Remember that to allow remote clients to connect, you must have enabled the Listen on All Addresses feature during the PostgreSQL installation (see Chapter 2). If you did not do that, and now want to allow remote clients to connect, you must change the `listen_addresses` entry in the `postgresql.conf` configuration file, discussed later in this chapter.

Database Field

The *database* field defines which PostgreSQL databases the record controls access to. There are several formats that can be used for this field:

▼ A single database name

■ A comma-separated list of database names

■ The keyword `all`, for all databases configured on the system

■ The keyword `sameuser`, for a database with the same name as the user account

■ The keyword `samerole`, for a database with the same name as a role the user is a member of

▲ A filename, preceded by an at sign (@), to specify a file containing a text list of database names

The record only applies to the databases specified in this field. Clients matching this record will not be given access to any nonmatching database in the system, unless specified in a separate record in the configuration file.

User Field

The *user* field defines which PostgreSQL user accounts are controlled by this record. Remember, this applies to the PostgreSQL username, and not to the logged-in username on the operating system. Similar to the *database* field, there are a few different formats you can use for this field:

▼ A single username

■ A comma-separated list of usernames

■ A role name, preceded by a plus sign (+), to enable all users who are members of the role

▲ A filename, preceded by an at sign (@), to specify a file containing a text list of usernames

The user accounts listed in the record are allowed access to the databases listed in the record. This does not override normal PostgreSQL database security on tables (discussed in Chapter 4) once a client is connected to the database, but provides a front-end access control method for remote clients to gain initial entry into the database.

Network-address Field

The *network-address* field defines which network hosts clients are allowed to connect to the PostgreSQL system from. This is a handy way to restrict access to your system to clients on your local network, or even to just one specific host on your network.

The network address cannot be written using a host's domain name. The *network-address* field must be entered in one of two formats:

▼ A host address and subnet mask pair

▲ A Classless Inter-Domain Routing (CIDR)-formatted address

The old method of specifying host addresses is the host address/subnet mask pair method. This uses two separate values: a dotted-decimal host or network address, and a dotted-decimal subnet mask address. The subnet mask defines how many bits of the address are used to define the network address and host address. For example, the subnet mask 255.255.255.255 is used to define a single host on the network. The subnet mask 255.255.255.0 defines a subnet of hosts that uses the fourth octet in the network address for the host address.

The CIDR format is becoming more popular in the networking world. This method uses a host or network address in dotted-decimal notation, along with a single integer value to define the number of bits enabled in the subnet mask. For example, the CIDR address 192.168.0.10/32 indicates the host at address 192.168.0.10, using all 32 bits for the subnet mask, or 255.255.255.255. This defines a single host address on the network. The CIDR address 192.168.0.0/27 indicates all of the hosts on subnet 192.168.0.0, using subnet mask 255.255.255.0. This provides for any host whose address is from 192.168.0.1 to 192.168.0.254 to connect to the databases listed in the record.

Login-method Field

The *login-method* field defines the method the client must use to authenticate with the PostgreSQL system. PostgreSQL supports quite a few different login methods. Unfortunately, though, some of the supported methods are only available on Unix platforms. The values available on Windows installations are as follows:

▼ trust

■ reject

- ident
- password
- md5
- crypt
- ▲ krb5

The `trust` authentication method provides for no password requirement. It assumes that any client that connects to the PostgreSQL server should be allowed to access database items. It relies on the PostgreSQL database restrictions to handle the actual restrictions. This feature works fine in a single-user environment, but is not recommended in a multiuser environment.

The `reject` authentication method specifically prohibits clients matching the record from accessing the PostgreSQL system. This is often used for temporarily restricting access to the system for a specific user or host.

The `ident` authentication method uses the client userid from the client's host system. The system assumes that all client authentication has been performed by the remote host system to verify the userid supplied is valid. The remote client userid is then mapped to a valid PostgreSQL user account using a separate configuration file. This will be discussed in more detail later in "The pg_ident.conf File" section.

The next three authentication methods provide for a client to send a separate password through the TCP/IP connection to the PostgreSQL server. The password can be in one of three forms, as described for the following authentication methods:

- ▼ `password`   Sends password in plain text through the connection
- `md5`   Sends an MD-5-encrypted version of the password through the connection
- ▲ `crypt`   Sends a crypt-encrypted version of the password through the connection

Obviously, if you are working on an open network such as the Internet, it is best to use one of the encrypted authentication methods (unless you are connecting using an SSL connection). If you are just experimenting on your own home network or internal corporate network, the `password` authentication method works just fine.

The `krb5` authentication method uses secure Kerberos technology to send an encrypted password key between the client and PostgreSQL server. This is the most secure method of authentication.

Options Field

The *options* field provides an area for options to be supplied when using the `ident` authentication method. The keyword `sameuser` is used to bypass the `pg_ident.conf` configuration file and pass the received client userid to PostgreSQL as the logged on user account. This assumes that PostgreSQL user account names match the userids assigned to users by the remote host.

If this is not the case, a map name can be specified as the option to point to a specific entry class in the `pg_ident.conf` configuration file. PostgreSQL matches the remote client userid within the map name class to a PostgreSQL user account defined in the configuration file. The upcoming section "The pg_ident.conf File" explains this process in more detail.

Example pg_hba.conf Records

Now that you have seen what all of the record fields look like, it is time to take a look at a few examples. If you look at the default `pg_hba.conf` configuration file created by the PostgreSQL install, you should see the following record:

```
host    all    all    127.0.0.1/32    md5
```

This entry applies to all host connections originating from the local loopback address (127.0.0.1) of the PostgreSQL server for all users connecting to all databases. Basically, this applies to every time you connect to the PostgreSQL server from the local system. This record specifies that these types of connections must use the md5 authentication method to authenticate PostgreSQL user accounts. Thus, you must supply an appropriate password when you try to log into the PostgreSQL system from the local server.

Here is another sample record that can be created:

```
host    all    postgres    192.168.0.10/32    md5
```

This record only allows the `postgres` user account to connect to any database from the single network host address of 192.168.0.10. The `postgres` user account will not be allowed to log in from any other network address.

Finally, take a look at this example:

```
host    all    all    192.168.1.0/27    password
```

This record allows any client on the local 192.168.1.0 subnetwork to connect as any user to any database using plain-text authentication. Of course, once the client connection is made, PostgreSQL database restrictions still apply for database access (discussed in Chapter 4). Again, be very careful when using the `password` authentication method, as it can be susceptible to network snooping.

The pg_ident.conf File

As discussed earlier in the "The `pg_hba.conf` file" section, the `pg_ident.conf` configuration file provides a method for you to map remote client user accounts to PostgreSQL user accounts. The format of records in this configuration file is

```
map-name    ident-name    PostgreSQL-user-account
```

The *map-name* field contains the name associated with the pg_hba.conf ident field option. This allows you to set up different maps if you have users accessing the system using the same userids from different remote host systems.

The *ident-name* field contains the userid that is passed from the client system to PostgreSQL in the connection. The account is mapped to the specific PostgreSQL user account specified in the record.

As an example, assume you have the following record in your pg_hba.conf file:

```
host   all   all   192.168.0.10/32   ident   testhost
```

All users from the host 192.168.0.10 will have access to all PostgreSQL databases. User accounts from this host are mapped to PostgreSQL user accounts using the testhost ident mapping. Now, we need to look at how the pg_ident.conf file maps these user accounts. Assume you have the following records in your pg_indent.conf file:

```
testhost   rich   richard
testhost   mike   michael
testhost   dan    daniel
```

When the user rich connects from the host 192.168.0.10, he is automatically mapped to the richard PostgreSQL user account on the system. The same process happens for users mike and dan. If any user other than rich, mike, or dan attempts to connect from this host, they will be denied access to the PostgreSQL system.

PROGRAMS

All of the PostgreSQL main program files are located in the bin directory. While most Unix administrators live and die by these utilities, Windows administrators will want to use the graphical tools available in the pgAdmin III application (discussed next in Chapter 4). However, even in Windows it is sometimes easier to just use a simple command-line program than to start up a full Windows program just to perform a single function.

To run the PostgreSQL utilities, you either need to be in the PostgreSQL bin directory or set your Windows PATH environment variable to include this directory. The easiest method to run these programs is to use the Command Prompt item in the PostgreSQL menu (Start | Programs | PostgreSQL 8.2 | Command Prompt). This creates a command prompt window that defaults to the bin directory.

This section describes some of the more popular PostgreSQL command-line utilities that are available, and demonstrates how to use them.

PostgreSQL Server Commands

PostgreSQL provides several server commands that are used to perform specific system functions directly on the PostgreSQL server. These commands are stand-alone programs, interacting directly with the PostgreSQL server. Obviously, for these commands to work, the PostgreSQL server must be running.

pg_config

The `pg_config` program provides a quick way to see the current configuration values on the running PostgreSQL system. These are not the configuration values that are defined in the three configuration files shown earlier. Instead, these are configuration values that were used to compile and install the PostgreSQL package.

pg_ctl

The `pg_ctl` program is used to control the PostgreSQL system. It is used to stop, start, or reload the configuration files for PostgreSQL. To perform one of these functions, though, you must specify the database cluster area used by PostgreSQL using the `-D` command-line option:

```
C:\>pg_ctl stop -D "c:\Program Files\PostgreSQL\8.2\data"
waiting for postmaster to shut down..... done
postmaster stopped

C:\>
```

Notice that if the database cluster pathname includes spaces, you must enclose the pathname with double quotes. To start the database, you must either be logged in as a user account without administrator privileges or use the Windows `runas` command to run as another user:

```
C:\>runas /user:postgres "pg_ctl start -D \"c:\Program Files\PostgreSQL
\8.2\data\""
Enter the password for postgres:
Attempting to start pg_ctl start -D "c:\Program Files\PostgreSQL\8.2\data"
 as user "EZEKIEL\postgres" ...

C:\>
```

If you use the `runas` command to run `pg_ctl`, the command line gets even more complicated. Since the `runas` command line includes spaces, you must enclose the entire command in double quotes. However, the `pg_ctl` command also requires double quotes. As you can see in the preceding code, the solution is to use the backslash character (\) to escape out the double quotes required for the `pg_ctl` command.

pg_dump

The `pg_dump` program provides an easy way for you to dump (or back up) the contents of a database on the PostgreSQL system to a file.

The `pg_dump` program can output the dump in one of two dump file formats:

▼ Script

▲ Archived

The Script dump format creates a text file that contains SQL statements that will re-create the database and insert the appropriate data. The Script dump file can be run on any system that can read SQL statements, such as the `psql` program described in the next section.

The Archived dump format creates a compressed binary file of the database that can only be restored using the `pg_restore` program, discussed a bit later in the chapter.

There are lots of command-line options used to control how `pg_dump` works. The `-F` option is used to specify the backup type (c for compressed binary, t for uncompressed binary, or p for plain SQL). You can specify the filename to write the backup to using the `-f` command-line option. To produce a compressed backup file of the database `test`, you would use the following command:

```
C:\>pg_dump test -f test.backup -Fc -U postgres
Password:

C:\>dir *.backup
```

As you can see from the example, you can also specify the user account to use for the backup by using the `-U` option. The `pg_dump` program does not provide any status, it just quietly performs the backup and exits. If you want to see what it is doing, you can use the verbose option, `-v`.

pg_dumpall

The `pg_dumpall` program is similar to the `pg_dump` program, except it dumps all of the databases in a PostgreSQL database cluster to a file that can later be used to restore the entire PostgreSQL system. This also includes all system tables and user accounts, so you must log in as the PostgreSQL superuser account to run this program.

By default, the `pg_dumpall` utility produces the SQL statements necessary to re-create the entire system, and sends them to the standard output (the console window display). You can redirect this output to a file by using the standard Windows redirect symbol:

```
C:\>pg_dumpall -U postgres > backup.sql
```

When you run this command, it will ask several times for the `postgres` user password (each time it connects to a different database). This command creates the file `backup.sql`, which contains SQL statements for creating the user accounts, databases, tables, and all other database objects in your PostgreSQL system.

It is recommended that you run the `pg_dump` utility on a regular basis, and copy the resulting backup file to a removable storage medium. The PostgreSQL system allows you to run the `pg_dump` program without having to stop the database. It manages all user transactions during the backup process, and applies them when the backup is complete.

The backup file produced by the `pg_dumpall` program is in Script format. The database can be restored using a standard SQL command-prompt interface, such as `psql`. You must also be logged into the system as the superuser account to restore database and user objects.

pg_restore

After using the `pg_dump` program to dump a database to an archived dump format file, reason would have it that at some point you may need to restore that data. The `pg_restore` program is just the tool for that job. It allows you to restore a database from a file created by the `pg_dump` program.

The `pg_restore` program also provides command-line options that allow you to select which parts of a total database dump you want to restore.

postmaster

The `postmaster` program is the main program that controls the PostgreSQL system. It must be running in the background at all times for anyone to be able to access data in the PostgreSQL database cluster. All applications (both local and remote) must connect to the `postmaster` program to interface with the database. In the Windows implementation of PostgreSQL, the PostgreSQL installer can configure the `postmaster` program to run as a Windows service to ensure that it is always running on the host system.

Each instance of the `postmaster` program references a single database cluster area. It is possible to have two or more `postmaster` programs running on the same server, each referencing different database cluster areas.

postgres

The `postgres` program is the database engine part of PostgreSQL. The `postmaster` program spawns multiple copies of the `postgres` program to handle database queries. As seen in Chapter 2, when you look at the running processes on your Windows system, you will see one copy of the `postmaster` program and several copies of the `postgres` program running.

It is possible to use the `postgres` program on the command line as a stand-alone program to query the database, but this is not an easy task. With the `psql` program available, you should never need to use `postgres` from the command prompt.

SQL Wrapper Commands

You can perform most database operations by interfacing with the procedural language interfaces installed on the PostgreSQL system. The `psql` interface provides a platform for you to use standard SQL commands to do things such as create and delete databases and user accounts.

However, sometimes it is nice to be able to do some functions directly without having to use the procedural language interface. The PostgreSQL SQL wrapper commands allow you to do just that. Some basic SQL commands are incorporated into separate Windows commands you can use both at the Windows command prompt and within Windows batch files. Table 3-4 describes the SQL wrapper commands that are available for you to use.

Since all of these commands are duplicated in the graphical pgAdmin III program, they are almost never used in the Windows environment.

Command	Description
clusterdb	Reclusters tables in a database
createdb	Creates a new database
createlang	Adds a programming language to a database
createuser	Creates a new user in the PostgreSQL system
Dropdb	Deletes an existing database
droplang	Removes an existing programming language from a database
reindexdb	Rebuilds indexes in the database
vacuumdb	Removes deleted records from a database, and generates statistics

Table 3-4. The PostgreSQL SQL Wrapper Commands

PostgreSQL Applications

Finally, there are two special applications that are included in the PostgreSQL installation. These applications help you interface with the PostgreSQL server and provide an easy way for you to administer and use your databases.

psql

The psql application provides a command-line interface to the PostgreSQL system. From here you can execute standard SQL commands, as well as special psql commands used for querying the database to see what tables, indexes, and other features are available in the database. The psql program is examined in detail in Chapter 5.

pgAdmin III

The pgAdmin III application is a program that provides a fancy graphical interface for administering a PostgreSQL system. The pgAdmin III program is a separately developed Open Source application. The home page for pgAdmin III is www.pgadmin.org.

This application allows you to perform any database function from a graphical front end. You can add or remove databases, users, tables, and tablespaces easily using the graphical icons. The pgAdmin III program also includes a SQL command interface, allowing you to enter SQL queries and view the results. It is the Swiss Army knife for PostgreSQL systems. Chapter 4 covers the pgAdmin III program and how to use it to completely manage your PostgreSQL system.

SUMMARY

This chapter covered a lot of ground. The PostgreSQL installation includes lots of files and directories to support all of its functions. The main PostgreSQL directory is located by default at `C:\Program Files\Postgresql`. Each update release has its own directory under the main directory. Within the update release directory, PostgreSQL divides files into several directories. The `data` directory contains the database cluster files and directories necessary for the database engine. The `data` directory also contains the PostgreSQL configuration files. The `postgresql.conf` configuration file defines all of the features available in the PostgreSQL system. You can edit this file to fine-tune your PostgreSQL installation. The `pg_hba.conf` configuration file allows you to define which PostgreSQL users can log in from remote workstations, as well as control which databases they have access to. The `bin` directory contains the utilities and programs that you use to interact with PostgreSQL. There are several SQL wrapper commands that provide command-prompt programs that implement standard SQL commands. This allows you to execute SQL commands without having to use a SQL interface.

The next chapter discusses the pgAdmin III application, which allows you to perform all of your database administration functions from a graphical interface. You will see that you can do all of your administration work from a single interface, making your life much easier.

CHAPTER 4

Managing PostgreSQL on Windows

The previous chapter showed you where all of the database, configuration, and program files are located on your PostgreSQL system. It is now time to dive in and start working with the actual PostgreSQL system. This chapter walks you through the basic functions required to manage your PostgreSQL server. The pgAdmin III program provides an easy interface for you to perform all of the management functions required to keep your PostgreSQL server running. There are many pieces to manage within a PostgreSQL system, and trying to keep track of them all can be a challenge. This chapter walks you through each of the parts in the system, and shows how to manage them using pgAdmin III.

THE pgADMIN III PROGRAM

For the PostgreSQL database administrator, the pgAdmin III tool is the Swiss Army knife of utilities. Any function you need to perform on your PostgreSQL system you can do from within the pgAdmin III graphical interface.

The pgAdmin III program is installed within the main PostgreSQL installer program (see Chapter 2). To start pgAdmin III, you can either choose Start | Programs | PostgreSQL 8.2 | pgAdmin III or double-click the executable file (pgadmin3.exe) located in the PostgreSQL bin directory. When pgAdmin III starts, the main window appears, shown in Figure 4-1.

By default, pgAdmin III is configured to connect to a PostgreSQL server running on the local system (using the special localhost IP hostname), and use the default PostgreSQL TCP port of 5432. You can also use pgAdmin III to connect to remote PostgreSQL servers, by choosing File | Add Server from the main window menu bar. You can use pgAdmin III to manage multiple PostgreSQL servers located on multiple systems.

When pgAdmin III starts, notice that the default server (the localhost) is shown with a red X mark. This means that you are not currently connected to the server. To connect, right-click the server entry and select Connect from the menu. By default, pgAdmin III will attempt to connect to the server using the standard postgres superuser account. If you need to change the default login account or the default TCP port number for a server, right-click the server entry in the main window and select Properties from the menu. In the Properties window you can set the IP address, TCP port, the default database name, and the user account to log into the PostgreSQL server with.

After setting your configuration values, right-click the server entry and select Connect to log into the PostgreSQL system. In the Connect window, enter the password for the superuser account you are using with the PostgreSQL system (if this was a new installation, hopefully you remembered the password you assigned to the account during the installation process; if not, you will have to reinstall PostgreSQL—ouch!). When pgAdmin III establishes a connection with the PostgreSQL server, you will see a graphical representation of all the objects created on the server, as shown in Figure 4-2.

Once you are connected to a server, the pgAdmin III window splits into three frames. The left frame shows a graphical representation of all the objects contained on the

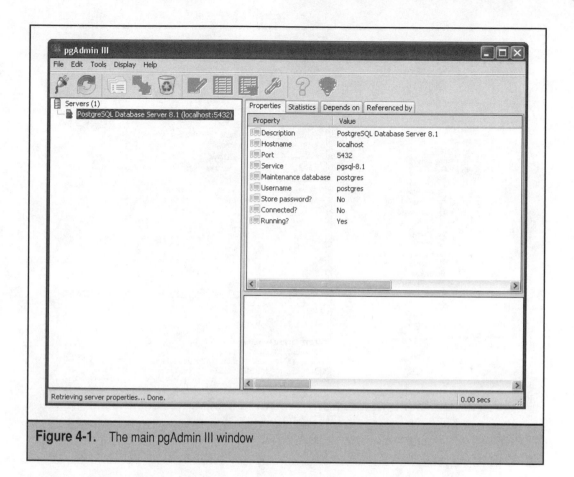

Figure 4-1.   The main pgAdmin III window

PostgreSQL server. The top-right frame shows detailed configuration values of the object currently selected in the left frame. The lower-right frame shows the SQL code used to create the object currently selected in the left frame.

There are lots of objects contained in the PostgreSQL system. To help you manage all of these objects, pgAdmin III divides the objects into categories. The next section describes the objects in the PostgreSQL system based on the category they are displayed under.

PARTS OF THE POSTGRESQL SYSTEM

Chapter 3 walked through the physical files that are required in a PostgreSQL installation. From that viewpoint we were not able to really see what the internal components are that make up the PostgreSQL server. As you saw in that chapter, the database cluster

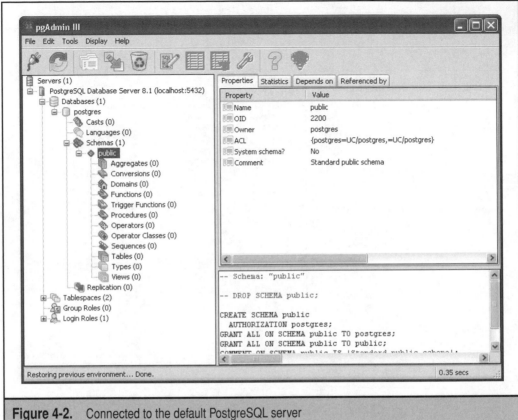

Figure 4-2. Connected to the default PostgreSQL server

contains all of the files necessary to run the database. Now it is time to see what these files contain.

There are five basic components that make up the PostgreSQL server (which are listed in the directory on the left side of pgAdmin III, as shown in Figure 4-2):

▼ Tablespaces

■ Databases

■ Schemas (listed under each individual database)

■ Group Roles

▲ Login Roles

Before you dive into managing your PostgreSQL server, you need to be familiar with each of these components. This section walks through each of these components, describing how they interact to form the PostgreSQL server.

Tablespaces

Tablespaces are the physical locations where objects are stored. Objects can be anything from database tables, indexes, functions, and triggers.

The database cluster area you saw while examining files in Chapter 3 is the default location where PostgreSQL creates its tablespaces. Remember, by default this location is c:\Program Files\Postgresql\8.2\data, but you can create the default Data Dictionary in a different location when you install PostgreSQL (described in Chapter 2).

When you initialized the PostgreSQL system, either when you installed it from the PostgreSQL installer or initialized it using the *initdb* command, it created two default tablespaces within the database cluster area:

▼ pg_default

▲ pg_global

When you expand the Tablespaces object in the directory on the left side of pgAdmin III, you see both of these tablespaces listed. The pg_default tablespace is the default location for all database objects created on the PostgreSQL system. When you create new database objects, you should use the pg_default tablespace area to store them. You can store as many database objects as you want in a single tablespace (provided you have enough disk space available).

The pg_global tablespace is used to hold PostgreSQL system catalogs. The system catalogs contain internal Data Dictionary information for the PostgreSQL system to operate. You should not create new database objects within this tablespace.

You can also create new tablespace areas within the PostgreSQL system. Often, database administrators create new tablespaces on separate hard disk devices to distribute the database load between disk systems. When new database objects are created, you must specify which tablespace area they are stored in. It is possible (and sometimes even beneficial) to store different objects within the same database in different tablespaces.

The pgAdmin III program provides an easy interface for creating new tablespaces. Before you can create a new tablespace, though, you must set up its physical location on your system.

The new tablespace must point to an empty directory on the system. If there are any files currently located in the directory, PostgreSQL will refuse to create the tablespace. Also, the PostgreSQL system account (called postgres by default) must have permission to write to the directory. Remember from Chapter 2 that the system account is created as a normal user account for security purposes. Most likely you will have to specifically grant the postgres user account access to the directory. Unfortunately, Windows XP and Vista Home Editions do not provide a method for you to grant special permissions to directories for user accounts. You have to use the location specified during the installation. The other Windows operating systems supported by PostgreSQL allow you to use the Security property of a directory to set privileges for users on the directory. You can view the Security property of a directory by right-clicking the directory in Windows Explorer, and selecting Properties.

After creating the directory and assigning the `postgres` account permissions, right-click the Tablespaces object in pgAdmin III and select New Tablespace from the menu. The New Tablespace window appears, providing an interface for you to create the new tablespace. In the form, you must specify a name for the new tablespace, the location (directory) where the new tablespace will be located, and the user account that will be the owner of the tablespace. After you create the new tablespace, you can use it to store new database objects.

Databases

Databases are the core objects in PostgreSQL. They hold all of the data objects used in PostgreSQL. When a user account connects to a PostgreSQL server, it connects to a database object, and has access to all the objects contained within the database, restricted by the privileges that are granted on the objects. A user account can only access objects within a single database in a single connection. You cannot access objects in two separate databases in one connection. Of course, there is no restriction as to how many database connections a single user can have within an application at the same time, but each individual connection can only be connected to a single database.

A PostgreSQL system can (and usually does) have multiple databases defined on the system. The default database created during the PostgreSQL installation (or when you use the `initdb` command) is called *postgres*. The `postgres` database contains the default system tables for handling the internal PostgreSQL Data Dictionary. These tables are not shown in pgAdmin III, but can be accessed via SQL queries.

There are two additional databases that are configured by default in PostgreSQL, but not shown in pgAdmin III: `template0` and `template1`. These are, as their names suggest, generic templates that are used to create new databases. Values assigned to these templates (such as the tablespace location and database owner) are assigned to new databases created using the template. As you will see in the "Creating a New Database" section later in this chapter, the pgAdmin III interface allows you to choose any database to base a newly created database on.

The difference between `template0` and `template1` is that `template1` can be modified. If you need to create lots of database objects with certain features or objects, you can modify the `template1` database template to include the features and objects, then use it as the master template to create all of your new databases. Each new database will have the same features and objects as the `template1` database template. The `template0` database template cannot be modified and always describes a generic PostgreSQL database object. This template uses the `pg_default` tablespace, and any new databases created with this template will always use the `pg_default` tablespace.

As you can see from the pgAdmin III display (shown in Figure 4-2), each database object contains four types of objects:

▼   Casts

■   Languages

■   Replications

▲   Schemas

Casts allow you to specify conversions from one data type to another. Once a cast is defined, it is active for the entire database and can be used in any table object defined in the database. Casts are often used to create unique data types for a database. By default there are no casts defined in the database.

Languages define procedural programming languages that can be used for functions and triggers within the database. In Chapter 2, you had the opportunity to install new procedural languages at installation time.

Replications define copies (or replicas) of the PostgreSQL database in a fault-tolerant operation. PostgreSQL uses an add-on package called Slony-I to control database replicas distributed among remote servers. This is not part of the standard PostgreSQL package.

Schemas are the most important objects within the database. As you can see from Figure 4-2, a schema contains the tables, triggers, functions, views, and other objects for handling data in the database. Table 4-1 describes the different objects contained within a schema.

Schema Object	Description
Aggregates	Defines functions that produce results based on processing input values from multiple records in a table (such as a sum or average)
Conversions	Defines conversions between character set encodings
Domains	User-defined data types
Functions	User-defined functions
Trigger Functions	User-defined table triggers
Procedures	User-defined functions that manipulate data but do not return a value
Operators	User-defined operators used to compare data
Operator Classes	Defines how a data type can be used within an index
Sequences	Defines a sequenced number generator
Tables	User-created data repositories
Types	User-defined data types used in the database
Views	User-created queries combining data from multiple tables

Table 4-1.   Schema Objects in PostgreSQL

A database can contain several different schemas, each with its own set of tables, triggers, functions, and views. While users can only access objects within one database at a time, they can access all of the schemas within that database (restricted by assigned privileges). Sometimes related applications can share the same database, but use different schemas to hold their separate data. This makes it easier for users to find data tables related to the applications within the database. This is especially true if tables have the same names.

Table names must be unique within a schema, but can be duplicated between schemas. Tables are referenced in SQL statements using the format:

```
schemaname.tablename
```

This format specifies exactly which table in which schema is being accessed. Depending on your naming conventions, this format can become quite cumbersome. However, PostgreSQL provides a shortcut for us.

Much like a Windows PATH environment variable, PostgreSQL uses the search_path variable for defining default schema names. If you specify a table name alone within a SQL statement, PostgreSQL attempts to find the table by searching the schemas in your search_path. In Chapter 6, you will see how you can set your search_path variable for your particular schema configuration.

The schema objects created in a new database are based on the template used to create the database. By default, the template0 and template1 templates contain a schema called *public*. By default, all user accounts that have permission to a database have permission to create and access objects in the public schema. Most applications do not use the public schema, but instead create their own schemas to control data used in the application. You will see how to do that in the "Creating a New Schema" section later on in this chapter.

Group Roles

Group Roles are used to create access permissions for groups of users. While you can grant an individual user account access directly to a database object, the preferred method is to use Group Roles (in fact, pgAdmin III only allows you to grant Group Roles access to database objects). A Group Role is not allowed to log into the PostgreSQL server, but controls access for user accounts that do log in.

Group Roles are defined at the PostgreSQL server level and used by all databases controlled by the PostgreSQL server. By default, there is one Group Role configured in PostgreSQL. The *public* group role applies to all users on the PostgreSQL system. You are not able to remove any user account from the public Group Role. Because of this, the public Group Role does not appear in the pgAdmin III Group Roles listing.

You can create your own Group Roles using pgAdmin III to control access to your application schemas and tables. This process is described in detail in the "Working with User Accounts" section later in this chapter.

Login Roles

Login Roles are roles that are allowed to log into the PostgreSQL server. They are also known as user accounts. The Login Roles section is where you define accounts for individual users for the PostgreSQL system.

Each database user should have an individual account for logging into the Post-greSQL system. That account is then assigned as a member of the appropriate Group Roles that grant privileges to the database objects required. In a large database environment, this allows you to easily change access for database objects without having to touch hundreds (or even thousands) of individual user Login Roles.

CREATING A NEW APPLICATION

Now that we have looked into the different parts within the PostgreSQL system, it is time to start working with them. To help demonstrate managing a database application using pgAdmin III, this section walks through creating a simple application environment. It uses the store example described in Chapter 1. In this example we will create a new database for the application and a new schema to control access to the data. Within the schema, we will create three tables to hold the data required for the store:

▼   **Customer**   Contains information on the store customers

■   **Product**   Contains information on the products the store sells

▲   **Order**   Contains information on orders placed by customers

To control access to the data, we will create two Group Roles. The *Salesman* Group Role will be given write permission on the Customer and Order tables, but only read permission on the Product table. The *Accountant* Group Role will be given write permission on the Product and Order tables, and read permission on the Customer table. To round out our application, we will create two Login Roles. Our store will consist of a salesman, called Barney, and an accountant, called Fred. The following sections create our new store application.

Creating a New Database

The first step for the application is to create a new database object. While you can use the standard `postgres` database object to hold the application data, it is usually best programming practice to create a separate database object that contains your applications. Remember, each client connection to the PostgreSQL server can connect to only one database object. By using a separate database object for your applications, you help isolate application users from the system tables.

To create the new database, first start pgAdmin III and log into your PostgreSQL server. Right-click the Databases object and select New Database from the menu. The New Database window, shown in Figure 4-3, appears.

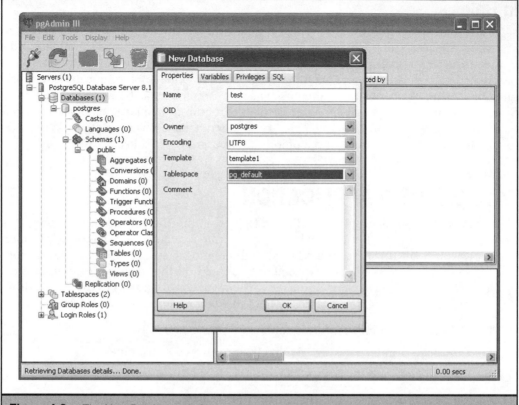

Figure 4-3.   The New Database window

The New Database window contains four tabs for entering information for the new database. The Properties tab contains a form for entering the required information to create the new database. The Variables tab is a generic tab used in pgAdmin III, but does not apply to the New Database function.

By default, only the database owner will be able to create or modify objects in the database. The Privileges tab allows you to assign privileges to other Group Roles configured in the PostgreSQL server.

The SQL tab shows the SQL statement generated by your selected options in the other tabs to create the database. Creating a new database uses the CREATE DATABASE SQL statement. pgAdmin III fills in the appropriate statement parameters for you automatically based on your entries in the configuration tabs.

Go to the Properties tab and assign a name to your new database (for this example, I use the database name test). You must select an owner for your database. At this point, you might not have any users other than the postgres superuser created on your server, so you can make that user the owner of the database. Remember, the database owner has complete control over all objects in the database. You never want to make a normal database user owner of the entire application database.

After entering the database owner, you must select the encoding to use for the database. By default, pgAdmin III uses the SQL_ASCII encoding. The ASCII character set is an old 7-bit character set that has been around almost since the dawn of computers. This value has worked fine for simple, English-language databases. However, if you plan on creating tables that contain advanced data types or using languages with more complicated character sets, the 7-bit ASCII character set will not work. You need to use a full 8-bit character encoding.

In the past this has been a problem with running PostgreSQL on Windows. However, since version 8.1, PostgreSQL supports the UTF8 encoding format on Windows systems. If you are not sure what type of data your application will ultimately hold, it is always safest to use the UTF8 encoding.

The next setting on Properties tab is the template to use to create the new database. If this is the first database you have created, all that will be available to you are the `template0` and `template1` templates. As you create new databases, pgAdmin III provides those to be used as templates as well. For now you can use the `template1` template to create your new database.

After the template choice comes the tablespace. In most situations, you should use the `pg_default` tablespace for your new database. Although pgAdmin III offers the `pg_global` tablespace as an option, you should never create new objects in the `pg_global` tablespace. It is generally not a good idea to mix your application objects with the system objects. If you had created a new tablespace on your system, it would also appear in the list of options available.

The Comment section is another area that does not apply to creating databases. PostgreSQL allows you to add comments to many objects when they are created, but databases are not one of them.

After filling out the Properties tab, look at the SQL tab. It contains the complete SQL statement used to create the database. This is shown in Figure 4-4.

The `CREATE DATABASE` SQL statement (see Figure 4-4) is what pgAdmin III runs to create the new database. In Chapter 6, you will learn how to manually create and enter these types of SQL commands. However, with pgAdmin III it is as easy as filling out a form and clicking a button.

Speaking of clicking a button, go back to the Properties tab and, if it is complete, click the OK button. PostgreSQL will create the new database object, which then appears in your pgAdmin III main window object listing. By default, you are not connected to the new database object, so it is shown with a red X over it. Clicking the new object connects you to the database and expands the database object in the window.

Creating a New Schema

When you open the newly created database object, you see that it contains the `public` schema by default. While it is perfectly acceptable to create data tables and other objects

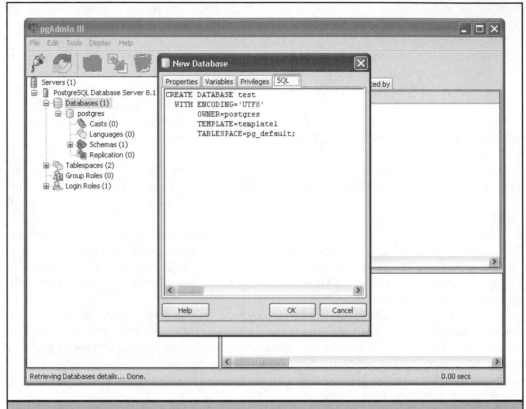

Figure 4-4. The CREATE DATABASE SQL statement

within the public schema, we will create a new schema to hold our application data objects. Unlike the public schema, the newly created schema will be protected by default. No users will have access to the schema until we specifically grant them access. This helps provide better security for the application by default.

There are a couple of ways to create a new schema in the database. The first method is to right-click the newly created database object that will contain the new schema and select New Object | New Schema. The second method is to expand the newly created database object, right-click the Schemas object contained within the database object, and select New Schema from the menu. Either method opens the New Schema window, shown in Figure 4-5.

Just like the New Database window, the New Schema window provides an easy form (Properties tab) for you to fill out to define the new schema. You must provide a unique name for the schema within the database in which it is created. For this example, use the schema name store. Just as with the new database, you must also provide the owner

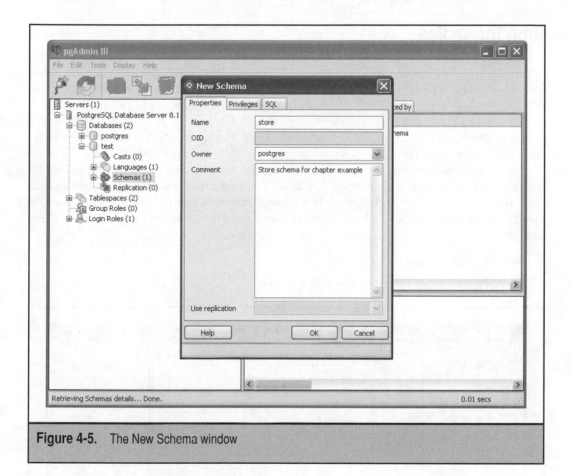

Figure 4-5. The New Schema window

of the schema, which should be set to the `postgres` user account. Unlike the new database, you do not specify the tablespace for the schema. PostgreSQL creates the schema object in the same tablespace where the parent database object resides. Also unlike the new database, you can supply a comment in the Comment field of the Properties tab. Note that the OID field is grayed out. PostgreSQL automatically assigns a unique OID to the database once it is created.

The New Schema window also allows you to assign permissions to the newly created schema. By default, only the superuser account has permissions to create and modify data in the schema. We will change that later after we create some user accounts.

After entering the information, click OK to create the new schema. The new schema automatically appears within the database object in pgAdmin III. You can expand the new schema object to see the listing of objects contained within the schema. At this point there should not be any new objects within the schema. Now it is time to create some tables.

Creating the Tables

Tables are the meat and potatoes of our database. They hold all of the data used in the application. As mentioned in Chapter 1, in a relational database model, data is divided into tables that contain related information. As specified for the example application, we will create three separate tables to hold the data required for this application.

To create a new table, expand the newly created database object and then the newly created schema object. In this listing, right-click the Tables object and select New Table from the menu. The New Table window appears, shown in Figure 4-6.

There are several steps involved in creating a new table, and you do not necessarily have to perform them all at the same time. The first tab is the Properties tab. Just as with the New Database and New Schema windows, this tab is where you define the basic properties for the new table. There are a few rules for defining table names in PostgreSQL:

▼   Must be unique within a schema

■   Must start with a letter or an underscore (_)

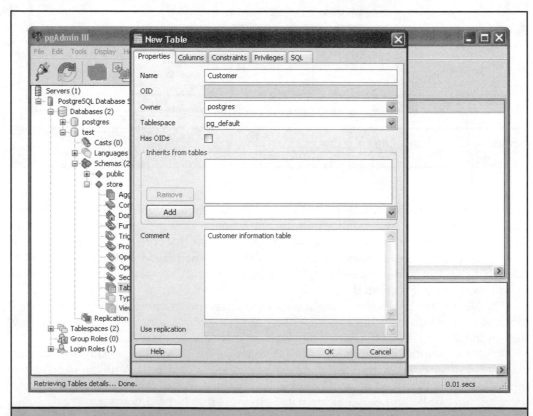

Figure 4-6.   The New Table window

- Subsequent characters can be letters, numbers, underscore, or a dollar sign ($)
- Must be 63 or fewer characters long
- ▲ Case sensitive

The last rule is often what gets novice database administrators in trouble. This means that you can have a table named Customer as well as another table named customer in the same schema. This is almost always a recipe for disaster when running SQL statements, and should be avoided if at all possible. For this exercise, we will capitalize the first character in the table names and make the rest lowercase. When creating this new table, use the name Customer.

As with the other database objects, you must define the owner of the table. Again, we will use the `postgres` user for this exercise.

When creating a new table, you must specify the tablespace where the table will be stored. You may store tables in different tablespaces within the same database if you desire. For this exercise, you should just use the `pg_default` tablespace.

The Has OIDs check box indicates whether PostgreSQL will assign an object ID (OID) to the newly created table. By default, PostgreSQL does not assign an OID to user-created tables. If you plan on using the PostgreSQL inheritance feature (discussed in Chapter 1), you must assign an OID to the table. Since our tables will not use this feature, we can leave this check box unchecked.

The Inherits from Tables section allows you to specify whether the newly created table will inherit any columns (fields) from parent tables. The parent table must have an OID assigned to it. Again, since none of our tables will do this, we will leave this section blank.

Finally, the Comment section allows us to place a comment in the table that can be seen from pgAdmin III when we view the properties of the table. This is extremely handy when designing a large system with lots of tables.

After filling in the required information in the Properties tab, click the OK button to create the table. The new table appears under the Tables list in the new schema. You have created a new table, but there is no data defined within the table. We will do that shortly.

Before entering new data, look at the table objects created with the new table. Expand the new Customer table object that was created in the new schema. Each table consists of five categories of objects:

- ▼ **Columns** Hold data elements in the table
- **Constraints** Add further restrictions on data in the columns
- **Indexes** Speed up data searching in the table
- **Rules** Define functions performed on data in other tables based on events
- ▲ **Triggers** Define functions performed on data in the table based on events

The next step to complete your table is to define columns for the data. Each column defines a data element that will be stored in the table. Each column must be declared as

Column	Data Type	Description
CustomerID	char—six characters	Unique identifier for each customer
LastName	varchar	Last name of customer
FirstName	varchar	First name of customer
Address	varchar	Street address of customer
City	varchar	City of customer
State	char—two characters	State of customer
Zip	char—five characters	Postal ZIP code of customer
Phone	varchar	Phone number of customer

Table 4-2.   Customer Table Columns

a specific data type, depending on the type of data you intend to store in the column. Which data elements are placed in which tables is a subject of many relational database theories. For the purposes of this exercise, we will try to keep things somewhat simple. Table 4-2 shows the columns that will be used for the Customer table.

The Customer table contains the necessary contact information for the customer. It also contains a unique value added to the customer information to uniquely identify the customer in the database (in case you get two customers named John Smith, for example). There are two different data types used for the columns in the Customer table. The *char* data type holds a fixed-length character string. The length of the character string must be stated when the column is created. The CustomerID column will be created as a six-character string, the State column as a two-character string, and the Zip column as a five-character string.

The *varchar* data type holds a variable-length character string. This is for fields where you do not know the length of the data that could be entered. The columns where the data lengths can vary widely, such as the street address, are set to use the varchar data type.

There are lots of data types defined within PostgreSQL. Table 4-3 shows some of the more popular data types that are used.

This is just a small sampling of the many data types available. The PostgreSQL Help window (in pgAdmin III, choose Help | PostgreSQL Help) contains information on all of the PostgreSQL data types available.

You can create the data columns either when you first create the table or after the table has already been created. If you created the Customer table earlier, there are a couple of different methods you can use for adding columns. You can double-click the new

Data Type	Description
int2	Two-byte integer (−32768 to +32768)
int4	Four-byte integer (−2147483648 to +2147483648)
int8	Eight-byte integer (−9223372036854775808 to +9223372036854775808)
bool	Logical True/False Boolean value
float4	Single-precision floating-point number
float8	Double-precision floating-point number
numeric	User-defined-precision floating-point number
money	Two-decimal place floating-point number
char	Fixed-length character string
varchar	Variable-length character string
date	Calendar date
time	Time of day
timestamp	Date and time

Table 4-3.   Common PostgreSQL Data Types

table object in pgAdmin III to bring up the standard Table Properties window or you can right-click the Columns object under the Customer table entry and select New Column. I prefer to double-click the new table object, as it provides the entire Table Properties window to view. In the Table Properties window, click the Columns tab to access the columns list.

In the Columns tab, click the Add button to add a new column. The New Column window appears, shown in Figure 4-7.

Fill in the forms for the information to define the column. The Data Type textbox includes a handy drop-down menu that contains all of the available data types. Select the appropriate data type for the column you are creating. For the CustomerID and Phone columns, check the Not NULL check box. This feature requires that these fields must be filled for the data record to be added to the table. If either of these fields is missing, the new data record will be rejected.

As you enter columns in the table, they appear in the columns list in the Columns tab. When you have entered all of the columns for the Customer table, click the Constraints tab. The Constraints tab allows you to specify further constraints on the data in the columns.

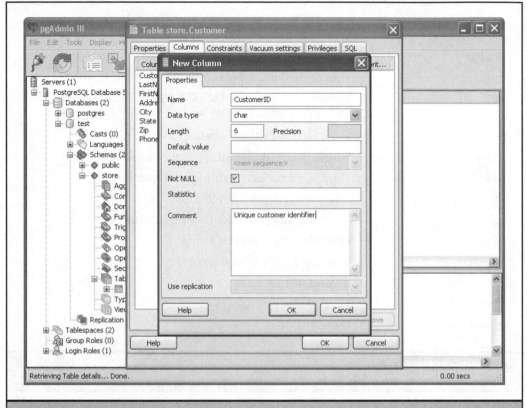

Figure 4-7. The New Column window

There will be one constraint in the Customer table. You want to ensure that no two customers have the same CustomerID column value. To do that, you can make this column a *primary key* for the table. Primary keys are used to uniquely identify each record in the table. Each table can have only one primary key assigned to it. A column (or column combination) used for the primary key is guaranteed to be unique. The PostgreSQL system will not allow users to enter records with a duplicate primary key.

On the Constraints tab, ensure that the Primary Key value is set in the drop-down box, and click the Add button. The New Primary Key window appears. On the Properties tab, set the name of the primary key (call it CustomerKey) and define which tablespace it should be located in. You do not have to place a primary key in the same tablespace as the data table (and, in fact, many database administrators do not for performance purposes). The primary key object creates an index of the database that is accessed during queries to help speed things up. PostgreSQL can quickly search the index looking for the key value without having to read all of the table columns.

After filling out the information on the Properties tab, click the Columns tab. On this tab, you must select the columns that are used for the primary key. For this exercise, select

Column Name	Data Type	Description
ProductID	char—six characters	Unique primary key identifier that is not NULL
ProductName	varchar	Name of the product
Model	varchar	Product model number
Manufacturer	varchar	Name of the manufacturer
UnitPrice	money	Current price of product
Inventory	int4	Number of units in inventory

Table 4-4. The Product Table Columns

the CustomerID column. You can choose to make a constraint *deferrable*, which means PostgreSQL does not check the constraint at the end of each command, but rather at the end of a transaction. When you have defined the primary key, click the Add button.

After filling out the forms, click OK to add the constraint to the Table Properties window. When you have all of the columns and the constraint configured, click the SQL tab to view the generated SQL statements required to implement your selections. In this case, you can see how pgAdmin III saves you from lots of typing by not having to manually enter the SQL code to create the table columns. After reviewing the SQL statements, click OK to create the columns and constraint. Back in the pgAdmin III window, you should see the new columns and constraint added to the table objects.

Now you can create the other two tables for the application. The Product table columns are shown in Table 4-4.

Create the Product table using the same procedures used to create the Customer table. Do not forget to add the primary key constraint to the table for the ProductID column.

The last table is the Order table. This one is a little different from the other two tables. It uses column values derived from the other two tables. Table 4-5 describes the Order table.

Create the Order table as you did the other two tables. Create the CustomerID and ProductID columns using the same data type and length as with the associated columns in the other tables. The difference with the Order table is in the constraints. There are two additional constraints that must be created. You must create constraints to ensure that the CustomerID and ProductID values entered into the Order table are valid.

Click the Constraints tab in the New Table window for the Order table. First, create the primary key on the OrderID column as normal. After creating that, from the drop-down menu on the Constraints tab, select Foreign Key and click Add. The New Foreign Key window appears, shown in Figure 4-8.

For the first constraint, we will match the CustomerID column to the CustomerID column in the Customer table, so call the new constraint Customer. In the References textbox, click the drop-down arrow and select the store. Customer table (remember,

Column Name	Data Type	Description
OrderID	char—six characters	Unique primary key identifier that is not NULL
CustomerID	char—six characters	The CustomerID from the Customer table (not NULL)
ProductID	char—six characters	The ProductID from the Product table (not NULL)
PurchaseDate	date	Date of purchase
Quantity	int4	The number of items purchased
TotalCost	money	The total cost of the purchase

Table 4-5.   The Columns for the Order Table

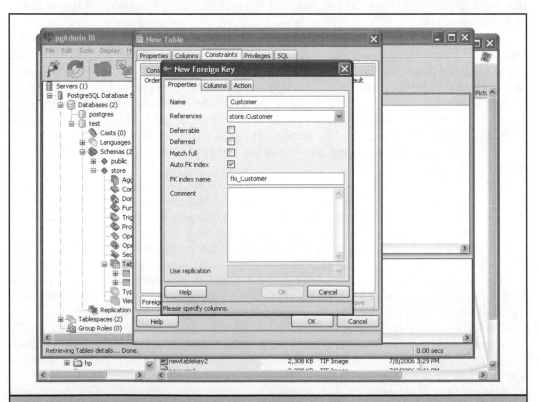

Figure 4-8.   New Foreign Key window for the Order table

tables are referenced by *schemaname.tablename*). Next, click the Columns tab. The Local Column textbox references the column in the Order table you want to match. Select the CustomerID column. The Referencing textbox references the column in the Customer table you want to constrain the column to. Select the CustomerID column, click Add, then click OK. Do the same with the ProductID column (except reference the ProductID column in the Products table).

The Action tab allows you to specify an action to take on the related data when an event occurs on the table. If the foreign key column value is updated or deleted from the table, the related value in the foreign key table can also be updated or deleted. For now we will not worry about that, so leave the settings at the default No Action. When you are finished, click OK to create the table.

Entering and Viewing Data

Now you have a running database system with three configured tables. The next step is to put data in your tables. Our friend pgAdmin III can help us do that as well.

Right-click the table object you want to enter data into and choose the View Data menu item. The pgAdmin III Edit Data window appears, shown in Figure 4-9.

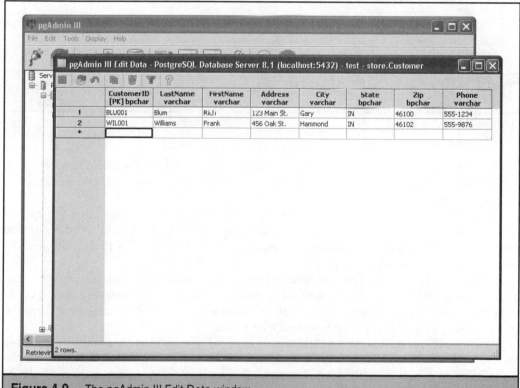

Figure 4-9. The pgAdmin III Edit Data window

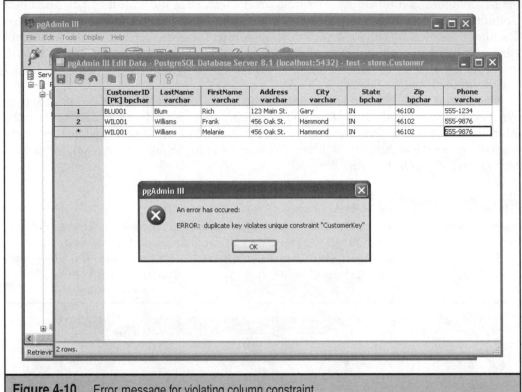

Figure 4-10.   Error message for violating column constraint

The table columns are shown as columns across the top of the Edit Data window. Within the window are grids showing the individual records within the table. You can enter data directly into the next available row in the window.

When you have entered data for all of the columns in a record, press ENTER to submit the data. All constraints applied to the columns apply to the Edit Data window. If you violate any of the constraints, an error message appears when you try to submit the data, as shown in Figure 4-10.

In Figure 4-10, I attempted to enter a record with the same CustomerID column value as an existing record. The Edit Data window produced an error message informing me of my error. Unfortunately, when you get an error message, all of the data entered into the record is lost, and you must start over on that record.

By default, the Edit Data window displays all of the records contained in the table and sorts them in ascending order based on the defined primary key. You can use the Sort/Filter option button (the funnel icon) to change this. Clicking this button produces the View Data Options window (a slight misnaming of windows and icons), which has two tabs:

▼ **Data Sorting** Allows you to specify how to sort data as it is displayed in the Edit Data window.

▲ **Filter** Allows you to specify what data to view using simple expressions. You can use standard comparison expressions within the Filter tab to filter the data you are looking for.

After entering your expressions, click the Validate button to see if your filter expressions will work.

One warning about using column names in the Filter tab (actually, this applies to all of PostgreSQL). If you use the filter expression `LastName = 'Blum'` you will get an error when you click the Validate button, as shown in Figure 4-11.

All the error message says is that the column "lastname" is invalid. This error throws many novice administrators off, as they assume that indeed they do have a column named lastname. What has happened is that PostgreSQL assumes all column names are

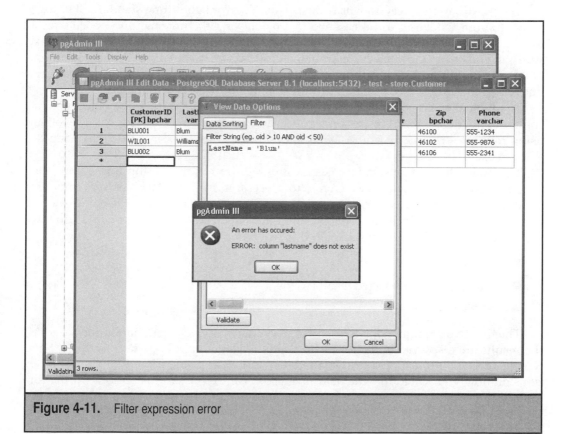

Figure 4-11. Filter expression error

in lowercase. Unfortunately, I created my column name in mixed case. Notice that even though I entered the filter expression correctly, PostgreSQL converted the column name to all lowercase letters, which did not match the real column name.

To solve this problem, you should always place double quotes around column and table names that use uppercase letters. If you use the *schemaname.tablename* format, make sure that each one has quotes around each individual name instead of the whole name (for example, `"Store"."Customer"` and not `"Store.Customer"`). Notice, however, that character strings use single quotes. This feature can get confusing, as well as annoying.

Do not get too hung up on the filter expressions at this point. Chapter 6 discusses this topic in greater detail.

THE pgADMIN III QUERY TOOL

While the pgAdmin Edit Data window is a handy way to display and enter data, it is not all that sophisticated. For more advanced queries to your PostgreSQL system, pgAdmin III includes its own query program.

The pgAdmin III Query Tool provides an interface for submitting standard SQL statements to your database. You access the tool by clicking the notepad-and-pencil icon in the top toolbar or by choosing Tools | Query Tool. Before you start the Query Tool, make sure that you have the database you want to query data from selected in the left-side frame of the pgAdmin III window. You are only allowed to query tables from one database at a time using the Query Tool. The main Query Tool window is shown in Figure 4-12.

The toolbar at the top of the Query Tool window shows the database object you are connected to. Remember, you can only query tables in the connected database. If you are using multiple schemas in your database, you need to reference your tables using the *schemaname.tablename* format.

The main Query Tool window is split into two frames. In the top frame you enter SQL commands for the database engine to process. In this interface you can enter any valid SQL command (see Chapter 6 for SQL commands) and as many SQL commands as you need to process. Once you have the SQL commands created, click one of the following three execution buttons in the toolbar to run them:

▼ Execute query

■ Execute query and save results to file

▲ Explain query

The first two are somewhat self-explanatory. When the SQL commands are executed, the results are displayed in the lower frame in the Data Output tab. If you use the Save Results to File button, an Export Data to File window appears, providing you with options on how you would like the data saved. You can select various options for the format the data is stored in, such as what character is used to separate record fields, and the type of quotes used to delineate string values.

The third option, Explain Query, is somewhat different. Instead of running the query, the Query Tool uses the PostgreSQL explain plan. The *explain plan* describes the steps

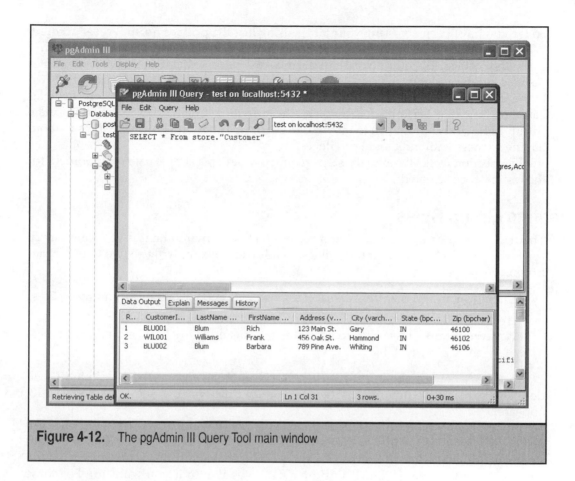

Figure 4-12.   The pgAdmin III Query Tool main window

the PostgreSQL database engine takes to process the query, and how long the individual steps would take to process.

The steps appear as icons in the Explain tab of the lower frame. For a simple one-step query, the results are not too interesting. You will see just a single icon. When you click the icon, a textbox appears, showing the statistics for processing the SQL command. For more complicated SQL commands, you see multiple step icons within the Explain tab. This feature enables you to determine which steps take the most amount of time when processing the SQL commands, and possibly allow you to alter your commands to be more efficient. These will be covered in more detail in Chapter 10.

WORKING WITH USER ACCOUNTS

If you have been following the exercise in this chapter on your own computer, you have the makings of a real application. However, there is one important piece still missing.

So far you have been accessing your tables using just the `postgres` superuser account. While this works okay in development, this is a major no-no in the production world.

In the real world, you want each of the database users to have their own Login Roles (user accounts) assigned to them. This ensures that you can track database activity down to the individual user. You also want to create Group Roles to grant permissions to tables based on functions performed, then assign the individual Login Roles to the appropriate Group Roles. This allows you to move user Login Roles around between tables without having to mess with individual privileges.

This section walks through the steps required to set up a simple user environment for the test database created.

Creating Group Roles

The first step toward implementing a secure database environment is to create Group Roles to control access to your data tables. In this example, we will use two Group Roles to control access:

▼ **Salesman**   Has write access to the Customer and Order tables, and read access to the Product table

▲ **Accountant**   Has write access to the Product and Order tables, and read access to the Customer table

To create a new Group Role, right-click the Group Roles entry in the pgAdmin III window and select New Group Role. The New Group Role window, shown in Figure 4-13, appears.

By now you should be familiar with the drill. In the window, there is a simple form on the Properties tab to fill out the information pertinent to the Group Role you want to create. Group Roles do not have login privileges, so you do not need to create a password for the role (although PostgreSQL allows you to if you want to). For these Group Roles, you also do not need to check any of the check boxes in the Role Privileges area of the Properties tab. We obviously do not want the members of this group to be superusers, and there will not be any objects or roles that these users need to create. You can cascade Group Roles, assigning one group as a member of another group, and allowing it to inherit all of the permissions assigned to the parent group. We will not get that complicated in this simple example. You also have the option of setting a date when the group will expire. This is convenient for setting up temporary testing groups for applications.

Go ahead and create the Salesman and Accountant roles using the New Group Role window. You should see the new roles added to the PostgreSQL system as you create them.

After creating the new Group Roles, you must assign the proper permissions to the tables for them. This is done in the individual Table Properties windows.

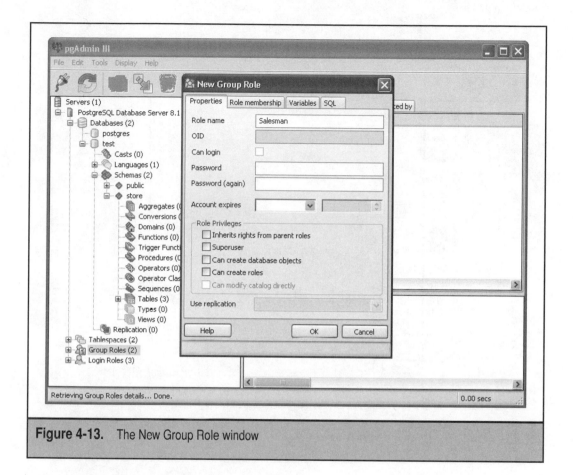

Figure 4-13.   The New Group Role window

Double-click the Customer table icon in pgAdmin III. The Table Properties window appears for the table. Click the Privileges tab, showing the configuration window to set permissions on the table, shown in Figure 4-14.

In the lower section, you must select the role to grant permissions for. Select the Salesman Group Role. Next, select the permissions you want to grant for that Group Role. For the Salesman role, we want to grant them INSERT, SELECT, UPDATE, and DELETE privileges, so check those check boxes. The WITH GRANT OPTION check box allows members in the Group Role to reassign the same privileges to other users. We do not want our users going behind our backs and giving other users privileges to the tables, so leave those check boxes empty.

When you are done, click the Add/Change button to assign the selected privileges. You will see the Salesman Group Role name added to the list in the top frame, along with a code showing the privileges assigned. The codes are shorthand for the privileges set. Table 4-6 shows the codes that are used.

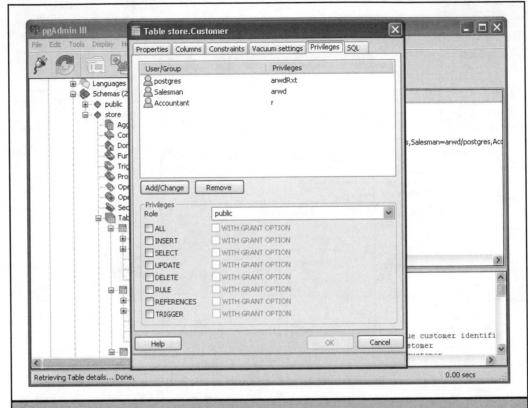

Figure 4-14. The Customer Table Privileges tab

Next, do the same for the Accountant Group Role, assigning them only SELECT privileges for the table.

When you have finished, do the same for the Product table, assigning INSERT, SELECT, UPDATE, and DELETE privileges for the Accountant role, and only SELECT privileges for the Salesman role. Finally, assign privileges for the Order table, giving both the Salesman and Accountant roles INSERT, SELECT, UPDATE, and DELETE privileges.

Now that you have all of the table privileges created, you might think that you are done. Unfortunately that is not the case. There is one more privilege you need to address.

As a security feature, a newly created schema does not grant any privileges to any groups (not even the public group). Only the superuser (postgres by default) has privileges to modify the schema. By default, pgAdmin III does not show individual user privileges in the listing until after you add group privileges, so you will not see the postgres user privileges displayed. You must specify if your new Group Roles should have access to the store schema. Double-click the store schema in pgAdmin III, then

Code	Privilege
a	INSERT (append)
r	SELECT (read)
w	UPDATE (write)
d	DELETE
R	RULE
x	REFERENCES
t	TRIGGER
X	EXECUTE
U	USAGE
C	CREATE
T	TEMPORARY

Table 4-6.   pgAdmin Object Privilege Codes

click the Privileges tab. You should not see any group privileges shown for the schema. Select the group to add privileges for from the drop-down menu. The USAGE privilege allows the group to use existing objects in the schema. The CREATE privilege allows groups to create new objects in the schema.

You must add the USAGE privilege to both the Salesman and Accountant Group Roles for those users to have access to objects in the schema. Just select the appropriate Group Role from the drop-down menu, check the USAGE check box, and click the Add/Change button. When you are done, click OK. Now your application should be all set for user accounts.

Creating Login Roles

Now that you have created a security environment, you can start creating user accounts and assigning them to Group Roles. In PostgreSQL, user accounts are called Login Roles.

Right-click the Login Roles entry in pgAdmin III and select New Login Role. The New Login Role window appears, as shown in Figure 4-15.

As expected, on the Properties tab, you need to fill in the role name (user account name) that will be used to log into the server, and assign a password for the account (do not create Login Role accounts without passwords). If needed, you can also set an expiration date for the account.

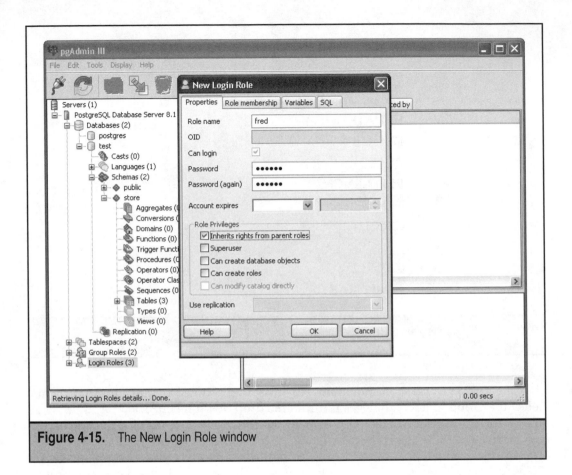

Figure 4-15. The New Login Role window

In the Role Privileges section, you must select the Inherits Rights from Parent Roles check box. This ensures that the Login Role will inherit the privileges assigned to the Group Role it is assigned to.

After filling in the Properties tab, click the Role Membership tab. This is where you assign the Login Role to one or more Group Roles. For a Salesman account, click the Salesman group name in the left box and click the right arrows. The Salesman group name is added to the Member In list.

To complete this example, create two Login Roles, user `barney` and user `fred`. Add `barney` to the Salesman group and add `fred` to the Accountant group.

While it is not necessary, it is best practice to create Login Roles using all lowercase letters. As mentioned before, PostgreSQL is case sensitive in all things, so creating a Login Role `Barney` can result in future problems if the user does not remember to capitalize the first letter. Using all lower case letters is a standard practice on database systems.

Testing Privileges

You can now test your new user environment by logging into the PostgreSQL server using the newly created Login Roles. The easiest way to do that is to use the `psql` program. Chapter 5 describes this program in great detail, but for now we will just use it to see if we can get to the new tables.

The easiest way to start the `psql` program is to choose Start | Programs | PostgreSQL 8.2 | Command Prompt. This creates a command prompt window in the default `bin` directory of PostgreSQL, where all of the utilities are located. From here you can run the `psql` command-line program. There are lots of command-line options for `psql` (as you will see in Chapter 5). For now we will just use a basic format:

```
psql databasename username
```

The first option specifies the database to connect to. The second option specifies the Login Role to log in as. Assuming you have been following the example names in this chapter, log in using the `test` database and the `fred` Login Role:

```
psql test fred
```

After entering the password for the `fred` Login Role, you will be greeted by the `psql` welcome screen and given a command prompt, showing the database name you are connected to.

The `fred` Login Role is a member of the Accountant Group Role, so he should have write privileges for the Product table. We can test this by using a simple SQL `INSERT` statement:

```
test=>INSERT into store."Product" VALUES ('LAP001', 'Laptop', 'TakeAlong',
'Acme', '500.00', 100);
INSERT 0 1
test=>
```

The details of the `INSERT` SQL statement will be explained in Chapter 6. For now, all you need to know is that this command attempts to enter a new record into the Product table (again, note the double quotes required around Product). Note that, using this command format, you must enter a value for each column in the table, in the order the column appears in the table. Character values must be surrounded by single quotes. Also, be aware of the semicolon at the end of the SQL statement. This is required to let `psql` know the SQL statement is finished. As you will see in Chapter 6, you can create SQL statements that go on for several lines.

The result of the SQL statement indicates that one record was added to the Product table, so indeed Fred has his necessary privileges. You can use a `SELECT` SQL statement to ensure the record really was added to the table. Now you can see if Fred can add a record to the Customer table (which he should not be allowed to do, based on the Accountant Group Role privileges):

```
test=> INSERT into store."Customer" VALUES ('BLU001', 'Blum', 'Rich',
'111 Main St', 'Gary', 'IN', '46100', '555-1234');
ERROR:  permission denied for relation Customer
test=>
```

As expected, Fred was prevented from adding a new Customer record. You can try the same tests for the barney Login Role. When you are ready to exit psql, just type the command \q by itself on a line and press ENTER.

DATABASE MAINTENANCE

Once your application goes into production mode, there will most likely be lots of activity on the tables. When lots of records are deleted and updated, dead space appears in the tables. This is a result of deleted or updated records being marked for deletion but not physically removed from the table. Remember, at any time, a transaction could be rolled back, meaning that previously deleted records need to be recovered. PostgreSQL accomplishes this by keeping internal information about each record, such as if it is marked for deletion or not.

Over time, an active table could possibly contain more records marked for deletion than actual live records. Because of this, dead space should be cleaned out at regular intervals.

PostgreSQL provides a method called *vacuuming* to remove records marked for deletion. Chapter 3 showed the postgresql.conf file settings for the autovacuum function. By default, PostgreSQL vacuums all database tables at a regular interval, controlled by the autovacuum_naptime setting in the postgresql.conf file. However, you can also manually vacuum a table. There is a special utility just for this function.

The vacuum utility can be accessed directly from the pgAdmin III main window. There are a few different ways to vacuum records from a table:

▼ Set a table to automatically vacuum at preset intervals, different from the default autovacuum settings in the postgresql.conf file

■ Manually vacuum a table

▲ Manually vacuum all tables in a database

To set a table to be automatically vacuumed at a different interval from the system setting, double-click the table object and select the Vacuum Settings tab in the Table Properties window. The top check box allows you to enable the Custom Autovacuum feature. When this feature is enabled, you are allowed to modify the vacuum configuration parameters (described in Chapter 3) for the table. This is demonstrated in Figure 4-16.

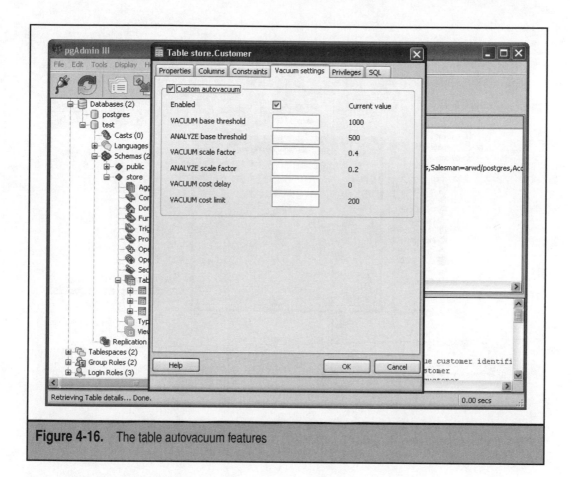

Figure 4-16.   The table autovacuum features

If there is not a lot of activity on a particular table, you can turn off the autovacuum feature in the `postgresql.conf` file and manually vacuum your tables when necessary. To manually vacuum a table or database, right-click the table or database object and select Maintenance. The Maintain Table (or Database) window appears, as shown in Figure 4-17.

The Maintain Table and Database windows allow you to

▼   Vacuum the table

■   Analyze the table to determine if vacuuming is necessary

▲   Reindex all indexes for the table

Besides vacuuming deleted records from a table, reindexing any created table indexes can also speed up query performance for a table. As new records are added, the index can become disjointed. By reindexing, PostgreSQL can reorganize the index values to maximize query performance.

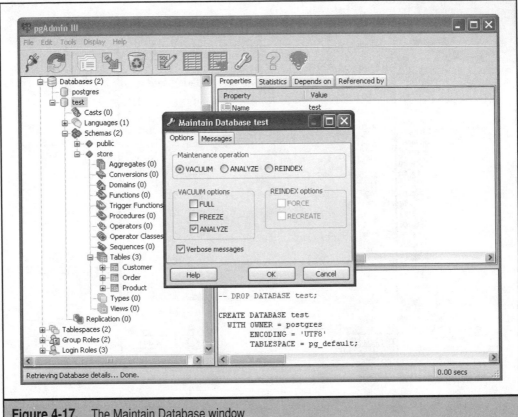

Figure 4-17. The Maintain Database window

BACKUPS AND RESTORES

Part of the ACID test of durability (discussed in Chapter 1) is if the database is able to recover from a catastrophic event, such as a disk crash. To plan for those types of events, it is always a good idea to have a backup of the database. In Chapter 3, the pg_dump and pg_dumpall utilities were discussed. These programs allow you to back up the database structure and data to an alternative location. The pg_dumpall utility allows you to back up the entire PostgreSQL system, including Login and Group Roles. The pg_dump utility is used to back up individual databases.

The pgAdmin III program tries to make your life even easier by incorporating a graphical front end to the pg_dump utility. Unfortunately, it does not provide an interface to the pg_dumpall utility, so you should still manually create a full backup of the entire PostgreSQL system on a regular basis. However, backing up your databases is as easy as filling in the proper forms and submitting the job. This section describes how to back up and restore a database using the pgAdmin III utility.

Performing a Backup

To back up a database, right-click the database object and select Backup from the menu. The Backup Database window appears, as shown in Figure 4-18.

From this window you can select the options for your backup, including the file-name of the backup file, the type of backup (as discussed in the "pg_dump" section in Chapter 3), and the parts backed up. By default, the pg_dump utility uses the COPY SQL commands to restore table data. If you need to restore the database on a different data-base system, you should use the INSERT commands feature by checking the check box. If you do select the Insert Commands check box, you will not be able to store OIDs either, since OIDs cannot be copied using standard SQL INSERT commands. After the backup completes, click the Messages tab and view the backup results.

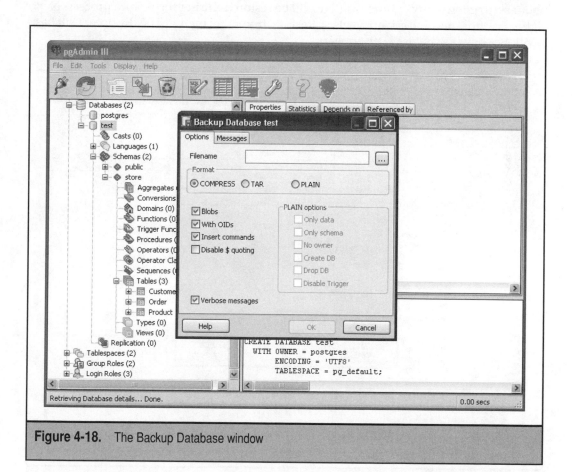

Figure 4-18.   The Backup Database window

Restoring a Database

The other side of backing up your database is the ability to restore the database. The backup file created by the pgAdmin III program can be restored using the `pg_restore` utility, discussed in Chapter 3. This file can be used to restore the database on any PostgreSQL platform on any server. This makes for a powerful tool in migrating databases to larger servers on different platforms.

With the `pg_restore` utility, all you need to do is run the utility with the backup file. The objects that are contained in the backup file are automatically restored. Unfortunately, in pgAdmin III, to restore a database, schema, or table, you must have a similar skeleton object available to perform the restore. First, create a new object using the same name as the original object that was lost (you can easily copy an object by creating an object with a different name and performing the restore on that object). You do not have to worry about setting too many options, as they will be restored during the restore process. Next, right-click the new object and select Restore from the menu. The Restore Database window, shown in Figure 4-19, appears.

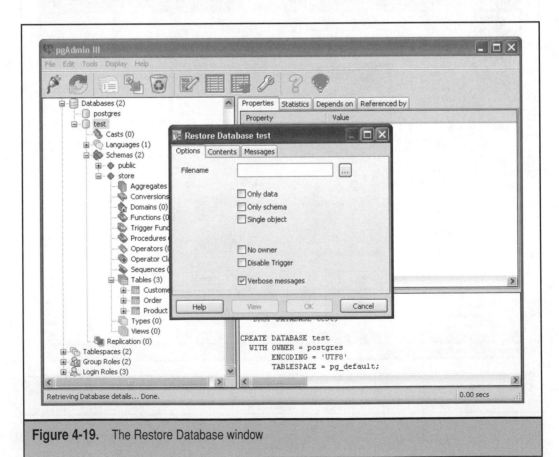

Figure 4-19. The Restore Database window

From the Restore Database window, select the appropriate backup file to restore, and the options you need (for a complete restore, you do not need to check any of the options). The restore process starts, and the results are shown in the Messages tab.

Please do not wait until you have lost important data to find out that you missed something in the process. Now that you have a few sample tables and data, try doing a backup of your test database. After you back up the database, remove it by right-clicking the database object and selecting Delete/Drop from the menu.

After removing the database, create a new skeleton database, then perform the restore process using your backup file. After the restore, you will have to click the database object and then click the Refresh icon in the toolbar. The new (or rather old) database objects should now be present. View the data in the new tables to make sure the data has also been restored. You should also try a few table queries using psql to ensure that the privileges have been restored as well.

It is important to remember that this backup and restore did not affect any of the Login or Group Roles created in the PostgreSQL system. While the backup preserved the privileges assigned to objects, it did not create the roles themselves. To fully back up your entire PostgreSQL system, use the pg_dumpall utility. This creates the SQL statements to restore your entire PostgreSQL system, including Login and Group Roles.

SUMMARY

This chapter walked through the many features of the pgAdmin III program, and demonstrated how to use it to perform all of your database administration needs. You can use pgAdmin III to create new tablespaces, databases, schemas, tables, and user accounts (Login Roles). From each new table, you can create new columns to hold data, as well as define constraints, indexes, rules, procedures, and triggers. After you create new tables and data, you can create Group Roles to assign group privileges to tables and schemas. Finally, you use pgAdmin III to create Login Roles (also known as user accounts), and assign them to the appropriate Group Roles.

An important part of managing a PostgreSQL system is to maintain the database data. You can do this using the table maintenance features provided in pgAdmin III. The vacuum and reindex functions are essential to maintaining your database performance as you accumulate more data. Backing up the database is another important function of the database manager. pgAdmin III provides a simple way to back up and restore individual databases, but to back up and entire PostgreSQL system, you must still use the pg_dumpall utility.

In this chapter, you got a taste of the other powerful PostgreSQL application, psql. The next chapter expands on the psql program, showing all of the functions you can perform using the simple command-line interface.

PART II

Using PostgreSQL in Windows

CHAPTER 5

The psql Program

After you have installed the PostgreSQL system and created user accounts, databases, and tables using pgAdmin III, it is time to start interacting with your new system. While PostgreSQL provides many interfaces to interact with the system, none is as simple as the `psql` program. This simple console application provides full access to the entire PostgreSQL system using both internal meta-commands and SQL statements. This chapter dissects the `psql` program and shows how to use it for all of your database needs.

THE PSQL COMMAND-LINE FORMAT

The `psql` program is a simple Windows console application that provides a command-line interface to the PostgreSQL system. Unlike the pgAdmin III program, discussed in Chapter 4, which enables you to see graphically all of the database objects and access information with the click of a mouse button, in the `psql` program you must enter text commands to view and manipulate data. While this method may seem old-fashioned by today's computing standards, a knowledgeable database administrator can be more productive just by entering the desired commands and quickly seeing results.

The `psql` program is one of the PostgreSQL utility programs located in the `bin` directory of the PostgreSQL installation directory (see Chapter 3). The easiest way to get to the PostgreSQL `bin` directory is to use the Command Prompt link provided by the PostgreSQL installer in the Windows Start menu. Choose Start | Programs | PostgreSQL 8.2 | Command Prompt. (Do not use the Command Prompt link in the Windows Accessories menu area, because it does not point to the PostgreSQL `bin` directory.)

By default, when you enter `psql` by itself at the Windows command prompt, `psql` attempts to connect to the default `postgres` database on the PostgreSQL server running on the local system and uses the Windows operating system user account you are currently logged in with as the PostgreSQL user account. If you want to log directly into another database, or log in using a different PostgreSQL user account, you have to include some command-line options with the `psql` command. There are lots of command-line options available for `psql`. The following sections walk through all of them.

Connection Options

The `psql` program uses command-line options and parameters to control its features. The format of the `psql` command line is

```
psql [options] [databasename [username] ]
```

where *options* can be one or more options that define additional information that controls the various psql features. The *databasename* and *username* parameters allow you to directly specify these values on the command line without having to use the *options* format.

To simply start `psql` and connect to a specific database on the local system as a specific user, all you need to do is list the database name and user account name on the command line. As was demonstrated in Chapter 4, you can connect to the database named `test` on the local system using the PostgreSQL user account `fred` with the `psql` command:

```
psql test fred
```

The PostgreSQL `pg_hba.conf` configuration file on the server defines what authentication method the `psql` connection needs to use to authenticate the connection (see Chapter 3). If the entry in the `pg_hba.conf` file defining this connection requires password authentication, `psql` asks you for the password for the `fred` account. Once you enter the correct password, the `psql` command prompt appears, ready for action.

You may have also noticed the *psql* link available in the PostgreSQL 8.2 Start menu. This link provides a quick way to start `psql` as the `postgres` superuser account and connect to the `postgres` database. This link is handy if you need to do any quick database administration work, but I would not recommend using it for normal database activity. It is always easy to enter wrong commands, and always logging in as the superuser account can cause problems if you do the wrong things, such as accidentally delete the wrong database. It is much safer to just log in as a normal user account unless you absolutely have to be the superuser.

Feature Options

The `psql` command-line options allows you to control what features are enabled when you start `psql`. The format for a feature option is

```
optionname [value]
```

The *value* parameter is required for some options to further define the option behavior, such as specifying a filename or a variable name. There are two formats that can be used to specify the *optionname* parameter:

▼ **Long-name format**   Uses a common name to represent the option, preceded by a double dash, such as —`echo-queries`.

▲ **Short-name format**   Uses a single character to represent the option, preceded by just a single dash, such as `-e`. Be careful when using the short-name options, as they are case sensitive.

Table 5-1 describes all of the feature options that are available on the `psql` command line.

You can see from this table that many of the `psql` command-line options focus on controlling how table data is displayed. You will see later in this chapter in the "The psql Meta-commands" section that many of these command-line options can also be set using `psql` meta-commands at the `psql` prompt. Sometimes it is easier to include a quick command-line option than to use the internal meta-commands. For example, if you just

Short Name	Long Name	Description
-a	—echo-all	Displays all SQL lines processed from a script file in the output.
-A	—no-align	Sets output format to unaligned mode. Data is not displayed as a formatted table.
-c *statement*	—command *statement*	Executes the single SQL statement *statement* and exits.
-d *database*	—dbname *database*	Specifies the database to connect to.
-e	—echo-queries	Echoes all queries to the screen.
-E	—echo-hidden	Echoes hidden `psql` meta-commands to the screen.
-f *filename*	—file *filename*	Executes SQL commands from file *filename* and exits.
-F *separator*	—field-separator *separator*	Specifies the character to use to separate column data when in unaligned mode. The default is a comma.
-h *hostname*	—host *hostname*	Specifies the IP address or hostname to connect to.
-H	—html	Generates HTML code for all table output.
-l	—list	Displays a list of available databases on the server and exits.
-o *filename*	—output *filename*	Redirects query output to the file *filename*.
-p *port*	—port *port*	Specifies the PostgreSQL server TCP port to connect to.
-P *variable=value*	—pset *variable=value*	Sets the table printing option *variable* to *value*.

Table 5-1.   The psql Command-Line Options

Short Name	Long Name	Description
-q	—quiet	Quiet mode; no output messages are displayed.
-R *separator*	—record-separator *separator*	Uses the character *separator* as the record separator. The default is a newline.
-s	—single-step	Prompts to continue or cancel after every SQL query.
-S	—single-line	Specifies that the ENTER key defines the end of a SQL query instead of a semicolon.
-t	—tuples-only	Disables column headers and footers in table output.
-T *attribute*	—table-attr *attribute*	Uses HTML table tag *attribute* when in HTML mode.
-U *username*	—username *username*	Specifies the user account to connect as.
-v *name=value*	—variable *name=value*	Sets the variable *name* to *value*.
-V	—version	Displays the psql version number and exits.
-W	—password	Forces a password prompt.
-x	—expanded	Enables expanded table output to display additional information for records.
-X	—nopsqlrc	Specifies to not process the psql startup file, called psqlrc.conf.
-?	—help	Displays the psql command-line help and exits.

Table 5-1. The psql Command-Line Options *(continued)*

want to execute some SQL statements stored in a file, you could use the following `psql` command:

```
C:\Program Files\PostgreSQL\8.2\bin>psql -f test.sql test fred
Password for user fred:
Customer Query result
 CustomerID | LastName | FirstName |  Address  |  City   | State |  Zip  | Phone
------------+----------+-----------+-----------+---------+-------+-------+----------
 BLU001     | Blum     | Rich      | 123 Main  | Chicago | IL    | 60633 | 555-1234
(1 row)

Product Query result
 ProductID | ProductName |   Model   | Manufacturer | UnitPrice | Inventory
-----------+-------------+-----------+--------------+-----------+----------
 LAP001    | Laptop      | Takealong | Acme         |       500 |        10
(1 row)

C:\Program Files\PostgreSQL\8.2\bin>
```

The `-f` option specifies the text file to read SQL statements from. By default, `psql` assumes the text file is located in the same directory you started `psql` from. You can also supply a full pathname for the file. If the pathname includes spaces, you must use double quotes around the pathname. The `psql` command connected to the database `test` using the user account `fred`, then executed the SQL commands in the file `test.sql`.

Using the Command-Line Options

You can use more than one option within the command line, but any values associated with the command-line option must be included after the specific command-line option. For example:

```
C:\Program Files\PostgreSQL\8.2\bin>psql -U fred -l
Password for user fred:

        List of databases
    Name    |  Owner   | Encoding
------------+----------+----------
 postgres   | postgres | UTF8
 template0  | postgres | UTF8
 template1  | postgres | UTF8
 test       | postgres | UTF8
(4 rows)

C:\Program Files\PostgreSQL\8.2\bin>
```

In this example, the -l option is used to obtain a list of all the databases created in the local PostgreSQL server, and the -U option is used to specify the user account to log in with. If you do not specify a database name as an option, you cannot specify the user account to log in with unless you use the -U option.

Once you have started your psql session, it greets you with a simple welcome message, then the psql command prompt:

```
C:\Program Files\PostgreSQL\8.2\bin>psql test fred
Password for user fred:
Welcome to psql 8.2.0, the PostgreSQL interactive terminal.

Type:   \copyright for distribution terms
        \h for help with SQL commands
        \? for help with psql commands
        \g or terminate with semicolon to execute query
        \q to quit

test=>
```

If this gets old, you can use the -q command-line option to disable the welcome message.

The default psql prompt shows the database you are currently connected to. If you are connected as a normal user, the prompt ends with a greater-than sign (>). If you are connected to the database as a superuser (such as the postgres user), the prompt ends with a pound sign (#):

```
test=#
```

This provides a warning to let you know of your superuser capabilities. Again, use extreme caution when deleting objects as the superuser.

At the psql prompt you can enter psql commands to control and query objects in the database. There are two different types of psql commands:

▼ Standard SQL commands

▲ Special psql meta-commands

Chapters 6 and 7 cover the SQL commands you can use in psql. The following section describes the special psql meta-commands.

THE PSQL META-COMMANDS

The psql *meta-commands* are predefined shortcuts in psql that save you from typing more complex SQL commands. Each meta-command is preceded by a backslash (thus they are sometimes referred to as *slash commands*). The commands are combinations of one or more characters referencing specific SQL commands. You can see a list of the available meta-commands from the psql prompt by typing \?. The psql meta-commands are divided into the following categories based on their functions:

▼ General meta-commands

■ Query buffer meta-commands

■ Input/output meta-commands

■ Informational meta-commands

■ Formatting meta-commands

▲ Copy and large object meta-commands

The following sections describe the psql meta-commands.

psql General Meta-commands

The psql general meta-commands display information about the psql system. These commands are listed and described in Table 5-2.

There are a couple of handy meta-commands included in this set. The most obvious is the \q meta-command, which is used to exit psql when you are done. The \c meta-command is great if you need to switch to another database while already logged in. Remember that you can only connect to one database at a time (at least within the same session). When you use the \c meta-command, PostgreSQL uses the same user account

Command	Description
\c *dbname*	Connect to different database
\cd *dir*	Change to a different working directory on the local system
\copyright	Display the PostgreSQL copyright information
\encoding *encoding*	Display or set the current psql encoding
\h *statement*	Display help on a SQL statement
\q	Exit (or quit) psql
\set *name value*	Set variable value (same as -v command-line option)
\timing	Display total time a command takes
\unset *name*	Unset variable value
\! *command*	Execute *command* on host system

Table 5-2. psql General Meta-commands

you are currently connected as (which has already been authenticated) to connect to the specified database. If you do not have privileges to connect to the database, your previous database connection is restored. Here is an example of connecting to a database from within psql.

```
C:\Program Files\PostgreSQL\8.2\bin>psql -q test fred
Password for user fred:
test=> \c postgres
You are now connected to database "postgres".
postgres=>
```

Notice that the prompt changes to reflect the database in use.

Another meta-command in this general group that is handy is \set. This is used to set values to variables used in the psql session. There are default variables that are preset within the psql sessions, and you can also create your own variables that can be used within the psql session. You can use this feature to save you from lots of typing.

To view the variables that are currently set, enter the \set meta-command by itself with no parameters:

```
test=> \set
VERSION = 'PostgreSQL 8.2.0 on i686-pc-mingw32, compiled by GCC gcc.exe
  (GCC) 3.4.2 (mingw-special)'
AUTOCOMMIT = 'on'
VERBOSITY = 'default'
PROMPT1 = '%/%R%# '
PROMPT2 = '%/%R%# '
PROMPT3 = '>> '
DBNAME = 'test'
USER = 'fred'
PORT = '5432'
ENCODING = 'UTF8'
test=>
```

The PROMPT1, PROMPT2, and PROMPT3 variables allow you to set the prompts used in the psql session to descriptive text, giving you hints about where you are in the database process. The reason for the three prompts is the three levels of input modes in psql:

▼   PROMPT1 is for normal prompt input.

■   PROMPT2 is for entering continued SQL lines.

▲   PROMPT3 is for manually entering data in a COPY statement.

As you can see in the \set variable output, the prompts use substitution characters (characters preceded by a percent sign, %) to represent variable information. Table 5-3 lists and describes the prompt variable substitution characters that can be used.

Substitution Character	Description
%~	Inserts the database name, or a tilde (~) if it is the default database
%#	Inserts a pound sign (#) if the user is a superuser, or a greater-than sign (>) if the user is a normal user
%>	Inserts the TCP port number of the PostgreSQL server
%/	Inserts the name of the database you are connected to
%m	Inserts the nonqualified hostname of the PostgreSQL server
%M	Inserts the fully qualified hostname of the PostgreSQL server
%n	Inserts the user account currently logged in
%R	Inserts mode character: = for normal mode, ^ for SQL completion mode, and ! if disconnected
%:*variable*	Inserts the `psql` variable *variable*

Table 5-3.   psql Prompt Substitution Characters

The `psql` prompts can be customized to reflect many features of your database connection:

```
test=>\set PROMPT1 %n@%~%R%#
fred@test=>
```

Besides setting the default variables, you can create your own variables that are used during the `psql` session. Here is an example of creating your own variable:

```
test=> \set cust 'store."Customer"'
test=> select * from :cust;
 CustomerID | LastName | FirstName | Address  |  City   | State | Zip   | Phone
------------+----------+-----------+----------+---------+-------+-------+----------
 BLU001     | Blum     | Rich      | 123 Main | Chicago | IL    | 60633 | 555-1234
(1 row)

test=>
```

The variable `cust` is set to the full pathname of the Customer table. The variable can then be referenced in any SQL statement by preceding it with a colon (:).

Query Buffer Meta-commands

The query buffer meta-commands display and control the contents of the internal `psql` query buffer. This buffer contains the most recently submitted SQL query statement processed by `psql`. These commands are listed and described in Table 5-4.

These commands allow you to manipulate the query buffer by editing the query currently in the buffer. Here is an example of using the query buffer commands:

```
test=> \set pr 'store."Product"'
test=> select * from :pr;
 ProductID | ProductName |   Model    | Manufacturer | UnitPrice | Inventory
-----------+-------------+------------+--------------+-----------+-----------
 LAP001    | Laptop      | Takealong  | Acme         |       500 |        10
(1 row)

test=> \p
select * from store."Product";
test=> \g
 ProductID | ProductName |   Model    | Manufacturer | UnitPrice | Inventory
-----------+-------------+------------+--------------+-----------+-----------
 LAP001    | Laptop      | Takealong  | Acme         |       500 |        10
(1 row)

test=> \r
Query buffer reset (cleared).
test=> \p
Query buffer is empty.
test=>
```

Command	Description
\e [*file*]	Edit the query buffer (or *file*) with an external editor (Windows Notepad).
\g [*file*]	Send the query buffer to the PostgreSQL server. Place the results in *file* if specified. This can be a full pathname, or a file located in the directory `psql` was started from.
\p	Display the current contents of the query buffer.
\r	Reset the contents of the query buffer.
\w *file*	Write the contents of the query buffer to *file*. This can be a full pathname, or a file located in the directory `psql` was started from.

Table 5-4. psql Query Buffer Meta-commands

Notice that even though a variable is used for the SQL statement, the query buffer contains the expanded variable text. The \g command is used to rerun the SQL statement in the query buffer. The \r command resets (empties) the query buffer.

Input/Output Meta-commands

The input/output meta-commands control the way SQL statements are input to psql and how output should be handled. Table 5-5 lists and describes these commands.

The \i command is extremely helpful. This command allows you to run SQL statements stored in files on the system. This includes any files created by the pg_dump backup program (described in Chapter 3) that were created using the *plain* backup format. By default, the file must be located in the same directory you started psql from. If it is not, you must specify the full pathname for the file. If the pathname includes spaces, you must enclose the filename in double quotes.

While in interactive mode the \echo command may seem silly, it is often used to insert comments within stored SQL statements. The echoed strings appear within the standard command output. As an example, create the file test.sql, and enter the following lines:

```
\echo Customer query result
select * from store."Customer";
\echo Product query result
select * from store."Product";
```

Now, within a psql session, use the \i meta-command to run the SQL file:

```
test=> \i test.sql
Customer Query result
 CustomerID | LastName | FirstName | Address  |  City   | State |  Zip  |  Phone
------------+----------+-----------+----------+---------+-------+-------+----------
 BLU001     | Blum     | Rich      | 123 Main | Chicago | IL    | 60633 | 555-1234
(1 row)

Product Query result
 ProductID | ProductName |  Model    | Manufacturer | UnitPrice | Inventory
-----------+-------------+-----------+--------------+-----------+-----------
 LAP001    | Laptop      | Takealong | Acme         |       500 |        10
(1 row)

test=>
```

Command	Description
\echo *string*	Display *string* on the standard output
\i *file*	Execute commands from the specified *file*
\o *file*	Redirect all query output to the specified *file*
\qecho *string*	Write *string* to the output specified in the \o command

Table 5-5.   psql Input/Output Meta-commands

The commands entered in the `test.sql` file were processed by `psql`, and the output was displayed on the console. Notice that the commands themselves were not displayed in the output. This is where the `\echo` command comes in handy to help produce nice titles for the displayed data.

Informational Meta-commands

The `psql` informational meta-commands provide a wealth of information about the PostgreSQL system. You can use the informational meta-commands to display the tables, views, and users created in the connected database. These commands are listed and described in Table 5-6.

Command	Description
\d *name*	Display detailed information about the table, index, sequence, or view *name*.
\da [*pattern*]	List aggregate functions matching *pattern*
\db [*pattern*]	List tablespaces matching *pattern*
\dc [*pattern*]	List conversions matching *pattern*
\dC	List casts
\dd [*pattern*]	Show comments for objects matching *pattern*
\dD [*pattern*]	List domains matching *pattern*
\df [*pattern*]	List functions matching *pattern*
\dg [*pattern*]	List Group Roles matching *pattern*
\di [*pattern*]	List indexes matching *pattern*
\dn [*pattern*]	List schemas matching *pattern*
\do [*pattern*]	List operators matching *pattern*
\dl [*pattern*]	List large objects matching *pattern*
\dp [*pattern*]	List table, view, and sequence access privileges matching *pattern*
\ds [*pattern*]	List sequences matching *pattern*
\dS [*pattern*]	List system tables matching *pattern*
\dt [*pattern*]	List tables matching *pattern*
\dT [*pattern*]	List data types matching *pattern*
\du [*pattern*]	List users matching *pattern*
\dv [*pattern*]	List views matching *pattern*
\l	List all databases
\z [*pattern*]	List table, view, and sequence access privileges matching *pattern*

Table 5-6. psql Informational Meta-commands

As you can see from Table 5-5, there are lots of informational meta-commands available for you. These are great tools for viewing the layout of a PostgreSQL database.

Be careful when using these commands, though, as the information they produce is dependant on your schema search path (described in detail in Chapter 6). By default, the \dt command displays a list of tables in the schemas contained in your search path. If you want to display the tables from a schema not in your search path, you must specify it within the option pattern:

```
test=> \dt store.
            List of relations
  Schema  |   Name    | Type  |  Owner
----------+-----------+-------+----------
  store   | Customer  | table | postgres
  store   | Order     | table | postgres
  store   | Product   | table | postgres
(3 rows)

test=>
```

The period at the end of the schema name is important. A very useful meta-command is the \d command.

This meta-command allows you to view the columns available within a table:

```
test=> \d store."Customer"
            Table "store.Customer"
   Column   |        Type        | Modifiers
------------+--------------------+-----------
 CustomerID | character varying  | not null
 LastName   | character varying  |
 FirstName  | character varying  |
 Address    | character varying  |
 City       | character varying  |
 State      | character(2)       |
 Zip        | character(5)       |
 Phone      | character(8)       |
Indexes:
    "CustomerKey" PRIMARY KEY, btree ("CustomerID")

test=>
```

Notice that all of the information related to the table is displayed, including any indexes created.

For a quick look at what Group Roles a Login Role belongs to, the \dg meta-command is handy:

```
test=>\dg fred
                              List of roles
 Role name | Superuser | Create role | Create DB | Connections |  Member of
-----------+-----------+-------------+-----------+-------------+-------------
 fred      | no        | no          | no        | no limit    | {Accountant}
(1 row)

test=>
```

This output tells you what database privileges the Login Role has, as well as what Group Roles it is a member of.

Formatting Meta-commands

The formatting meta-commands control how table data is displayed in psql. These commands control the format of the table output when displaying the results from queries. The formatting meta-commands are listed and described in Table 5-7.

You should have noticed by now that in the normal query output, the table column names are displayed, followed by the record data, each record being on one row, immediately followed by the data for the next record. These meta-commands allow you to change the way the data is displayed.

For starters, if you want to see only the data rows, without the column headings, use the \t meta-command. If you would like to create a special title for the table, use the \C meta-command. If you do not even want the data displayed in a table format, use the \a meta-command. This outputs only the table headings and data, without the table formatting.

Command	Description
\a	Toggle between aligned (table) and unaligned (raw) output mode.
\C *string*	Set table title to *string*. Unsets the title if *string* is empty.
\f [*string*]	Show the field separator character, or set it to *string*.
\H	Toggle HTML output mode.
\pset *parameter value*	Set table printing option *parameter* to *value*. Same as -P command-line option.
\t	Toggle display of table headings.
\T *string*	Set HTML <table> tag attribute to *string*.
\x	Toggle expanded output.

Table 5-7.   psql Formatting Meta-commands

If you would like to use a character other than the pipe symbol (|) to separate fields in the unaligned output, use the \f meta-command and specify the character to use.

The \x command provides for a completely different style of table output. Each record is displayed individually, with the column names on the left, and record values on the right:

```
test=> \x
Expanded display is on.
test=> select * from :cust;
-[ RECORD 1 ]-------
CustomerID | BLU001
LastName   | Blum
FirstName  | Rich
Address    | 123 Main
City       | Chicago
State      | IL
Zip        | 60633
Phone      | 555-1234

test=>
```

This format is called *extended* frames. This also applies to other commands that display data, such as using the informational meta-commands such as \dt and \l.

The \pset meta-command is your one-stop-shopping place for all table formatting commands. It provides an interface to control all of the table formatting possibilities in one place. It can be used to fine-tune exactly how you want the table output to look. Table 5-8 lists and describes the \pset parameters that are available.

As you can see, you can control just about every aspect of the table output using the \pset meta-command. Also, these same controls can be set using the psql -P command-line option. The special HTML formatting controls are great tools that allow you to easily incorporate psql output in web pages.

Copy and Large Object Meta-commands

The final group of meta-commands control importing and exporting large objects into PostgreSQL tables, and copying data directly from text files into tables. Table 5-9 lists and describes these commands.

The \copy meta-command is a great tool for importing data directly into tables. This is covered in detail in the "Importing Data with psql" section later in this chapter.

The large object meta-commands help you handle large objects in a PostgreSQL database. Large objects are binary objects, such as picture, video, and audio files. PostgreSQL allows you to enter them in the database, but because of their size, they cannot be placed directly in a table.

Instead, PostgreSQL manages large objects separately, in a special table called pg_largeobject. A link called the Large Object Object ID (LOBOID) is placed in the

\pset Parameter	Description
Format	Set the table format to aligned, unaligned, html, or latex.
border *val*	Set a number for the type of border used by the table. Higher numbers have more pronounced borders.
Expanded	Toggle between regular and extended frames. Regular frames display each record as a row. Extended frames display each record column as a separate line.
Null	Set a string to use when a NULL field is displayed.
Fieldsep *character*	Specify the column separator when in unaligned mode (default is pipe).
Recordsep *character*	Specify the record separator when in unaligned mode (default is newline).
tuples_only	Display only table data, with no column headers.
Title	Set a title to display before the table is displayed.
Tableattr	When in HTML format, define additional <table> tags.
Pager	Toggle paging the output. Paging stops the display after each screen of information is displayed.

Table 5-8.   psql \pset Meta-command Parameters

Command	Description
\copy	Copy data from a file to a table
\lo_export *LOBOID file*	Export the large object *LOBOID* to a file named file
\lo_import *LOBOID file*	Import the large object in the file file to the large object *LOBOID*
\lo_list	List all large objects defined in the database
\lo_unlink *LOBOID*	Unlink the large object *LOBOID*

Table 5-9.   The psql Copy and Large Object Meta-commands

data table that references the large object. The LOBOID points to the location of the large object in the `pg_largeobject` table.

THE PSQLRC.CONF FILE

You may have noticed that the `-X` `psql` option specifies that `psql` will not process the `psqlrc` startup file. The `psqlrc` startup file allows you to place commonly used meta-commands and SQL statements in a file that is processed every time you start `psql`.

In the Windows environment, the standard PostgreSQL `psqlrc` file has been re-named to `psqlrc.conf` and is located in somewhat of an odd place. To find it, you must know the value of the `APPDATA` Windows environment variable. To find this value, use the Windows `echo` command:

```
C:\Documents and Settings\RICH>echo %APPDATA%
C:\Documents and Settings\RICH\Application Data

C:\Documents and Settings\RICH>
```

To display the value of the environment variable, place percent signs (`%`) around it within the `echo` statement. Now that you know the value of the `APPDATA` environment variable, the `psqlrc.conf` file is located in the following path:

```
%APPDATA%\postgresql\psqlrc.conf
```

The PostgreSQL installer doesn't create this file automatically, so you have to manually create it using the Windows Notepad application. The `psqlrc.conf` file is a standard text file that contains the meta-commands and SQL statements you want to automatically run. Here is an example of a `psqlrc.conf` file:

```
\set cust 'store."Customer"'
\set prod 'store."Product"'
```

Now every time `psql` is run, these variables will automatically be set:

```
C:\Program Files\PostgreSQL\8.2\bin>psql -q test fred
Password for user fred:
test=> select * from :cust;

 CustomerID | LastName | FirstName | Address  |  City   | State |  Zip  |  Phone
------------+----------+-----------+----------+---------+-------+-------+----------
 BLU001     | Blum     | Rich      | 123 Main | Chicago | IL    | 60633 | 555-1234
(1 row)

test=>
```

In the `psql` session, the `cust` variable was already set for us by the `psqlrc.conf` file. To reference the variable, just precede it with a colon. This can be a great typing saver, especially if you (or your customers) choose to have long schema and table names.

IMPORTING DATA WITH PSQL

Chapter 4 showed how the pgAdmin III program could help us insert data into our tables. Chapter 6 shows how to use the SQL INSERT statement to insert data into tables as well. Unfortunately, both methods are somewhat tedious if you must enter lots of data. PostgreSQL provides a great solution to this problem.

Many times you will already have data provided in spreadsheets that must be entered into the tables. Instead of having to manually retype all of the information, PostgreSQL provides a way for us to automatically push the data into tables. This is a great feature to have available.

The \COPY meta-command is used to copy data from files directly into tables. Each row of data in the file relates to a record of data for the table. The data in the row must be in the same order as the table columns. You can determine the order of the table columns by using the \d meta-command, as shown earlier in this chapter in the "Informational Meta-commands" section.

The format of the \copy commands is

```
\copy tablename from filename [using delimiters 'delim' with null as 'string']
```

The *tablename* value must be the full table name. In my version of psql, it appears that you cannot use a variable name in the \copy command. The *filename* value must include the full pathname for the data file if it is not located in the same directory you started psql from.

By default, the \copy command assumes column data is separated by a tab character. If your data uses any other character as a separator, you must use the USING DELIMITERS option to specify it. Be careful when specifying a delimiter character. You must ensure that the character is not found within the normal data. If it is, the \copy command will not parse the column data correctly.

Also, by default the \copy command assumes that blank column data entries are empty strings, and not the special NULL character. To enter a NULL character, use a \N value, or specify the NULL character to use in the WITH NULL option.

These days, it is common to receive from customers data within Microsoft Excel spreadsheets. Using the \copy command, it is easy to import this data directly into your PostgreSQL tables. Before using the \copy command, you must convert the Excel spreadsheet data to a format that \copy can read. This is accomplished by saving the spreadsheet in either the Text (tab-delimited) or CSV (comma-delimited) format. The following is an example of a comma-delimited text file:

```
BLU002,Blum,Barbara,879 Oak,Gary,IN,46100,555-4321
BLU003,Blum,Katie,342 Pine,Hammond,IN,46200,555-9242
BLU004,Blum,Jessica,229 State,Whiting,IN,46300,555-0921
```

Since the data is separated by commas, you must specify the proper delimiter in the \copy command:

```
test=> \copy store."Customer" from data.txt using delimiters ','
\.
test=> select * from :cust;
 CustomerID | LastName | FirstName | Address   |  City    | State |  Zip  | Phone
------------+----------+-----------+-----------+----------+-------+-------+----------
 BLU001     | Blum     | Rich      | 123 Main  | Chicago  | IL    | 60633 | 555-1234
 BLU002     | Blum     | Barbara   | 879 Oak   | Gary     | IN    | 46100 | 555-4321
 BLU003     | Blum     | Katie     | 342 Pine  | Hammond  | IN    | 46200 | 555-9242
 BLU004     | Blum     | Jessica   | 229 State | Whiting  | IN    | 46300 | 555-0921
(4 rows)

test=>
```

The data converted perfectly for the import. If any of the data rows in the text file do not convert properly (such as if they do not satisfy any constraints placed on the columns), the \copy command will produce an error message:

```
test=> \copy store."Customer" from data.txt using delimiters ','
\.
ERROR:  duplicate key violates unique constraint "CustomerKey"
CONTEXT:  COPY Customer, line 1: "BLU002,Blume,Judy,111 Maple,Hobart,IN,
46700,555-5577"

test=>
```

Notice that both the error message and the row that produced the error are displayed. There is another very important thing to know about errors in the \copy command. The \copy command is processed as a single transaction by the database. This means that the \copy command is either committed as a whole or rolled back as a whole. If you import a 1000-row data file, and row 999 has an error, all of the previously inserted 998 rows will be rolled back and not entered into the database, and the one remaining row will not be processed.

SUMMARY

This chapter walked through the features of the psql program, which provides a simple console interface to your PostgreSQL system. You can perform database administration functions as well as input, delete, modify, and query the data contained in the database. The psql program uses command-line options to allow you to set features used within the application. Besides the command-line options, psql also provides its own internal meta-commands. These commands consist of shortcuts for performing complex SQL statements (such as copying data from a data file to a table) and commands for setting the format of query results.

The main language used to interface with the PostgreSQL database is SQL. Chapter 6 dives into the basics of the SQL language and shows you how to use psql to perform administration and user functions using SQL statements.

CHAPTER 6

Using Basic SQL

C hapter 5 showed how to use the `psql` program to interact with the PostgreSQL system. One of the ways to interact with PostgreSQL is to use the standard SQL query language. Whether you are accessing your PostgreSQL system from the `psql` program interface or from a fancy Java or .NET application, knowing how to use SQL is an important skill to have. The better your SQL skills, the better your application will perform. This chapter shows the basics of using SQL to control your PostgreSQL system, and how to insert, delete, and query data.

THE SQL QUERY LANGUAGE

When you look at the PostgreSQL feature descriptions on the PostgreSQL web site (www .postgresql.org), they state that PostgreSQL conforms to the ANSI SQL 92/99 standards. Unless you are familiar with the database world, you might not know exactly what that means. This section explains what the SQL query language is, and how it is used to interact with the database.

SQL History

The Structured Query Language (SQL) has been around since the early 1970s as a language for interacting with relational database systems. As database systems became more complex, it was clear that a simpler language was needed to interact with databases. The first commercial SQL product, called Structured English Query Language (SEQUEL), was released by IBM in 1974. As its name suggests, it was intended to provide a query interface to the database system using simple English words. Over the next few years the SEQUEL language was modified, and eventually became known as SQL (which often is pronounced "sequel").

As other database vendors attempted to mimic or replace SQL with their own query languages, it became evident that SQL provided the easiest interface for both users and administrators to interact with any type of database system. In 1986 the American National Standards Institute (ANSI) formulated the first attempt to standardize SQL. The standard was adopted by the United States government as a federal standard, and was named ANSI SQL89. This SQL standard was adopted by most commercial database vendors.

As you can probably guess from there, additional updates have been made to the ANSI SQL standard over the years, resulting in SQL92 (also called SQL2) and SQL99 (also called SQL3) versions, which are the versions PostgreSQL supports. At the time of this writing there is also an ANSI SQL 2003 version that has been published, but PostgreSQL does not claim compatibility with it.

SQL Format

The main feature of SQL is that it provides a standard way of defining commands that the database engine can understand. A SQL command (also called a statement) consists of *tokens*, separated by white space, and terminated by a semicolon (although PostgreSQL can be configured to allow a SQL statement to be terminated by pressing the ENTER key, defined in the `postgresql.conf` file).

The command tokens identify actions, and data used in the command. They consist of:

▼ Keywords

■ Identifiers

▲ Literals

SQL Keywords

SQL keywords define the actions the database engine takes based on the SQL statement. Table 6-1 lists and describes the standard SQL keywords supported by PostgreSQL.

SQL Keyword	Description
ALTER	Change (alter) the characteristics of an object.
CLOSE	Remove (close) an active cursor in a transaction or session.
COMMIT	Commit a transaction to the database.
CREATE	Create objects.
DELETE	Remove database data from a table.
DROP	Remove an object from the database.
END	Define the end of a transaction.
GRANT	Set object privileges for users.
INSERT	Add data to a table.
RELEASE	Delete a savepoint defined in a transaction.
REVOKE	Remove object privileges from users.
ROLLBACK	Undo a transaction.
SAVEPOINT	Define a point in a transaction where commands can be rolled back. This allows transactions within transactions.
SELECT	Query database table data.
START TRANSACTION	Start a set of database commands as a block.
UPDATE	Alter database data stored in a table.

Table 6-1.   Standard SQL Keywords

These standard SQL keywords are common among all database products that follow the ANSI SQL standards. However, besides the standard ANSI SQL commands, many database vendors implement nonstandard commands to augment the standard commands and to differentiate their product from others. Besides the standard SQL keywords, PostgreSQL provides a few nonstandard SQL keywords, listed and described in Table 6-2.

SQL keywords are case insensitive in PostgreSQL. You can enter keywords in any case (including mixed case) and PostgreSQL will interpret them properly.

Besides these keywords there are also modifying keywords, such as FROM, WHERE, HAVING, GROUP BY, and ORDER BY. These keywords are used to modify the command defined in the main keyword. The various modifying keywords are described later in this chapter as the main keywords are introduced.

SQL Identifiers

SQL command *identifiers* define database objects used in the command. This is most often a database name, schema name, or table name. Identifiers are case sensitive in PostgreSQL, so you must take extreme care to enter the case correctly. By default, PostgreSQL changes all unquoted identifiers to all lowercase. Thus the identifiers Customer, CUSTOMER, and CusTomer all become customer to PostgreSQL. To use uppercase letters in an identifier, you must use double quotes around the individual identifiers. For example, to reference the table Customer in the schema store, you must type store."Customer" in the SQL statement. However, to reference the table Customer in the schema Store, you must type "Store"."Customer" in the SQL statement.

Also, identifier names cannot be keywords. Thus, you cannot create a table named select and expect to use it in a SQL statement as

```
SELECT * from SELECT;
```

This will produce an error message from PostgreSQL. However, you can get around this rule by using a quoted identifier. PostgreSQL allows you to reference a table called select by using the format "select". The SQL statement

```
SELECT * from "select";
```

is perfectly permissible in PostgreSQL. While this is perfectly legal in PostgreSQL, this format is not supported by all database systems, and using keywords as table names is an extremely bad habit to acquire. Try to avoid using keywords as identifiers at all cost.

SQL Literals

SQL command *literals* define data values referenced by the keyword command. These are constant values, such as data that is to be inserted into tables, or data values for referencing queries.

Literals can be any type of data supported by PostgreSQL. There are hundreds of various data types recognized by PostgreSQL (as demonstrated in Chapter 4).

PostgreSQL SQL Keyword	Description
ABORT	Roll back the current transaction.
ANALYZE	Collect statistics about database tables.
BEGIN	Mark the start of a transaction.
CHECKPOINT	Force all data logs to be written to the database.
CLUSTER	Reorder table data based on an index.
COMMENT	Store a comment about a database object.
COPY	Move data between system files and database tables.
DEALLOCATE	Deallocate a previously prepared SQL statement.
DECLARE	Define a cursor used to retrieve a subset of data records from a table.
EXECUTE	Execute a previously prepared transaction.
EXPLAIN	Display the execution plan generated for a SQL statement.
FETCH	Retrieve data rows based on a previously set cursor.
LISTEN	Listen for a NOTIFY command from another user.
LOAD	Load a shared library file into the PostgreSQL address space.
LOCK	Perform a lock on an entire table.
MOVE	Reposition a table cursor without retrieving data.
NOTIFY	Send a notification event to all users listening on the same name.
PREPARE	Create a prepared SQL statement for later execution using EXECUTE.
REINDEX	Rebuild an index file for a table.
RESET	Restore configuration parameters to their default value.
SET	Set configuration parameters to an alternative value.
SHOW	Display the current value of a configuration parameter.
TRUNCATE	Quickly remove all rows from a set of tables.
UNLISTEN	Stop listening for a NOTIFY command from another user.
VACUUM	Reclaim storage space used by deleted table records.

Table 6-2.   PostgreSQL Nonstandard SQL Keywords

String data types, such as characters, variable-length characters, time strings, and date strings, must be enclosed in single quotes in the SQL statement. You can include a single quote within a string data type by preceding it with a backslash (such as `'O\'Leary'`). You can also embed special ASCII control characters into the string literal using C-style references:

▼   `\n` for newline

■   `\r` for carriage return

■   `\f` for form feed

■   `\t` for tab

▲   `\b` for backspace

Numerical literal values must be entered without quotes, otherwise PostgreSQL will interpret them as string values. Numerical values use standard math notations for entry, such as 10, 3.14, .005, and 10e3. PostgreSQL will interpret these values as numerical and attempt to enter them into the database table field using the format defined in the column (such as integer, floating point, or scientific).

CREATING OBJECTS

Chapter 4 showed how to use the graphical pgAdmin III program to create database, schema, table, Group Role, and Login Role objects. All of these objects can also be manually created using standard SQL statements. While most PostgreSQL administrators will find the graphical tools much easier to work with, sometimes knowing how to manually create an object comes in handy. This section walks through the SQL CREATE statement, showing how to manually create objects in the PostgreSQL system.

Creating a Database

As mentioned in Chapter 4, the PostgreSQL installation program creates a default database called `postgres`. It is advisable to create at least one other database for your applications to use, separate from the default database. The following is the format of the SQL CREATE statement used for creating databases:

```
CREATE DATABASE name [WITH
                    [OWNER owner]
                    [TEMPLATE template]
                    [ENCODING encoding]
                    [TABLESPACE tablespace]
                    [CONNECTIONLIMIT connlimit]]
```

The parameters enclosed in brackets are optional, and not required to create the database. The only required parameter for the CREATE DATABASE command is the name of the new database, *name*. By default, PostgreSQL makes the database owner the Login Role that creates the database. The Login Role must have privileges to create a new database on the PostgreSQL system. In practice, only the `postgres` superuser should create new databases.

The default template used to create the database will be `template1` (see Chapter 4 for details on templates), and the encoding, tablespace, and connection limit values will be the same as those defined for the `template1` database. You can specify alternative values for any or all of these parameters.

When you create a database, PostgreSQL returns either the CREATE DATABASE message on success or an error message on failure:

```
C:\Program Files\PostgreSQL\8.2\bin>psql postgres postgres
Password for user postgres:
postgres=# create database test2;
CREATE DATABASE
postgres=# create database test2;
ERROR: database "test2" already exists
postgres=# \c test2
You are now connected to database "test2".
test2=#
```

The first database creation command completed successfully, but the second attempt failed, as the proposed database name already existed. You can display a listing of all the existing database objects by using the PostgreSQL \l meta-command:

```
test2=# \l
          List of databases
    Name    |   Owner   | Encoding
------------+-----------+-----------
 postgres   | postgres  | SQL_ASCII
 template0  | postgres  | SQL_ASCII
 template1  | postgres  | SQL_ASCII
 test       | postgres  | UTF8
 test2      | postgres  | SQL_ASCII
(5 rows)

test2=#
```

If you need to remove an existing database, use the DROP DATABASE SQL command. This command cannot be used while anyone (including yourself) is currently in the database. All objects contained in the database (schemas, tables, functions, and so on) are removed from the PostgreSQL system. Be careful when using this command. The only way to recover from the DROP DATABASE command is to restore the database from the last backup.

Creating a Schema

After creating a database object, next up is the schema. As described in Chapter 4, a database can contain multiple schemas, which in turn contain the tables, views, and various functions. Often a database administrator will create separate schemas for each application within the database.

Just as with the database, normally only the superuser should create schemas for database users. The format of the CREATE SCHEMA command is

```
CREATE SCHEMA [schemaname] [AUTHORIZATION username [schema elements]]
```

The first oddity you may notice with this command format is that the *schemaname* value is optional. If it is not listed, PostgreSQL uses the Login Role value as the schema name.

The AUTHORIZATION parameter defines the user who will be the schema owner. By default, the schema owner is the user who creates the schema. Only the superuser can use the AUTHORIZATION parameter to specify a different user as the schema owner.

A unique feature of the CREATE SCHEMA command is that you can add additional SQL commands to the CREATE command to create schema objects (tables, views, indexes, sequences, and triggers) and grant privileges to users for the schema.

The new schema is created in the database you are currently connected to. By default, this is shown in the psql command prompt. A list of existing schemas in the database can be displayed using the PostgreSQL \dn meta-command:

```
test2=# \dn

        List of schemas
        Name        |   Owner
--------------------+-----------
 information_schema | postgres
 pg_catalog         | postgres
 pg_toast           | postgres
 public             | postgres
(4 rows)

test2=#
```

The information_schema, pg_catalog, and pg_toast schemas are internal PostgreSQL system schemas, created when the database object is created. The public schema is also created by PostgreSQL automatically when the database object is created, and is used as the default schema for the database.

The following example creates a new schema named store in the test2 database created earlier, and makes the Login Role fred the schema owner:

```
test2=# create schema store authorization fred;
CREATE SCHEMA
test2=# \dn
        List of schemas
        Name        |  Owner
--------------------+----------
 information_schema | postgres
 pg_catalog         | postgres
 pg_toast           | postgres
 public             | postgres
 store              | fred
(5 rows)

test2=#
```

If you need to remove a schema, use the DROP SCHEMA command:

```
DROP SCHEMA schemaname [CASCADE | RESTRICT]
```

By default, the RESTRICT parameter is enabled. This allows the schema to be re-moved only if it is empty. If there are any objects (such as tables, views, and triggers) created in the schema, by default the DROP SCHEMA command will fail. Alternatively, if you really want to remove the schema and all of the objects it contains, you must use the CASCADE parameter.

Creating a Table

By far the most common CREATE SQL command you will need to use is the CREATE TABLE command. Tables hold all of the application data. Advanced planning must be used to ensure that the application tables are created properly. Often, poor table design is the cause of many failed applications. Whenever possible, use standard relational da-tabase techniques to match related data elements together within the same table (such as all customer data in the Customer table, and all product data in the Product table).

Each data table must define the individual data elements (columns) contained in the table, the data type used for each data element, whether any of the columns will be used as a primary key for the table, whether any foreign keys need to be defined, and whether any table constraints should be present (such as requiring a column to always have a value). All of this information can make the CREATE TABLE command extremely complex.

Instead of trying to include all of the information required to create a table in one SQL CREATE command, often database administrators utilize the ALTER TABLE SQL command. This command is used to alter the definition of an existing table. Thus, you can create a base definition of a table using the CREATE TABLE command, then add ad-ditional elements using ALTER TABLE commands.

The following sections go through the process of creating a new table and adding additional elements to the base table.

Defining the Base Table

For the basic table definition, you need to define the table name and the individual data columns contained in the table. For each data column, you also need to declare the data type of the data. The format of a basic table definition looks like this:

```
CREATE TABLE tablename (column1 datatype, column2 datatype, ...);
```

For tables with lots of columns, this can become quite a long statement. Database administrators often split the statement into several command-line entries. Remember, by default, PostgreSQL does not process the SQL command until it sees a semicolon. Here is an example of creating a simple table in `psql`:

```
C:\Program Files\PostgreSQL\8.2\bin>psql test2 fred
Password for user fred:
test2=> create table store."Customer" (
test2(> "CustomerID" varchar,
test2(> "LastName" varchar,
test2(> "FirstName" varchar,
test2(> "Address" varchar,
test2(> "City" varchar,
test2(> "State" char,
test2(> "Zip" char(5),
test2(> "Phone" char(8));
CREATE TABLE
test2=> \dt store.
          List of relations
 Schema  |    Name    |  Type  |  Owner
---------+------------+--------+---------
 store   | Customer   | table  | fred
(1 row)
test2=> \d store."Customer"
          Table "store.Customer"
   Column    |        Type         | Modifiers
-------------+---------------------+-----------
 CustomerID  | character varying   |
 LastName    | character varying   |
 FirstName   | character varying   |
 Address     | character varying   |
 City        | character varying   |
 State       | character(2)        |
 Zip         | character(5)        |
 Phone       | character(8)        |

test2=>
```

There are lots of things to watch for in this example. First, by default, PostgreSQL creates all new tables in the public schema for the database you are connected to. If you want to create a table in a different schema, you must include the schema name in the CREATE TABLE command. Next, notice that the psql command prompt changes when additional input is required to finish the SQL statement as it is entered on multiple lines. This helps you keep track of what is expected next when entering commands. As you enter the definitions for each column, remember that if you want to use mixed-case letters in the column names, you must enclose the names in double quotes.

When the CREATE TABLE command is finished, a message is displayed showing the command was successful (if you use the -q command-line option, the command prompt returns with no message if the command is successful).

Besides the column data type, you can also add constraints to the column data definition:

```
postgres=> create table Employee (
postgres(> EmployeeID int4 primary key,
postgres(> Lastname varchar,
postgres(> Firstname varchar,
postgres(> Department char(5) not null,
postgres(> StartDate date default now(),
postgres(> salary money);
NOTICE:  CREATE TABLE / PRIMARY KEY will create implicit index "employee_pkey"
for table "Employee"
CREATE TABLE
postgres=>
```

In this example, notice that the keyword PRIMARY KEY is used to define a primary key used for indexing the data. The PRIMARY KEY keyword forces each data entry in the employeeid column to be both unique and not empty (called *null* in database terms). An additional constraint is added to the department column, requiring an entry for this column. The startdate column uses the PostgreSQL now function (discussed in Chapter 8) to enter today's date as a default value each time a record is entered.

Adding Additional Table Elements

Once the basic table is created, you can add additional columns, keys, and constraints by using the ALTER TABLE SQL command. The format of the ALTER TABLE command is

```
ALTER TABLE tablename action
```

The *action* parameter can be one or more SQL commands used to modify the table. Table 6-3 lists and describes the commands available.

Be careful when altering a table that contains data. Altering column information applies to all records already present in the table. With the Customer table added earlier,

ALTER Action	Description
ADD COLUMN *columnname*	Add a new column to the table.
DROP COLUMN *columnname*	Remove an existing column from the table.
ALTER COLUMN *columnname action*	Change the elements of an existing column. Can be used to change data type, add keys, or set constraints.
SET DEFAULT *value*	Set a default value for an existing column.
DROP DEFAULT	Remove a defined default value of an existing column.
SET NOT NULL	Define the NOT NULL constraint on an existing column.
DROP NOT NULL	Remove a NOT NULL constraint from an existing column.
SET STATISTICS	Enable statistic gathering used by the ANALYZE command.
SET STORAGE	Define the storage method used to store the column data.
ADD *constraint*	Add a new constraint to the table.
DROP *constraint*	Remove a constraint from the table.
DISABLE TRIGGER	Disable (but not remove) a trigger defined for the table.
ENABLE TRIGGER	Define a new trigger for the table.
OWNER *loginrole*	Set the table owner.
SET TABLESPACE *newspace*	Change the tablespace where the table is stored to *newspace*.
SET SCHEMA *newschema*	Change the schema location of the table to *newschema*.
RENAME COLUMN *oldname* TO *newname*	Change the name of table column *oldname* to *newname*.
RENAME TO *newname*	Change the name of the table to *newname*.

Table 6-3. ALTER TABLE Actions

I did not specify the primary key, and the constraint on the Phone column. I can now add those using the ALTER TABLE command:

```
test2=> alter table store."Customer" add primary key ("CustomerID");
NOTICE:  ALTER TABLE / ADD PRIMARY KEY will create implicit index
"Customer_pkey" for table "Customer"
ALTER TABLE
test2=> alter table store."Customer" alter column "Phone" set not null;
ALTER TABLE
test2=> \d store."Customer"
          Table "store.Customer"
   Column   |       Type        | Modifiers
------------+-------------------+-----------
 CustomerID | character varying | not null
 LastName   | character varying |
 FirstName  | character varying |
 Address    | character varying |
 City       | character varying |
 State      | character(2)      |
 Zip        | character(5)      |
 Phone      | character(8)      | not null
Indexes:
    "Customer_pkey" PRIMARY KEY, btree ("CustomerID")

test2=>
```

Here are a few other examples of using the ALTER TABLE command:

```
postgres=> alter table employee rename to employees;
ALTER TABLE
postgres=> alter table employees add column birthday date;
ALTER TABLE
postgres=> alter table employees rename column birthday to bday;
ALTER TABLE
postgres=> alter table employees alter column bday set not null;
ALTER TABLE
postgres=> \d employees
          Table "public.employees"
   Column   |       Type        | Modifiers
------------+-------------------+-------------
 employeeid | integer           | not null
 lastname   | character varying |
 firstname  | character varying |
 department | character(5)      | not null
 startdate  | date              | default now()
 salary     | money             |
 bday       | date              | not null
Indexes:
    "employee_pkey" PRIMARY KEY, btree (employeeid)

postgres=> alter table employees drop column bday;
ALTER TABLE
postgres=>
```

As a final check of your work, you can start the pgAdmin III program (as demonstrated in Chapter 4) and look at the newly created database, schema, and tables in the graphical display.

Creating Group and Login Roles

Once you have your tables created, you probably need to create some Group and Login Roles to control access to the data. As was discussed in Chapter 4, PostgreSQL uses *Login Roles* to act as user accounts that can log into the system, and *Group Roles* to control access privileges to database objects. Login Roles are assigned as members of the appropriate Group Roles to obtain the necessary privileges. Both of these roles are created using the CREATE ROLE SQL command.

The basic form of the CREATE ROLE command is

```
CREATE ROLE rolename [[WITH] options]
```

As expected, there are lots of options that can be used when creating a role. Table 6-4 lists and describes the options that can be used.

Option	Description
ADMIN *rolelist*	Add one or more roles as administrative members of the new role.
CONNECTION LIMIT *'value'*	Limit the number of connections the role can have to the database. The default is -1, which is unlimited connections.
CREATEDB	Allow the role to create databases on the system.
CREATEROLE	Allow the role to create new roles on the system.
ENCRYPTED	Encrypt the role password within the PostgreSQL system tables.
IN ROLE *rolelist*	List one or more roles that the new role will be a member of.
INHERIT	Specify that the role will inherit all of the privileges of roles it is a member of.
LOGIN	Specify that the role can be used to log into the system (a Login Role).
NOLOGIN	Specify that the role cannot be used to log into the system (a Group Role).
PASSWORD *passwd*	Specify the password for the role.
ROLE *rolelist*	List one or more roles that will be added as members to the new role.
SUPERUSER	Specify that the new role will have superuser privileges. Only the superuser can use this option.
VALID UNTIL *'date'*	Specify a date when the role will expire.

Table 6-4.   The CREATE ROLE SQL Command Options

By default, the CREATE ROLE command uses the NOLOGIN option to create a Group Role (although it also does not hurt to specify it). Remember, you must have superuser privileges to create new roles in the database. This is a job usually done with the postgres user account:

```
test2=# create role management with nologin;
CREATE ROLE
test2=# create role technician nologin;
CREATE ROLE
test2=#
```

Notice that the WITH keyword is optional in the command. If it makes things easier for you, go ahead and use it.

To create a new Login Role, the command can get somewhat complex. Just as in creating tables, you can also use the ALTER ROLE command to help break up the options. Unfortunately, you cannot use the IN ROLE option in the ALTER TABLE command, so that must be entered in the CREATE ROLE command:

```
test2=# create role wilma in role management;
CREATE ROLE
test2=# alter role wilma login password 'pebbles' inherit;
ALTER ROLE
test2=# create role betty in role technician;
CREATE ROLE
test2=# alter role betty login password 'bambam' inherit;
ALTER ROLE
test2=# \du wilma
                        List of roles
 Role name | Superuser | Create role | Create DB | Connections |  Member of
-----------+-----------+-------------+-----------+-------------+--------------
 wilma     | no        | no          | no        | no limit    | {management}
(1 row)

test2=#
```

The INHERIT parameter tells PostgreSQL to allow the Login Roles to inherit any privileges assigned to the Group Roles they belong to.

If you need to remove any Login or Group Roles, you can use the DROP ROLE command. However, PostgreSQL will not let you remove a role if it is the owner of any database objects, such as schemas or tables. You must perform an ALTER command to change the owner of the object to another role.

Assigning Privileges

Now that you have some Login and Group Roles created, it is time to assign privileges to database objects. In the SQL language, the command to assign privileges is GRANT:

```
GRANT privlist ON object TO roles
```

The *privlist* parameter contains a list of the privileges you want *roles* to have on the object *object*.

Granting privileges can be a complex function to perform. There are two types of GRANT commands, depending on what the *object* specified in the command is:

▼   Granting privileges to database objects

▲   Granting privileges to role objects

Granting Privileges to Database Objects

Granting privileges to database objects involves allowing Login and Group Roles to create, access, and modify the object. Table 6-5 lists and describes the privileges that can be assigned to database objects.

Database Object Privilege	Description
ALL PRIVILEGES	Allow role to have all privileges to the specified object.
CREATE	Allow role to create schemas within a specified database, or create tables, views, functions, and triggers within a specified schema.
DELETE	Allow role to remove data from a row in a specified table object.
EXECUTE	Allow role to run a specified function object.
INSERT	Allow role to insert data into a specified table object.
REFERENCES	Allow role to create a foreign key constraint in a table object.
RULE	Allow role to create rules for a specified table object.
SELECT	Allow role to query columns to retrieve data from the table object.
TEMPORARY	Allow role to create temporary table objects.
TRIGGER	Allow role to create a trigger on the specified table object.
UPDATE	Allow role to modify any column within a specified table object.
USAGE	Allow role to use a specified language, or access objects contained in a specified schema.

Table 6-5.   GRANT Command Database Object Privileges

When using the GRANT command on database objects, by default the command assumes you are using table objects. If you are granting privileges to any other database object, you must specify the object type before the object name:

```
test2=# grant usage on schema store to management;
GRANT
test2=#
```

This is an extremely important privilege that many novice administrators overlook. It is easy to get caught up in figuring out privileges for tables and forget to give your users access to the schema. If you forget to do that, even with table privileges their SQL commands will fail!

Once your users have access to the schema, you can start granting privileges to individual tables for your Group Roles:

```
test2=# grant select, insert, update on store."Customer" to management;
GRANT
test2=# grant select on store."Customer" to technician;
GRANT
test2=#
```

To see the assigned privileges for a table, use the \z meta-command:

```
test2=# \z store."Customer"
                     Access privileges for database "test2"
  Schema |    Name    |  Type  |                  Access privileges
---------+------------+--------+-----------------------------------------------
  store  |  Customer  |  table |  {fred=arwdRxt/fred,management=arw/fred,
technician=r/fred}
(1 row)

test2=#
```

The \z command shows all of the roles that have been assigned privileges for the table, along with the privilege codes (described in Chapter 4). The Login Role listed after the privilege is the one who granted the privileges.

To grant a privilege to all users on the system, use the special public Group Role:

```
test2=# grant select on store."Customer" to public;
GRANT
test2=#
```

Now all users on the system have the ability to query data from the Customer table. If you try to view the privileges for the table, you may be confused by what you now see. Instead of seeing an entry for public, you will see an entry with no name, assigned the r privilege:

```
{fred=arwdRxt/fred,management=arw/fred,technician=r/fred,=r/fred}
```

The empty privilege is the default for everyone on the system, which is the `public` group.

Granting Privileges to Roles

Granting privileges to roles is similar to using the `ALTER ROLE` command. You can use the `GRANT` command to specify a role to be a member of another role:

```
test2=# grant management to wilma;
NOTICE:  role "wilma" is already a member of role "management"
GRANT ROLE
test2=#
```

To revoke privileges already granted, use the `REVOKE` SQL command. You can revoke all assigned privileges on an object, or just a single assigned privilege for a single role:

```
test2=# revoke update on store."Customer" from management;
REVOKE
test2=#
```

HANDLING DATA

Now that you have your tables created, your user Login and Group Roles created, and the proper privileges assigned, you probably want to start manipulating data in the database. There are three SQL commands that are used for handling data in PostgreSQL:

- ▼ INSERT
- ■ UPDATE
- ▲ DELETE

The following sections describe these commands, and show how to use them in your application.

Inserting Data

The `INSERT` command is used to insert new data into the table. Each row of data in the table is called a *record*. Sometimes in database books and publications you will see the term *tuple*, which is just a fancy way of saying record.

A record consists of a single instance of data for each column (although it is possible that one or more columns in a record can be empty, or null). If you think of the table as a spreadsheet, the columns are the table columns, and the rows are the individual table records.

The basic format of the `INSERT` command is

```
INSERT INTO table [(columnlist)] VALUES (valuelist)
```

By default, the INSERT command attempts to load values from the *valuelist* into each column in the table, in the order the columns appear in the table. You can view the column order by using the \d meta-command. To enter data into all columns, you use the following command:

```
test2=# insert into store."Customer" values ('BLU001', 'Blum', 'Rich',
test2(# '123 Main St.', 'Chicago', 'IL', '60633', '555-1234');
INSERT 0 1
test2=#
```

Notice that you can separate the INSERT command into separate lines. The statement is not processed until the semicolon is entered. The response from psql shows two values. The first value is the object ID (OID) of the table record if the table was defined to use OIDs. If not, then the value is zero. The second value is the number of records that were entered into the table from the command.

If you do not want to enter all of the values into a record, you can use the optional *columnlist* parameter. This specifies the columns (and the order) that the data values will be placed in:

```
test2=# insert into store."Customer" ("CustomerID", "LastName", "Phone")
test2-# values ('BLU002', 'Blum', '555-4321');
INSERT 0 1
test2=#
```

Remember that the table constraints defined when creating the table apply, so you must enter data for columns created with the NOT NULL constraint. If a column was created with a DEFAULT VALUE constraint, you can use the keyword DEFAULT in the *valuelist* to assign the default value to the column data. You can also skip columns that have default values by not listing them in the *columnlist* parameter. Those columns will automatically be assigned their default values.

Modifying Data

If data entered into the table needs to be changed, all is not lost. You can modify any data in the table, as long as your Login Role has UPDATE privileges for that table.

The UPDATE SQL command is used for updating data contained in tables. The UPDATE command is another one of those commands that, while the idea is simple, can easily get complex. The basic format of the UPDATE command is

```
UPDATE table SET column = value [WHERE condition]
```

The basic format of this command finds the specified *column* in the *table* and changes the data in that column to the *value* specified in the command. However, using that basic format gets many database administrators into lots of trouble. Here is the way the scenario usually plays out. Suppose you want to go back to a data record previously inserted into the store.Customer table, and add some data that might have been left out in the original INSERT command, such as the customer's first name. It is not uncommon to see this erroneous SQL code:

```
test2=# update store."Customer" set "FirstName" = 'Barbara';
UPDATE 2
test2=#
```

Your first clue that something bad happened would be the output of the UPDATE command. The value after the update message shows the number of rows affected by the update process. Since this value is 2, you know that more than just the one row you wanted to change has been changed. Obviously something went wrong. Doing a simple query on the data shows what went wrong:

```
test2=# select * from store."Customer";
 CustomerID | LastName | FirstName |   Address    |  City   |State| Zip  | Phone
------------+----------+-----------+--------------+---------+-----+------+----------
 BLU001     | Blum     | Barbara   |123 Main St.|Chicago| IL | 60633|555-1234
 BLU002     | Blum     | Barbara   |            |       |    |      |555-4321
(2 rows)

test2=#
```

Ouch. We managed to change the FirstName column in both records in the table. This is an all-to-common mistake made by even the most experienced database programmers and administrators when in a hurry. Without the WHERE clause portion of the UPDATE command, the update is applied to every record in the table. In almost all cases, this is not what you intend to do.

The WHERE clause allows you to restrict the records that the UPDATE command applies to. The WHERE clause is a logical statement that is evaluated by PostgreSQL. Only records that match the condition contained within the WHERE clause are updated. Here is an example of a simple WHERE clause:

```
test2=# update store."Customer" set "FirstName" = 'Rich'
test2-# WHERE "CustomerID" = 'BLU001';
UPDATE 1
test2=# select * from store."Customer";
 CustomerID | LastName | FirstName |   Address    |  City   |State| Zip  | Phone
------------+----------+-----------+--------------+---------+-----+------+----------
 BLU002     | Blum     | Barbara   |            |       |    |      |555-4321
 BLU001     | Blum     | Rich      |123 Main St.|Chicago| IL |60633|555-1234
(2 rows)

test2=#
```

Every record in the table is examined to determine if it meets the condition defined in the WHERE clause. In this simplistic example, there is only one record that could possibly match the condition, as the primary key column cannot be duplicated in the table. Only the record that met the WHERE clause condition was updated with the new information.

You can add as many elements within the condition to the WHERE clause as you need to restrict the records to a specific subset within the table, such as updating employee records for everyone making more than $100,000.

You can also update more than one column in a single UPDATE command:

```
test2=# update store."Customer" set "Address" = '123 Main St.',
test2-# "City" = 'Chicago',
test2-# "State" = 'IL', "Zip" = '60633'
test2-# where "CustomerID" = 'BLU002';
UPDATE 1
test2=#
```

The WHERE option is where things can start to get complex. You can specify expressions for just about any column from any table in the database to determine which columns are updated. To use columns from other tables, you must precede the WHERE option with the FROM option, listing the tables the foreign columns come from:

```
test=# update store."Order" set "Quantity" = 5 from store."Customer"
test-# where "Order"."CustomerID" = "Customer"."CustomerID";
UPDATE 1
test=#
```

Deleting Data

The last data function discussed is removing data that is no longer needed in the table. Not surprisingly, the DELETE command is used to do this. The format for the DELETE command is

```
DELETE FROM table [WHERE condition]
```

This command is similar to the UPDATE command. Any records matching the condition listed in the WHERE clause are deleted. As with the UPDATE command, extreme caution is recommended when using the DELETE command. Another all-too-common mistake is to quickly type the DELETE command and forget the WHERE clause. That results in an empty table, as all records are deleted.

Here are a couple of examples of using the DELETE command:

```
test2=# delete from store."Customer" where "CustomerID" = 'BLU001';
DELETE 1
test2=# delete from store."Customer" where "CustomerID" = 'BLU003';
DELETE 0
test2=#
```

Notice that when the DELETE command fails to find any records to delete it does not produce an error message. Instead, it just reports back that the total number of records deleted was zero.

Similar to the UPDATE command, you can also specify columns in other tables in the WHERE clause. Before doing that you must precede the WHERE clause with the USING option, specifying a list of tables the columns come from. (Note that since the DELETE command already uses the FROM keyword, it uses the USING keyword to specify the tables. This is different from the UPDATE command.)

QUERYING DATA

Quite possibly the most important function you will perform in your applications is to query existing data in the database. While many application developers spend a great deal of time concentrating on fancy GUI front ends to their applications, the real heart of the application is the behind-the-scenes SQL used to query data in the database. If this code is inefficient, it can cause huge performance problems and make an application virtually useless for customers.

As a database application programmer, it is essential that you understand how to write good SQL queries. The SQL command used for queries is SELECT. Because of its importance, much work has been done on the format of the SELECT command, to make it as versatile as possible. Unfortunately, with versatility comes complexity.

Because of the complexity of the SELECT command, the command format has become somewhat unwieldy and intimidating for the beginner. To try and keep things simple, the next few sections demonstrate how to use some of the more basic features of the SELECT command. Some more advanced features of the SELECT command format will be presented in Chapter 7, after you have had a chance to get somewhat familiar with it here.

The Basic Query Format

The SQL SELECT command is used to query data from tables in the database. The basic format of the SELECT command is

```
SELECT columnlist from table
```

The *columnlist* parameter specifies the columns from the table you want displayed in the output. It can be a comma-separated list of column names in the table, or the wildcard character (the asterisk) to specify all columns, as was shown in the SELECT examples used earlier in this chapter:

```
SELECT * FROM store."Customer";
```

Sorting Output Data

The output of the SELECT command is called a *result set*. The result set contains only the data columns specified in the SELECT command. The result set is only temporary, and by default is not stored in any tables.

By default, the records are not displayed in any particular order. As records are added and removed from the table, PostgreSQL may place new records anywhere within the table. Even if you enter data in a particular order using INSERT commands, there is still no guarantee that the records will display in the same order as a result of a query. If you need to specify the order of the displayed records, you must use the ORDER BY clause:

```
test=> select "CustomerID", "LastName", "FirstName" from store."Customer"
test-> order by "FirstName";
 CustomerID | LastName | FirstName
------------+----------+-----------
 BLU002     | Blum     | Barbara
 BLU004     | Blum     | Jessica
 BLU003     | Blum     | Katie
 BLU001     | Blum     | Rich
(4 rows)

test=>
```

In this example (taken from the test database used in Chapter 5), only the columns specified in the SELECT command are displayed, ordered by the FirstName column. The default order used by the SELECT command is ascending order, based on the data type of the column you selected to order by. You can change the order to descending by using the DESC keyword after the column name in the ORDER BY clause.

Filtering Output Data

As you can see from the output in the preceding section, by default all of the records from the table are displayed. The power of the database query comes from displaying only a subset of the data that meets a specific condition.

The WHERE clause is used to determine what records satisfy the condition of the query. This is the meat-and-potatoes of the SELECT command. You can use the WHERE clause to break down complex tables to extract specific data. For example, you can check for all of the customers that live in Chicago by using the following query:

```
test=> select "CustomerID", "LastName", "FirstName" from store."Customer"
test-> where "City" = 'Gary';
 CustomerID | LastName | FirstName
------------+----------+-----------
 BLU001     | Blum     | Rich
(1 row)

test=>
```

Notice that the string literal Gary uses single quotes to signify that it is a string value, while the mixed-case column names require double quotes to preserve the uppercase letters. It is easy to get these two things confused.

Writing Advanced Queries

The next step in the query process is to extract data from more than one table using a single `SELECT` command. This section demonstrates some advanced queries that can be used when handling data contained in multiple tables, such as in a relational database application.

Querying from Multiple Tables

In a relational database, data is split into several tables in an attempt to keep data duplication to a minimum. In the store example described in Chapter 5, we created the Customer and Product tables to keep the detailed customer and product information separate. The Order table then only needed to reference the CustomerID and ProductID fields to identify the customer and the product ordered, eliminating the need to duplicate all of the customer and product information for each order.

Now, if you are trying to query the information for an individual order, you may need to extract the customer's detailed information for delivery purposes. This is where being able to query two tables at the same time comes in handy.

To query data from two tables, you must specify both tables in the `FROM` clause of the `SELECT` statement. Also, since you are referencing columns from both tables, you must indicate which table each column comes from in your `SELECT` statement:

```
C:\Program Files\PostgreSQL\8.1\bin>psql test barney
Password for user barney:
test=> select "Order"."OrderID", "Customer"."CustomerID",
test-> "Customer"."LastName", "Customer"."FirstName",
"Customer"."Address"
test-> from store."Order", store."Customer"
test-> where "Order"."OrderID" = 'ORD001'
test-> and "Order"."CustomerID" = "Customer"."CustomerID";
 OrderID | CustomerID | LastName | FirstName | Address
---------+------------+----------+-----------+---------
 ORD001  | BLU001     | Blum     | Rich      | 123 Main
(1 row)

test=>
```

As you can see, it does not take long for a seemingly simple SQL command to get fairly complex. The first part of the command defines the data columns you want to see in the output display. Since you are using columns from two tables, you must precede each column name with the table it comes from. As always, remember to use double quotes around names that use mixed-case letters.

Next, you must define which tables the columns come from in the `FROM` clause. If they are not located in the `public` schema, you must also indicate the schema where they are located. Finally, the `WHERE` clause must define a query to filter out the records you want to display. In this example, there are two conditions to the `WHERE` clause. The `AND` operator means that both conditions must be met for a record to be displayed.

The first condition states that you are looking for the record in the Order table where the OrderID column value is ORD001. The second condition states that you are looking for records in the Customer table that have the same CustomerID column value as the records retrieved from the Order table. For each record where both of these conditions are matched, the information in the data columns is displayed. Since only one record in the Order table has that OrderID value, only the information for that record is displayed.

Using Joins

In the previous example, you had to write a lot of SQL code to match the appropriate record from the Customer table to the Order record information. In a relational database, this is a common thing to do. To help programmers out, the SQL designers came up with an alternative way to perform this function.

A database *join* matches related records in relational database tables without you having to perform all of the associated checks. The format of using the join in an SELECT command is

```
SELECT columnlist FROM table1 jointype JOIN table2 ON condition
```

The *columnlist* parameter lists the columns from the tables to display in the output. The *table1* and *table2* parameters define the two tables to perform the join on. The *jointype* parameter determines the type of join to perform. There are three types of joins available in PostgreSQL:

▼ INNER JOIN   Only display records found in both tables

■ LEFT JOIN   Display all records in *table1* and the matching records in *table2*

▲ RIGHT JOIN   Display all records in *table2* and the matching records in *table1*

The LEFT and RIGHT JOIN join types are also commonly referred to as *outer joins*. The condition parameter defines the column relation to use for the join operation.

It is common practice to use the same column name for columns in separate tables that contain the same information (such as the CustomerID column in the Customer and Order tables). You can use the NATURAL keyword before the join type to inform PostgreSQL to join using the common column name. Here is the same query as used before, but this time using a NATURAL INNER JOIN:

```
test=> select "Order"."OrderID", "Customer"."CustomerID",
test-> "Customer"."LastName", "Customer"."FirstName", "Customer"."Address"
test-> from store."Order" natural inner join store."Customer";

OrderID | CustomerID | LastName | FirstName | Address
--------+------------+----------+-----------+----------
ORD001  | BLU001     | Blum     | Rich      | 123 Main
ORD002  | BLU002     | Blum     | Barbara   | 879 Oak
(2 rows)

test=>
```

That is a lot less typing to do! The result shows all of the records in the Order table that have matching CustomerID records in the Customer table. To display all of the records in the Customer table with their matching records in the Order table, use a RIGHT JOIN:

```
test=> select "Order"."OrderID", "Customer"."CustomerID",
test-> "Customer"."LastName","Customer"."FirstName", "Customer"."Address"
test-> from store."Order" natural right join store."Customer"

 OrderID | CustomerID | LastName | FirstName |   Address
---------+------------+----------+-----------+--------------
         | BLU004     | Blum     | Jessica   | 925 Dogwood
 ORD001  | BLU001     | Blum     | Rich      | 123 Main
 ORD002  | BLU002     | Blum     | Barbara   | 879 Oak
         | BLU003     | Blum     | Katie     | 342 Pine
(4 rows)

test=>
```

Notice in the result set that two records in the Customer table do not have any records in the Order table, but are still displayed as the result of the RIGHT JOIN.

Using Aliases

Use table aliases to help keep down the clutter in your SELECT commands. A table alias defines a name that represents the full table name within the SELECT command. The basic format for using aliases is

```
SELECT columnlist FROM table AS alias
```

When the table name is defined as an alias, you can use the alias anywhere within the SELECT command to reference the full table name. This is especially handy when you have to use schema names and double quotes for all of your table names. Here is a typical example:

```
test=> select a."OrderID", b."CustomerID", b."LastName", b."FirstName",
test-> b."Address" from store."Order" as a, store."Customer" as b
test-> where a."OrderID" = 'ORD001' and a."CustomerID" = b."CustomerID";
 OrderID | CustomerID | LastName | FirstName | Address
---------+------------+----------+-----------+-------------
 ORD001  | BLU001     | Blum     | Rich      | 123 Main
(1 row)

test=>
```

The alias a is used to represent the store."Order" table, and the alias b is used to represent the store."Customer" table. Notice that you can use the aliases anywhere in the SELECT statement, even before they are defined.

SUMMARY

SQL is at the heart of the PostgreSQL system. All interaction with PostgreSQL, whether you are using a fancy GUI or a simplistic command-line interface, is via SQL commands. This chapter introduced the basic SQL commands necessary to create database objects, insert and modify data, and query data.

The CREATE SQL family of commands allows you to create new database objects. The CREATE DATABASE command is used to start a new database area separate from the default area set up for system tables. The CREATE SCHEMA command allows you to provide a separate working area for each application within a single database. And, of course, the CREATE TABLE command is used for creating tables to hold the application data. The CREATE TABLE command is by far the most complex, as you are required to define all of the data elements and constraints contained within the application.

After creating the database environment, you must use the CREATE ROLE command to create Group and Login Roles. These roles are used for allowing users access to database objects. The GRANT and REVOKE commands are used to assign the appropriate privileges to the Group Roles.

The next step in the process is managing data within the tables. The INSERT command is used to insert new data records into a table. Table columns can be set to provide default values when a data element is not provided. The UPDATE command is used to modify data contained in existing tables. The WHERE clause of the UPDATE command is crucial in restricting the update to specific records within the table. Likewise, the DELETE command is almost always modified with the WHERE clause when used for removing data elements from the table.

Possibly the most important SQL command available is the SELECT command. This command allows you to create complex queries on the data stored within database tables. The SELECT command has lots of features, which require lots of command-line parameters used to fine-tune the query.

The next chapter continues coverage of the SELECT command. Advanced uses for SELECT are covered, as well as tips on how to maximize data retrieval using SELECT commands. The chapter also covers how to create views, combining data elements from multiple tables into a single object that can be used in queries, and triggers, which allow you to perform table functions based on database events. The chapter closes out on how to define SQL command transactions, grouping multiple SQL commands into a single transaction that is either accepted or denied by PostgreSQL.

CHAPTER 7

Using Advanced SQL

Chapter 6 covered the basics of interacting with your PostgreSQL system using SQL. This chapter extends that thought, presenting some more advanced SQL topics that will help you handle data within your PostgreSQL system. As was mentioned in Chapter 6, the SELECT command is possibly the most complex of the SQL commands. This chapter picks up on the discussion of the SELECT command and shows all of the options that can be used when querying a database. After that, table views are discussed. Views allow you to group data elements from multiple tables into a single virtual table, making querying data much easier. Following views, indexes are covered. Creating indexes on heavily queried columns can greatly speed up the query process. Next, the idea of transactions is demonstrated. Transactions allow you to group SQL commands together in a single operation that is processed by the database engine. The chapter finishes by discussing cursors. Cursors are used to help maneuver around a result set produced by a SELECT command. They can be used to control how you view the result set.

REVISITING THE SELECT COMMAND

Chapter 6 showed how easy it can be to query data from database tables using the SELECT command. Now that you have a rough idea about how to handle the SELECT command, it is time to dig a little deeper and look at all of the features it offers.

The official format of the SELECT command can be somewhat daunting. Besides the many standard ANSI SQL SELECT command parameters, there are also a few features that PostgreSQL has added that only apply to PostgreSQL. Here is the SELECT command format as shown in the official PostgreSQL documentation:

```
SELECT [ALL | DISTINCT [ON (expression [,...] ) ] ]
       * | expression [AS output_name ] [,... ]
       [ FROM from_list [, ...] ]
       [ WHERE condition ]
       [ GROUP BY expression [,...] ]
       [ HAVING condition [,...] ]
       [ (UNION | INTERSECT | EXCEPT) [ ALL ] select ]
       [ ORDER BY expression [ ASC | DESC | USING operator ] [,...] ]
       [ LIMIT ( count | ALL ) ] [ OFFSET start ]
       [ FOR (UPDATE | SHARE ) [ OF table_name [,...] [ NOWAIT ] ]
```

This is about as complex of a command as you can possibly get in the SQL command world. The best way to look at this is to walk through the various parameters one by one and discuss each feature individually. The following sections do just that.

The DISTINCT Clause

```
[ALL | DISTINCT [ON (expression [,...] ) ] ]
```

The DISTINCT clause section defines how the SELECT command handles duplicate records in the table. The ALL parameter defines that all records that are returned in the result set will be displayed in the SELECT command output, even if there are duplicates. This is the default behavior if neither of these parameters is specified in the DISTINCT clause.

The DISTINCT parameter specifies that when more than one record in a result set has the same values, only the first record is displayed in the output. The duplicate records are suppressed. This can be beneficial if you have tables that may contain duplicate information.

By default DISTINCT only eliminates records that are complete duplicates (all the column values match). You can use the ON option to define which column (or a comma-separated list of columns) to compare for duplicates.

The most common use for the DISTINCT clause is to display a list of the distinct number of values for a specific data column. For example, if you need to produce a report on all the cities you have customers in, you would want only one occurrence of each individual city, not one for each customer. To do this you could use the following SQL command:

```
test=> select distinct on ("City") "City", "State" from store."Customer";
  City    | State
----------+-------
 Chicago  | IL
 Gary     | IN
 Hammond  | IN
(3 rows)

test=>
```

Each city is displayed only once, no matter how many customers are located in that city.

The SELECT List

```
* | expression [AS output_name ] [,... ]
```

The SELECT list is the portion of the SELECT command between the SELECT and FROM keywords. The SELECT list section lists the columns you want displayed in the result set. The columns can all be from the same table, or they can be columns from multiple tables, preceded by the table name. The asterisk is used to indicate that all columns in a table should be displayed in the output.

The AS option allows you to change the column heading label in the output to a value different from the column name. For example:

```
test=> select "CustomerID" as "ID", "LastName" as "Family",
test-> "FirstName" as "Person" from store."Customer";
   ID   | Family | Person
--------+--------+--------
 BLU004 | Blum   | Jessica
 BLU001 | Blum   | Rich
 BLU002 | Blum   | Barbara
 BLU003 | Blum   | Katie
(4 rows)

test=>
```

Instead of the generic column names, the output display now shows the alternative column headings specified in the AS option.

The FROM Clause

```
FROM from_list [,...]
```

Despite its innocent looks, the FROM clause can be the most complex part of the SELECT command, as the *from_list* parameter has several different formats all of its own. Here are the different formats, each one on its own line:

```
[ONLY ] table_name [ * ] [ [ AS ] alias [ (column_alias [,...] ) ] ]
( select ) [ AS ] alias  [ (column_alias [,...] ) ]
function_name ( [argument [,...] ]) [ AS ] alias [ (column_alias [,...] |
    column_definition [,...] ) ]
function_name ( [ argument [,...]) AS (column_definition [,...] )
from_item [ NATURAL ] join_type from_item [ ON join_condition | USING
    (join_column [,...]) ]
```

Just as with the SELECT command, it is easier to break the FROM clause options down one by one to discuss them.

Standard Table Names

```
[ONLY ] table_name [ * ] [ [ AS ] alias [ (column_alias [,...] ) ] ]
```

First, by now you should be familiar with most of the first line of parameters. The *table_name* parameter specifies the tables to find the requested columns in. The ONLY option directs PostgreSQL to search only the table specified, and not any tables that inherit the specified table (child tables, often created for partitioning, discussed in Chapter 1). An asterisk after the table name directs PostgreSQL to search all child tables of the specified table (this is the default behavior in PostgreSQL version 7.1 and later). As seen in

Chapter 6, the AS parameter allows you to define an alias for the table name that can be used anywhere within the SELECT command.

The Sub-select

```
( select ) [ AS ] alias  [ (column_alias [,...] ) ]
```

The second format shows features that allow you to define a sub-query (called a sub-select) to extract data from. The sub-select is evaluated first, then the result set is used in the original select.

The result set from the sub-select acts as a temporary table, which is queried using the original SELECT command. It is required that the sub-select be enclosed in parentheses and assigned an alias name. You can optionally provide aliases to the result set columns for the sub-select:

```
test=> select * from (select "CustomerID", "FirstName" from store."Customer")
test-> as test ("ID", "Name");
   ID   |  Name
--------+--------
 BLU004 | Jessica
 BLU001 | Rich
 BLU002 | Barbara
 BLU003 | Katie
(4 rows)

test=>
```

Functions

The next two formats describe the use for querying the result of a PostgreSQL function:

```
function_name ( [argument [,...] ]) [ AS ] alias [ (column_alias [,...] |
    column_definition [,...] ) ]
function_name ( [ argument [,...]]) AS (column_definition [,...] )
```

The result set of the declared function is used as the input to the first SELECT command. Just as with the sub-select, you must define an alias name for the function result set, and optionally declare column names for multicolumn function output. The SELECT command queries the function output just as if it were a normal database table.

Using PostgreSQL functions is discussed in detail in Chapter 8.

Joins

```
from_item [ NATURAL ] join_type from_item [ ON join_condition | USING
    (join_column [,...]) ]
```

The last format of FROM parameters handles joins. As discussed in Chapter 6, joins allow you to easily match relational data between tables in the database. The NATURAL keyword is used to join tables on common column names. Alternatively, you can use the ON keyword to define a join condition, or the USING keyword to define specific matching column names in both tables.

```
test=> select "Customer"."LastName", "Customer"."FirstName",
test-> "Product"."ProductName", "Order"."TotalCost" from
test-> store."Order" natural inner join store."Customer"
test-> natural inner join store."Product";
LastName | FirstName | ProductName | TotalCost
---------+-----------+-------------+-----------
 Blum    | Rich      | Laptop      | $5,000.00
 Blum    | Barbara   | Laptop      | $1,000.00
 Blum    | Katie     | Desktop     |   $300.00
(3 rows)

test=>
```

This example shows the use of two inner joins to obtain data from tables related to the Order table via defined foreign keys. The Customer and Order tables are joined on the CustomerID column, while the Order and Product tables are joined on the ProductID column. The Customer table matches the LastName and FirstName values related to the CustomerID value stored in the Order table. The Product table matches the Product-Name value related to the ProductID stored in the Order table.

The WHERE Clause

```
WHERE condition [,...]
```

The elements of the WHERE clause were discussed in detail in Chapter 6. The WHERE clause specifies one or more conditions that filter data from the result set. While the concept is simple, in reality the WHERE clause conditions can get somewhat complex, specifying multiple conditions joined using Boolean operators, such as AND, OR, or NOT.

The GROUP BY Clause

```
GROUP BY expression [,...]
```

The GROUP BY clause specifies one or more columns of data to group together in the result set. Unlike the DISTINCT clause, the GROUP BY clause allows you to aggregate values of the grouped records. This is almost always used with a PostgreSQL function that aggregates values from similar records. This example shows how to produce a report showing the total number of products currently ordered by customers:

```
test=> select sum("Order"."Quantity"), "Order"."ProductID" from
test-> store."Order" group by "ProductID";
 sum | ProductID
-----+-----------
  12 | LAP001
   1 | DES001
(2 rows)

test=>
```

The GROUP BY clause must declare which column is used to sort the records. The sum() function adds the values of the Quantity column of each record (This will be discussed further in Chapter 8). Be careful with the GROUP BY and ORDER BY clauses. It is important to remember that the GROUP BY clause groups similar records before the rest of the SELECT command is evaluated, while the ORDER BY clause orders records after the SELECT commands are processed. The sum() function would not work properly using the ORDER BY clause, since the records would not be ordered until after the sum() function executes.

The HAVING Clause

```
HAVING condition [,...]
```

The HAVING clause is similar to the WHERE clause, in that it is used to define a filter condition to limit records used in the GROUP BY clause. Records that do not satisfy the WHERE conditions are not processed by the GROUP BY clause. The HAVING clause filters the records contained in the result set after the GROUP BY clause groups the records.

The Set Operation Clauses

```
select1 [ (UNION | INTERSECT | EXCEPT ]) [ ALL ] select2
```

The Set Operation clauses use mathematical set theory to determine the result set of two separate SELECT commands. The Set Operation clause types are:

▼ UNION   Display all result set records in both *select1* and *select2*

■ INTERSECT   Display only result set records that are in both *select1* and *select2*

▲ EXCEPT   Display only result set records that are in *select1* but not in *select2*

By default, duplicate records in the output set are not displayed. The ALL keyword is used to display all records from the output, including duplicate records.

The set operation is performed on the result sets of the SELECT commands. The result sets must have the same number of columns, and the columns must have the same data types.

The ORDER BY Clause

```
[ ORDER BY expression [ ASC | DESC | USING operator ] [,...] ]
```

As seen in Chapter 6, the ORDER BY clause is used to sort the result set based on one or more column values. One or more *expression* parameters are used to define the column (or columns) used to order the result set records. If two records have the same value for the first expression listed, the next expression is compared, and so on.

By default, the ORDER BY clause orders records in ascending order, either numerically if the expression column is a numeric data type, or using the locale-specific string sorting if the column is a string data type. The USING parameter declares an alternative operator to use for ordering. The less-than operator (<) is equivalent to the ASC keyword, and the greater-than operator (>) is equivalent to the DESC keyword.

The LIMIT Clause

```
[ LIMIT ( count | ALL ) ] [ OFFSET start ]
```

The LIMIT clause specifies a maximum number of records to return in the result set. For queries that may produce a large number of records, this is used to help manage the output. The default behavior is LIMIT ALL, which returns all records in the result set. When you specify a value for *count*, the output only displays *count* records.

The OFFSET parameter allows you to specify the number of result set records to skip before displaying records in the output. Be careful with this parameter. It is easy to get confused with the orientation of the *start* value. The first record in the result set is at *start* value 0 (no records are skipped), not 1. *Start* value 1 is the second record in the result set (one record is skipped). This can cause a problem if you are not careful.

The OFFSET parameter goes hand-in-hand with the LIMIT clause. If you limit the output to ten records, you can rerun the query with *start* equal to 10 (remember, skip the first ten records), so the output starts where the previous output ended.

Using the LIMIT clause on a query may produce inconsistent results, as by default there is no ordering to the records returned in the result set. It is advised that you use the ORDER BY clause whenever you use the LIMIT clause to ensure the output is sorted into a specific order:

```
test=> select * from store."Customer" order by "CustomerID" limit 3 offset 0;
 CustomerID | LastName | FirstName | Address  | City   |State| Zip  | Phone
------------+----------+-----------+----------+--------+-----+------+----------
 BLU001     | Blum     | Rich      | 123 Main |Chicago| IL  |60633|555-1234
 BLU002     | Blum     | Barbara   | 879 Oak  | Gary  | IN  |46100|555-4321
 BLU003     | Blum     | Katie     | 342 Pine |Hammond| IN  |46200|555-9242
(3 rows)

test=> select * from store."Customer" order by "CustomerID" limit 3 offset 3;
 CustomerID | LastName | FirstName |  Address  | City   |State| Zip | Phone
------------+----------+-----------+-----------+--------+-----+-----+----------
 BLU004     | Blum     | Jessica   |925 Dogwood| Gary  | IN  |46100|555-3241
(1 row)

test=>
```

When using the LIMIT and OFFSET parameters, you must be careful that you do not overlap the records in the listing.

The FOR Clause

```
[ FOR (UPDATE | SHARE ) [ OF table_name [,...] [ NOWAIT ] ]
```

By default, the SELECT command does not lock any records during its operation. The FOR clause allows you to change that behavior. It is not uncommon during a transaction (discussed later in this chapter) to perform a SELECT command to obtain the current data values, then immediately perform an INSERT, DELETE, or UPDATE command to alter the values in the database. Between those operations, you may not want the current values to be changed by other database users. This is where the FOR clause comes in.

The FOR UPDATE clause causes the records returned in the result set to be locked in the table. This prevents other users from viewing, deleting, or modifying any record returned in the result set until the transaction that contains the SELECT command finishes.

Using the FOR UPDATE clause causes the SELECT command to wait until any other table locks set by other users are completed. If you specify the NOWAIT parameter, the SELECT command does not wait, but instead exits with an error stating that the records are locked.

The FOR SHARE clause behaves similarly to the FOR UPDATE clause, except it allows other users to view the records while they are locked. However, they will not be able to delete or modify any of the records.

By default, the FOR clause locks all records that are returned in the result set. If you do not want to lock all of the records returned in the result set, you combine the FOR clause with the LIMIT clause to limit the number of records locked in the transaction.

TABLE VIEWS

As described in Chapter 1, table views allow you to combine columns from multiple tables into a "virtual table" for querying. The combination of columns is performed as the result of a query using the SELECT command. This feature allows you to create a result set and use it just as if it were a physical table. This is demonstrated in Figure 7-1.

Views are often used to help simplify complex sub-selects within SELECT commands. Instead of constantly having to type a complex sub-select, you can assign it to a view, then use the view in your SELECT commands.

Views are created using the CREATE VIEW SQL command. The format of this command is

```
CREATE [ OR REPLACE ] [ TEMP | TEMPROARY ] VIEW viewname
     [ (column_name,...] ) ] AS query
```

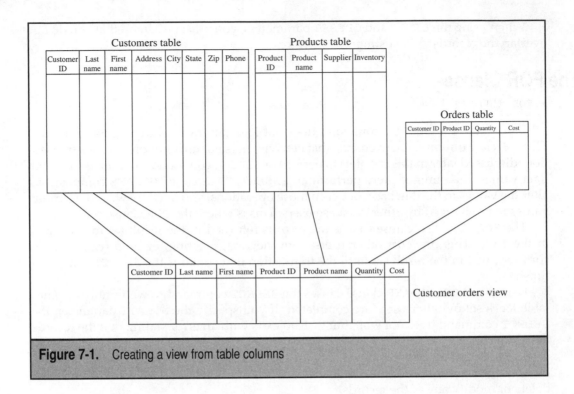

Figure 7-1.   Creating a view from table columns

The `CREATE OR REPLACE VIEW` command allows you to overwrite an existing view. When you do this, the column names and data types for the new view must match the column names and data types of the existing view.

By default, PostgreSQL creates the view in the default schema within the active database. You can save the view in another schema within the database by using the full *schemaname.viewname* format for the *viewname* parameter.

Remember, to create a new view in a schema, the Login Role must have `CREATE` privileges in the schema. The superuser can grant this privilege to trusted users. Once the view is created, the view owner can assign privileges to the view to Group Roles, just like a normal table object.

Alternatively, if you do not need to create a permanent view, you can use the `TEMP` or `TEMPORARY` keyword. This makes the view available only within the current session. Once you quit the session, PostgreSQL automatically drops the view.

By default, PostgreSQL assigns column names to the view columns based on the result set columns names of the specified *query*. You can alter the column names by including the column name list *column_name* in the command.

Here is an example of creating a view based on a complex `SELECT` command:

```
test=# create view store."CustomerOrders" AS
test-# select "Customer"."LastName", "Customer"."FirstName",
```

```
test-# "Product"."ProductName", "Order"."TotalCost" from
test-# store."Order" natural inner join store."Customer"
test-# natural inner join store."Product";
CREATE VIEW
test=# grant select on store."CustomerOrders" to "Salesman";
GRANT
test=#
```

After creating the view (remember, you need the proper privileges to do this) and as-signing privileges to allow Group Roles to use it, other users can query the view just as if it were a table. PostgreSQL only allows you to query views. As of the time of this writing, you are not able to insert, remove, or modify data directly from a view.

To display the views available in a database, use the \dv meta-command (plus the schema name if the view was created in specific schema):

```
test=> \dv store.
               List of relations
  Schema  |       Name        | Type  | Owner
----------+-------------------+-------+----------
  store   | CustomerOrders    | view  | postgres
(1 row)

test=>
```

Once created, users can query the view just as if it were a normal table:

```
test=> select * from store."CustomerOrders";
 LastName  | FirstName | ProductName | TotalCost
-----------+-----------+-------------+------------
  Blum     | Rich      | Laptop      | $5,000.00
  Blum     | Barbara   | Laptop      | $1,000.00
  Blum     | Katie     | Desktop     |   $300.00
(3 rows)

test=>
```

If you no longer need the view, the view owner can remove it using the DROP VIEW command.

TABLE INDEXES

Querying tables is the most computer-intensive part of using a database. For each query, PostgreSQL must compare each record contained in the table with any conditions de-fined in the SELECT command. This can consume both time and processor power, espe-cially when working with large amounts of data.

Customer table

BLU001	Blum	Rich	123 Main St.	Chicago	IL	60633	555-1234
WIL001	Williams	Frank	9582 Oak St.	Granger	IN	46100	555-4342
WIS001	Wisecarver	Emma	4332 Pine Ave.	Valparaiso	IN	46500	555-4352
WIS002	Wisecarver	Ian	4938 Rose Terr.	Hammond	IN	46500	555-4322
SNE001	Snell	Haley	731 Maple Ln.	Fowler	IN	46302	555-9184
WIL002	Williams	Melanie	5439 Evergreen way	Hammond	IN	46500	555-6832
BLU002	Blum	Barbara	219 Dogwood Ave.	Gary	IN	46200	555-6728
WIL003	Williams	Nick	2819 Cherry St.	Granger	IN	46100	555-3298

City column index

Chicago	BLU001
Fowler	SNE001
Gary	BLU002
Granger	WIL001
Granger	WIL003
Hammond	WIS002
Hammond	WIL002
Valparaiso	WIS001

Figure 7-2. Using an index for a column

Why Use Indexes?

The primary goal of database performance tuning is to speed up queries. One method that is often used for this is to create an index for columns in the table. Just like the index in a book, a column index lists just the data elements in that column, and references the record where that value is located. This is shown in Figure 7-2.

Now, instead of having to read the entire Customer table looking for all the customers located in Hammond, PostgreSQL can scan the much smaller City index to look for the desired column value. Each record in the index file only contains the key value and a pointer to the location in the table that contains the key value. When the values are found in the index, PostgreSQL then knows immediately which records to include in the output result set based on the related primary key values.

However, there is a trade-off for this feature. When an index exists on a column, every time a new record is created, PostgreSQL must also update the index file, adding overhead to every `INSERT`, `UPDATE`, and `DELETE` command. For applications that do lots of data manipulation, this overhead may outweigh the performance increase for queries.

Creating an Index

Chapter 6 showed how to create one type of index when using the `CREATE TABLE` command. Part of creating a table is often defining a column to use as the primary key. The primary key is a special index that causes PostgreSQL to automatically create an index for the primary key column. You can see the index created using the `\d` meta-command:

```
test=> \d store."Customer"
            Table "store.Customer"
    Column   |        Type         |  Modifiers
-------------+---------------------+------------
 CustomerID  | character varying   | not null
 LastName    | character varying   |
 FirstName   | character varying   |
 Address     | character varying   |
 City        | character varying   |
 State       | character(2)        |
 Zip         | character(5)        |
 Phone       | character(8)        |
Indexes:
    "CustomerKey" PRIMARY KEY, btree ("CustomerID")

test=>
```

The CustomerKey index was automatically created for the CustomerID column when the primary key was defined.

You can manually create indexes for any column within the table that might be used in a query. To create an additional index, you must use the CREATE INDEX command:

```
CREATE [ UNIQUE ] INDEX name ON table [USING method ]
    ( ( column | ( expression ) ) [ opclass ]  [,...] )
    [ TABLESPACE tablespace ]
    [ WHERE condition ]
```

When creating an index, you have the option of specifying several things. First off, if you specify the UNIQUE keyword, each entry in the index file must be unique, so every record must have unique data for the specified column. While using a UNIQUE index is allowed in PostgreSQL, the preferred method of forcing a column value to be unique is to add a constraint to the column (see "Creating a Table" in Chapter 6).

One or more *columns or expressions* that use columns are specified as the value to create the index on. You can specify as an index value not only a column, but also a function that uses a column. The classic example of this is the lower() string function (described in Chapter 8). This function converts a string to all lowercase letters. By default, the index on a string value is case sensitive. String values in uppercase are considered different from string values in lowercase. In some applications this can be a problem, as you never know when a customer will enter data values such as names in upper- or lowercase. By creating an index using the lower() function, you can eliminate this problem by converting all string data values to lowercase for the index.

Picking which columns to create indexes for is often a science in itself. For each index you define, there is overhead associated with it. Every time a new record is added to the table, PostgreSQL must automatically determine where in the index file to place the indexed column value. The trick is balancing which indexes will improve your query performance without having too much of a negative impact on data entry. For applications that do a lot of data input and little querying, it is often best to not mess with indexes.

An example of creating a simple index follows:

```
test=# create index "Customer_City_Index" on store."Customer" ("City");
CREATE INDEX
test=# \di store.
                    List of relations
 Schema |          Name          | Type  |  Owner   |  Table
--------+------------------------+-------+----------+----------
 store  | CustomerKey            | index | postgres | Customer
 store  | Customer_City_Index    | index | postgres | Customer
 store  | OrderKey               | index | postgres | Order
 store  | ProductKey             | index | postgres | Product
(4 rows)

test=# \d store."Customer_City_Index"
Index "store.Customer_City_Index"
 Column |       Type
--------+------------------
 City   | character varying
btree, for table "store.Customer"

test=#
```

Notice that the naming rules apply to indexes as well. If you use uppercase letters in the index name, remember to use double quotes. Also, notice that by default the index was created in the same schema as the data table it references.

You can also create indexes based on more than one column:

```
test=# create index "Customer_City_State_Index" on store."Customer"
test-# ("City", "State");
CREATE INDEX
test=# \d store."Customer_City_State_Index"
Index "store.Customer_City_State_Index"
 Column |       Type
--------+------------------
 City   | character varying
 State  | character(2)
btree, for table "store.Customer"

test=#
```

PostgreSQL will automatically use the resulting index on queries where the WHERE condition references both the City and State columns.

The TABLESPACE parameter allows you to create the index file on a tablespace different from where the original table is located. By default, the index is placed on the default system tablespace, usually pg_default. On a heavily loaded system, it is common for database administrators to place table indexes on a separate hard drive from the data table. This helps minimize the head movement on a specific hard drive as PostgreSQL searches the index file and the table data.

The WHERE parameter allows you to create a *partial index*, which indexes only a subset of the full table data. Only the data that meets the WHERE condition is placed in the index. As mentioned, creating an index does have a performance cost. If there is a particular subset of data that is queried more so than other data, you can create the index using only this data.

```
test=# create index "Customer_State_IN_Index" on store."Customer"
test-# ("City", "State") where "State" = 'IN';
CREATE INDEX
test=# \d store."Customer_State_IN_Index"
Index "store.Customer_State_IN_Index"
 Column |        Type
--------+--------------------
 City   | character varying
 State  | character(2)
btree, for table "store.Customer", predicate ("State" = 'IN'::bpchar)

test=#
```

If you determine that the created index is detrimental to your database performance, you can remove the index by using the DROP INDEX command. If lots of data is added to the table, you may consider using the REINDEX command. The REINDEX command is used to, obviously, reindex the index files associated with the table. In very active tables, often the index can get somewhat out of wack, and reindexing can help speed up performance of the index. The REINDEX command is part of the table maintenance tools provided by pgAdmin III.

Determining the Index Method

I saved the most complex indexing parameter for last. The USING keyword allows you to specify the indexing algorithm used to sort the index values. The sorting algorithm determines how column values are placed in the index for access. Different sorting algorithms are used in different situations in order to speed up the search. Knowing which indexing method to use can often help improve the performance of your application. The following are the indexing methods currently available in PostgreSQL:

▼ btree

■ rtree

■ hash

▲ gist

The btree option is the default value used by PostgreSQL. It uses the balanced-tree (B-Tree) sorting algorithm to create links between index values. The B-Tree sorts the data based on the index value, then references index values with links. Each index value links to values both less than and greater than the value.

The B-Tree index contains a root value, which is usually in the middle of the data range. The B-Tree index compares the desired result value to the root value and determines if it is less than, greater than, or equal to the root value. Obviously, if the desired value is equal to the root value, the search is complete. If the value is less than the root value, a link to the midpoint of the lower range is given. In a similar manner, if the desired value is greater than the root value a link to the midpoint of the higher range is given. Each of the resulting sides is then split in half, and so on until the desired value is found in the index. This is demonstrated in Figure 7-3.

The B-Tree links allow PostgreSQL to quickly scan through the index looking for the appropriate values. The City index starts with the middle value, Gary. If the city that is being searched is greater than Gary, the right-side link is followed to Hammond. If the desired value is less than Hammond (but greater than Gary), the left-side link is followed to Granger. Thus, instead of having to read every record in the table, PostgreSQL was able to find the proper record in just a couple of reads in the City index file.

The B-Tree index method is useful for indexing numerical and string values. If you are querying a table for values equal to, less than, or greater than a value, the B-Tree index can quickly produce results, as this is the core basis of the underlying data sort in the index. If you are in doubt about what indexing method to use, it is safe to use the default B-Tree method.

The rtree option uses an *R-Tree (real tree) index,* and is often used for data ranges (such as television programs that span a timeframe) or multidimensional data (such as spatial data or combinations of data). It uses a recursion tree-indexing method. The layout of the R-Tree index is similar to the B-Tree, but the benefit of the R-Tree is that it can group data elements together within the individual nodes. An example of an R-Tree index is shown in Figure 7-4.

The spatial points are first grouped into two groups, R1 and R2. The points are then further grouped into smaller groups, R3, R4, R5, and R6. The R-Tree index is organized by the individual groups, and shows which spatial groups are subsets of other spatial groups.

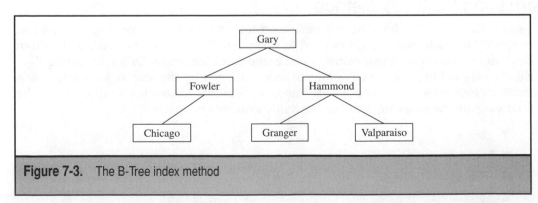

Figure 7-3. The B-Tree index method

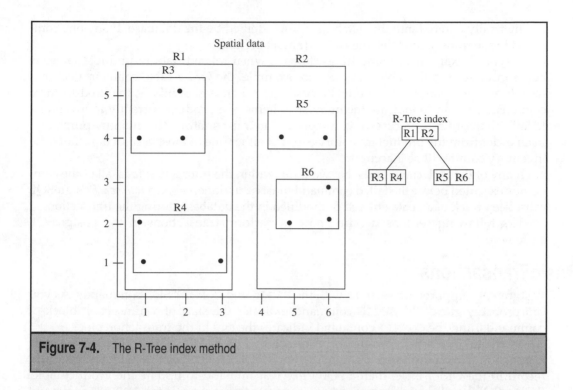

Figure 7-4. The R-Tree index method

If you are specifically working with multidimensional point values, use the R-Tree index method. Otherwise, it is not any benefit over the standard B-Tree method.

The hash option uses a *hash index,* and is the oldest and least-used indexing algorithm available in PostgreSQL. It uses simplified hashing techniques to sort data elements. The hash index is only useful for comparing value equalities, and is less useful than the standard B-Tree method. PostgreSQL recommends using the default B-Tree method instead of the hash index method. The hash index method is mainly available for compatibility purposes with older systems.

The gist option uses a *Generalized Search Tree (GiST) index.* This is a relatively new indexing method that utilizes several different indexing techniques in a conglomeration of algorithms. This method is supported by PostgreSQL starting in version 7.3.

The GiST index method allows administrators to define indexes for many different types of data, indexing on many different user-defined features. Some examples of advanced GiST indexes are indexing three-dimensional objects and full-text indexing of complete text articles.

TRANSACTIONS

As described in Chapter 1, PostgreSQL supports the database concept of *transactions.* Transactions allow you to bundle multiple SQL commands together into one event that is either fully entered into the database or fully denied by the database. If any one command in the transaction fails, the entire transaction fails.

A typical example of using transactions is when related data in multiple tables is being inserted into the tables. In the store example, the Order table contains a column to indicate the quantity of a product a customer purchases. Similarly, the Product table contains a column to indicate the number of items of a product currently in inventory. Ideally, if an order is processed, your application must subtract the quantity purchased in an order from the product inventory count. If either one of these transactions fails, the inventory count will be inaccurate.

If any of the SQL commands that were run within the transaction fails, all of the commands executed before the failed command must be undone, called a *rollback*. PostgreSQL must keep track of all data entered or modified in the database during the transaction.

The following sections describe how to perform transactions in the PostgreSQL system.

Basic Transactions

PostgreSQL supports transactions with the BEGIN and COMMIT SQL commands. As you can probably guess, the BEGIN command indicates the start of a transaction block of commands, and the COMMIT command indicates the end of the transaction block.

By default, each SQL command processed by PostgreSQL is handled as a separate transaction. If you are using psql and enter a SQL INSERT command to enter a new record in the Order table, then a SQL UPDATE command to update the Product table, PostgreSQL handles each command as a separate transaction. If the INSERT command fails because the data entry clerk forgot to enter the OrderID column data, but the UPDATE command succeeds on the Product table, you will have a problem.

To force PostgreSQL to handle the two commands as a single transaction, use the BEGIN and COMMIT commands. Here is an example of a failed transaction:

```
test=> begin;
BEGIN
test=> insert into store."Order" values ('BLU001', 'LAP001', 2, '1000.00',
test(> 'ORD004');
INSERT 0 1
test=> update store."Product" set "Inventory" = 9 where "ProductID" = 'LAP001';
ERROR:  permission denied for relation Product
test=> commit;
ROLLBACK
test=> select * from store."Order";
 CustomerID | ProductID | Quantity | TotalCost  | OrderID
------------+-----------+----------+------------+---------
 BLU001     | LAP001    |       10 | $5,000.00  | ORD001
 BLU002     | LAP001    |        2 | $1,000.00  | ORD002
 BLU003     | DES001    |        1 |   $300.00  | ORD003
(3 rows)

test=>
```

The INSERT command to add the new record to the Order table was processed within in the transaction, but the UPDATE command to change the inventory total failed, as the user did not have permission to update the Product table. When the COMMIT statement was processed to commit the transaction, it produced the ROLLBACK message, which indicates the transaction was rolled back and not processed. Looking at the Order table, you can see that the record that was inserted during the transaction was removed (rolled back) from the table.

Advanced Transactions

Besides the auto-rollback feature, PostgreSQL also allows you to perform a manual rollback at any point within the transaction using the ROLLBACK command:

```
test=> begin;
BEGIN
test=> insert into store."Order" values ('BLU001', 'LAP001', 2,
test(> '1000.00', 'ORD004');
INSERT 0 1
test=> select * from store."Order" where "OrderID" = 'ORD004';
 CustomerID | ProductID | Quantity | TotalCost | OrderID
------------+-----------+----------+-----------+----------
 BLU001     | LAP001    |        2 | $1,000.00 | ORD004
(1 row)

test=> rollback;
ROLLBACK
test=> select * from store."Order" where "OrderID" = 'ORD004';
 CustomerID | ProductID | Quantity | TotalCost | OrderID
------------+-----------+----------+-----------+----------
(0 rows)

test=> commit;
WARNING:  there is no transaction in progress
COMMIT
test=>
```

When the INSERT command is processed, the record is added to the table, but only within the confines of the transaction. PostgreSQL hides the changes from other users using the Multi-version Concurrency Control (MVCC) feature, discussed in Chapter 1. If another user should query the table at this point in time, the record would not be visible to them. After inserting the new record, the ROLLBACK command is executed. This removes any previously executed commands since the start of the transaction. The newly added record is removed from the table, and the transaction is aborted.

In this example, once the ROLLBACK command is executed, the entire transaction is aborted. Sometimes in extremely long and complex transactions, you may need to perform sub-transactions—that is, little mini transactions within the larger transaction. In a normal transaction, if any of the commands within the transaction fail, the entire transaction is doomed for failure. To demonstrate this, look at this example:

```
test=> begin;
BEGIN
test=> update store."Product" set "Inventory" = 9
test-> where "ProductID" = 'LAP001';
ERROR:  permission denied for relation Product
test=> insert into store."Order" values ('BLU001', 'LAP001', 2, '1000.00',
test(> 'ORD004');
ERROR:  current transaction is aborted, commands ignored until end of
transaction block
test=> commit;
ROLLBACK
test=>
```

In this example, the failed command was the first command in the transaction. When the second command was processed, even though it should have succeeded, PostgreSQL indicated that it was ignored, as the transaction as a whole was already on its way to being rolled back. No other commands will be processed by PostgreSQL until the COMMIT command is entered, completing the rollback of the transaction.

In some cases, though, you may want the parts of a transaction that succeed to be committed, even if commands farther down in the transaction fail. PostgreSQL allows you to create mini transactions within the larger transaction. If any of these mini transactions fails, PostgreSQL can still process the previous commands within the larger transaction.

The SAVEPOINT command allows you to set places within the transaction block where PostgreSQL can roll back to instead of aborting the entire transaction. This allows you to save steps along the transaction process, and roll back to those steps if a future command fails, thus salvaging the work that was completed.

You can set multiple savepoints within the transaction. You must assign each savepoint a name, and then use that name in the ROLLBACK command. Here is an example of using a SAVEPOINT command to salvage a failed transaction:

```
test=> begin;
BEGIN
test=> insert into store."Order" values ('BLU001', 'LAP001', 2,
test(> '1000.00', 'ORD004');
INSERT 0 1
test=> SAVEPOINT first_point;
SAVEPOINT
test=> update store."Product" set "Inventory" = 9
test-> where "ProductID" = 'LAP001';
ERROR:  permission denied for relation Product
```

```
test=> rollback to first_point;
ROLLBACK
test=> commit;
COMMIT
test=> select * from store."Order" where "OrderID" = 'ORD004';
 CustomerID | ProductID | Quantity | TotalCost | OrderID
------------+-----------+----------+-----------+---------
 BLU001     | LAP001    |        2 | $1,000.00 | ORD004
(1 row)

test=>
```

In this example, a savepoint named `first_point` was declared after the `INSERT` command. When the `UPDATE` command failed, the `ROLLBACK` command was entered, using the specific savepoint name. The transaction was rolled back to that point, and the `COMMIT` command was entered. The transaction was processed just as if the command after the `SAVEPOINT` was never entered.

CURSORS

Earlier, the "Revisiting the SELECT Command" section of this chapter showed how to use the `LIMIT` and `OFFSET` parameters to walk your way through large result sets. However, even these features can get cumbersome when working with large result sets. Fortunately for us, there is an easier solution available.

SQL cursors are used as pointers within a result set returned from a `SELECT` command. The cursor points to a specific row of data within the result set. There is a subset of SQL commands available that allows you to work with the cursor, return data from a result set based on where the cursor is located, and move the cursor around within the result set.

A cursor is a temporary object and, by default, only exists within a transaction, although you can specify that the cursor stay active within an entire session. When the transaction is terminated (either from a rollback or a commit) or the user terminates the session, PostgreSQL automatically deletes the cursor object. You can also manually close a cursor object within a transaction if you need to.

The following sections show how to create and use a cursor in your transactions.

Creating a Cursor

The `DECLARE` SQL command is used to create a new cursor. The format of the `DECLARE` command in PostgreSQL is

```
DECLARE cursorname [BINARY] [ [NO] SCROLL]
        CURSOR [ (WITH | WITHOUT) HOLD ] FOR query
```

As you can tell from the command format, there are a few options available when you create the cursor:

▼ BINARY   Allows you to use the result set as binary data instead of the default text data.

■ SCROLL   Allows you to move backward within the result set (specifying NO SCROLL may increase performance if you do not need this feature).

▲ WITH HOLD   Allows the cursor to stay active for the entire session (the default is WITHOUT HOLD, which deletes the cursor at the end of the transaction).

The *query* parameter defines the SELECT command used to produce the result set. Any valid SELECT command (including sub-selects) can be used to produce the result set for the cursor.

If you create a cursor without the hold property (which is the default), you must start a transaction using the BEGIN command before you can create the cursor:

```
test=> begin;
BEGIN
test=> declare all_customers cursor for select * from store."Customer";
DECLARE CURSOR
test=>
```

Notice that the result set for the SELECT command is not displayed automatically. The cursor all_customers contains the data from the result set. The next step is to use the cursor to view the data.

Using a Cursor

When the cursor is created, it points to the first record in the result set. You can now display records from the result set based on the location of the cursor. As records are displayed, the cursor moves on to the next record. There are a few commands that can be used for handling active cursors:

▼ FETCH   Retrieves (displays) records from the result set and sets the cursor to the next record in the result set

■ MOVE   Moves the cursor to another record without displaying records

▲ CLOSE   Removes the cursor before the end of the transaction

The FETCH command is the workhorse for cursors. This is the command you use to maneuver around the result set and view the data. The basic format for the FETCH command is

```
FETCH direction [ FROM | IN ] cursor
```

Direction	Description
NEXT	Fetch the next record in the result set (the default if no direction is specified)
PRIOR	Fetch the previous record in the result set
FIRST	Fetch the first record of the result set
LAST	Fetch the last record of the result set
ABSOLUTE *count*	Fetch the *count*'th record in the result set
RELATIVE *count*	Fetch the *count*'th record from the current location in the result set
Count	Fetch the next *count* records in the result set
ALL	Fetch all remaining records in the result set
FORWARD	Fetch the next record in the result set (same as NEXT)
FORWARD *count*	Fetch the next *count* records in the result set
FORWARD ALL	Fetch all of the remaining records in the result set
BACKWARD	Fetch the previous record in the result set (same as PRIOR)
BACKWARD *count*	Fetch the previous *count* records in the result set
BACKWARD ALL	Fetch all of the previous records in the result set

Table 7-1. FETCH Direction Options

Obviously *cursor* is the cursor name used in the DECLARE command to open the cursor. The *direction* parameter specifies the direction within the result set to get the next record from. Remember, if the cursor was created using the NO SCROLL option, you can only move forward in the result set. Table 7-1 shows the various direction values you can use.

The MOVE command uses the exact same format and parameters as the FETCH command, but only moves the cursor to the new location without displaying any of the result set records.

To test out the cursor functions, you should insert some records into one of your test tables and play around with the various direction parameters. Here are a few examples of using the FETCH and MOVE commands in a result set:

```
test=> begin;
BEGIN
test=> declare all_customers cursor for select "CustomerID",
```

```
test-> "LastName","FirstName" from store."Customer"
test-> order by "CustomerID";
DECLARE CURSOR
test=> fetch all from all_customers;
 CustomerID |  LastName   | FirstName
------------+-------------+-----------
 BLU001     | Blum        | Rich
 BLU002     | Blum        | Barbara
 WIL001     | Williams    | Frank
 WIL002     | Williams    | Melanie
 WIL003     | Williams    | Nick
 WIS001     | Wisecarver  | Emma
 WIS002     | Wisecarver  | Ian
 WIS003     | Wisecarver  | Bryce
(8 rows)
```

When the DECLARE command is executed, the cursor points to the first record in the result set. The FETCH command displays all of the records in the result set, leaving the cursor at the end of the result set. If you try to fetch the next record, no error will be produced, but you will not get any records returned:

```
test=> fetch next from all_customers;
 CustomerID | LastName | FirstName
------------+----------+-----------
(0 rows)
```

To retrieve the first record in the result set, you can use the FIRST direction:

```
test=> fetch first from all_customers;
 CustomerID | LastName | FirstName
------------+----------+-----------
 BLU001     | Blum     | Rich
(1 row)
```

Now the cursor points to the first record in the result set. When you use another FETCH command, you will retrieve records relative to the first record, where the cursor points to:

```
test=> fetch 3 from all_customers;
 CustomerID | LastName | FirstName
------------+----------+-----------
 BLU002     | Blum     | Barbara
 WIL001     | Williams | Frank
 WIL002     | Williams | Melanie
(3 rows)
```

The three records after the first record are displayed, and the cursor is set to the last record that is displayed.

So far so good, but look at what happens when you display the previous two records:

```
test=> fetch backward 2 from all_customers;
 CustomerID | LastName | FirstName
------------+----------+-----------
 WIL001     | Williams | Frank
 BLU002     | Blum     | Barbara
(2 rows)
```

The previous two records were displayed, but in reverse order from how they were in the result set. This is an important thing to realize when moving backward in the result set. The records are displayed in the order based on the direction the cursor is moving. When the cursor is moving backward, the records are displayed in reverse order. When the cursor is moving forward, the records are displayed in normal order.

Another common mistake happens when using the MOVE command. The MOVE command moves the cursor to a particular record within the result set without displaying any records. Often you will see a beginner try to move the cursor to the first record of the result set, then attempt to use a FETCH command to display the record:

```
test=> move first in all_customers;
MOVE 1
test=> fetch next from all_customers;
 CustomerID | LastName | FirstName
------------+----------+-----------
 BLU002     | Blum     | Barbara
(1 row)

test=>
```

Notice that the FETCH command retrieved the second record in the result set, not the first. Most likely this is not the result that was intended. The MOVE FIRST command moves the pointer to the first record in the result set, but the FETCH NEXT command retrieves the next record, which is actually the second record in the result set.

If you need to retrieve the record that the cursor currently points to, you can use the FETCH 0 command:

```
test=> move first in all_customers;
MOVE 1
test=> fetch 0 from all_customers;
 CustomerID | LastName | FirstName
------------+----------+-----------
 BLU001     | Blum     | Rich
(1 row)

test=>
```

Now the FETCH command displays the first record in the result set.

When the transaction is ended (using the COMMIT command), the all_customers cursor goes away. You can also close the cursor before the transaction ends by using the CLOSE command.

Be careful when using cursors in transactions where you insert, delete, or modify data. Remember, the cursor only returns the records (and their values) at the time of the query in the DECLARE command (sort of a snapshot of the table). Any modifications to the data after that time, even if the cursor is still open, do not appear in the cursor results. This can cause huge problems if you do not remember this rule.

The best way to get comfortable with cursors is to play around with them. It is usually not until you make a few mistakes that you will get a true understanding of how cursors work within the result set.

SUMMARY

This chapter continued the journey through SQL commands. First, a recap of the SELECT command was presented, along with the full command format and descriptions. There are lots of features involved in the SELECT command for producing queries. Next, using views was discussed. Views allow you to create temporary tables combining columns from multiple tables. This can help simplify complex queries, and also give your customers a single place to look for data, rather than having to hunt through several tables in the database.

After views, helping speed up queries using table indexes was shown. Just as a book index helps you to find topics in a book, table indexes help PostgreSQL to find data in tables quicker and easier. Indexes on columns that are often used for queries can often speed up the query process. However, overusing indexes can be a detriment to database performance. As each new record is inserted into a table, all of the associated table indexes must be updated as well.

Transactions can be used to help keep the data in tables consistent. A transaction groups a set of SQL commands into a single block that is either processed or rejected by PostgreSQL. If a single command within the block fails, PostgreSQL undoes, or rolls back, the results of all the previous commands in the transaction. Savepoints can be set within long transactions to provide places for PostgreSQL to roll back to within the transaction. This allows some commands within the transaction to succeed, even if future commands fail.

Finally, cursors were discussed. Cursors allow you to walk through the result set from a SELECT command. They allow you to move both forward and backward through the result set to examine the records contained in the result set.

The next chapter continues showing how to use SQL in PostgreSQL. PostgreSQL provides many built-in functions that can be used in your SQL commands. Chapter 8 discusses these functions, and shows how to use them to simplify your applications.

CHAPTER 8

PostgreSQL Functions

W hen handling data in a table, applications are often required to perform functions with the data, such as obtaining the square root of a value, totaling the values in a column, or converting a text value to all upper- or lowercase letters. Instead of having to write code in your application to do these types of functions, PostgreSQL provides many commonly used functions for you. All you need to do is include the PostgreSQL functions directly in your SQL commands. This chapter walks through the built-in PostgreSQL data functions and shows how to use them in your applications.

WHAT IS A FUNCTION?

Functions are used by the database engine to manipulate data contained in the tables. The database engine provides functions to help database programmers minimize the amount of code required in an application program to manipulate data contained in tables. Instead of having to write code for basic calculations, such as adding numbers to a column data value, summing column data values, determining averages, or converting strings to integers, the programmer can utilize functions already provided by the database engine.

While the ANSI SQL standards include some generic functions that should be implemented, they do not specify the exact format of the functions. Thus, any functions available within a particular database engine are designed purely by the database engine developers. There is no guarantee that a function present in one database engine is portable to other database engines. That said, many functions available within current database engines are somewhat consistent between vendors.

The PostgreSQL developers have included many functions within the PostgreSQL database engine to assist you with your database programming needs. The following sections describe the basics of functions in the PostgreSQL database engine.

Operators

Operators are the most basic form of data functions. They include the standard mathematical operators you are familiar with (such as addition, subtraction, multiplication, division, and Boolean operators), along with some you might not be familiar with (such as cubed roots and factorials). The \do meta-command in psql displays all of the operators available in the PostgreSQL database engine. You can also specify a single operator with the \do meta-command to see the format for just that operator:

```
test=> \do &
                        List of operators
   Schema   | Name | Left arg type | Right arg type | Result type | Description
------------+------+---------------+----------------+-------------+-------------
 pg_catalog | &    | bigint        | bigint         | bigint      | binary and
 pg_catalog | &    | bit           | bit            | bit         | bitwise and
```

```
pg_catalog | &       | integer     | integer     | integer    | binary and
pg_catalog | &       | smallint    | smallint    | smallint   | binary and
(4 rows)

test=>
```

Notice that there are several entries for the Boolean AND operator, based on the input value data type. It is crucial that you use the proper data types when using operators. Each operator specifies a set of data types that can be used for the input, and the data type of the resulting output. You must follow these rules. You cannot mix and match data types, such as add a character string to an integer data type.

There are three basic groups of data type operators:

▼ Numeric values

■ String values

▲ NULL values

The following sections describe how to use operators within each of these data types.

Using Numerical Operators

Numerical operators are used on any numeric data type, such as integer, floating-point, and even money data types. They can be used anywhere within the SQL command where an expression is allowed. You can even use mathematical operators in the expression within the SELECT list:

```
test=> select 2 + 2 as result;
 result
--------
      4
(1 row)

test=> select (10 * 35) - (14 * 20) as output1,
test-> (14 * 20) - (10 * 35) as output2;
 output1 | output2
---------+---------
      70 |     -70
(1 row)

test=>
```

One thing you should notice in these simple examples is that if you are not using data from a table, you do not need a FROM clause when working with operators and functions. The result of the function appears within the result set, just as with a SELECT statement that queries tables.

While these are cute examples, in real life they are not too practical. A common use for operators is within the UPDATE command to update values in the table. For example, if you need to increase the price of all the products in the store by 3 percent, you would do the following:

```
test=> update store."Product" set "UnitPrice" = "UnitPrice" * 1.03;
UPDATE 2
test=> select * from store."Product";
 ProductID | ProductName |   Model    | Manufacturer | UnitPrice | Inventory
-----------+-------------+------------+--------------+-----------+----------

 DES001    | Desktop     | Standard   | Acme         |  $309.00  |        25
 LAP001    | Laptop      | Takealong  | Acme         |  $515.00  |        10
(2 rows)

test=>
```

Since no WHERE clause was specified, the expression within the UPDATE command changed the UnitPrice data values in all records in the table. Notice that you can use column names within the expressions as well as constant values. This provides for a wealth of possibilities for manipulating data within the tables using SQL commands, without having to write any separate code in your application!

Besides the standard numerical operators, PostgreSQL also provides a few operators that you might not be familiar with. A complete list of numerical operators supported in PostgreSQL is shown in Table 8-1.

Using String Operators

Unfortunately, PostgreSQL does not allow you to use the standard numerical operators on strings, such as adding or subtracting strings. However, there are two types of operators that PostgreSQL does provide for your use:

▼   String concatenation operator

▲   String comparison operators

The concatenation operator (||) allows you to splice multiple string values together into a single string value:

```
test=> select "LastName" || ', ' || "FirstName" as "Customer"
test-> from store."Customer";
   Customer
------------------

 Blum, Jessica
 Blum, Rich
 Blum, Barbara
 Blum, Katie
(4 rows)

test=>
```

Numerical Operator	Description
+	Addition
−	Subtraction
*	Multiplication
/	Division
%	Modulo (remainder of the division)
^	Exponent (one value to the power of another)
| /	Square root
| | /	Cube root
!	Factorial
!!	Factorial, when used as a prefix
@	Absolute value
&	Boolean AND
|	Boolean OR
#	Boolean XOR
-	Boolean NOT
<<	Bitwise shift left
>>	Bitwise shift right

Table 8-1.   PostgreSQL Numerical Operators

The concatenation operator merged the two column string values along with a constant string value to produce the desired output in the result set. Again, it is important to notice that the constant string value uses a single quote, and the column names use a double quote. The concatenation operator is an extremely useful tool to have available when creating reports from a query.

The most popular type of string operators available in PostgreSQL are *comparison operators*. Comparison operators are used to (obviously) compare string values. This allows you to do such things as query a table looking for a specific name or address.

There are three categories of string comparison operators available in PostgreSQL:

▼ Unix-style regular expression operators

■ The ANSI SQL LIKE operator

▲ The ANSI SQL SIMILAR TO operator

Each type uses a slightly different method for comparing strings, as discussed in the following sections.

Unix-style Regular Expressions   The Unix-style regular expression comparison operators provided by PostgreSQL are listed and described in Table 8-2.

The first seven comparison operators compare two string values. The alphabetical comparison used for strings depends on the locale setting set in the `postgresql.conf` configuration file (configured during the installation, as described in Chapter 2).

Each of the comparison operators can be used anywhere within the expression of a SQL command:

```
test=> select * from store."Order" where "OrderID" > 'ORD002';
 CustomerID | ProductID | Quantity | TotalCost | OrderID
------------+-----------+----------+-----------+---------
 BLU003     | DES001    |        1 |   $300.00 | ORD003
 BLU001     | LAP001    |        2 | $1,000.00 | ORD004
(2 rows)

test=>
```

String Operator	Description
=	Check if two string values are exactly identical
!=	Check if two string values are not exactly identical
<>	Check if two string values are not exactly identical
>	Check if one string value is alphabetically greater than another
<	Check if one string value is alphabetically less than another
>=	Check if one string value is alphabetically equal to or greater than another
<=	Check if one string value is alphabetically equal to or less than another
~	String matches regular expression
~*	String matches regular expression without regard to case
!~	String does not match a regular expression
!~*	String does not match a regular expression without regard to case

Table 8-2.   PostgreSQL String Comparison Operators

The greater-than string comparison operator worked as expected on the OrderID column string data. It examined the string values and compared the entire string and filtered only the strings that were alphabetically greater than the ORD002 constant value (numbers in strings are still considered characters, and are compared using their encoding value such as ASCII or UTF8).

The last four string comparison operators shown in Table 8-2 compare a single string value against a Unix-style *regular expression*. Regular expressions are coded sequences of characters and symbols that allow you to specify ranges of character values to compare a string against. The expression is matched against the entire data string value, and is true if the expression is found within the string value as specified by the regular expression.

Regular expressions use special symbols to indicate where in the string to locate characters. Table 8-3 lists and describes the regular expression special symbols available.

Regular expressions can become quite complex (entire books have been written on how to use them). The best way to get a feel for using regular expressions is to see them in action. Here is a simple example of a regular expression:

```
test=> select "LastName", "FirstName" from store."Customer"
test-> where "FirstName" ~ '[RB]';
 LastName | FirstName
----------+-----------
 Blum     | Rich
 Blum     | Barbara
(2 rows)

test=>
```

Regular Expression Symbol	Description
[*abc*]	Match any one of the characters listed between the brackets anywhere in the string
[*a-b*]	Match any of the characters alphabetically between *a* and *b* anywhere in the string
^*a*	Match the character *a* at the beginning of the string
a$	Match the character *a* at the end of the string
a?	Match zero or one instance of the character *a* anywhere within the string
*a**	Match zero or more instances of the character *a*
a+	Match one or more instances of the character *a*
a | *b*	Match either expression *a* or expression *b*

Table 8-3. PostgreSQL Unix-style Regular Expression Symbols

The regular expression used in the WHERE clause compares the FirstName column value to the regular expression [RB]. This expression matches any string that contains either an *R* or a *B* anywhere within the string.

Here is another example of using a regular expression on a string:

```
test=> select "LastName", "FirstName" from store."Customer"
test-> where "FirstName" ~ '[A-K]';
 LastName | FirstName
----------+-----------
 Blum     | Jessica
 Blum     | Barbara
 Blum     | Katie
(3 rows)

test=>
```

This regular expression checks for strings that contain any letter between capital *A* and capital *K*.

The ANSI SQL LIKE Operator   The LIKE operator is an ANSI SQL standard operator that compares string values using a limited version of a regular expression. The LIKE regular expression allows character matching, but uses only two special symbols within the expression:

▼   The underscore (_), to represent a single character

▲   The percent symbol (%), to represent zero or more characters

Thus the expression 'c%' matches any string that begins with the letter *c*, the expression 'c_t' matches three-character strings that start with the character *c* and end with the letter *t* (such as cat, cot, or cut), and the expression '%tion' matches any string that ends with the characters *tion*.

Here is an example of using the LIKE operator:

```
test=> select "LastName", "FirstName" from store."Customer"
test-> where "FirstName" LIKE '_a%';
 LastName | FirstName
----------+-----------
 Blum     | Barbara
 Blum     | Katie
(2 rows)

test=>
```

The LIKE parameter uses the expression '_a%' to filter out records where the FirstName value has a lowercase *a* in the second character position (anything can be in the first position), followed be zero or more characters.

You can use the NOT LIKE operator to filter strings that do not match the indicated string pattern. PostgreSQL also supports the ILIKE operator to compare strings without case sensitivity.

The ANSI SQL SIMILAR TO Operator   The SIMILAR TO operator is a relatively new addition to the ANSI SQL standard. It uses the underscore and percent symbols used in the LIKE operator, along with a few symbols found in the Unix-style regular expressions discussed earlier. The operators allowed in the SIMILAR TO operator are listed and described in Table 8-4.

As an example, if you want to display the records where the FirstName column value starts with either a *J* or a *K*, you would use the following expression:

```
test=> select "LastName", "FirstName" from store."Customer"
test-> where "FirstName" similar to '(J|K)%';
 LastName | FirstName
----------+-----------
 Blum     | Jessica
 Blum     | Katie
(2 rows)

test=>
```

The parentheses in the regular expression group the expression to represent one character. The percent sign at the end of the regular expression matches zero or more characters in the string.

Using NULL Operators

The NULL value is a special data type that indicates a record column contains an unknown data value. Often this means that there is no data value in the column, but that is not always the case. The NULL data type must be handled differently than other data types.

Operator	Description
_	Match any one character at that position
%	Match zero or more characters
*	Match repetitions of the previous character zero or more times
+	Match repetitions of the previous character one or more times
[abc]	Match one or more characters listed between the brackets
( )	Group items into a single logical item

Table 8-4.   The SIMILAR TO Regular Expression Symbols

Testing if a column data value is NULL can be tricky. You cannot use standard mathematical operators to check if a value is NULL, as you cannot compare two unknown values. Another thing to remember is that the NULL value is not the same thing as either an empty string or the numeric value of zero. This confuses and traps many a novice database programmer.

To add insult to injury, there is some controversy between the various database engine vendors as to exactly how to handle NULL values (see Chapter 12). This can often make porting a database application from one vendor's database engine to another's extremely complicated.

The ANSI SQL standard provides the IS NULL and IS NOT NULL operators to help you determine when a column value is NULL. PostgreSQL fully supports the IS NULL operator. The IS NULL operator is the only way to determine if a column value is empty.

Here is an example of using the IS NULL operator to check a column value. First, you must create a record that contains a NULL value for a column value. This can be done by inserting a new record and not assigning a value to one or more data columns (remember, some of the columns were created so that they cannot be NULL):

```
test=> insert into store."Customer" ("CustomerID", "LastName", "Phone")
test-> values ('MUL001', 'Mullen', '555-4829');
INSERT 0 1
test=>
```

Now you can perform a query on the table, looking for records that contain a NULL value for one of the missing data columns:

```
test=> select * from store."Customer" where "FirstName" IS NULL;
 CustomerID | LastName | FirstName | Address | City | State | Zip |  Phone
------------+----------+-----------+---------+------+-------+-----+----------
 MUL001     | Mullen   |           |         |      |       |     | 555-4829
(1 row)

test=>
```

The preceding SQL command queries the table, looking for records that do not have a value in the FirstName column. Sure enough, the new record appears in the result set.

To see how easy it is to confuse NULL values with empty strings, we can create a record containing an empty string value, then try to use the IS NULL operator to find it:

```
test=> update store."Customer" set "FirstName" = ''
test-> where "CustomerID" = 'MUL001';
UPDATE 1
test=> select * from store."Customer" where "FirstName" IS NULL;
 CustomerID | LastName | FirstName | Address | City | State | Zip | Phone
------------+----------+-----------+---------+------+-------+-----+-------
(0 rows)

test=>
```

Since the FirstName column has a value now, even though it is an empty string, the IS NULL operator does not filter the record out. You can also set a column value to NULL by using the NULL keyword:

```
test=> update store."Customer" set "FirstName" = NULL
test-> where "CustomerID" = 'MUL001';
UPDATE 1
test=> select * from store."Customer" where "FirstName" IS NULL;
 CustomerID | LastName |FirstName| Address | City | State | Zip |  Phone
------------+----------+---------+---------+------+-------+-----+----------
 MUL001     | Mullen   |         |         |      |       |     | 555-4829
(1 row)

test=>
```

Setting the FirstName column value to NULL has the same effect as creating the new record with a column value.

Built-in Functions

Besides all of the standard operators, the PostgreSQL developers also included many useful functions for use with various data types. As with operators, functions can be used in any expression value within the SQL command.

To get an idea of the number of functions available in PostgreSQL, try the following \df meta-command from psql. The output goes on for quite a long time. Just as with the operators listing, you can specify a specific function to view information on only that function. Also just as with operators, notice that within the functions available, there are often several versions of the same function, depending on the input data types.

```
test=> \df area
                     List of functions
   Schema   | Name | Result data type | Argument data types
------------+------+------------------+---------------------
 pg_catalog | area | double precision | box
 pg_catalog | area | double precision | circle
 pg_catalog | area | double precision | path
(3 rows)

test=>
```

The area() function has three different versions, depending on the data type of the input data. Even though the three formats use different input data types, they all use the same data type for the result.

Just as with operators, it is imperative that you use the correct input data types with the correct functions. There is not much sense in trying to calculate the square root of a string. The PostgreSQL functions can be divided into groups based on the data types they handle:

▼ String functions

■ Date and time functions

■ Math functions

■ Data conversion functions

▲ Aggregate functions

The following sections describe each of these groups of functions and show a few basic examples of how to use the different types of functions.

STRING FUNCTIONS

Along with the standard string comparison operators discussed earlier, PostgreSQL provides a wealth of functions that can be used to manipulate string values. The ANSI SQL standard specifies some standard string functions that all database vendors must implement to be ANSI standard. Table 8-5 lists and describes the ANSI SQL string functions.

The upper() and lower() functions are commonly used to convert strings to all one case:

```
test=> select upper("LastName"), lower("FirstName") from store."Customer";
 upper  |  lower
--------+---------
 BLUM   | jessica
 BLUM   | rich
 BLUM   | barbara
 BLUM   | katie
 MULLEN |
(5 rows)

test=>
```

Notice that by default the column names in the result set change to the function name used (upper and lower), and not the table column name of the data used in the function (LastName and FirstName).

Besides the standard ANSI SQL string functions, PostgreSQL provides some of its own string functions, listed and described in Table 8-6.

Using string functions within SQL commands is fairly simple. Just provide the required number of parameters for the function. You should also be careful of what the function returns. Some functions return the result as a string, and some return the result as an integer value. Remember that an expression within a WHERE clause must compute

String Function	Description
bit_length(*string*)	Return the number of bits in *string*.
char_length(*string*)	Return the number of characters in *string*.
Convert(*string* using *encoding*)	Convert the *string* encoding to another *encoding*.
lower(*string*)	Convert the *string* characters to lowercase.
octet_length(*string*)	Return the number of bytes in *string*.
Overlay(*string1* placing *string2* from *int1* [for *int2*])	Replace the *string1* elements with *string2*, starting at position *int1* to position *int2*.
Position(*string1* in *string2*)	Return the location of substring *string1* within string *string2*.
Substring(*string* [from *int1*] [for *int2*])	Extract a substring from *string*, starting at position *int1* to position *int2*. By default, it starts at position 0.
Substring(*string* from *pattern*)	Extract a substring from *string* matching the regular expression *pattern*.
Substring(*string* from *pattern* for *escape*)	Extract a substring from *string* matching the regular expression *pattern* using escape character *escape*.
trim([leading | trailing | both] [*characters*] from *string*)	Remove the leading, trailing, or both *characters* from *string*. Default character is a space.
upper(*string*)	Convert the *string* characters to uppercase.

Table 8-5. PostgreSQL ANSI SQL String Functions

to a Boolean TRUE/FALSE result, so you cannot use string functions by themselves within a WHERE clause. You can however use them within the expression:

```
test=> select "FirstName", ascii("FirstName") from store."Customer"
test-> where ascii("FirstName") = 74;
 FirstName | ascii
-----------+-------
 Jessica   |    74
(1 row)

test=>
```

PostgreSQL String Function	Description
ascii(*string*)	Return the ASCII value of the first character of *string*.
btrim(*string* [, *characters*])	Remove *characters* (or a space by default) from the start and end of *string*.
chr(*int*)	Convert the value *int* to the corresponding ASCII character value.
decode(*string, encoding*)	Convert binary data in *string* using the *encoding* type of base64, hex, or escape sequences.
encode(*string, encoding*)	Convert *string* to binary data using the *encoding* type of base64, hex, or escape sequences.
initcap(*string*)	Convert the first character of *string* to uppercase.
length(*string*)	Return the number of characters in *string*.
lpad(*string, length* [, *fill*])	Make *string length* characters long by adding *fill* character to the beginning of the string (uses a space by default).
ltrim(*string* [, *characterlist*])	Remove characters found in *characterlist* (the default is a space) from the beginning (left side) of *string*.
md5(*string*)	Calculate the MD5 hash of *string*. The result is in hexadecimal format. Used for generating passwords.
quote_ident(*string*)	Convert *string* to a quoted string for use as a column identifier.
quote_literal(*string*)	Convert *string* to a quoted string for use as a string literal value.
repeat(*string, int*)	Return a string containing *string* repeated *int* number of times.
Replace(*string, outstring, instring*)	Replace all occurrences of *outstring* with *instring* within *string*.
rpad(*string, length* [, *fill*])	Make *string length* characters long by adding *fill* character to the end (right side) of the string (uses space by default).

Table 8-6. PostgreSQL Nonstandard String Functions

PostgreSQL String Function	Description
rtrim(*string* [, *characterlist*])	Remove characters found in *characterlist* (the default is a space) from the end (right side) of *string*.
split_part(*string, delimiter, int*)	Split *string* based on *delimiter* character and return the resulting *int* field.
strpos(*string, substring*)	Return the location of *substring* in *string* (note this is the reverse order of the `position()` function).
substr(*string, location* [, *count*])	Return the substring of *count* characters starting at *location* within *string*.
to_ascii(*string* [, *encoding*])	Return the ASCII representation of *string* using *encoding* (the default is the normal string encoding).
to_hex(*int*)	Convert *int* value into a hexadecimal value.
translate(*string, fromstring, tostring*)	Replace every occurrence of *fromstring* within *string* with *tostring*.

Table 8-6.   PostgreSQL Nonstandard String Functions *(continued)*

DATE AND TIME FUNCTIONS

The PostgreSQL date and time functions allow you to use date and time values in your applications. These functions all manipulate data using the `date` data type. Table 8-7 lists and describes the date and time functions supported by PostgreSQL.

The most important part of the date and time functions is to become comfortable with the way PostgreSQL deals with dates and times. The format used depends on the `datestyle` parameter setting in the `postgresql.conf` configuration file (see Chapter 3). By default, PostgreSQL uses the date and time style appropriate for your locale setting. Here is an easy way to see how dates and times will look in your setting:

```
test=> select current_date, current_time, current_timestamp;
    date    |      timetz       |              now
------------+-------------------+-------------------------------
 2006-08-15 | 19:51:31.837-04   | 2006-08-15 19:51:31.837-04
(1 row)

test=>
```

Date/Time Function	Description
age(*timestamp*)	Return the time between the current date and time and *timestamp*
age(*timestamp1, timestamp2*)	Return the time between *timestamp1* and *timestamp2*
current_date	Return the current date
current_time	Return the current time
current_timestamp	Return the current date and time
date_part(*field, timestamp*)	Return the subfield *field* from *timestamp*
date_part(*field, interval*)	Return the subfield *field* from a time *interval*
date_trunc(*precision, timestamp*)	Return a truncated value of *timestamp*, rounded to the nearest *precision*
extract(*field* from *timestamp*)	Return the subfield *field* from *timestamp*
extract(*field* from *interval*)	Return the subfield *field* from a time *interval*
isfinite(*timestamp*)	Return TRUE if *timestamp* is infinity
isfinite(*interval*)	Return TRUE if time *interval* is infinity
justify_hours(*interval*)	Adjust time *interval* to convert 24-hour values to days
justify_days(*interval*)	Adjust time *interval* to convert 30-day values to months
localtime	Return the current time of day
localtimestamp	Return the current date and time
now()	Return the current date and time
timeofday()	Return the current date and time

Table 8-7.   PostgreSQL Date and Time Functions

Besides these functions, there is also the now() and timeofday() functions:

```
test=> select now(), timeofday();
          now             |           timeofday
--------------------------+-------------------------------------
 2006-08-15 13:56:01.776-04 | Tue Aug 15 13:56:01.807000 2006 EDT
(1 row)

test=>
```

The date_part() and extract() functions allow you to extract individual date or time values from larger timestamp values. This is handy when trying to combine or compare items by date, such as looking for all items purchased in September. These functions use common words such as year, day, month, hour, minute, second, and millisecond, to extract the desired value:

```
test=> select date_part('month', current_timestamp);
 date_part
-----------
         8
(1 row)

test=>
```

MATH FUNCTIONS

It is not surprising that PostgreSQL includes lots of math functions. There are math functions for just about every common math utility you could require in your application. Table 8-8 lists and describes the various math functions supported by PostgreSQL.

All of the math functions return numeric values. If you need to use a math function within a WHERE clause, remember to place it in an expression that evaluates to TRUE or FALSE.

The random() function is often used to produce random numbers for applications. The random() function only returns a random number between 0 and 1. It is your job to extrapolate that value to the range you require for your application. If you need to produce a random integer value between 10 and 50, you would use

```
test=> select round(random() * 40) + 10;
 ?column?
----------
       23
(1 row)

test=>
```

By multiplying the random number times 40, you are producing a random floating-point number between 0 and 40. The round() function is used to round the result to the nearest integer value. Adding 10 makes the range go from 10 (if the random number was 0) through 50 (if the random number was 1).

AGGREGATE FUNCTIONS

The functions covered so far in this chapter work on a single value within a record. Often there are times when you need to extract information based on the data contained in all of the records in a table. An *aggregate function* is a function that PostgreSQL performs on all values contained within a specified column for all records.

Math Function	Description
abs(x)	Return the absolute value of x
acos(x)	Return the arc cosine of x
asin(x)	Return the arc sine of x
atan(x)	Return the arc tangent of x
atan2(x, y)	Return the arc tangent of x / y
cbrt(x)	Return the cube root of x
ceil(x)	Return the smallest integer not less than x
ceiling(x)	Same as `ceil()`
cos(x)	Return the cosine of x
cot(x)	Return the cotangent of x
Degrees(x)	Convert x radians to degrees
exp(x)	Return the exponential of x
floor(x)	Return the largest integer not greater than x
ln(x)	Return the natural logarithm of x
log(x)	Return the base10 logarithm of x
log(b, x)	Return the base$b$ logarithm of x
mod(x, y)	Return the remainder of x / y
pi()	Return the pi constant as a double-precision value
power(x, y)	Return x raised to the y power
Radians(x)	Convert x degrees to radians
Random()	Return a random value between 0.0 and 1.0
round(x)	Round x to the nearest integer
round(x, d)	Round x to d decimal places
Setseed(x)	Set a double-precision seed number for the random-number generator
sign(x)	Return -1 for negative values of x, and +1 for positive values of x
sin(x)	Return the sine of x
sqrt(x)	Return the square root of x
tan(x)	Return the tangent of x
trunc(x)	Truncate x toward zero
trunc(x, d)	Truncate x to d decimal places toward zero
width_bucket (x, $count$, $b1$, $b2$)	Return the histogram bucket that the value x would be assigned to, using $count$ buckets, with lower bound $b1$ and upper bound $b2$

Table 8-8. PostgreSQL Math Functions

These functions are helpful when you need to perform a statistical analysis of data contained within a table. Instead of having to read every record in the table and perform calculations within your application, the PostgreSQL aggregate functions can produce the statistical results automatically for you (and usually much quicker).

The aggregate functions supported in PostgreSQL are listed and described in Table 8-9.

These functions are used within the SELECT list portion of the SELECT SQL command and are displayed in the result set as a separate column, similar to the other functions:

```
test=> select * from store."Order";
 CustomerID | ProductID | Quantity | TotalCost | OrderID
------------+-----------+----------+-----------+---------
 BLU001     | LAP001    |       10 | $5,000.00 | ORD001
 BLU002     | LAP001    |        2 | $1,000.00 | ORD002
 BLU003     | DES001    |        1 |   $300.00 | ORD003
 BLU001     | LAP001    |        2 | $1,000.00 | ORD004
(4 rows)

test=> select sum("TotalCost") from store."Order";
    sum
-----------
 $7,300.00
(1 row)

test=>
```

Aggregate Function	Description
avg(*expression*)	Return the average of all values matching *expression*
bit_and(*expression*)	Return the bitwise AND of all values matching *expression*
bit_or(*expression*)	Return the bitwise OR of all values matching *expression*
bool_and(*expression*)	Return TRUE if all values matching *expression* are true
bool_or(*expression*)	Return TRUE if any value matching *expression* is true
count(*expression*)	Return the number of records matching *expression*
every(*expression*)	Return TRUE if all values matching *expression* are true
max(*expression*)	Return the maximum value matching *expression*
min(*expression*)	Return the minimum value matching *expression*
stddev(*expression*)	Return the standard deviation of values matching *expression*
sum(*expression*)	Return the sum of all values matching *expression*
Variance(*expression*)	Return the variance of the values matching *expression*

Table 8-9. PostgreSQL Aggregate Functions

The sum() aggregate function automatically added the TotalCost column values in one easy command. For more advanced calculations, you can use the GROUP BY clause to sum individual groups of data values found in a column:

```
test=> select "ProductID", sum("Quantity")
test-> from store."Order" group by "ProductID";
 ProductID | sum
-----------+-----
 LAP001    |  14
 DES001    |   1
(2 rows)

test=>
```

This produces two records, one for each type of ProductID value that appears in the table. If you are working with aggregate functions on column data, the GROUP BY clause is almost always needed to produce the correct aggregate values. Be careful that you use the correct column to group the data by, or you may not get the results you intend.

SUMMARY

This chapter discussed the functions that PostgreSQL provides for programmers to help make their lives easier. PostgreSQL provides lots of common functions for all data types for you to use in your SQL programming. The simplest type of functions are called operators. Operators allow you to easily add, subtract, and multiply numeric values within your SQL commands. There are comparison operators provided that allow you to compare complex string values. PostgreSQL provides three methods for comparing string values. The Unix-style regular expressions use wildcard symbols to match one or more characters within a string value. The ANSI SQL LIKE operator is used for comparing a string value to a basic simplified regular expression. The ANSI SQL SIMILAR TO operator is a combination of the simplicity of the LIKE operator with some of the advanced features of the Unix-style regular expression.

Finally, the chapter discussed the math, string, date and time, and aggregate functions. Date and time functions allow you to easily manipulate and compare date and time values in your SQL commands. The aggregate functions allow you to perform statistical analysis, such as sums, standard deviations, and averages, on all or a subset of records in a table.

The next chapter discusses how to use stored procedures and triggers in your tables. Both stored procedures and triggers allow you to create complex table environments that can be utilized in your database applications.

CHAPTER 9

Stored Procedures
and Triggers

Chapter 8 showed how to use the built-in functions provided by PostgreSQL in SQL commands, making the life of database programmers much easier. This chapter goes a step further in the process by showing how to create your own functions. PostgreSQL supports a number of different programming languages that can be used to create functions. This chapter concentrates on using the PL/pgSQL procedural language. After walking through how to use the PL/pgSQL language, the chapter demonstrates how to use it to create functions that are unique to your specific applications and available for all of the application users. The chapter discusses how to create and use both stored procedure functions, which allow you to create functions for commonly used actions within your own specific applications, and trigger functions, special functions that are performed when a predefined event occurs in a table.

POSTGRESQL PROCEDURAL LANGUAGES

The PostgreSQL database engine provides a method for you to create your own functions for use in your SQL commands. These custom functions are built using a *procedural language.* Procedural languages are specialized programming languages used by the database engine to manipulate and extract data within database tables. The procedural languages execute directly inside the database engine, instead of remotely in a separate application program. Running programs inside the database engine can greatly improve performance by reducing the execution time of your application, as well as provide a standard place to store functions that is accessible to anyone who uses the database.

As seen in Chapter 2, PostgreSQL supports five procedural languages:

▼ PL/pgSQL

■ PL/Tcl

■ PL/Perl

■ PL/Python

▲ PL/Java

Before you can use a procedural language in PostgreSQL, it must be installed on the system supporting the PostgreSQL server. The default procedural language in PostgreSQL (and by far the most popular) is the PL/pgSQL language. This procedural language is installed within the PostgreSQL installer program without having to install a separate programming environment package. The Tcl, Perl, Python, and Java procedural languages all require installing a separate software package (see Chapter 2) before they can be used within PostgreSQL.

The downside to using PL/pgSQL is that it is not a standard language—it is specific to PostgreSQL. Any functions created using PL/pgSQL are not portable to other database engines. If you are familiar with the Oracle database environment, you may notice that the PL/pgSQL name is very close to Oracle's default procedural language, PL/SQL. Not only is the name similar, but the layout and operation of the two procedural languages are also similar. Very little effort is required to port functions created in PL/SQL to PL/pgSQL, and visa versa.

The function examples in this chapter all use the PL/pgSQL procedural language. If you want to run these examples within your PostgreSQL database, you must have opted to install the PL/pgSQL procedural language during the PostgreSQL install. If you did not, you can still install it using the normal PostgreSQL installation, this time just select the PL/pgSQL procedural language to install (just remember to uncheck the PostgreSQL database installation, or you will overwrite your existing database structure).

TYPES OF FUNCTIONS

There are two types of functions that can be created using procedural languages:

▼ Stored procedures

▲ Triggers

Stored procedures are probably the thing you would normally think of when thinking of creating a new function. They behave exactly as do the built-in PostgreSQL functions within common SQL command expressions. They appear in the \df meta-command listing of functions, and can be used by other database users in their SQL commands to easily manipulate data within the database tables.

The benefit of creating stored procedures is that instead of each individual user having to create a lot of SQL commands to perform an action on table data, you can create a specialized stored procedure that performs multiple SQL commands as one function. Each user can then execute the stored procedure as a single function within a SQL command. When the function executes, the entire block of SQL commands contained in it is processed by the database engine.

Triggers are functions that are executed directly by the database engine, based on an event that occurs in a table. PostgreSQL monitors each action performed on tables (such as inserts, updates, and deletes). If an action is performed on a table that has a trigger linked to it, the database engine automatically performs the trigger function assigned to the trigger. Trigger functions are often used to update related data in tables automatically when a table value is inserted or updated in a single table. This allows you to maintain data relations automatically, without having to worry about that in your application code.

THE PL/PGSQL LANGUAGE

The PL/pgSQL procedural language uses standard SQL commands to build programs that can query data from tables, as well as insert, modify, and delete data. This makes learning the language easier for database programmers, as they already know how to interface with a database using SQL.

Besides SQL commands, the PL/pgSQL language also uses standard programming statements to define and evaluate variables, accept input values for the function, supply output values from the function, and use control logic, such as conditional loops and IF/THEN statements, to control execution flow within the program. The PL/pgSQL language is an *interpreted* programming language. This means that it is not compiled into a binary form, but rather the database engine executes the text program lines one by one as the function is executed. That said, there is a catch to the way PostgreSQL handles PL/pgSQL code, and you should be aware of it.

The first time a PL/pgSQL program is run in the database engine, an *execution plan* is prepared (see Chapter 10). The execution plan is the roadmap PostgreSQL uses to interact with tables, indexes, and result sets. Once the execution plan is created for a function, PostgreSQL keeps the plan and uses it every time the function is called (during the lifetime of the PostgreSQL server session). This feature increases performance, as the PL/pgSQL code does not have to be interpreted each time the function is run.

The downside to this is that you must be careful when making dynamic changes to functions. Normally PostgreSQL detects if a function's code has changed, and creates a new execution plan when necessary. What it does not know, though, is whether a function calls another function, and whether that function's code has been changed. This can often cause problems when working with stored procedures, as the old execution plan for the called function will be used. It is up to you to know when this situation may occur. The only way to solve the problem is to re-create the original function (even though it has not changed) so that PostgreSQL knows to create a new execution plan, or manually stop and restart the database server session (see the discussion of the pg_ctl program in Chapter 3).

The following sections describe the PL/pgSQL procedural language and show how to use it to create your own functions for your applications.

Creating a PL/pgSQL Function

To create a new function, you must use the CREATE FUNCTION command. If you need to modify an existing function, you have two options. One method is to use the CREATE OR REPLACE FUNCTION command to redefine the program code for an existing function. You can not, however, change any input or output variables or data types when using this method. This only works for modifying the function code within the function.

The other way to modify an existing function is to use the DROP FUNCTION command to completely remove the function from the database. You can then use CREATE FUNCTION to build a new function with the same name and modify whatever you need to change. It is important to remember, though, that the new function is a new database object. Any objects referencing the original function by its object ID (OID) must be changed to point to the new function, even if the function name stays the same.

The basic format of the CREATE FUNCTION command is

```
CREATE [ OR REPLACE ] FUNCTION
 functionname ( [ [argmode] [argname] argtype [,...] )
 [RETURNS returntype] AS $$
```

```
DECLARE
    <variable declarations>
BEGIN
    <code section>
END;
$$ LANGUAGE languagename
[ IMMUTABLE | STABLE | VOLATILE
  | CALLED ON NULL INPUT| RETURNS NULL ON NULL INPUT | STRICT
  | SECURITY INVOKER | SECURITY DEFINER ]
```

The *languagename* parameter defines the procedural language used to create the function. For functions created using PL/pgSQL, this value is `plpgsql`. The first line of the function declares the *functionname* parameter, which defines the unique name used to identify the function. By default, the function will be created in the `public` schema. If you need to create the function for a different schema, you must specify a schema name along with the function name.

You can define for the function both input and output arguments that are used to pass input and output variables between the function and the SQL code that uses the function. There are three components used to define a function argument:

```
argmode argname argtype
```

The *argmode* value defines the direction of the argument, `IN` for input variables, `OUT` for variables returned by the function, or `INOUT` for variables that can be used for both. The *argname* value defines the name of the variable. In PL/pgSQL this variable name can be used within the program code of the function. The *argtype* value defines the data type of the argument. You may define as many input and output variables as you need (each separated by a comma).

For compatibility with previous versions of PostgreSQL, PostgreSQL 8 also supports defining a single output variable using the `RETURNS` keyword in the command. The *returntype* parameter defines only the data type of the returned output variable. The last line of code in the function must be a `RETURN` statement. This statement specifies which variable is used to return a value to the calling program.

The `AS` section defines the program code used in the function. Since PL/pgSQL is an interpreted language, all of the lines of program code must be in text format. The double dollar signs (`$$`) signify the start and end of the function code text.

PostgreSQL interprets the function code as a single literal text string. If you remember from Chapter 6, literal text strings are normally enclosed with single quotes, and that is certainly permissible in this case as well. However, when creating a function, this could be a problem, as you often need to use single quotes to define other literal strings used within the function.

Working with literal strings embedded within literal strings can quickly become confusing, as quotes for embedded literal strings must be identified with multiple single quotes. PostgreSQL has provided the double dollar sign since version 7.3 as an alternative method for signifying literal strings. This allows the programmer to use the double dollar sign to delineate the function code literal string, then use single quotes within the BEGIN code section to delineate other literal strings.

The program code is divided into two sections. The DECLARE section of the code is used to declare variables used within the function. Each variable declaration statement uses the following format:

```
variablename datatype [ := value];
```

The *variablename* identifies the variable and can be used anywhere within the function. The *datatype* identifies the data type of the variable. Any of the available data types used in table columns can be used here. Optionally, you can also assign a default *value* to the variable. Notice that the symbol for assigning a value is : = and not just an equal sign. Be careful to note that in PL/pgSQL equal signs are preceded by a colon. The equal sign is used for a comparison, and not for an assignment. Also make sure that each statement in the DECLARE section ends with a semicolon, another syntax requirement.

The BEGIN and END keywords are used to delineate the code section of the function. This is where you enter the SQL commands and programming statements to manipulate table data and variables. If the function uses the RETURN parameter, this statement must be the last statement before the END keyword, indicating the variable to return.

There are two methods for returning values from functions. The old-fashioned RETURN statement can be used within the function, or you can specify an output argument using the OUT keyword. Do not let this confuse you; both methods perform the same action, to return an answer from the function. As discussed later in this chapter, the pgAdmin III program makes a distinction between functions that use the RETURN keyword and those that use the OUT keyword (calling functions that use the RETURN keyword "functions" and functions that use the OUT keyword "procedures"). In reality, there is no difference between the two methods.

After the LANGUAGE keyword, there are several parameters that can be used to further define the behavior of the function. These parameters are listed and described in Table 9-1.

The easiest way to get the hang of using stored procedure functions is to watch one in action. Here is a simple example of defining and using a stored procedure function in psql:

```
test=# create function store.test(IN val1 int4, IN val2 int4, out result int4)
test-# AS $$
test$# DECLARE
test$# multiplier int4 := 3;
test$# BEGIN
test$# result := val1 * multiplier + val2;
test$# END;
test$# $$ language plpgsql;
CREATE FUNCTION
test=# select store.test(10, 5);
 test
-----
   35
(1 row)

test=#
```

Function Parameter	Description
IMMUTABLE	The function always returns the same result when given the same input values.
STABLE	The function always returns the same results when scanning a table.
VOLATILE	The function may return different values for the same input values. This is a default behavior.
CALLED ON NULL INPUT	The function will be called normally if an input is NULL. This is a default behavior.
RETURNS NULL ON NULL INPUT	The function always returns NULL if any of the input values are NULL. This is the same as STRICT.
STRICT	The function always returns NULL if any of the input values is NULL.
SECURITY INVOKER	The function is run using the security level of the user who calls it. This is a default behavior.
SECURITY DEFINER	The function is run using the security level of the user who created it.

Table 9-1. CREATE FUNCTION Parameters

This stored procedure function defines two input arguments of int4 data type, and one output argument, also of int4 data type. The DECLARE section also declares an additional variable, multiplier, and assigns it a default value of 3. The actual code section performs a simple assignment, assigning a simple mathematical equation using the variables to the variable result. Since this variable was identified as the OUT argument, this is the value the function returns. Remember, you could just as easily use the RETURN keyword to return this value.

After creating a stored procedure function, you most likely want to share it with other database users. You must use the GRANT SQL command and grant the EXECUTE privilege to Group or Login Roles before other users can use the new stored procedure function.

Notice that in this example I entered each line of the program one at a time directly at the psql command prompt. Any typing mistakes would have ruined the entire function, and I would have had to start entering the function from the start. That is not a good thing if you are working with a 100-line function (unless you are an impeccable typist).

There are two recommended methods for creating complex functions. The first method is to create a text file that contains the complete CREATE FUNCTION command. If you are in development mode and need to experiment with various program code, you often have to constantly rewrite a function. It is advised to use the CREATE OR REPLACE FUNCTION format when creating your function code in the text file, so any code updates will replace the function without you having to manually delete the function. Also, remember you must end the CREATE FUNCTION command with a semicolon, or psql will not process it. After the text file is created, you can load it into the database using the psql -f option:

```
C:\Program Files\PostgreSQL\8.2\bin>psql -f test.sql test postgres
Password for user postgres:
CREATE FUNCTION

C:\Program Files\PostgreSQL\8.2\bin>
```

The function code was loaded into the database engine and the new function was created.

The other recommended method for creating a function is to use a graphical development environment that allows you to alter program code within an editing window. It just so happens that our friend pgAdmin III contains a graphical environment for creating functions. The next section describes how to use this to create and modify functions.

Creating a Stored Procedure Using pgAdmin III

Besides the databases, schemas, and table objects, the pgAdmin III program also displays function objects that are created within each schema. There are three types of function objects shown in the main window:

▼ **Functions** Define functions that use the RETURNS keyword to return a single value

■ **Procedures** Define functions that use the OUT keyword to return one or more values

▲ **Triggers** Define functions that are used to manipulate tables based on a table event

Notice that pgAdmin III makes a distinction between functions and stored procedures. This is a new feature within pgAdmin III. It considers functions that were created using the RETURNS keyword as functions, and functions created using the OUT parameter as stored procedures. This is somewhat important to know when looking for a function that was manually created in psql. Remember, in reality, both functions and procedures are the same thing, just with different methods of returning values to the calling program.

If you created the example function in the previous section, it should appear in the Procedures section of the `store` schema, since it uses the `OUT` parameter to return a value. Right-clicking the `test` procedure name and then selecting Properties produces the Procedure window, shown in Figure 9-1.

The Properties tab shows all of the `CREATE FUNCTION` options that were used to create the function. Notice that check boxes are used to define the `STRICT` and `SECU-RITY DEFINER` parameters. Clicking the Parameters tab shows the parameters defined for the function, as well as the function code used to define the function, as shown in Figure 9-2.

The function code appears in a windowed textbox. You can add new lines, remove existing lines, and even move lines around using standard Windows cut-and-paste techniques. This makes the job of modifying functions almost easy.

You can create a new procedure or function by right-clicking the appropriate object type in the main window and selecting New Procedure or New Function from the menu.

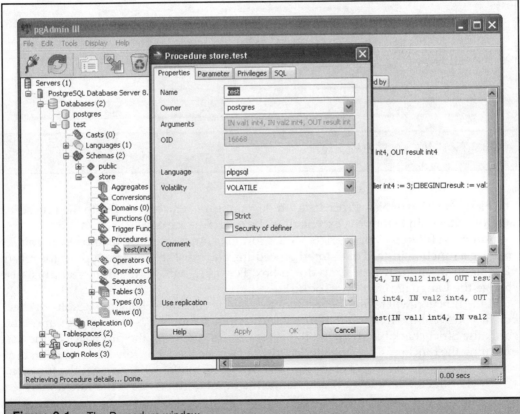

Figure 9-1.   The Procedure window

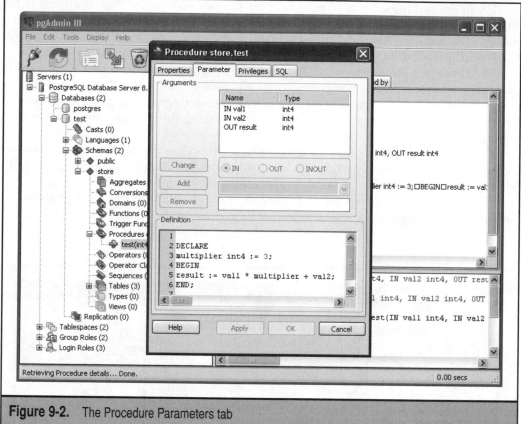

Figure 9-2. The Procedure Parameters tab

The New Function or New Procedure window appears, which is similar to the Procedure window shown in Figure 9-1, except all of the textboxes are empty.

You must fill in the appropriate values for your function in the textboxes. If you are creating a function instead of a stored procedure, you must set the data type of the return variable in the Return Type drop-down box. For a PL/pgSQL function, you must also change the Language entry to `plpgsql`.

If the function will return the result from a query, you must check the Result Set check box. If you want the function to return a `NULL` value if any of the input values are `NULL`, check the Strict check box. By default, the function is run using the privileges of the user executing the function. Checking the Security of Definer check box forces the function to always run using the privileges of the function owner, no matter who executes the function.

The Parameter tab allows you to define the input arguments for the function. If you are creating a new stored procedure, you must also select whether the argument is `IN`, `OUT`, or `INOUT`. The Definition textbox is where the program code goes. You can use standard Windows cut-and-paste functions to move code lines around the textbox.

The Privileges tab allows you to define what Group Roles are allowed to execute the function. By default, only the function owner is allowed to use it. If you want everyone to be able to use the function, you must grant `execute` privileges for the `public` Group Role.

PL/pgSQL Function Code

The PL/pgSQL procedural language allows you to create complex functions using simple SQL commands and standard programming statements. It helps to know the syntax for the PL/pgSQL programming environment to develop complex functions. This section describes the commands that are used within a PL/pgSQL function definition.

Assigning Values to Variables

Since most functions are used to manipulate data, being able to assign values to variables is a crucial feature. The PL/pgSQL assignment operator is used to assign values and expressions to variables:

```
variable := expression;
```

The *expression* can be any normal mathematical expression that uses constant values as well as other variables. The result of the expression is assigned to *variable*.

Since functions often work with table data, PL/pgSQL provides a method for assigning table column data values to variables. The `SELECT INTO` statement is used to perform a typical `SELECT` command against a table, assigning the output to a variable. The format of the `SELECT INTO` statement is

```
SELECT INTO variable [, ... ] column [, ... ] clause;
```

One or more variables can be used to receive column data from the `SELECT INTO` statement. Each *variable* is matched against a *column* from the column list. The variables used in the `SELECT INTO` statement must have the same data types as the columns listed. The *clause* parameter defines a normal `SELECT` clause used to filter data into a result set.

You can create a single variable that holds all of the data columns of a table. The variable must be declared using the table's `%ROWTYPE` table attribute:

```
customervar store."Customer"%ROWTYPE
SELECT INTO customervar * FROM store."Customer" where "CustomerID" = 'BLU001';
```

This statement assigns the contents of the result set record to the `customervar` variable. Each individual column data value can then be retrieved as an individual element of the variable:

```
result := customervar."FirstName" || ' ' || customervar."LastName";
```

Of course, this method assumes that only one record of data will be returned in the result set. Later, this chapter discusses the `FOR` loop, showing how to deal with multiple records returned in the result set.

Condition Statements

Just like any other language, PL/pgSQL supports the use of IF/THEN/ELSE statements to allow program code branching based on conditions:

```
IF condition THEN
    <statements1>
ELSE
    <statements2>
END IF;
```

Notice that the IF and ELSE statements do not contain a semicolon. The *condition* can be any expression that evaluates to a Boolean result. You can also combine additional IF statements after the ELSE statement to continue the comparisons:

```
IF condition1 THEN
    <statements1>
ELSE IF condition2 THEN
    <statements2>
ELSE
    <statements3>
END IF;
```

This series can continue to check each set of conditions. If none of the conditions evaluates to a TRUE value, the ELSE statements are performed.

Loop Statements

PL/pgSQL provides three ways to loop through data:

▼ The LOOP statement

■ The WHILE loop

▲ The FOR loop

The LOOP statement by itself provides a continuous loop:

```
LOOP
    <statements>
    EXIT [ WHEN expression];
END LOOP;
```

The statements inside the LOOP structure are executed continuously. To exit this loop, you must execute an EXIT statement. The EXIT statement may also include a WHEN clause. The loop is followed until the WHEN clause expression returns a TRUE value.

The WHILE loop works the opposite way. The WHILE loop continues looping until an expression is FALSE:

```
WHILE condition LOOP
    <statements>
END LOOP;
```

The FOR loop allows you to iterate through a set range of values:

```
FOR variable IN [REVERSE] value1..value2 LOOP
    <statements>
END LOOP;
```

The *variable* value is an integer that is incremented (or decremented if REVERSE is specified) by one in each loop iteration, starting at *value1* and stopping after *value2*. The variable does not have to be declared within the function, but if it is not, it will only be available within the FOR loop.

There is another neat feature to the FOR loop in PL/pgSQL. You can use it to iterate through a result set that returns more than a single data record. The format for doing this is

```
FOR variable IN select_clause LOOP
    <statements>
END LOOP;
```

The *variable* value must be defined with the %ROWTYPE attribute of the table used in the *select_clause*. An example of this would be

```
customervar store."Customer"%ROWTYPE;
FOR customervar IN SELECT * FROM store."Customer" LOOP
    <statements>
END LOOP;
```

In this example, the customervar variable would contain the values of each record for each FOR loop iteration. This is an extremely handy tool to have for evaluating data when a result set returns multiple records.

TRIGGERS

A *trigger* defines an operation that is performed when a specific event occurs on a table. A trigger can be defined for when a user inserts a new record, updates an existing record, or deletes a record. The trigger is configured to execute a specific function when the event occurs. The function executed as a result of a trigger is called a *trigger function*. This section describes what trigger functions are and demonstrates how to use them.

Trigger Function Format

A trigger function looks similar to the stored procedure function. Trigger functions use the same CREATE OR REPLACE FUNCTION command as a stored procedure to define the procedural language code executed by the trigger. There are, however, two things that are different between the two:

▼ Trigger functions do not use input arguments in the function, but rather are passed arguments from a trigger event.

▲ Trigger functions have access to special variables from the database engine.

Since trigger functions are not executed by SQL commands, you are not able to send input arguments to the function through the function definition. Instead, arguments are passed from the trigger to the trigger function using special variables. Similarly, since the trigger function does not send output to the calling program, there are no output data type arguments to define. The trigger returns either a NULL value or a record having the same columns as the table the trigger was defined for.

When a trigger function is called, the database engine passes a group of special variables to the trigger function to define the environment the trigger function is working in. The special variables can be used within the trigger function to determine environment features, such as how the function was called, what data is present when the trigger was fired, and when the trigger was fired. Table 9-2 lists and describes the trigger special variables available for use in a trigger function.

After the trigger function is created, you must define the actual trigger event that executes the function. This is done using the CREATE TRIGGER command:

```
CREATE TRIGGER name { BEFORE | AFTER } {event [OR ... ] }
   ON table [ FOR [ EACH ] { ROW | STATEMENT }]
   EXECUTE PROCEDURE function (arguments)
```

The trigger can be defined to occur either before or after the *event* occurs. The event can be an INSERT, UPDATE, or DELETE SQL command on the *table* the trigger is defined for.

There are two methods for firing triggers. You can select to fire the trigger once for each row that is affected by the event (such as multiple rows in an UPDATE or DELETE command) by specifying the ROW parameter. Alternatively, you can select to fire the trigger only once for each statement that triggers the event, no matter how many rows are returned (even if no rows are returned) by specifying the STATEMENT parameter.

Finally, the *function* to execute when the trigger is fired is declared. This defines the trigger function created using the CREATE FUNCTION SQL command. The arguments listed in the *function* parameter are not passed to the function within the normal function definition (remember, trigger functions do not define input arguments). Instead, the arguments in the CREATE TRIGGER command are passed using the TG_ARGV special variable.

Special Variable	Description
NEW	The record column data values present in the INSERT or UPDATE command
OLD	The record column data values present in the table before an UPDATE or DELETE command is executed
TG_NAME	The name of the called trigger
TG_WHEN	When the trigger was fired, either BEFORE or AFTER the SQL command
TG_LEVEL	The trigger definition, either ROW or STATEMENT
TG_OP	The event that fired the trigger, either INSERT, UPDATE, or DELETE
TG_RELID	The OID of the table that fired the trigger
TG_RELNAME	The name of the table that fired the trigger
TG_NARGS	The number of arguments in the CREATE TRIGGER command
TG_ARGV[]	An array containing the arguments used in the CREATE TRIGGER command

Table 9-2.   The Trigger Function Special Variables

Creating a Trigger Function

Just as with stored procedures, you can use the pgAdmin III program to create trigger functions. The trigger functions are grouped together within each schema. The individual triggers are shown as objects under the table object they are defined for.

To create a trigger function, right-click the Trigger Functions object and select New Trigger Function. The New Trigger Function window appears, shown in Figure 9-3.

Just as with the stored procedure, the New Trigger Function window provides text-boxes and check boxes to allow you to define the trigger function features. Remember to set the Language textbox to plpgsql. For a trigger function that updates table records, you must define it as a VOLATILE function.

On the Parameter tab, notice that you are not allowed to define arguments. The Definition textbox is available to enter the function code.

As an example, let's revisit the store database objects created in Chapter 4. Suppose you now need to create a trigger that automatically updates the inventory count for a product in the Product table every time an order is entered into the Order table. This is a perfect example of showing how an event on one table can alter data in a totally different table.

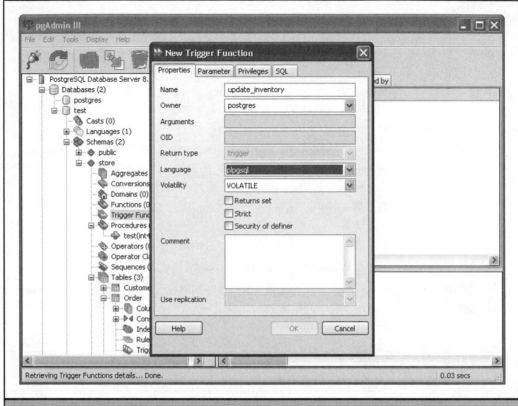

Figure 9-3. The New Trigger Function window

In the Trigger Function object within the `store` schema in the `test` database created in Chapter 4, create a new trigger function called `update_inventory`. Set the Owner value to `postgres`, set the Language to `plpgsql`, keep the Volatility set to VOLATILE, and check the Security of Definer check box (this allows anyone with access to the Order table to run the trigger, which will modify the Product table). On the Parameter tab, type the following function code:

```
DECLARE
  onhand int4;
BEGIN
  SELECT into onhand "Inventory" from store."Product" where
     "Product"."ProductID" = NEW."ProductID";
  IF TG_OP = 'INSERT' THEN
     update store."Product" set "Inventory" = onhand - NEW."Quantity"
     where "ProductID" = NEW."ProductID";
  END IF;
END;
```

When a new record is inserted into the Order table, the NEW special variable will be set by the database engine to the data values of the inserted record. The individual column values are referenced as if the NEW keyword were the table name.

This function code uses the SELECT INTO command to extract the current inventory value from the Product table that matches the same ProductID value as the new record's value, and places it into the onhand variable.

Next, the TG_OP special variable is checked to ensure that the event was indeed an INSERT (this is a common practice, so you can use the same trigger function for multiple trigger events). If the event is an INSERT event, the UPDATE command is executed. Again, the NEW special variable is used to retrieve the Quantity column data value inserted into the Order table, and to ensure the proper Product record is updated.

Now that the trigger function is created, you must define a trigger event for the Order table that automatically executes the trigger function whenever someone inserts a new record.

Under the Order table object is the Triggers object. Right-click Triggers and select New Trigger. The New Trigger window appears, shown in Figure 9-4.

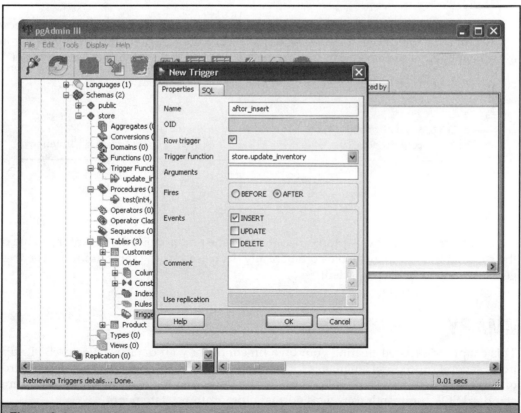

Figure 9-4. The New Trigger window

The textboxes and check boxes represent the parameters available for the CREATE TRIGGER function. After entering the trigger name, you must check the Row Trigger check box so that the trigger is fired for each record inserted into the Order table. Next, select the store.update_inventory trigger function from the drop-down box. Since we do not want to update the product inventory until after we are sure the order has been entered, click the AFTER radio button, and then check the INSERT check box. If the INSERT command for the Order table fails, the trigger will not fire. That is all there is. Click OK to create the trigger.

Testing the Trigger Function

Now it is time to test our work. Use psql to insert data into the Order table, and then see what happens to the Product table. First, though, make sure you have a valid customer in the Customer table and a valid product in the Product table:

```
test=# insert into store."Product" values ('LAP001', 'Laptop',
test(# 'Takealong', 'Acme', '1,000', 10);
INSERT 0 1
```

This command inserts a record showing there are ten laptops in inventory. Once you know you have valid data, try entering a new record in the Order table (remember, you must be logged in as someone in the Salesman Group Role, such as the barney user):

```
test=> insert into store."Order" values ('ORD001', 'BLU001', 'LAP001',
test(> 2, '2,000');
INSERT 0 1
test=> select * from store."Product";
 ProductID | ProductName |   Model    | Manufacturer | UnitPrice  | Inventory
-----------+-------------+------------+--------------+------------+-----------
 LAP001    | Laptop      | Takealong  | Acme         | $1,000.00  |         8
(1 row)

test=>
```

After the order for two laptops was added to the Order table, the inventory value of the product in the Product table automatically decreased by the same amount. The trigger function worked as expected!

SUMMARY

This chapter discussed creating your own functions for your database. PostgreSQL supports several procedural languages for creating functions. PL/pgSQL is the default procedural language provided by PostgreSQL. It allows you to create function code using standard SQL commands as well as normal programming statements.

There are two types of functions: stored procedures and trigger functions. Stored procedures are used just like the PostgreSQL built-in functions within SQL commands. You can create a stored procedure in a schema and make it available for any database user to use. Trigger functions are special functions that manipulate table data based on a table event. A trigger is defined for a specific table event, such as inserting a new record, updating an existing record, or deleting a record. When the trigger event occurs, the database engine automatically executes the trigger function.

The next chapter discusses the security and performance issues that often occur in PostgreSQL systems. It is important that you exercise proper security procedures to ensure the safety of your application data. It is also important that database customers have the quickest response time as possible for the application.

CHAPTER 10

Security

Security is an important, but often misunderstood, concept for database administrators. These days database security is not an option, it is a requirement, especially if your PostgreSQL database is running on a system attached to a network. Knowing how to allow your customers into the database while blocking the bad guys is something that all database administrators must know how to do. This chapter shows the basic security pieces required for putting your PostgreSQL database on a network for multiple customers to access.

Back in the early days of network computing, as a system administrator, you could put a database system onto a network and safely assume that only your customers would connect to it. In today's environment, though, every database server connected to the network becomes a target for unscrupulous individuals, both from outside the network and, unfortunately, sometimes even from inside your own network.

This section discusses three methods that can be used in multi-user database systems to help control the security environment of the database server:

▼ Controlling network users

■ Encrypting network sessions

▲ Monitoring database users

Each method provides a different level of security for the database, and each is invaluable in your arsenal in protecting your application data.

CONTROLLING NETWORK USERS

The first method available for protecting the database is controlling network access. You have total control over who can access what databases from the network. It is your job to ensure not only that your customers can get to the appropriate databases, but also that unauthorized clients are prevented from accessing the databases. There are two components available for controlling access for network database users:

▼ Using a server firewall system

▲ Using the PostgreSQL configuration files

Each component provides a different way of controlling access. The combination of the components helps you to implement a secure database server environment.

Controlling Access via Firewalls

The most basic way of protecting network services on a server is through a *firewall*. The firewall allows you to configure which clients are allowed to pass packets through the firewall to specific applications. While it is common to think of network firewalls protecting entire networks from outside intruders, individual servers can also contain firewalls.

The server firewall is the front door of the system on the network. It can block attempts to access individual services on the server before the packets even get passed to the server applications. This is the first line of defense in protecting your PostgreSQL databases from attack and intrusion.

There are many different network firewall products available on the market today, both free and commercial. Microsoft Windows XP Home and Professional workstations with Service Pack 2 installed, as well as Microsoft 2003 servers, include a basic firewall application built into the operating system.

When the Windows Firewall application is enabled, it blocks all access to the PostgreSQL server service by default. If you want network clients to be able to access your PostgreSQL server, you must manually configure the firewall application to allow access to the PostgreSQL server TCP port.

To start the Windows Firewall application on a Windows XP workstation, choose Start | Control Panel, click Network and Internet Connections, and then click Windows Firewall. On a Windows 2003 server, choose Start | Control Panel and click the Windows Firewall icon.

When the Windows Firewall application is started, the main window appears, shown in Figure 10-1.

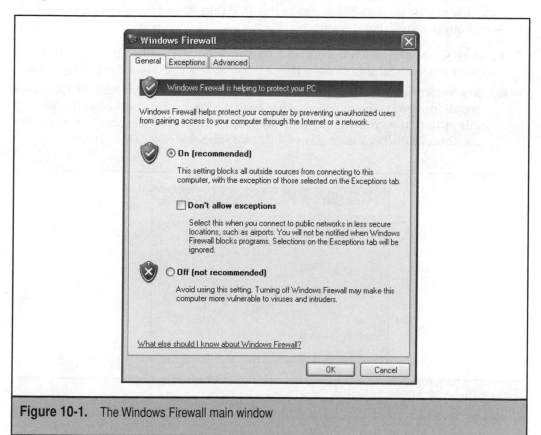

Figure 10-1. The Windows Firewall main window

To block all unauthorized access, enable the firewall. Once the firewall is enabled, all but the basic network TCP ports are blocked. You must configure an exception to allow network traffic onto the server. Enable exceptions by unchecking the Don't Allow Exceptions check box.

When exceptions are allowed, you can then click the Exceptions tab to see the programs and services that are allowed access through the firewall to the system.

To enable remote clients access to your PostgreSQL server, you must add a new port exception to the firewall for PostgreSQL. Click the Add Port button to open the Add a Port window, shown in Figure 10-2.

Select a name to call the new port (such as "PostgreSQL"), then enter the PostgreSQL TCP port number that is configured in the `postgresql.conf` configuration file (discussed in Chapter 3). The default TCP port for PostgreSQL is 5432. After entering the port number, ensure that the TCP radio button is selected, to indicate that this is a TCP port.

Next you must define which remote network clients will be allowed through the firewall to this TCP port. Click the Change Scope button to open the Change Scope window, shown in Figure 10-3.

The Change Scope window offers you the following three options for defining the network clients that are allowed access to the TCP port. Which you should choose depends on your network requirements.

▼ **Any Computer (Including Those on the Internet)**   Select this option if you want any computer from anywhere to be able to access your PostgreSQL server.

■ **My Network (Subnet) Only**   If the customers accessing your PostgreSQL server are all located on the same subnetwork as the PostgreSQL server, you can select this option. If your company network is split into multiple subnets, you cannot use this option, because it allows only one subnet access to the service.

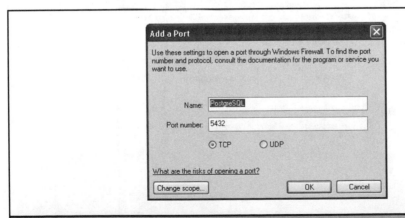

Figure 10-2.   The Windows Firewall Add a Port window

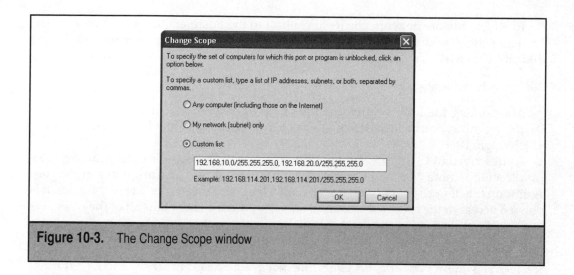

Figure 10-3.   The Change Scope window

▲   **Custom List**   Most likely, you do not want everyone to be able to access the
    server. In this scenario, you must add your customer client address ranges in-
    dividually by using this option. In the host list, you can add either individual
    IP addresses, such as 192.168.10.21, or an IP address/subnet mask combination,
    such as 192.168.10.0/255.255.255.0, which allows all hosts on the 192.168.10.0
    network. You may add multiple entries to the list, separated by commas. This
    allows you to configure subnet ranges that are allowed access to the PostgreSQL
    TCP port.

Once you have chosen the appropriate option for your network environment, click
the OK button to accept the new scope, then click the OK button on the Add a Port window. This enters the newly defined exception in the Exceptions list. Now any remote
customer whose network address is accepted by the scope will be allowed through the
firewall to your PostgreSQL server. This finishes the firewall configuration. Next you
must configure the PostgreSQL configuration files to enable customers to connect.

Controlling Access via Configuration Files

Once your Windows Firewall application is configured to allow your customers access
to the server, your PostgreSQL server must be configured to accept remote connections.
This is done using the `postgresql.conf` and `pg_hba.conf` configuration files, described in Chapter 3.

The `postgresql.conf` file contains a single entry that controls which network interfaces PostgreSQL listens for connections on. By default, the `listen_addresses` setting is set to the value `localhost`. This value prevents remote clients from connecting
to the PostgreSQL server.

To enable remote network clients to connect to the PostgreSQL server, you must either enter the IP addresses of the network interfaces to activate or enter the asterisk (*) wildcard character to enable all network ports, as follows:

```
listen_addresses = '*'
```

After setting the listen addresses in the `postgresql.conf` file, the next step is to use the `pg_hba.conf` file to define which clients can connect to which database, using which Login Role.

As described in Chapter 3, the `pg_hba.conf` configuration file defines access rules for allowing remote customers access to the PostgreSQL server. Each entry in the configuration file defines an individual access rule. If a client meets any one of the rules, it is allowed access to the specified resources on the server. If a client fails all of the rules, it is prevented from accessing the databases on the server.

As shown in Chapter 3, the format of each rule entry is

```
connection-type  database  user  network-address  login-method  options
```

The *connection-type* field defines the method used by the remote client to connect to the server. For network hosts, there are three possible values:

▼ `host`   Allows a remote client to connect using either a plain-text TCP connection or an SSL-encrypted TCP connection

■ `hostssl` Requires that a remote client connect to the server using an SSL-encrypted TCP connection

▲ `hostnossl` Requires that a remote client connect to the server using a plain-text TCP connection

After the connection type, you must define the *database* the network client is allowed to connect to, along with the *user* Login Role allowed to connect. You can either specify individual database and Login Role names or use the `all` keyword to allow the network address defined in the rule to connect to any database using any Login Role on the server.

The *network-address* field specifies which network clients the rule applies to. It can specify a single network client IP address, or an IP address and subnet mask combination to define an entire subnet of clients. When a client connects to the PostgreSQL server, its network address is compared with the *network-address* field in the `pg_hba.conf` file. Only rules that match that network address are applied to the client.

Finally, the *login-method* field specifies the method the remote client must use to authenticate the Login Role name sent by the client to the PostgreSQL server. The most common methods are `password` and `md5`. The `password` method passes a plain-text password, which, while not recommended in plain-text TCP sessions, is just fine if used in an SSL-encrypted TCP session. The md5 method allows for encrypting the password before sending it to the server, which is recommended if using a plain-text TCP session.

Here are a few sample entries in the pg_hba.conf file:

```
hostssl    all     all       10.0.1.0/28      password
host       test    barney    192.168.120.5    md5
host       test2   barney    192.168.120.5    md5
host       test    all       10.0.2.0/28      md5
```

This first example allows any client on the 10.0.1.0 subnetwork to connect to any database using any Login Role. The client must connect using SSL encryption. In the second example, the 192.168.120.5 network client can only log into the test database using the Login Role barney (and using an encrypted password). The third example, however, lets the barney Login Role from the same network client also log into the test2 database as well. The final example allows any client from the 10.0.2.0 subnet to log in using any Login Role to the test database. This allows multiple customers from that network to connect to the test database.

After editing the configuration files, the PostgreSQL server must be either stopped and started or reloaded for the changes to become active. You can do this either from the pgAdmin III interface or from the pg_ctl command-line program.

Testing Remote Connectivity

After configuring your network environment in PostgreSQL, it is usually a good idea to test it out. You can use the psql program to test connections to the PostgreSQL server from a remote client. The -h option is used to specify the hostname (or IP address) of the remote PostgreSQL server:

```
C:\Program Files\PostgreSQL\8.2\bin>psql -h 10.0.1.33 test barney
Password for user barney:
Welcome to psql 8.2.0, the PostgreSQL interactive terminal.

Type:  \copyright for distribution terms
       \h for help with SQL commands
       \? for help with psql commands
       \g or terminate with semicolon to execute query
       \q to quit

test=>
```

Once the connection to the remote host is established, you can perform all of the normal psql meta-commands and SQL commands just as if you were connected to a local PostgreSQL server.

ENCRYPTING NETWORK SESSIONS

By default, the PostgreSQL server is configured to accept remote client connections using a standard TCP text connection. There is a downside to connecting to a remote PostgreSQL server using this type of connection. Figure 10-4 demonstrates the problem.

This network trace shows a single TCP packet going from the client running the `psql` application to the PostgreSQL server. Notice that the SQL command sent by the `psql` application is shown within the packet in plain text, visible in the lower window of the Wireshark network sniffer display shown in Figure 10-4. This could be a security problem, especially if your customers connect to your server across public networks. Anyone with access to the network can intercept the data packets and see the query. Even worse, not only are the SQL commands sent in clear text, but the result set generated by the SQL command is also sent from the PostgreSQL server to the `psql` client in clear-text format. This enables a network snooper to see your table data as well.

To solve this problem, PostgreSQL supports *Secure Sockets Layer (SSL)-encrypted TCP sessions*. SSL-encrypted TCP sessions use an encryption key to encrypt data before it is

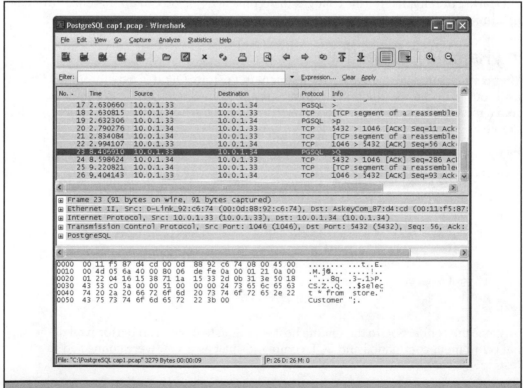

Figure 10-4. Network trace of a PostgreSQL TCP connection

sent out on the network. The PostgreSQL server and the remote client pass an encryption key that is used to encrypt the data. Theoretically, only those two devices should be able to decrypt the data that is encrypted and sent out on the network. Figure 10-5 shows a network trace of a SQL command contained in an SSL-encrypted TCP session.

The text SQL command has been encrypted and is unintelligible to the naked eye while it is on the network. The PostgreSQL server is able to receive the encrypted packet, decrypt the text, and process the SQL command just as normal. The process is then reversed when the PostgreSQL server sends the result set back to the client. While encrypting data is not 100 percent foolproof (the SSL encryption can be broken using a brute-force technique, which could take a few days), it does provide a basic level of security for clients connecting to the PostgreSQL server across public networks. By the time the encryption key is cracked, the database connection is most likely no longer active, and the key is useless.

The following sections describe the process of how to set up your Windows PostgreSQL server to accept SSL-encrypted TCP sessions.

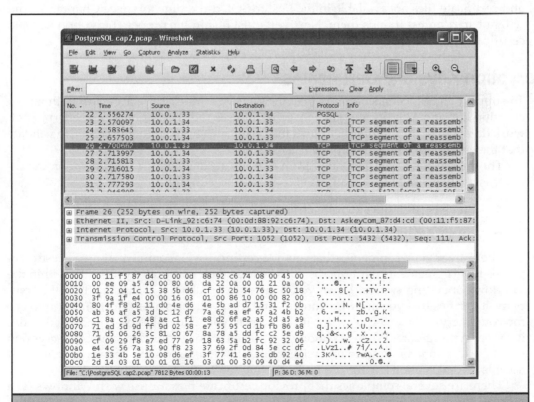

Figure 10-5. Network trace of an SSL-encrypted PostgreSQL TCP session

Enabling SSL in PostgreSQL

The first step is to ensure that your PostgreSQL installation is capable of supporting SSL connections. Fortunately, the PostgreSQL server installation package created for Windows is already compiled for SSL encryption support, so you do not need to recompile anything. All you need to do is enable SSL support in the configuration file and provide the appropriate encryption key and certificate files for the server to use.

Enabling SSL support in the configuration file is simple. Just modify the `ssl` parameter value in the `postgresql.conf` configuration file. In the default `postgresql.conf` configuration file, the `ssl` parameter is present but commented out. To enable SSL connections, just change the line to enable SSL support:

```
ssl = on
```

When PostgreSQL is restarted, it will recognize the configuration change and enable SSL connections. The PostgreSQL server now listens for both normal TCP sessions and secure SSL TCP sessions on the same TCP port (port 5432 by default). However, once SSL is enabled, the PostgreSQL server will look to make sure that the encryption key and certificate files are available in the PostgreSQL `data` directory (see Chapter 3), and will not start unless it finds them. Next you must obtain the proper encryption key and certificate files.

Encryption Keys and Certificates

To support an SSL connection, the PostgreSQL server must have access to both an encryption key and a certificate. The SSL protocol uses the encryption key to encrypt network data, while the remote client uses the certificate supplied by the server to validate that the encryption key came from a trusted source.

The encryption key is generated from a certificate signed by an organization the client trusts. There are two methods used to obtain a certificate:

▼ Purchase a certificate from a trusted commercial company

▲ Create a self-signed certificate

There are several companies that provide certificates for commercial use. These companies have agreements with Microsoft to include their corporate certificates within the Windows operating system. When you register to purchase a certificate from the company, it verifies that you are who you are, and then validates a certificate for you to use for your encryption key. The certificate belongs to you, and only you are allowed to use it for encrypting data. When a Windows workstation or server sees an SSL encryption key signed by one of these commercial companies, it assumes the key is authentic and accepts the encryption key for use in decrypting the TCP session.

There are several companies that provide certificate files for use with Windows. The most popular is the VeriSign corporation. In a production database environment, using a commercially assigned certificate is recommended.

Instead of purchasing a certificate from a well-known, trusted company, you can create your own certificate, validating that the encryption key came from you. This is called a *self-signed certificate*. This certificate is not automatically validated by the Windows system. It is up to your clients to determine whether they can trust your certificate, and accept any connection encrypted using the encryption key provided with the certificate.

This method is not recommended for production environments where you expect external customers to connect to your database, as it requires your customers to accept your certificate on faith. However, if you are just testing your PostgreSQL server, or providing a database that will only be used by a few internal customers, it works just fine. By self-signing a certificate, the server validates that the encryption key was sent by the specific host that generated it. If the encryption key is received from any other host on the network, it is assumed to be invalid.

Once you obtain a valid encryption key and certificate pair, you must place them in the PostgreSQL `data` directory. The encryption key file must be named `server.key`, and the certificate file must be named `server.crt` (these are the only filenames PostgreSQL recognizes). After this is done, the PostgreSQL server can be started.

The following section describes how to create your own `server.key` and `server.crt` files.

Creating an SSL Encryption Key

You can create your own self-signed certificate and encryption key using an Open Source software package called OpenSSL, a popular free tool for working with encryption keys and certificates. The OpenSSL package source code is available for download at the www.openssl.org web site.

The OpenSSL web site only provides the source code for the application. For a Windows environment, you will most likely prefer to use a binary executable package so you do not have to compile the software. Fortunately, the OpenSSL web site provides a resource for obtaining a precompiled Windows executable package of OpenSSL.

From the OpenSSL home page, click the Related link. On the Related web page, click the Binaries link (tab) at the top of the page. Click the OpenSSL for Windows link to go to the web page for Shining Light Productions (www.slproweb.com).

Shining Light Productions is a company committed to providing resources for programmers. Its web page provides a link to download a precompiled Windows binary executable package of the latest OpenSSL package, along with one previous release. At the time of this writing, the latest version of this package is called `Win32OpenSSL-v0.9.8d.exe`. Click the package link to download the installation package to your hard drive.

After downloading the `Win32OpenSSL` package, run the installation program by double-clicking the package from Windows Explorer. The installation process is pretty simple; just read and accept the license agreement, select the location to install the OpenSSL files (by default in the `c:\openssl` directory), and select the name of the Program group to create in your Start menu. After installing the program, you are ready to create your encryption key and certificate files.

The `openssl.exe` program is used to create the encryption key and self-signed certificate files. By default, it is located in the `c:\openssl\bin` directory. Since this is a command-line program, it is best to work from a command prompt window. Start a command prompt window and navigate to this directory using the `cd` command:

```
C:\Documents and Settings\RICH>cd \openssl\bin
C:\OpenSSL\bin>
```

There are three steps required to create the encryption key and self-signed certificate files:

1. Create a pass phrase-protected encryption key.
2. Remove the key pass phrase (for when using the PostgreSQL automatic startup feature).
3. Create the self-signed certificate.

The first step is to create the encryption key used by PostgreSQL for encrypting SSL sessions. This is done using the `req openssl` option:

```
openssl req -new -text -out server.req
```

OpenSSL will respond by asking lots of questions. Each of these questions is present in the encryption key and certificate, identifying you to your clients. Make sure you enter as much information as necessary to enable your clients to properly identify you:

```
C:\OpenSSL\bin>openssl req -new -text -out server.req
Loading 'screen' into random state - done
Generating a 1024 bit RSA private key
...............................................++++++
......++++++
writing new private key to 'privkey.pem'
Enter PEM pass phrase:
Verifying - Enter PEM pass phrase:
----
You are about to be asked to enter information that will be incorporated
into your certificate request.
What you are about to enter is what is called a Distinguished Name or a DN.
There are quite a few fields but you can leave some blank
For some fields there will be a default value,
If you enter '.', the field will be left blank.
----
Country Name (2 letter code) [AU]:US
State or Province Name (full name) [Some-State]:Indiana
Locality Name (eg, city) []:Indianapolis
```

```
Organization Name (eg, company) [Internet Widgits Pty Ltd]:Blum
Organizational Unit Name (eg, section) []:
Common Name (eg, YOUR name) []:ezekiel
Email Address []:rich@demo.lan

Please enter the following 'extra' attributes
to be sent with your certificate request
A challenge password []:
An optional company name []:

C:\OpenSSL\bin>
```

When answering the questions, you can choose to include the necessary information to identify yourself to your customers. The pass phrase is the encryption key's password. It ensures that only you can offer the encryption key to remote clients. You must enter at least a four-character pass phrase.

Another important item is the Common Name field. You must use the hostname of your PostgreSQL server as the Common Name. This identifies the host that issues the certificate. The hostname of your system can be determined by using the `ipconfig` Windows command in a command prompt window. You do not need to include the domain name, unless you want to use it to further identify your system to remote customers. It would not be a self-signed certificate if you were to use a different hostname from the one that will offer the certificate to remote clients. Finally, you do not have to enter a challenge password when prompted; just hit ENTER.

This process creates the file `privkey.pem`, which contains the encryption key, and the file `server.req`, which contains a basic certificate. Unfortunately, this key file is protected by the pass phrase, which you entered when the encryption key was created. This pass phrase must be entered every time the encryption key is used. This poses a problem if you automatically start PostgreSQL as a Windows service. Since the service is started by the operating system, you can not enter the pass phrase to enable the encryption key.

To solve this problem, you can remove the pass phrase from the encryption key by using another `openssl` option:

```
openssl rsa -in privkey.pem -out server.key
```

When this command is executed, OpenSSL asks for the pass phrase for the encryption key (hopefully you remember what you used to create it). It then creates a new encryption key, called `server.key`, which does not require the pass phrase to be entered.

Now you have an encryption key and a basic certificate. All that is left to do is to convert the certificate to a standard X.509 format (required by the SSL protocol) and self-sign it using the encryption key. This is done using the following command:

```
openssl req -x509 -in server.req -text -key server.key -out server.crt
```

The certificate is created in text mode using the standard X.509 format and is saved in the file `server.crt`. Since the certificate was created in text mode, you can look at it by using the `type` command:

```
C:\OpenSSL\bin>type server.crt | more
Certificate:
    Data:
        Version: 3 (0x2)
        Serial Number:
            94:c0:32:bb:ef:23:d9:d8
        Signature Algorithm: sha1WithRSAEncryption
        Issuer: C=US, ST=Indiana, L=Indianapolis, O=Blum,
                CN=CIN-exekiel/emailAddress=rich@demo.lan
        Validity
            Not Before: Aug 28 20:02:26 2006 GMT
            Not After : Sep 27 20:02:26 2006 GMT
        Subject: C=US, ST=Indiana, L=Indianapolis, O=Blum,
                CN=ezekiel/emailAddress=rich@demo.lan
        Subject Public Key Info:
            Public Key Algorithm: rsaEncryption
            RSA Public Key: (1024 bit)
                Modulus (1024 bit):
                    00:c7:e2:0f:b3:0e:12:84:bb:72:e3:5d:0a:ac:03:
```

The first part of the certificate file contains the information you entered when creating the encryption key. If you continue to scroll down through the text file, you will see the actual certificate section that contains the encrypted certificate.

Now copy the `server.key` and `server.crt` files to the PostgreSQL data directory (at the time of this writing, located at `C:\Program Files\PostgreSQL\8.2\ data`), then restart the PostgreSQL server service.

You can easily stop and restart the PostgreSQL server service from the pgAdmin III program. After starting the program, right-click the PostgreSQL server name and select Stop Service. After waiting a few seconds, you can right-click the server name and select Start Service. You should then be able to log into the PostgreSQL server from pgAdmin III as normal.

Testing SSL Encryption

After restarting the PostgreSQL server, you can use the `psql` application to test the SSL connection. The `psql` application attempts to connect to the PostgreSQL in SSL mode first, then tries to connect in plain-text mode if that fails. You can tell which method is used for the connection from the opening text after starting the connection:

```
C:\Program Files\PostgreSQL\8.2\bin>psql -h 10.0.1.33 test barney
Password for user barney:
Welcome to psql 8.2.0, the PostgreSQL interactive terminal.

Type:  \copyright for distribution terms
       \h for help with SQL commands
       \? for help with psql commands
       \g or terminate with semicolon to execute query
       \q to quit

SSL connection (cipher: DHE-RSA-AES256-SHA, bits: 256)

test=>
```

The message shows that the SSL connection has been established using the encryption key. Now your queries are safer from prying eyes on the network.

MONITORING USERS

The third method used for increasing server security is to monitor which users are connected to your PostgreSQL server. It always helps to know which users are connected from what network clients. Fortunately, the pgAdmin III application provides an excellent interface for this.

The Server Status tool is a window available from the pgAdmin III menu bar. After starting pgAdmin III and logging into the server, choose Tools | Server Status to open the pgAdmin III Server Status window, shown in Figure 10-6.

The Server Status window contains four tabs:

▼ **Status**   Shows information about the currently logged-in Login Roles

■ **Locks**   Shows information about the current table and record locks

■ **Transactions**   Shows information about pending database transactions

▲ **Logfile**   Displays the currently active PostgreSQL log file

Each of these tabs provides valuable information about the current status of the PostgreSQL databases. The Status tab provides a wealth of information about each Login Role that is connected to the server. The refresh rate textbox at the bottom of the Server Status window allows you to set how often the status information is updated in the window. This allows you to constantly monitor the Login Roles connected to the database and watch for problems.

Besides monitoring user connections, you can also monitor the transactions submitted by users. As described in Chapter 3, you can enable full transaction logging in the PostgreSQL server log file. Take care when doing this, though, because the log file can quickly fill up with logging transactions.

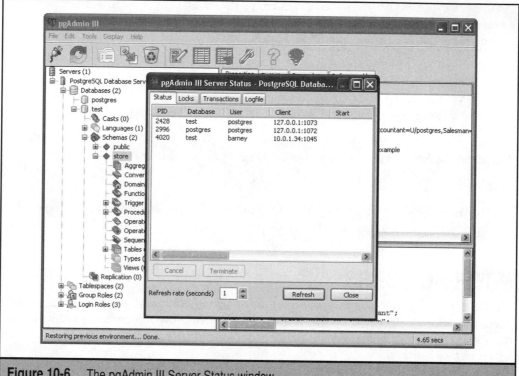

Figure 10-6. The pgAdmin III Server Status window

SUMMARY

This chapter dove into the world of database security. Database security has become a hot topic, and implementing a security plan for a database is a must. PostgreSQL allows remote clients to connect to the server using TCP communications. You can restrict which clients can connect to the PostgreSQL server by using both a firewall application on the system and the pg_hba.conf configuration file. The firewall application is used to block packets from unknown clients from entering the server. The pg_hba.conf configuration file is used to restrict what databases and Login Roles can be used from a network client.

Another aspect of security you must be concerned about is network security. When remote clients send data to the PostgreSQL server, that data is contained in TCP packets that can be intercepted. To protect data from remote clients, you should enable SSL encryption support on the PostgreSQL server. You can either purchase or generate an encryption key and certificate file that are used to communicate with remote clients using the SSL protocol. Data transported using SSL is encrypted and is more secure on the network because it cannot be read with a network sniffer.

The next chapter tackles another important issue for database administrators, the topic of database performance.

CHAPTER 11

Performance

D atabase performance is often a difficult concept for new database administrators to grasp, and even more difficult to implement. There are lots of variables involved in trying to troubleshoot and solve database performance issues. This chapter shows some tips that can be useful in trying to get the most performance out of your PostgreSQL database.

ENHANCING QUERY PERFORMANCE

The words "the database seems slow today" strike fear in the hearts of database administrators everywhere. There are lots of things that can cause a query or database transaction to be slow. This section describes some tools you can use to help both monitor and possibly increase performance of your PostgreSQL server.

The biggest source of performance problems is poorly written queries. Unfortunately, it is often the job of the database administrator to help troubleshoot database programmers' poorly written query code. The best tool for this function is the *query explain plan.*

The query explain plan maps out a query into its individual components, then estimates the time each component should take to complete. The database programmer can analyze this information to determine which components take the longest time to complete, and possibly alter the query to reduce or sometimes even eliminate the delay. This section describes how to use the EXPLAIN SQL command to produce query explain plans, and then shows how to perform query analysis graphically using the pgAdmin III application.

The EXPLAIN Command

Sometimes when entering SQL commands into the database engine, it seems like you are just working with a big black box. Queries go into the database engine, and result sets come out of the database engine, without you knowing exactly what is happening inside the database engine. The key to improving query performance is getting an idea of what is happening inside the database engine, and determining how to maximize the times each component takes.

The EXPLAIN SQL command allows us to peek inside the database engine and get a feel for how data is handled. If you use the EXPLAIN SQL command in front of a normal SELECT command, PostgreSQL returns estimated statistics from the database engine. Here is a simple example:

```
test=> explain select * from store."Customer";
                          QUERY PLAN
---------------------------------------------------------------
 Seq Scan on "Customer"   (cost=0.00..1.04 rows=4 width=232)
(1 row)

test=>
```

The SELECT query is not actually run in the database engine. The database engine goes through the motions of processing the query, and produces statistics on how it thinks it would handle the query. The EXPLAIN command output displays three sets of statistics:

▼ The estimated time cost of the SQL command

■ The estimated number of rows the result set would contain

▲ The estimated maximum character count in a result set record

The cost estimate is provided as two numbers. The first value estimates how much time it would take the database engine to return the first record of data for the query. In this example, the first value estimates it would take 0.00 time units to produce one record of the result set. The second value estimates how much time it will take the database engine to return the entire result set. In this example, PostgreSQL estimates it would take 1.04 time units to return the entire result set.

While these values represent time, they do not use standard time units, such as milliseconds. These time values are generic time references. While this sounds confusing, there is a reason for this.

Time within the system processor (or processors, if the system is a server with more than one processor) is inexact. Each application is provided time slices of the processor as the processor switches between multiple applications. At any given time, an application does not necessarily know how many time slices it will have for using the processor. Attempting to estimate the exact real time a query would take on any processor on any given system running multiple applications would be nearly impossible.

Instead, the PostgreSQL developers chose to provide values that represent the amount of "time" the database engine takes to work on the query. These values show how much actual work time the query components take, not necessarily how much real time. While these values are not exact, they are consistent. You can use these values to compare one query to another.

Besides the estimated time, you can also choose to view the actual time it takes the database engine to process a query. To see the actual time a query takes, use the ANALYZE parameter after EXPLAIN:

```
test=> explain analyze select * from store."Customer";
                                        QUERY PLAN
-------------------------------------------------------------------
 Seq Scan on "Customer"  (cost=0.00..1.04 rows=4 width=232)
                         (actual time=0.082..0.087 rows=5 loops=1)
 Total runtime: 0.135 ms
 (2 rows)

test=>
```

This produces two sets of values. The actual time shown in the output is still defined using relative units and not actual time. The real time the query took to complete is shown at the end of the statistics. Although the command actually runs the query to produce the time results, the output from the query is suppressed and not displayed.

This example showed that to produce the result set for this SELECT command, the database engine performed a sequential scan of the Customer table, looking for records that match the query. The entire query was processed in a single step. Things get more interesting with more complicated queries:

```
test=> explain analyze select * from store."Customer" order by "LastName";
                                          QUERY PLAN
-------------------------------------------------------------------------------
 Sort   (cost=1.08..1.09 rows=4 width=232)
            (actual time=0.148..0.150 rows=5 loops=1)
    Sort Key: "LastName"
    -> Seq Scan on "Customer"   (cost=0.00..1.04 rows=4 width=232)
                                 (actual time=0.010..0.015 rows=5 loops=1)
 Total runtime: 0.258 ms
(4 rows)

test=>
```

By using the ORDER BY clause, we force the database engine to perform two steps. One thing that you need to get used to when analyzing query explain plans is that you must work from the bottom up. The first step the database engine performs is the last item in the list.

Just as with the first example, the first step in this query was to scan the Customer table for the records that match the query. This process did not take all that long (relatively speaking).

The second step the database engine took was to sort the data records in the result set from the scan. This component is what slowed down the query. While the query explain plan estimated that it would not take much time, the actual numbers show that it took over 0.150 time units to complete sorting the data. Compared to the 0.015 time units for the scan, you can see how sorting your result set consumes more database engine time.

Now we can compare this query to a query that sorts the data based on a table key:

```
test=> explain analyze select * from store."Customer" order by "CustomerID";
                                          QUERY PLAN
-------------------------------------------------------------------------------
 Sort   (cost=1.08..1.09 rows=4 width=232)
          (actual time=0.032..0.034 rows=5 loops=1)
    Sort Key: "CustomerID"
    -> Seq Scan on "Customer"   (cost=0.00..1.04 rows=4 width=232)
                            (actual time=0.006..0.011 rows=5 loops=1)
 Total runtime: 0.077 ms
(4 rows)

test=>
```

By examining the query explain plan for this query, you can see the benefit of using indexes in queries. The query on the CustomerID column only took 0.077 millisecond, compared to the 0.258 millisecond for the query sorting the result set on a non-key value. While these values do not look all too much different, remember this example was for a table with only five records. If instead this table had five million records, these values would be multiplied many times over, creating quite a performance hit.

As you use the EXPLAIN command, you may notice that sometimes the database engine does not do things you expect it to do. Usually, the database engine keeps track of new database objects, such as table indexes, and utilizes them in the query explain plan. Sometimes, however, you must force the database engine to re-evaluate how to execute a query.

The ANALYZE SQL command (different from the ANALYZE parameter in the EX-PLAIN command) tells the database engine to re-examine all database objects. The table owner can use the ANALYZE command along with the table name to force PostgreSQL to re-examine the table and reset any query explain plans set for the table:

```
test=# analyze store."Customer";
ANALYZE
test=#
```

The normal output of the ANALYZE command is not too exciting. To get some information on what is happening, you can use the VERBOSE keyword:

```
test=# analyze verbose store."Product";
INFO:   analyzing "store.Product"
INFO:   "Product": scanned 1 of 1 pages, containing 2 live rows and 6 dead rows;
2 rows in sample, 2 estimated total rows
ANALYZE
test=#
```

The output now shows some information about the table. In this example, there are two records that contain live data, and six records that had been either deleted or updated. By performing a VACUUM command on the table, you can free up six records' worth of storage space. If your application performs lots of record updates and deletions, it is a good idea to regularly analyze the status of the table, and vacuum when necessary.

This is the basic idea behind using the EXPLAIN command. As your customers start using more complex queries, and your application starts containing more data, query performance can become a problem. Using the EXPLAIN command gives you (and the database programmers) a simple tool for examining how individual queries affect application performance.

Using pgAdmin III to Evaluate Queries

While using the EXPLAIN SQL command can provide useful information, the output can sometimes get confusing, especially as queries become more complex. Our old friend pgAdmin III comes to the rescue again, providing a great graphical interface for the EXPLAIN command output.

As discussed in Chapter 4, the pgAdmin III Query tool can be used to view the query explain plan in a graphical mode. Start the Query tool by clicking the SQL icon in the pgAdmin III toolbar.

In the top window of the Query tool, enter your SQL query command just as normal (without the EXPLAIN keyword). After entering the query, click the Explain Query icon on the toolbar. The lower window contains the result as if you used the EXPLAIN command for the query.

The Data Output tab shows the normal output you are used to seeing from the EXPLAIN command. The Explain tab shows a graphical representation of the EXPLAIN output. Each query component is shown as a separate icon in the diagram. If you click an individual icon, it displays the statistics for that component. Figure 11-1 shows a more complex query example displayed in the Explain tab.

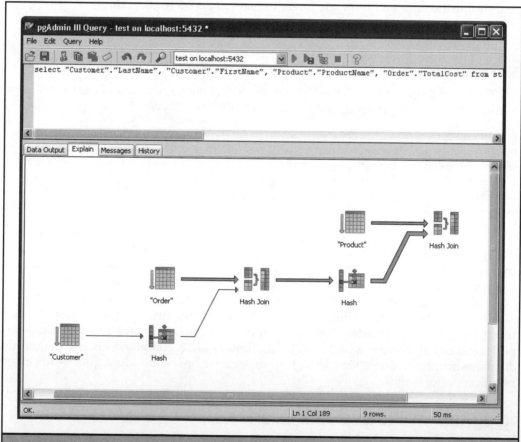

Figure 11-1.   Using the pgAdmin III Query Explain function

There are lots of components that were generated from this query. The SQL query used to produce this output contained two inner joins to join three tables:

```
select "Customer"."LastName", "Customer"."FirstName",
    "Product"."ProductName", "Order"."TotalCost" from
     store."Order" natural inner join store."Customer"
     natural inner join store."Product";
```

By looking at the graphical output, it is much easier to see how each of the components is used to process the query.

Just as with the EXPLAIN SQL command, you can set the Query tool query explain function to include actual performance data. Choosing Query | Explain Options | Analyze enables the ANALYZE keyword for the EXPLAIN command. Now when you click an icon in the graphical output, you can view the actual times as well as the estimated times.

THE POSTGRESQL.CONF PERFORMANCE PARAMETERS

After query performance, the next biggest performance problem is the PostgreSQL server itself. There are many factors, both hardware and software, that can affect the performance of the server as it processes queries and transactions. Some of the hardware factors were discussed in Chapter 2. Most of the software factors that affect performance revolve around how the PostgreSQL database engine handles queries and utilizes system resources.

Instead of hard coding these factors into the PostgreSQL program code, developers have added them to the postgresql.conf file so they can be fine-tuned for specific applications. This method enables the PostgreSQL developers to suggest default values to use for these parameters, but allows database administrators to customize their own PostgreSQL environment. If your database application is in a specialized environment, such as performing lots of complex queries or lots of data inputs and deletes, changing the PostgreSQL server performance is as easy as customizing the performance parameters in the configuration file.

Of course, the real trick is knowing which parameters to customize and what values to use. This has become more of an art form than a science. If you ask three database administrators for suggested values, you might possibly get three totally different answers. The solution is to become familiar with the parameters that may most likely affect your database environment, and experiment with different values to see what works best in your situation. To help that process, this section describes some of the more famous tunable parameters in the PostgreSQL configuration file.

Query Tuning

As shown earlier in the "Enhancing Query Performance" section, PostgreSQL creates a query explain plan for each query executed by the database engine. The postgresql.conf file contains parameters that can be used to control what components PostgreSQL uses when executing the query explain plan. Modifying these parameters can alter the way the database engine processes your queries, and sometimes can help increase the performance of your queries.

The individual components used by the database engine to process queries are called *planner methods*. Planner methods are the building blocks used within the query explain plan to obtain the result set, as we saw graphically in Chapter 10, Figure 10-7. The database engine puts these building blocks together to produce the result set for the query. Each icon in the explain query output is a separate planner method. The various planner methods used by the PostgreSQL database engine are described in Table 11-1.

You can select to disable individual planner methods in the database engine to force the database engine to utilize a different planner method combination to produce the result set. The Query Tuning section of the `postgresql.conf` configuration file contains entries for each of the planner methods (see Chapter 3). To disable a particular planner method, alter the appropriate setting in the `postgresql.conf` configuration file:

```
enable_bitmapscan = off
```

Planner Method	Description
Bitmap scan	Performs a binary scan of columns that are not conducive to indexing (such as Binary Large Objects, or BLOBs) to look for columns that match the query
Hashed aggregation	Performs an aggregation of table records based on a hash result
Hashed join	Performs a join of table records based on a hash result of two table columns
Indexed scan	Performs a scan of an indexed field using the associated table index file
Merged join	Performs a table join by merging all records in the tables
Nested loop	Performs multiple iterations of a function within the table
Sequential scan	Scans each individual table record in order within the table to find records that match the query
Sort	Manually sorts data values in memory as it reads table data
TID scan	Scans the tuple (record) ID (TID) looking for a specific tuple

Table 11-1. PostgreSQL Database Engine Planner Methods

By setting a parameter to off you are disabling that planner method in the database engine. You should use this feature with caution. Remember that disabling a planner method disables that method for all queries on the server. While this may increase the performance of one query, it may have severe adverse effects on other queries. This feature is not intended as a permanent method of altering the PostgreSQL query planner. It is most often used as a debugging tool. You can disable an individual planner method and see how your queries behave, then re-enable the planner method and determine how to rewrite the queries to work around that planner method.

Resource Usage

As described in Chapter 3, the Resource Usage section of the `postgresql.conf` file contains parameters that affect how the PostgreSQL server utilizes system memory. Memory usage is one of the biggest performance bottlenecks on a server. PostgreSQL provides lots of different configuration parameters that allow you to control how the server uses system memory.

There are a few parameters, described next, that are key for controlling how the PostgreSQL server performs in your particular environment.

```
shared_buffers = 1000
```

The `shared_buffers` parameter allows you to set how much memory (in 8KB blocks) the PostgreSQL server will use on the system. This is a somewhat controversial topic, and different administrators have different opinions on what this should be set to. The default setting of 1000 (8MB of memory) is often considered just fine for most normal Windows server environments. If you are working in a high-volume application with lots of customers connecting to the server and processing queries and transactions, you can increase this value to see if it helps performance in your specific environment. Remember, increasing this value may have adverse effects on other processes running on the system. I do not recommend making large increases to this parameter all at once, as it could severely affect other applications running on the server.

```
work_mem = 1024
```

This parameter limits the amount of working memory (in kilobytes) available for each PostgreSQL sort and hash function. If you are using an application that constantly sorts data, you can try to increase this value to increase performance of the sorts. Be careful when increasing this value, though, as it applies to each individual sort or hash function, not the system as a whole. If your application performs simultaneous sorts, each one is granted this amount of memory. The default value of 1MB of memory per sort or hash function is fine for most normal database environments.

```
max_fsm_pages = 20000
```

The `max_fsm_pages` parameter sets the number of free-space pages tracked by PostgreSQL. When a record is updated or deleted from a table, PostgreSQL does not remove the record immediately, it is just tagged internally as being deleted. The free-space map tracks these deleted records. The more free-space pages available, the more records PostgreSQL can track before requiring a vacuum of the table to remove deleted records. In applications that perform lots of deletes and record updates, the free-space pages fill up quickly, decreasing performance. Increasing this value means providing more free-space pages and having to perform fewer vacuum operations to clear out the free-space pages.

Runtime Statistics

The last set of parameters do not directly affect the server performance, but allow you to configure the server so that it logs performance data for you to analyze. The Runtime Statistics section of the postgresql.conf configuration file allows you to enable several different performance logs, as described next.

```
log_statement_stats = on
```

Setting this parameter to on enables logging statistics for each SQL command processed by the database engine. It is not hard to see that, for busy databases, this could lead to an enormous amount of data. The logging entries are placed in the standard PostgreSQL log file in the pg_log directory (see Chapter 3). A statement entry looks like this:

```
2006-08-30 12:09:40 DETAIL:  ! system usage stats:
        !      0.031000 elapsed 0.000000 user 0.000000 system sec
        !      [0.078125 user 0.078125 sys total]
        ! buffer usage stats:
        !  Shared blocks: 11 read,     0 written, buffer hit rate = 2.72%
        !  Local  blocks: 0 read,      0 written, buffer hit rate = 0.00%
        !  Direct blocks: 0 read,      0 written
```

These statistics show how much time the query took, how much data was read and written, and how much of the data was already contained in buffers. The buffer hit rate is an important factor in query performance. The more information the PostgreSQL server can retrieve from memory buffers, the faster the query will perform.

While the log_statement_stats parameter logs statistics for an entire SQL command, there are three other parameters that can log statistics for individual components within the database engine process:

```
log_parser_stats = off
log_planner_stats = off
log_executor_stats = off
```

If any of these three parameters is enabled, you must disable the log_statement_ stats parameter, or an error condition will occur. Each of these parameters can be used to log query statistics during the parsing, planning, and executing phases of the database engine. The statistics produced are placed in the currently active PostgreSQL server log file.

Instead of changing the run-time statistics settings in the configuration file and re-starting the PostgreSQL server, you can change the values on-the-fly in `psql` using the `set_config` command:

```
SELECT set_config(config, value, is_local);
```

The *config* parameter is the name of the configuration parameter, and *value* is the parameter value, either `on` or `off`. The *is_local* parameter defines whether the setting applies to the current transaction (`true`) or the entire `psql` session (`false`):

```
SELECT set_config('log_statement_stats', 'on', 'false')
```

This command enables statement statistics logging for the remainder of the `psql` session. Using this feature, you can enable logging for a single transaction, then turn logging off. This prevents you from having to pour over thousands of lines of logging information looking for the transaction stats.

SUMMARY

Database performance is an important topic for administrators. The key to database performance is often the queries used to produce reports. The ability to analyze queries and see how they are processed by the database engine is a vital tool in evaluating database performance. PostgreSQL supports the `EXPLAIN` SQL command to allow you to view how the database engine processes a query. You can view each step taken to produce the result set, and see the time required to complete the step. Using this information, it is often possible to either create objects, such as index files, or rewrite queries to utilize other factors to increase performance.

Finally, the chapter discussed some of the parameters available in the `postgresql.conf` configuration file that affect database performance. There are several parameters that control how the database engine processes queries, along with several parameters that control how the PostgreSQL server handles system resources, such as memory. Knowing how to fine-tune these parameters can often help increase the performance of the PostgreSQL server in your database environment.

The next (and final) part of this book deals with how to use PostgreSQL in your Windows programming environment. There are several different programming languages that PostgreSQL supports. The final chapters in this book provide details on how to use PostgreSQL as a back-end database in four different Windows programming environments. Chapter 12 discusses how to migrate your Microsoft Access databases to PostgreSQL, and how to use Microsoft Access as a front end to a PostgreSQL database.

PART III

Windows Programming with PostgreSQL

CHAPTER 12

Microsoft Access
and PostgreSQL

Microsoft Access is one of, if not the, most popular database packages available for the Windows platform. It provides an excellent, user-friendly graphical environment for creating tables, queries, data entry forms, and customized reports. The downside is that Access often gets used inappropriately in corporate environments. While Access is perfect for single-user database applications, it suffers from performance problems when used in a multi-user environment. The problem is that it is not uncommon to see users become proficient in Access on their local workstations, then port an Access application to a network environment and have dozens of other people using the application. This can create a problem, both in application performance and network load. However, trying to convert a multi-user application completely from Access to PostgreSQL can be time-consuming. This chapter shows how you can leverage your Access programming skills so that you can use your existing front-end Access applications while utilizing the PostgreSQL database on the back end to manage your data in a multi-user-friendly environment.

INTERFACING POSTGRESQL WITH ACCESS

In normal use, Access uses its own database format to store data tables, indexes, views, forms, reports, and queries created for an application. By default, all of these items are stored in a single file that uses an .mdb extension to identify it as an Access database file. As discussed in Chapter 1, the only way to share an Access database application between multiple users is to place the .mdb database file on a shared network drive and allow users to read and write to the file.

Besides working with standard .mdb database files, Access also has the capability of interfacing with other databases using the Open Database Connectivity (ODBC) standard. The ODBC standard defines a set of application programming interfaces (APIs) for applications to access databases. Any application that supports ODBC can access any database that supports ODBC.

PostgreSQL fully supports the ODBC protocol. This allows an Access application to interact with a PostgreSQL database server, accessing tables, views, and other database objects contained on the PostgreSQL server, from the queries, forms, and reports created in Access. All normal PostgreSQL security restrictions apply to ODBC connections, such as Login Role restrictions and network client address restrictions.

The following sections describe how to download, install, and use the PostgreSQL ODBC driver to a client workstation to allow your Access applications to connect to and use a PostgreSQL database.

Installing the ODBC Driver

PostgreSQL provides a separate ODBC driver for remote client connectivity using the ODBC API set called psqlODBC. Any Windows client that needs to connect to the

PostgreSQL server using ODBC must have the psqlODBC package installed and configured. There are two ways to obtain and install psqlODBC:

▼   Through the normal PostgreSQL package installation

▲   Through a special client PostgreSQL ODBC installation

The standard PostgreSQL installation package includes the psqlODBC package, along with all of the other parts of a PostgreSQL server. To install psqlODBC, you must make sure that the ODBC option is enabled in the PostgreSQL installation window, shown in Figure 12-1.

The ODBC drivers are a set of Windows `.dll` files installed in the Windows system directories. The ODBC documentation files are placed under the PostgreSQL installation directory (`C:\Program Files\PostgreSQL\8.2\doc\psqlODBC`).

For a remote client, however, all you need to install is the ODBC driver; you obviously do not need to install the entire PostgreSQL server package. This makes using the standard PostgreSQL installation package somewhat overkill for installing just the ODBC driver. To compensate for that, there is another installation package that only includes the psqlODBC package for Windows. This is obviously a much smaller package, and installing it is much easier for customers than extracting the ODBC drivers from the standard PostgreSQL installation package.

The psqlODBC driver package can be found by following the links on the main PostgreSQL web site (www.postgresql.org). From the main web page, click the Downloads link. On the Downloads page, click the FTP Browser link to go to the PostgreSQL FTP

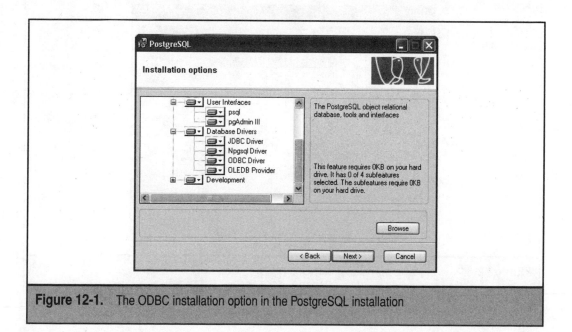

Figure 12-1.   The ODBC installation option in the PostgreSQL installation

Browser mirror site, www.postgresql.org/ftp/. Click the `odbc` folder, and then click the `versions` folder. This folder contains different binary installation packages for the psqlODBC program. The `msi` folder contains the full Windows installation packages, so click that link to open the folder.

The `msi` folder contains several versions of the psqlODBC package in zip format. Select the latest version (at the time of this writing it is 8_02_0200) to download. This link takes you to a list of available download sites for the file. Select a site, and download the zip file to your hard drive.

After the psqlODBC package is downloaded, you must extract the Windows installer file (`psqlodbc.msi`) from the zip file. Double-click the zip file from Windows Explorer and extract the file. Start the psqlODBC installer by double-clicking the `.msi` package from Windows Explorer. You must have administrative rights on the system you are installing this on. The main installation window appears. Click the Next button to walk through the welcome and license windows. The Feature Selection window shows the components available to install, as shown in Figure 12-2.

Notice that there are only two options to install: the ODBC driver and the psqlODBC documentation. By default, the installer will place the ODBC driver files and documentation in the `C:\Program Files\psqlODBC` directory. You can change that location by clicking the Browse button. Select the components you want to install, and click the Next button. After clicking another Next button to confirm the install, the installation process starts. Click the Finish button to complete the installation.

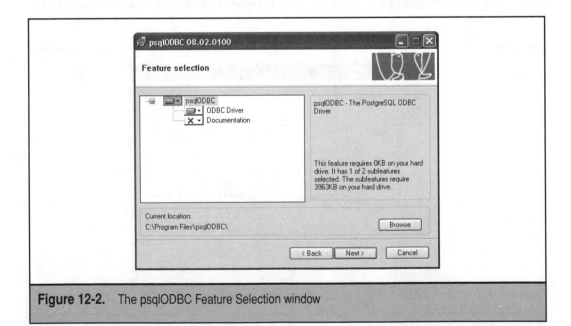

Figure 12-2. The psqlODBC Feature Selection window

Configuring a PostgreSQL ODBC Connection

After the PostgreSQL ODBC driver software is installed on the workstation, you must configure an ODBC session for each PostgreSQL database your applications must connect to (remember, a PostgreSQL session can connect to only one database at a time). Of course, you can always have multiple sessions to different databases open at the same time. Once the ODBC sessions are configured, Access applications will use them to access objects stored in the specified PostgreSQL databases.

For Windows 2000 and XP workstations, as well as Windows 2000 and 2003 servers, the way to configure ODBC sessions is through the ODBC Data Source Administrator program. On Windows XP Professional and 2000 and 2003 Server systems, you can start this program either by choosing Start | All Programs | Administrative Tools | Data Sources (ODBC) or going through the Control Panel and selecting Administrative Tools | Data Sources (ODBC). For Windows XP Home systems, it is a little harder to find. You must choose Start | Control Panel, click Performance and Maintenance, click Administrative Tools, and then double-click Data Sources (ODBC). The main ODBC Data Source Administrator window is shown in Figure 12-3.

The ODBC Data Source Administrator window contains several tabs that help you configure the ODBC data sources. The tabs are described in Table 12-1.

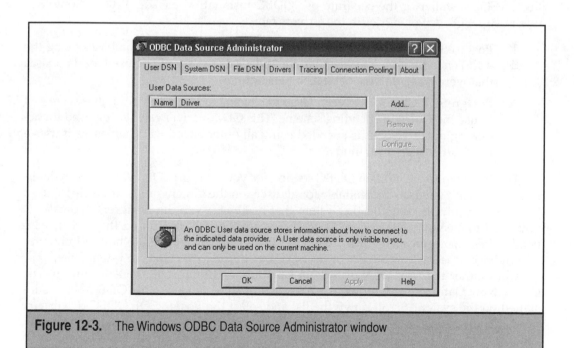

Figure 12-3.   The Windows ODBC Data Source Administrator window

Tab	Description
User DSN	User-level data sources available only to the user
System DSN	System-wide data sources available to all users, including services, on the system
File DSN	System-wide file data sources shared by users
Drivers	The ODBC drivers (and versions) currently installed on the system
Tracing	Start and stop an ODBC trace
Connection Pooling	Enable or disable connection pools, allowing applications to reuse a single open session to the ODBC driver
About	Information about the system ODBC environment

Table 12-1. ODBC Data Source Administrator Window Tabs

After installing the PostgreSQL psqlODBC driver package (through either the main PostgreSQL installer or the separate psqlODBC installation package), you should see two PostgreSQL driver entries in the Drivers tab:

▼ **PostgreSQL ANSI driver**   Used to connect to PostgreSQL databases using the ANSI encoding scheme (see Chapter 2). This driver should be used for databases that were created to use 7-bit ANSI encoding.

▲ **PostgreSQL Unicode driver**   Used to connect to PostgreSQL databases created to use the Unicode encoding scheme. This ODBC driver can also be used for accessing database objects encoded using all other encoding schemes, as it uses a full 8-bit encoding method.

The first step to creating an ODBC session for your PostgreSQL database is to determine whether it needs to be available for all users on the system or just for a single user. If there are multiple users on the system that need access to the PostgreSQL database, you need to create a new System DSN. If you are the only person on the system who needs access, you can just create a new User DSN. You do not need to have administrative rights on the system to create a User DSN, but you do to create a System DSN.

Click either the User DSN or System DSN tab, and then click the Add button. The Create New Data Source window appears, listing all of the available ODBC drivers installed on the system. Scroll down the list and select the PostgreSQL ODBC driver you need for your application (either ANSI or Unicode), and then click the Finish button. The PostgreSQL (Unicode or ANSI) ODBC Driver Setup configuration window, shown in Figure 12-4, appears.

As you can see in Figure 12-4, there are lots of textboxes that need to be filled out for the ODBC session. The Data Source textbox is used to identify the ODBC session. This is the

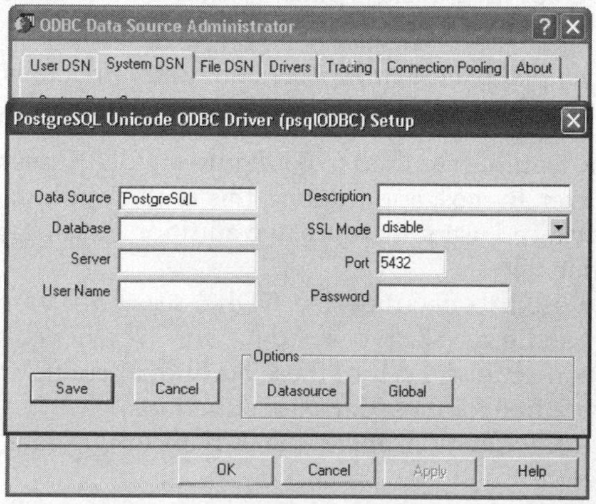

Figure 12-4. The PostgreSQL (Unicode or ANSI) ODBC Driver Setup configuration window

name you will see when searching through the User or System DSN list. It is a good idea to use a descriptive name, especially if you are creating multiple ODBC sessions for multiple PostgreSQL databases (remember, each session can connect to only one database).

The Description textbox is for information purposes. You can put a longer text phrase in the Description textbox to help identify the ODBC session.

The rest of the textboxes define the properties of the PostgreSQL database you need to connect to. These should be fairly self-explanatory. Put the name of the database that the ODBC session should connect to in the Database textbox, the Login Role used to connect to the database in the User Name textbox, and the password used for the Login Role in the Password textbox.

The value of the Server textbox defines the hostname or IP address of the PostgreSQL server. If the PostgreSQL server is running on the same system you are creating the ODBC session on, you can use the hostname `localhost`. Otherwise, enter the appropriate IP address or hostname of the system where the PostgreSQL server is running. In the Port textbox, enter the TCP port used by the PostgreSQL server to listen for connections (port 5432 by default).

The SSL Mode drop-down box allows you to determine the encryption method the ODBC session will attempt to use to connect to the PostgreSQL server (see Chapter 10). The SSL Mode options available are the following:

▼ **Prefer** Attempt an SSL encryption session first. If that fails, attempt a plain-text TCP session.

■ **Allow** Attempt a plain-text TCP session first. If the server requires an SSL-encrypted session, then attempt to connect using SSL.

■ **Require** Attempt an SSL encryption session first. If that fails, do not attempt any other connections.

▲ **Disable** Attempt a plain-text TCP session first. If that fails, do not attempt any other connections.

These are the basic features required to configure an ODBC session to communicate with a PostgreSQL server. In most applications, this is all you should have to configure. However, for more advanced users, there are two additional configuration buttons available in the configuration window.

These buttons are used to fine-tune the ODBC session parameters by telling the ODBC driver how to handle specific types of data, and whether or not to set up log files to log ODBC connection activity. Each of these additional configuration areas contains default values that work fine for most database situations.

Clicking the Datasource button opens the Advanced Options window, shown in Figure 12-5.

There are two pages of advanced options you can configure. Clicking the Page 2 button goes to the second page of options, and clicking the Page 1 button returns to the first page. Table 12-2 lists the advanced options available, along with a short description of their purpose.

The first group of options, up to the Read Only option, are located on page 1. The remaining options are on page 2. By default, these settings only apply to the specific ODBC session they are defined in. For testing, you can create multiple ODBC sessions pointing to the same database using different configuration settings. The Global button allows you to set the log files to be used for all psqlODBC sessions. This enables logging on all psqlODBC sessions, across all users on the system.

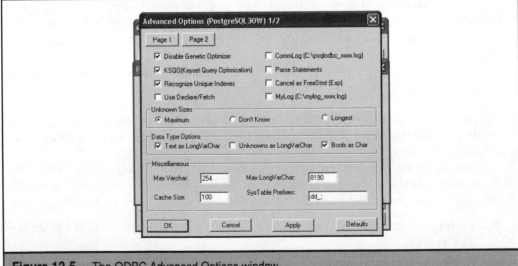

Figure 12-5. The ODBC Advanced Options window

Advanced Option	Description
Disable Genetic Optimizer	Automatically disables the query optimizer in PostgreSQL. This setting is recommended when working with Access.
KSQO	Optimizes Access keyset queries for the PostgreSQL database engine.
Recognize Unique Indexes	Allows Access to ask the user what the table index should be.
Use Declare/Fetch	Forces PostgreSQL to use a cursor to handle all SELECT result sets.
CommLog	Creates a log file (c:\psqlodbc.log) to log all communications between the Access system and the PostgreSQL server.
Parse Statements	Parses all SQL queries to identify columns and gathers statistics used by the execution planner.
Cancel as FreeStmt (Exp)	Canceling a query behaves as a CLOSE SQL command.
MyLog	Creates a log file (c:\mylog.log) to log all events for a specific ODBC session.
Unknown Sizes	Controls the precision used for variable character text strings. Used primarily in older versions of PostgreSQL, and not in version 8.
Data Type Options	Allows you to map specific Access data types to PostgreSQL data types. The Access text data type and any unknown data types (such as arrays) are normally mapped to a PostgreSQL varchar data type. You can instead make these longvarchar data types. The Access bool data type is normally mapped to a SQL_BIT data type. You can choose to make this a char data type to represent T and F values to match Access.
MaxVarchar	Sets the maximum length of the varchar data type. Be careful with this. If you set it higher than 254, Access will not allow you to create an index on a varchar column.
MaxLongVarChar	Sets the maximum length of the longvarchar data type. You can set this value to -4 to allow no limit.
Cache Size	Sets the number of records to allocate memory for, either in a cursor or in a result set.

Table 12-2.   The psqlODBC Advanced Options

Advanced Option	Description
SysTable Prefixes	Defines the prefixes used for system tables. PostgreSQL automatically considers pg_ as a system table prefix. The default value of dd_ is specified for Data Dictionary tables.
Read Only	Sets the ODBC session to only be able to read tables, regardless of the PostgreSQL security settings.
Show System Tables	Defines if PostgreSQL system tables appear in the table listings of the database session. System tables are identified by a prefix defined in SysTablePrefixes.
LF<->CRLF Conversion	Converts Unix linefeeds to Windows carriage return/linefeed combinations. This is set by default, and is required if your data values contain linefeeds.
Updatable Cursors	Enables updating records within a cursor.
bytea as LO	Treats binary string (bytea) data types as large objects (LOs).
Row Versioning	Allows applications to detect if a record has been updated by other users while the application is in the process of updating the record.
Disallow Premature	Compensates for some ODBC applications that use the PREPARE command before submitting a query. The PREPARE feature is not supported by PostgreSQL, and must be compensated for in the ODBC API. This is not required for Access.
True is –1	Some applications (such as Visual Basic) define a Boolean TRUE condition as a -1 numeric value. This is not required for Access.
Server side prepare	Allows the server to prepare an execution plan for queries before they are executed.
Int8 As	Defines how the PostgreSQL int8 data type is converted. The default setting is fine for Access.
OID Options	The Show Column option includes OID values in columns. This feature is not used in Access.
Connect Settings	Allows you to specify SQL commands to execute after the initial connection has been made to the PostgreSQL database. Any result sets returned by the server will be discarded. Multiple commands must be separated by a semicolon.

Table 12-2. The psqlODBC Advanced Options (*Continued*)

CREATING AN ACCESS APPLICATION USING POSTGRESQL

Now that you can connect to your PostgreSQL database using ODBC, you can utilize Access's full complement of query and report generators with your PostgreSQL database. This section walks through an example of connecting to a PostgreSQL database and creating queries and reports used for the application.

Data Type Considerations

The first part of creating any application is to create the database environment. There are a few things to consider when creating a PostgreSQL database that will be used with an Access front end. If you consider all of these things before designing the Access front end, life will be much simpler for you.

The biggest thing to consider when creating the PostgreSQL database is the data types used in tables. The psqlODBC driver has a problem handling some of the PostgreSQL data types. This can cause extremely painful situations for Access programmers.

The list of data types that psqlODBC directly supports is bool, int2, int4, int8, float4, float8, date, time, abstime, datetime, timestamp, char, varchar, and text. All other data types are accommodated by psqlODBC by converting the data into a varchar string. Depending on your specific situation, this can cause some problems.

A common example is the PostgreSQL money data type. In a PostgreSQL application, money data type values are entered as string values, but can be used within expressions as numbers, such as adding two money data values. When using the psqlODBC driver with Access, any columns defined as the money data type are treated as strings. You cannot use them in expressions. This is a big-time gotcha.

The NULL data value is another area of concern. Chapter 8 described the problems with handling NULL operators. This becomes even more complicated when you have two systems that define NULL differently.

As described in Chapter 8, PostgreSQL only considers an empty data value as a NULL value. Unfortunately, Access uses an older definition and considers data values of empty strings as a NULL value as well. This can cause lots of problems when using an existing Access front-end application and a PostgreSQL back-end database. You must take care when checking string data values in tables. If your Access application checks for empty strings by using the IS NULL constraint, you will have to rewrite those queries when migrating to a PostgreSQL database.

There is one additional data type problem that can appear between PostgreSQL and Access databases. The PostgreSQL bool data type may also cause you heartburn. From the ODBC session configuration parameters shown in Table 12-2, you can see there is an option to treat Boolean data types as a character data type. This option exists because Access can treat a Boolean value as the character strings true or false. In Access you can perform expressions such as WHERE TEST = 'true' to evaluate Boolean data values. By default, PostgreSQL only uses the bit values 1 for true and 0 for false. If your application uses the Access text strings for Boolean values, make sure you convert the PostgreSQL table column to a character data type.

Designing an Application Database

With these data type restrictions in mind, you can create a new PostgreSQL database environment for your Access application. It is best to create a new schema for the Access application, then create each existing Access table as a separate table in the new schema. Each query, form, and report designed in the Access application will be changed to point to the new PostgreSQL table.

As an example, I will use an Access application created for a silent auction. Many nonprofit organizations use the silent auction along with dinner parties to help raise money. Items are placed out on tables, and bidders are allowed to roam through the areas examining the items. A bidder places a bid on an item by writing an assigned bidder number along with the bid on a card next to the item. At the end of the evening, items are won by the bidder who wrote down the highest bid value for the item.

This application uses four tables. The Bidder table tracks personal information on each bidder, and assigns a unique bidder number to each bidder. The Donor table tracks information on people and companies who donate items for the auction. The Item table tracks information on the individual items donated, and tracks the winning bid information on the item. Finally, the Payment table tracks payments made by bidders at the end of the evening.

This application environment can be created as a separate schema in the test database used earlier in this book. If you have not created the test database, you can do that from pgAdmin III (see Chapter 4) or by using the CREATE DATABASE SQL command in psql (see Chapter 5). Remember, you must be logged in as the superuser account (postgres by default) to create a new database.

Once the test database is created, you can create the application tables and accounts using SQL commands. Here is the SQL used to create this application environment:

```
create schema auction;
create table auction.bidder (
bidderkey int4 primary key not null,
lastname varchar,
firstname varchar,
address varchar,
city varchar,
state char,
zip char(5),
phone varchar);

create table auction.donor (
donorkey char(6) primary key not null,
name varchar,
address varchar,
city varchar,
state char,
zip char(5),
phone varchar);
```

```
create table auction.item (
itemkey char(6) primary key not null,
description varchar,
donorkey char(6) not null,
resalevalue float4,
finalbid float4,
bidderkey int4,
foreign key (donorkey) references auction.donor,
foreign key (bidderkey) references auction.bidder);

create table auction.payment (
paymentid int4 primary key not null,
bidderkey int4,
amount float4,
foreign key (bidderkey) references auction.bidder);

create role auctioneer with nologin;
create role earl in role auctioneer;
alter role earl login password 'auction' inherit;

grant usage on schema auction to auctioneer;
grant all on auction.bidder to auctioneer;
grant all on auction.donor to auctioneer;
grant all on auction.item to auctioneer;
grant all on auction.payment to auctioneer;
```

To easily execute the SQL, copy the commands into a text file called `auction.sql`. Then you can use the `psql` program to load the commands into the database to create the objects:

```
C:\Program Files\PostgreSQL\8.2\bin>psql -f auction.sql test postgres
```

As `psql` processes the commands, you will see the output messages. This SQL code creates a new schema called `auction`, then the four tables in the `auction` schema (you may need to click the database server name, then click the Refresh button on the top menu bar to see the new items). A sample Login Role to use with the application (called `earl`) is created, along with a sample Group Role (`auctioneer`).

The `auctioneer` Group Role is assigned all privileges to all of the tables created, along with privileges to the schema. In a real application, you would probably have different levels of access, such as a group to control adding new bidders and donors, another group to update item information, and another group to update the Item table with the winning bids and insert bidder payments to the Payment table.

Setting Up the ODBC Session

Now that the database environment is created, you must create the ODBC session to connect to it from Access. Either from the same system that the PostgreSQL server is running

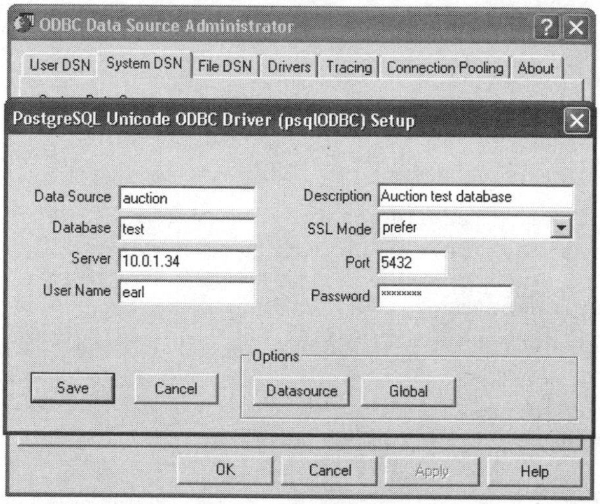

Figure 12-6. ODBC session settings for the example database

on or from a remote client system, start the ODBC Data Source Administrator program. From the ODBC Data Source Administrative window, click the System DSN tab, then click the Add button. From the Create New Data Source window, select either the ANSI or Unicode PostgreSQL driver, then enter the information for your new database in the PostgreSQL (Unicode or ANSI) ODBC Driver Setup dialog box, as shown in Figure 12-6.

Remember to set the SSL Mode settings as required in the pg_hba.conf configuration file of the PostgreSQL server for the client (see Chapter 3). In the Data Source text-box, enter **auction.** This value will be used to reference the auction schema tables in the Microsoft Access programs.

Unfortunately, there is no way to test the ODBC DSN configuration. Fortunately, if you try to connect using the ODBC source and it fails, an fairly detailed error message appears, giving you a good idea what value(s) needs to be changed.

Creating the Access Application

With the ODBC session created, you can now create a new Access application that uses the PostgreSQL database. Start Access and select the option to start a new database. Select a name for the new database project (even though the data tables will be located on the PostgreSQL server, Access must still create a .mdb file to store the queries, forms, and reports created).

Depending on the version of Access you are using, you may be asked if you want to use the wizard application to create the new database. Do not use the wizard application to create the database tables. Instead, choose the option to just create a blank database. You must select a name to call the new database object, such as auction-test.

The blank database does not contain any tables, queries, forms, reports, or macros. The next step is to create new tables that map to the PostgreSQL server tables. This is done by linking tables in Access.

Linking tables allows Access to retrieve table data directly from the remote table without having to actually have the data in the .mdb file on the system. Multiple systems can link to the same data sources. This enables you to have only one copy of the data on the data source and still allow multiple users to accessing the single data copy. Access retrieves the data using standard SQL commands. This greatly reduces network load, because the contents of an entire .mdb data file do not need to be moved across the network.

To create a new linked table, choose File | Get External Data | Link Tables. The Link window appears, pointing you to a default directory. Since this application will link to an ODBC connection instead of to an .mdb file, click the Files of Type drop-down arrow and select ODBC Databases. The Select Data Source window appears. Select the Machine Data Source tab. This shows a list of all the DSNs (both User and System) configured on the system.

The auction data source that was created in the previous step is available. Click that entry, then click OK. This produces the Link Tables window, shown in Figure 12-7.

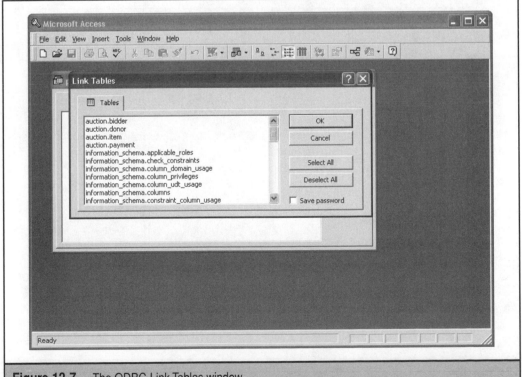

Figure 12-7. The ODBC Link Tables window

If you get an error message at this point, check your ODBC session configuration settings, especially the user and password values. Remember to use the earl Login Role, along with the auction password assigned to the Login Role. It is also important to ensure that your PostgreSQL server's pg_hba.conf file is configured to allow access from the network address of the remote client (see Chapter 3).

If the ODBC session connected to the PostgreSQL server properly, you will see a list of all tables available on the PostgreSQL database. Notice that there are lots of hidden tables in the database that appear in the table list, along with the schema tables you created earlier.

Click the four auction schema tables (you can select more than one table at a time to link to) and then click OK. The four tables (auction.bidder, auction.donor, auction.item, auction.payment) now appear in the Access tables list, as shown in Figure 12-8.

You can now treat these tables as any other Access tables. Double-clicking a table produces the Access Datasheet view, allowing you to easily enter new data into the table. You can also use the Access graphical Design View mode to view the properties of the table columns, although you will not be able to alter any of these properties.

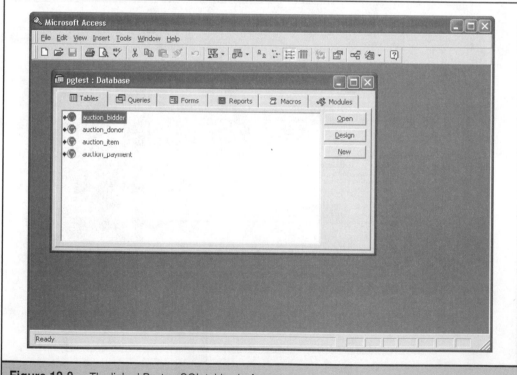

Figure 12-8.   The linked PostgreSQL tables in Access

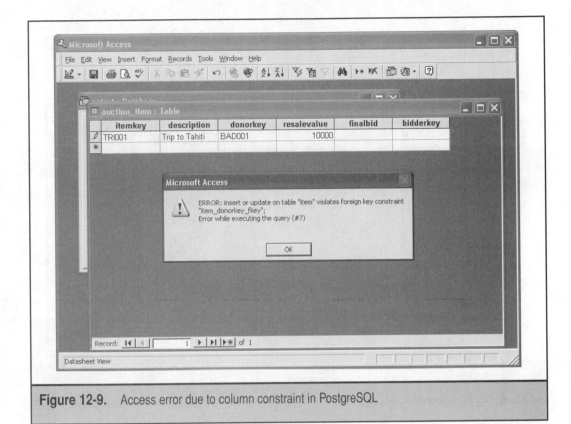

Figure 12-9.   Access error due to column constraint in PostgreSQL

Use the Access Datasheet view to add some sample data to your tables. Create a few sample bidders, one or two donors, then a few sample items to track. As you enter data, notice that all of the constraints defined in the tables apply to the Access Datasheet view. If you try adding an item with an invalid `donorkey` value, you get an error for the unmatched foreign key value, shown in Figure 12-9.

The errors returned by the ODBC driver are very descriptive, allowing you to easily identify problems.

After you have entered some sample data to work with, you are ready to create queries, forms, and reports in Access using the data tables from the PostgreSQL server. If you are familiar with how to use the Access environment, this should be a snap. All of the programming functions and features in Access behave exactly the same when using the linked PostgreSQL tables.

As an example, click the Reports tab, then click the New button to create a new report. Select the Design View mode to create the new report. In the Choose the Table or Query Where the Object's Data Comes From drop-down box, select the `auction_bidder` table created from the link to the PostgreSQL `auction.bidder` table. A blank report appears in the Design View window, linked to the `bidder` table.

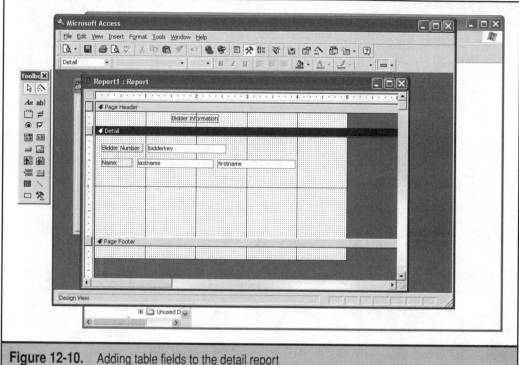

Figure 12-10.   Adding table fields to the detail report

In the new report, you can now add `bidder` table fields within the Detail section of the report. Select a textbox control and drag it into the Detail report area. Double-click the new textbox to produce the properties for the control. In the Properties window, the Control Source parameter contains all of the columns (fields) of the table. You can select any of the columns to include in the report, shown in Figure 12-10.

After adding the desired fields to the report, save the report and run it. The resulting report shows the data retrieved from the bidder table on the PostgreSQL server, shown in Figure 12-11.

Besides the standard arsenal of Access programming tools, you now can utilize PostgreSQL tools to help simplify your Access application. You now have triggers, functions, and views available for your PostgreSQL tables. You can use these features to help simplify and speed up your database applications.

Using PostgreSQL Views in Access

In Access, the only way to combine table columns for reports is to create queries. Unfortunately, the queries must now extract data across the network connection with the PostgreSQL server, causing additional delay. Now, however, you have the complete power

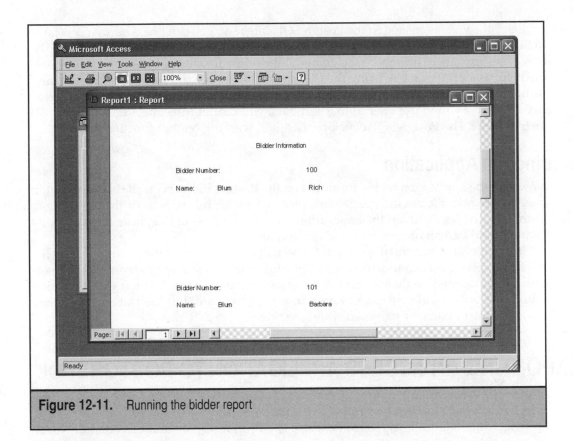

Figure 12-11.   Running the bidder report

of the PostgreSQL database at your disposal. Instead of using the old Access queries, you can create a PostgreSQL view that replicates the query by combining columns of multiple tables.

The difference is that once a view is created in the PostgreSQL database, it is available along with the regular tables as an external link. When the view is accessed by users, the query is processed internally on the PostgreSQL server, and only the result set data is returned. This greatly reduces the network overhead, and reduces the time required to process the query.

As an example, create the view `itemswon` in the `auction` schema:

```
create view auction.itemswon as
select item.itemkey, bidder.lastname, bidder.firstname, item.finalbid
from auction.item natural inner join auction.bidder;

grant all on auction.itemswon to auctioneer;
```

This view produces a result set that contains only the items that had successful winning bidders, and lists the names of the bidders instead of the bidder number.

Once the view is created in the PostgreSQL database, you can link a new Access table to the view by using the Get External Data feature described in the previous section. The new view appears in the table list along with the other database tables. You can now use the view as a regular table, using the Datasheet view to see the values in the view, and using the view in reports similar to the original query. The one drawback is that, whereas Access allows you to use queries to insert data, you cannot insert new data into a PostgreSQL view. The PostgreSQL developers are still working on that functionality.

Sharing the Application

Now that the application tables are stored on the PostgreSQL server, all that is shared in the Access `.mdb` file are the specialized queries, forms, and reports for the application. Each user that needs to run the application must have access to this file, either as a copy on their local system or from a shared network drive.

It is important to remember that the PostgreSQL tables are defined in the `.mdb` file as ODBC sessions. Each user that runs the application must have the same ODBC session names defined on their system. Each individual user can have their ODBC session configured with a different Login Role name and password, but the Data Source name assigned must match the one used when creating the `.mdb` file.

EXPORTING AN ACCESS APPLICATION TO POSTGRESQL

In many cases, if you are migrating from Access to PostgreSQL, you will already have existing Access database tables full of live data.

Migrating data from an Access database to a PostgreSQL database is often the hardest part of the application migration. There are many things that can go wrong in this process. You must take data type differences into consideration, as well as maintain table relationships, such as foreign keys, triggers, and indexes.

There are several commercial utilities available that automatically migrate data from Access tables to PostgreSQL tables. There are also a few free solutions available. In each case, you must take extreme care when working with live data so that no data loss occurs.

Of course, you can always perform the migration manually, by creating the tables in PostgreSQL and then exporting data from the Access database to the new PostgreSQL tables. The easiest solution is to export Access data as a CSV comma-delineated file. In a CSV file, a comma separates each record's column data. The CSV file can be imported into the PostgreSQL table using the `\copy psql` meta-command (described in Chapter 5).

To test this process, create an Access table using the same column data types as the `bidder` table created earlier. The table properties are shown in Figure 12-12.

After creating the table, enter some sample data. For this test, make sure you do not use any bidder numbers that duplicate what might already be in your PostgreSQL `bidder` table, or they will not copy over properly.

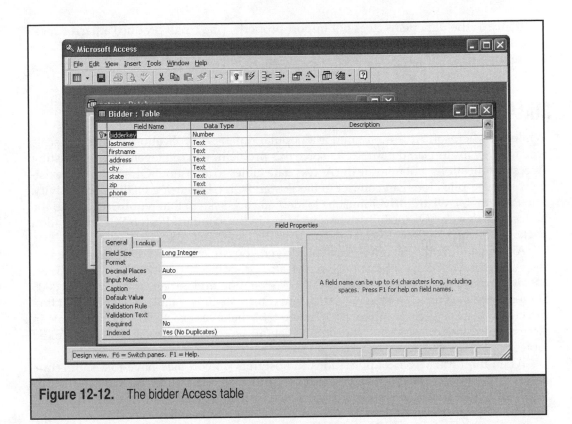

Figure 12-12.   The bidder Access table

After you have some sample data in the Access table, you can test exporting it to a PostgreSQL table. Right-click the Access table and select Save As/Export. In the Save As dialog box, select To an External File or Database, then click OK. Another dialog box appears, asking you for the filename and file type to save the data as. In the Save as Type textbox, select Text Files, choose a location and a filename, and click the Export button.

The Export Text Wizard dialog box then guides you through creating an export file of the table data. In the first wizard window, select that you want a delimited text file, then click Next. In the second wizard window, select the delimiter character you want to use. Remember, you should choose a delimiter character that is not present in any of the text data in the table. Also, select the Text Qualifier character in the drop-down box. In most cases, you can set this to **none,** as the \copy meta-command does not require text qualifiers. When done, click the Finish button to start the export.

After creating the export text file, you can copy it to the PostgreSQL server and use the \copy meta-command in psql to import the data into the new table:

```
test=> \copy auction.bidder from Bidder.txt using delimiters ','
\.
test=>
```

If any of the data items does not import properly, `psql` will produce an error message saying which line it is located in. Also, since the `\copy` command is treated as a single transaction, if any of the lines fails, the entire import will fail.

SUMMARY

While the Microsoft Access program is a popular database application, it does not scale well to large multi-user databases. To solve this problem, you can leverage your existing Access applications, but migrate the Access data tables to a PostgreSQL server. The existing Access applications can connect to the PostgreSQL tables using ODBC connectivity. The PostgreSQL ODBC driver must be loaded on each system that requires access to the tables. The PostgreSQL ODBC driver is included in the standard PostgreSQL installation package, or you can download it separately in the psqlODBC package.

After installing the PostgreSQL ODBC driver, you can create an ODBC session using the Windows ODBC Data Source Administrator program that is included in Windows XP Home and Professional, Windows 2000 Workstation and Server, and Windows 2003 Server. Once the ODBC session is created, you can create linked tables in Access that link directly to the PostgreSQL tables. Each linked table behaves exactly as a normal table in Access. Access queries, forms, and reports can all be used as normal using the linked tables.

When migrating Access applications to PostgreSQL, you may have to also migrate data. You can use the standard Access export feature to export table data to a text file. After creating the duplicate table in PostgreSQL, use the `\copy` meta-command included in `psql` to import the text data file into the new PostgreSQL table.

The next chapter describes how to access a PostgreSQL database from your Microsoft .NET applications. The .NET platform is the latest programming environment introduced by Microsoft. PostgreSQL includes a library that can be used by .NET applications to directly access a PostgreSQL database across a network.

CHAPTER 13

Microsoft .NET Framework

The Microsoft .NET Framework is the preferred programming environment for Microsoft Windows platforms. Microsoft has developed the .NET platform to allow multiple programming languages to interface using the same library files and development environment. PostgreSQL also provides a development library for .NET programmers. You can create .NET programs in Visual Basic .NET, C#, and Visual C++ that can communicate with a PostgreSQL server. This chapter describes the .NET programming environment and shows how to use the PostgreSQL .NET library to create Windows programs that interface with your PostgreSQL server.

THE MICROSOFT .NET FRAMEWORK

In its relatively short history, the Microsoft .NET technology has quickly become a popular programming platform for developing applications for Microsoft Windows workstations and servers. Although most of the media attention has focused around the web capabilities of .NET, there are many other features that are useful to Windows programmers.

The .NET technology includes an application development environment for creating applications for use in any type of Windows environment: command-prompt applications, Windows Forms applications, and web-based ASP.NET web applications and web services. The new Microsoft .NET development environment supports creating applications for each of these environments using different programming languages.

The popular Visual Basic .NET language incorporates .NET technology into the old Microsoft Visual Basic language that was the favorite of hobbyists and professional programmers alike. The new C# programming language incorporates advanced object-oriented programming techniques similar to Java, while incorporating the .NET technology libraries. And finally, the Visual C++ programming language uses the industry-standard C++ programming language along with .NET technology to create full-featured Windows and web applications.

The core of the .NET technology is the Common Language Runtime (CLR) environment. This environment enables programmers to create programs using a multitude of programming languages, and run them on any platform that supports the CLR. The idea of the CLR is to provide a middle layer of application programming interfaces (APIs) that operate between the low-level Windows operating system Win32 API functions and the application code. The layout of how application programs run in the CLR environment is shown in Figure 13-1.

High-level applications written in various .NET languages, such as Visual Basic .NET, Visual C++, and C#, are compiled into a special intermediate language called Microsoft Intermediate Language (MSIL). The MSIL code is interpreted by the CLR as the program runs, similar to how Java works. Any platform that supports the CLR can run application programs compiled into MSIL format. Of course, legacy programs that do not use the CLR can still run on Windows platforms and directly access the low-level Windows Win32 APIs as before.

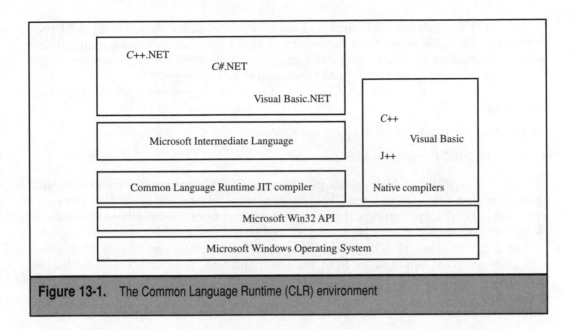

Figure 13-1.   The Common Language Runtime (CLR) environment

PostgreSQL includes a development library to support the .NET development environment. The Npgsql library provides the necessary APIs to allow a Visual Basic .NET, C#, or Visual C++ program to communicate with a PostgreSQL server using standard classes. These classes provide the necessary methods, properties, and data types for interfacing with a PostgreSQL server, and inserting, updating, deleting, and querying data within tables.

CREATING A .NET DEVELOPMENT ENVIRONMENT

Before you can start programming in a .NET language, you must have a .NET development environment. Microsoft offers two development environments for .NET programming:

▼   The Visual Studio .NET suite

▲   The .NET Framework Software Development Kit (SDK)

The Visual Studio .NET suite is the flagship development environment for Microsoft. This integrated development environment (IDE) offers many advanced features to assist your Windows application programming tasks. Microsoft describes the Visual Studio package as "a rapid application development (RAD) tool, enabling programmers to quickly code and debug .NET applications." It includes a complete graphical environment for creating Windows forms, console applications, and web applications, as well as providing a complete debugging environment for programmers.

The .NET Framework SDK offers an inexpensive way to get started with .NET programming. The SDK is available for free from Microsoft, and contains command-line tools for compiling and debugging .NET programs. This application allows you to get the feel for .NET programming without investing in an expensive IDE.

There are two components that make up the .NET Framework SDK development environment:

▼ The .NET redistributable package

▲ The .NET Framework SDK package

The .NET redistributable package provides the CLR libraries necessary to run .NET applications on a Windows system. This package must be installed on all Windows systems that run .NET applications. If you provide your application for other workstations to use, they must each have at least the .NET redistributable package installed.

The .NET Framework SDK package contains the compilers and library files necessary to create .NET applications from the command line. The .NET Framework SDK contains the Visual Basic .NET and C# compilers. This provides a single development environment for using the .NET programming language of your choice! This package needs to be installed only on the systems you use to develop your applications.

Downloading the .NET Packages

Both the .NET redistributable package and the .NET Framework SDK package can be downloaded for free from the Microsoft web site, or you can purchase a DVD at minimal cost from Microsoft. The .NET Framework SDK is a very large package (over 360MB), so I would not attempt the download unless you have access to a high-speed Internet connection.

The .NET Framework web site URL is currently www.microsoft.com/netframework/. This site contains lots of information about the SDK, including a link to a separate download section. Clicking the Downloads link takes you to the Downloads area. From there, click the SDKs, Redistributables, and Service Packs link. The latest versions (currently 2.0) of the redistributable and Framework SDK packages are available for three processor types. Download the appropriate package for your system processor (such as the x86 version for 32-bit Intel and Intel-compatible systems).

The .NET redistributable package downloads to a file called `dotnetfx.exe`, while the .NET Framework SDK downloads to a file called `setup.exe`. The next section describes how to install these packages.

Installing the .NET Packages

To start, you must install the .NET redistributable package first. To install the .NET redistributable package component, double-click the `dotnetfx.exe` file. The package is a compressed file that is automatically extracted into a temporary directory. After the installation files are extracted, the installation program greets you with a welcome screen. Click Next to go through the installation. When the installation is complete, click Finish.

You start the .NET Framework SDK package by double-clicking the `setup.exe` file. Similar to the redistributable package, the Framework SDK package is a compressed file that is automatically extracted into a temporary directory for installation. After the usual introduction and license windows, the Framework SDK installation options are displayed, shown in Figure 13-2.

The Framework SDK installation package contains three options:

▼ **QuickStart Samples**   Installs lots of Visual Basic .NET and C# program examples to help you learn and understand .NET programming

■ **Tools and Debugger**   Installs the compilers, library files, and debugging tools necessary for developing .NET programs

▲ **Product Documentation**   Installs HTML documentation for each of the .NET namespaces, as well as general information about the .NET platform

Select the options you want to install, then click Next. The next window asks for the location to install the Framework SDK. All of the library and executable files are stored in default directories on the system. You can, however, change the location where the product documentation and sample programs are stored.

After you select the installation location, the installation starts. The Framework SDK installation takes a long time to install, even on super-fast systems. When the installation

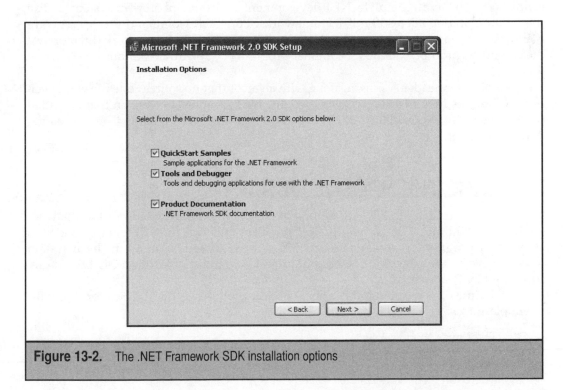

Figure 13-2.   The .NET Framework SDK installation options

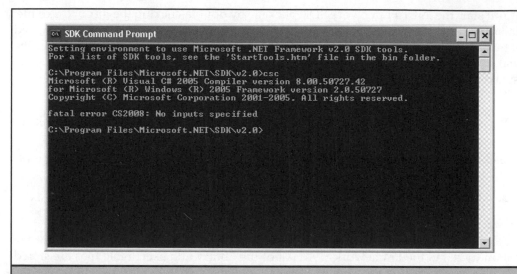

Figure 13-3.   Running the csc compiler from a command prompt

is finished, you have a complete .NET development environment on your system. To test this, choose Start | Microsoft .NET Framework v2.0 | SDK Command Prompt. A command prompt window opens, using the default location of the Framework directory. At the command prompt, run the C# compiler program (csc) with no options, as shown in Figure 13-3.

The compiler header is shown, along with an error that no source code file was specified to compile. In the header, you can see the .NET Framework version that is loaded (in this example, version 2.0.50727). If you get this result, you are ready to start creating .NET applications.

INTEGRATING THE NPGSQL LIBRARY

Now that you have a full .NET development environment, it is time to install the PostgreSQL .NET library. The Npgsql project provides a complete .NET data provider to allow .NET programs to access a PostgreSQL server running either on the local system or elsewhere on the network. The Npgsql project is not part of PostgreSQL, but is fully supported by PostgreSQL.

At the time of this writing, the Npgsql project provides .NET libraries for three different platforms:

▼   The Linux Mono project

■   Microsoft .NET version 1.1

▲   Microsoft .NET version 2.0

The Linux Mono project provides a development environment for creating and running .NET applications on Linux systems. This is the first attempt at cross-platform development using the .NET technology. While not 100 percent compatible with the Microsoft .NET environment, great strides have been made in Mono to make most .NET applications work seamlessly on a Linux system.

Npgsql supports two different Microsoft .NET platforms. The original .NET version 1.0 platform has been officially deprecated by Microsoft, and is not recommended for new development work. Customers who are using the .NET version 1.0 platform are recommended to upgrade to version 1.1. Recently, Microsoft has released the updated .NET version 2.0 platform. This platform contains a new CLR environment that supports many new features. It is recommended for all new .NET development to utilize this platform.

Downloading Npgsql

The Npgsql library download can be found from the PostgreSQL main web site (www .postgresql.org). From the main web page, click the Downloads link. On the Downloads page, click the FTP Browser link to go to the list of available downloads.

On the FTP Browser page, click the `projects` folder link, then click the `pgFoundry` folder link. This is the repository for projects that are not officially part of the PostgreSQL package, but are obviously related to PostgreSQL. In the `pgFoundry` area, click the `npgsql` folder link.

The `npgsql` folder contains all of the available Npgsql library formats currently supported. The filename for each package includes the npgsql version along with the package format. The Npgsql library can be download both as a source code package that must be compiled and as a binary distribution that is precompiled to run on a specific platform. Source code packages are identified by the filename tag `src`. Binary distribution packages use the filename tag `bin`, along with the platform they are compiled for.

For the Microsoft .NET platform, it is by far the easiest to download the binary distribution package. Look for the latest version available, and download the binary distribution for the .NET platform you have installed. For example, to download the binary Npgsql library for the .NET version 2.0 platform, get the following file:

```
Npgsql1.0-bin-ms2.0.zip
```

At the time of this writing the official 1.0 version of Npgsql had just been released. By the time you read this, there may be updates that have been released to fix any bugs or security issues. Please use the latest version available for download. After downloading the binary distribution package, you must use a zip program to unzip the contents into a directory. Windows XP Home and Professional, as well as Windows 2003 Server, can automatically detect and handle `.zip` files. For Windows 2000 workstations and servers, you must install a third-party `.zip` file handler.

Installing the Npgsql Library

Once you have downloaded the Npgsql binary package and extracted the files, you can install the library file in your .NET development environment. The entire Npgsql library is included in a single file: npgsql.dll. This file is located under the bin folder of the Npgsql installation package, in a folder named for the platform it was compiled for (such as ms1.1 or ms2.0).

There is also a second .dll file that is included with the Npgsql package. The Mono.Security.dll file contains the signed certificates used to validate the Npgsql library file for .NET.

For .NET applications to be able to use the Npgsql library, they must know where to find both the npgsql.dll and Mono.Security.dll files on the system. There are two options for accomplishing this.

The first option is to include the npgsql.dll and Mono.Security.dll files in the same directory as your .NET application code. By default, .NET applications check the local directory of the application for any required library files. If you include the npgsql.dll and Mono.Security.dll files with your application, just place them in the same directory as your application executable files and all will be fine.

Alternatively, you can add the npgsql.dll and Mono.Security.dll files to the standard .NET library on the system the application runs on. The CLR maintains a cache of available library files that is automatically searched whenever the CLR cannot find a library. This is called the *Global Assembly Cache (GAC)*.

Adding libraries to the GAC is done using the .NET Global Assembly Cache utility tool, gacutil. This tool is part of the .NET redistributable package, so it is available on every system that has the .NET platform installed.

To install the libraries into the GAC using the gacutil tool, go to the directory where you extracted the files, and use gacutil with the /i option:

```
C:\>gacutil /i npgsql.dll

Microsoft (R) .NET Global Assembly Cache Utility.  Version 2.0.50727.42
Copyright (C) Microsoft Corporation 1998-2002. All rights reserved.

Assembly successfully added to the cache

C:\>
```

Do the same for the Mono.Security.dll file included in the Npgsql binary distribution package. You are now ready to run a .NET PostgreSQL application.

Creating .NET Applications with Npgsql

The Npgsql library works with both the Visual Studio and the command-prompt compilers. However, when compiling programs, the library must be included in the library path of the compiler. In Visual Studio, this is done by adding the npgsql.dll file to the library list in Visual Studio. Every time you compile an application, the Npgsql library is automatically included. When using the command-prompt compilers, though, you must use the /r option to directly reference the npgsql.dll file in the compiler command each time you compile a program.

The format for compiling a C# application is

```
csc /r:npgsql.dll program.cs
```

This command adds the npgsql.dll library file as a resource for the compiler. The npgsql.dll file must be in a directory contained in the PATH environment variable of the current command-prompt session, or it must be in the same directory where the program source code file is located. To add the directory to the PATH environment variable, right-click My Computer, select Properties, click the Advanced tab, and then click the Environment Variables button, which takes you to the Environment Variable editor, where you can modify the PATH setting.

For a Visual Basic .NET program, you must use the /r option to reference the npgsql.dll file, and also reference the System.Data.dll file, which is standard in the .NET Framework SDK:

```
vbc /r:npgsql.dll /r:System.Data.dll program.vb
```

Again, the npgsql.dll file must be located in either the same directory as the source code file or in a directory listed within the PATH environment variable. The System.Data.dll file is already located in the standard .NET library directory.

Besides referencing the Npgsql library file in the compiler command, you must also include the Npgsql and System.Data namespaces in the Visual Basic .NET or C# programs that use the Npgsql library. By including the namespaces, you can directly reference any of the classes contained in the namespaces. In a C# program, this is done with the using statement at the start of a program:

```
using System.Data;
using Npgsql;
```

Now you can reference any class in the Npgsql namespace within the C# program. In a Visual Basic .NET program, this is done with the Imports statement:

```
Imports System.Data
Imports Npgsql
```

The next section walks through the classes included in the Npgsql library, and shows how to use them in both C# and Visual Basic .NET programs.

THE NPGSQL LIBRARY

The Npgsql library contains the classes necessary for establishing a connection with a PostgreSQL server, querying tables and views, inserting, updating, and deleting records, and performing transactions. Table 13-1 lists and describes the classes provided by the Npgsql library.

Class	Description
NpgsqlCommand	Contains a SQL statement or function to be executed on a PostgreSQL database
NpgsqlCommandBuilder	Builds commands for automatically inserting, updating, and deleting table records
NpgsqlConnection	Creates a connection to a PostgreSQL server
NpgsqlDataAdapter	Contains record data for SELECT, INSERT, UPDATE, and DELETE SQL commands
NpgsqlDataReader	Reads a result set from a query and makes the data values available
NpgsqlError	Contains error and notice messages returned by the PostgreSQL server
NpgsqlEventLog	Handles Npgsql event and debug logging
NpgsqlException	The exception that is thrown if an Npgsql error event occurs
NpgsqlNoticeEventArgs	Notice events for less important errors
NpgsqlNotificationEventArgs	Parameters for notification events
NpgsqlParameter	Contains parameters used for Npgsql commands
NpgsqlParameterCollection	A collection of parameters used in Npgsql commands and mappings to columns in a dataset
NpgsqlTransaction	Contains a set of SQL commands that are bundled into a complete transaction for the database
ServerVersion	Contains the version of the PostgreSQL server

Table 13-1.   Npgsql Classes

The classes contain members and properties that are used to interact with the PostgreSQL server to help you perform standard SQL commands and functions in your application code. The following sections describe these classes in more detail.

The NpgsqlConnection Class

The most basic operation provided by Npgsql is to allow your .NET program to connect with either a local or a remote PostgreSQL server. This is accomplished with the NpgsqlConnection class. The format for the NpgsqlConnection class constructor is

```
NpgsqlConnection(connectionstring)
```

The *connectionstring* parameter sets the values used to define the PostgreSQL server connection. This is stored in the ConnectionString property of the class. The ConnectionString property is a text string that can be built using standard string techniques. The ConnectionString property uses identifiers and values to define the connection properties. The identifiers and values are defined in the string using the following format:

```
ident1=value1;ident2=value2;ident3=value3...
```

Each identifier/value pair is separated by a semicolon. The identifiers used in the ConnectionString property are listed and described in Table 13-2.

Identifier	Description
Server	The hostname or IP address of the PostgreSQL server.
Port	The TCP port of the PostgreSQL server.
Protocol	The protocol to use if not automatic. May be 2 for pre-version 7.3 PostgreSQL servers or 3 for version 7.3 or later servers.
Database	The name of the database to connect to. The default is the username.
User Id	The Login Role to connect to the server as.
Password	The plain-text password for the Login Role specified.
SSL	Determines whether to use SSL (True or False), similar to Sslmode. The default is False.
Pooling	Controls connection pooling (True or False). The default is False.
MinPoolSize	Sets the minimum size of the connection pool when using pooling.
MaxPoolSize	Sets the maximum size of the connection pool when using pooling.
Encoding	Sets the encoding to use for the connection (ASCII or UNICODE). The default is ASCII.
Timeout	Sets the time to wait for the connection to open (in seconds). The default is 15 seconds.
CommandTimeout	Sets the time to wait for a command to finish executing (in seconds). The default is 20 seconds.
Sslmode	Sets the mode for the SSL connection (Prefer, Require, Allow, or Disable). The default is Disable.
ConnectionLifeTime	Sets the time to wait before closing unused connections if a connection pool is used (in seconds). The default is 15 seconds.
SyncNotification	Specifies whether Npgsql should use synchronous notifications.

Table 13-2. NpgsqlConnection ConnectionString Values

A typical `ConnectionString` string looks like this:

```
Server=127.0.0.1;Port=5432;User Id=earl;Password=auction;Database=test
```

The identifiers and values define the typical connection parameters used to connect to a PostgreSQL server database, using a specific Login Role. Remember, the PostgreSQL server must be configured to accept connections, and the `pg_hba.conf` configuration file must be configured to allow the specific Login Role to connect to the specified database (see Chapter 3).

After an `NpgsqlConnection` class instance is created, there are two class methods that are used to control the connection. The `Open()` class method is used to start a session with the PostgreSQL server. If the connection fails, the `Open()` method throws an `NpgsqlException` exception. This should be caught within a try-catch block and handled accordingly. If the exception is not caught by the program, the CLR will abort the application and produce an error message to the user—not exactly user-friendly.

When you are finished with the PostgreSQL session, use the `Close()` class method to stop the session. This disconnects from the PostgreSQL server and closes all of your session objects. Likewise, if the `Close()` method fails, it throws an `NpgsqlException` exception.

There are a few `NpgsqlConnection` class properties that come in handy after the connection is established:

▼ `ServerVersion`   Contains information on the PostgreSQL server version

■ `State`   Contains information on the state of the connection (`Opened` or `Closed`)

▲ `BackendProtocolVersion`   Contains information on the PostgreSQL protocol version used by the PostgreSQL server

An example of creating a new connection to a PostgreSQL server using the C# programming language is demonstrated in the `version.cs` program:

```csharp
using System;
using System.Data;
using Npgsql;

public class Version
{
    public static void Main(String[] args)
    {
        String connstring = "Server=127.0.0.1;Port=5432;SSL=True;";
        connstring = connstring + "User ID=earl;Password=auction;Database=test;";
        NpgsqlConnection conn = new NpgsqlConnection(connstring);
        try
```

```
    {
        conn.Open();
        ServerVersion sv = conn.ServerVersion;
        String vers = sv.ToString();
        Console.WriteLine("Connected to server, version: {0}", vers);
    } catch( NpgsqlException e)
    {
        Console.WriteLine("problem connecting to server: {0}", e.Message);
    } finally
    {
        conn.Close();
    }
  }
}
```

As you can see from the version.cs program, the ConnectionString property for the NpgsqlConnection object can be built as any type of String value, including a String that has been created from several pieces. Remember to include a semicolon between each value in the ConnectionString. This code example establishes a connection to the PostgreSQL server running on the local system (using the loopback network address 127.0.0.1), logging into the test database using the earl Login Role created in Chapter 12. You may have to change some of these values if your PostgreSQL environment is different. The ConnectionString value is long, so to split it up I built the string from two parts.

The NpgsqlConnection instance is created using the ConnectionString parameter. This does not need to be placed within a try-catch block, as the connection is not attempted until the Open() method is called.

Within the try-catch block section, after opening the connection using the Open() method, the program uses the ServerVersion property of the connection to retrieve the version of the PostgreSQL server. The ServerVersion property uses the Server-Version class to hold the version value.

This class contains a ToString() method that converts the version to a simple string value that can be displayed. You can also extract the individual major, minor, and patch values of the version as integer values for comparison. After displaying the version, the program uses the Close() method to stop the PostgreSQL session.

The try-catch block catches any NpgsqlException exceptions that are thrown by the methods, and displays the error message to the user. It is always a good idea to catch exceptions rather than letting the .NET CLR produce its own ugly error messages and abruptly terminate the program.

To compile the version.cs program from the command prompt, type

```
csc /r:npgsql.dll version.cs
```

Make sure that the version.cs and npgsql.dll files are available for the compiler. The resulting executable program, version.exe, can be run on any workstation that has the .NET redistributable package installed (of course, if it connects to a remote PostgreSQL server, you must use the correct server hostname or IP address in the

ConnectionString parameter). Here is an example of what you should see when running the program:

```
C:\>version
Connected to server, version: 8.2.0

C:\>
```

If the connection fails, an NpgsqlException exception is thrown, which the program catches and displays:

```
C:\>version
problem connecting to server: FATAL: 28000: password authentication
failed for
 user "earl"

C:\>
```

The NpgsqlCommand Class

The NpgsqlCommand class is used for creating SQL command strings that are sent to the PostgreSQL server. Each NpgsqlCommand instance contains a single SQL command.

Table 13-3 lists and describes the class properties available for the NpgsqlCommand class.

Property	Description
CommandText	Gets or sets the SQL command or function to execute on the PostgreSQL server
CommandTimeout	Gets or sets the time to wait (in seconds) for a command to complete
CommandType	Gets or sets the format of the CommandText property (either Text, the default, or StoredProcedure)
Connection	Gets or sets the NpgsqlConnection instance used by the command instance
LastInsertedIOD	Returns the OID of the last inserted row
Parameters	Gets the NpgsqlParametersCollection instance used for the command
Transaction	Gets or sets the NpgsqlTransaction instance within which the command executes

Table 13-3.   The NpgsqlCommand Properties

The constructor for an `NpgsqlCommand` instance can define the `CommandText` and `Connection` properties:

```
NpgsqlCommand(CommandText, Connection)
```

The SQL command is entered into the `CommandText` property of the `NpgsqlCommand` class instance. By default, the `CommandText` property is a text SQL command. You can also specify a stored procedure by setting the `CommandType` property to `Stored-Procedure`.

The `Connection` property contains an `NpgsqlConnection` instance that may or may not be already opened using the `Open()` method. These properties can also be set separately after an instance of the `NpgsqlCommand` class is created:

```
NpgsqlConnection conn = new NpgsqlConnection(connstring);
NpgsqlCommand command = new NplgsqlCommand();
command.Connection = conn;
command.CommandText = "DELETE from auction.bidder WHERE bidderid = 100";
```

After the `NpgsqlCommand` object is created, there are several methods that can be used to handle the command, listed and described in Table 13-4.

As you can see from Table 13-4, there are three different methods used to execute commands stored in an `NpgsqlCommand` object. The proper method to use depends on the expected results from the stored SQL command:

▼ SQL commands that do not return a value

■ SQL commands that return a single value

▲ SQL commands that return a result set

The following sections describe each of these methods.

Method	Description
Cancel	Attempts to cancel the execution of a command
Clone	Creates a new command based on this one
ExecuteNonQuery	Executes a SQL command that does not return a value
ExecuteReader	Executes a SQL command that returns a result set
ExecuteScalar	Executes a SQL command that returns a single value
Prepare	Sends the command to the PostgreSQL server before execution so it can be prepared by the server

Table 13-4.   The NpgsqlCommand Methods

The ExecuteNonQuery() Method

The `ExecuteNonQuery()` method does what it says, it allows you to send a nonquery SQL command to the server. This includes `INSERT`, `UPDATE`, and `DELETE` SQL commands. These commands do not return any data values, but do return a status value indicating the number of records affected by the SQL command. This status value is returned by the `ExecuteNonQuery()` method as an integer value, and can be captured by the program.

After the `NpgsqlConnection` and `NpgsqlCommand` objects are created, the `ExecuteNonQuery()` method sends the SQL command to the PostgreSQL server for processing. The resulting status of the SQL command is returned by the PostgreSQL server, and the `ExecuteNonQuery()` method returns an integer value of the number of records affected by the command:

```
int32 records;
records = comm.ExecuteNonQuery();
Console.WriteLine("Deleted {0} records", records);
```

If anything goes wrong with the SQL command on the PostgreSQL server, an `NpgsqlException` exception is thrown by the method, which can be caught in a try-catch section.

The `update.vb` program demonstrates using the `ExecuteNonQuery()` method to add a record to the Bidder table:

```
Imports System
Imports System.Data
Imports Npgsql

Public Class Update
   Public Shared Sub Main()

      Dim conn As NpgsqlConnection
      Dim comm as NpgsqlCommand
      Dim result as Integer
      Dim connstring as String
      Dim comstring as String

      connstring = "Server=127.0.0.1;Port=5432;SSL=True;User Id=earl;"
      connstring = connstring & "Password=auction;Database=test;"
      conn = New NpgsqlConnection(connstring)

      comm = New NpgsqlCommand()
      comm.Connection = conn
      comstring = "INSERT INTO auction.bidder values (150, 'Test', 'Ima',"
      comstring = comstring & "'329 State St.', 'Dyer', 'IN',"
      comstring = comstring & " '46602', '555-202')"
      comm.CommandText = comstring
```

```
        Try
            conn.Open()
            result = comm.ExecuteNonQuery()
            Console.WriteLine("Inserted {0} records", result)
        Catch e as NpgsqlException
            Console.WriteLine("Problem: {0}", e.Message)
        Finally
            conn.Close()
        End Try
    End Sub
End Class
```

The update.vb program declares the necessary variables using the Dim statement, then creates a connection to the local PostgreSQL server using the earl Login Role from Chapter 12. The CommandText string is built on three separate lines by concatenating a string value. You can also place the command string directly in the CommandText property of the NpgsqlCommand constructor.

The SQL command is not executed until the ExecuteNonQuery() method is executed in the program. This is done in a try-catch block to catch any possible errors without blowing up the program. The ExecuteNonQuery() method returns the number of records affected by the command. This value is displayed on the screen to verify that the INSERT command worked.

Compiling and running the example should look like this:

```
C:\>vbc /r:npgsql.dll /r:System.Data.dll update.vb
Microsoft (R) Visual Basic Compiler version 8.0.50727.42
for Microsoft (R) .NET Framework version 2.0.50727.42
Copyright (c) Microsoft Corporation.  All rights reserved.

C:\>update
Inserted 1 records

C:\>
```

The compile finished successfully, and the program indicated that the record was added with no problems. You can use pgAdmin III or psql to view the Bidder table to see if the record was indeed added. You can also try to run the update program again and see what happens:

```
C:\>update
Problem: ERROR: 23505: duplicate key violates unique constraint "bidder_pkey"

C:\>
```

This time an NpgsqlException exception was thrown. The exception indicates that the new record could not be added because it would violate the primary key constraint, which is what you would expect when trying to insert the same record again.

The ExecuteScalar() Method

The ExecuteScalar() method is used to execute a command that you know will return a single value, such as the output of a built-in function or stored procedure.

Since the SQL command executed can return any type of data type, the ExecuteScalar() method returns a generic object data type, which must be typecast into the expected data type. The getvals.cs program demonstrates using the ExecuteScalar() method in a C# application:

```
using System;
using System.Data;
using Npgsql;

public class GetVals
{
    public static void Main(String[] args)
    {
        String connstring = "Server=127.0.0.1;Port=5432;SSL=True;";
        connstring = connstring + "User ID=earl;Password=auction;Database=test;";
        NpgsqlConnection conn = new NpgsqlConnection(connstring);
        NpgsqlCommand comm = new NpgsqlCommand();

        comm.Connection = conn;
        comm.CommandText = "Select timeofday();";

        try
        {
            conn.Open();
            String servertime = (String)comm.ExecuteScalar();
            Console.WriteLine("The time on the server is: {0}", servertime);

            comm.CommandText = "Select pi();";
            Double result = (Double)comm.ExecuteScalar();
            Console.WriteLine("The value of pi on the server is: {0}", result);
        } catch( NpgsqlException e)
        {
            Console.WriteLine("problem: {0}", e.Message);
        } finally
        {
            conn.Close();
        }
    }
}
```

By now you should be familiar with the NpgsqlConnection and NpgsqlCommand parts. Within the try-catch block, after the connection to the PostgreSQL server is opened, the ExecuteScalar() method is used to execute the first SQL command. The return value is typecast into a String data type, and displayed.

Following that, the `NpgsqlCommand CommandText` property is changed to a new SQL command, and the `ExecuteScalar()` method is used again, this time typecast to a Double data type. This demonstrates that you can use the same `NpgsqlCommand` instance to send multiple SQL commands.

Compile and run the `getvals.cs` program as normal, and watch the output:

```
C:\>csc /r:npgsql.dll getvals.cs
Microsoft (R) Visual C# .NET Compiler version 8.00.50727.42
for Microsoft (R) .NET Framework version 2.0.50727
Copyright (C) Microsoft Corporation 2001-2005. All rights reserved.

C:\>getvals
The time on the server is: Mon Sep 18 19:20:01.343000 2006 EDT
The value of pi on the server is: 3.14159265358979

C:\>
```

The ExecuteReader() Method

Obviously, the type of SQL commands most often used in applications are `SELECT` commands, which query the database tables for data. The result of the `SELECT` command is most often a result set that returns more than one record of data. The key to being able to handle this situation in your .NET program is the `ExecuteReader()` method.

The `ExecuteReader()` method reads the result set returned by the PostgreSQL server, and returns the results in an `NpgsqlDataReader` object. Each record in the result set is contained in the `NpgsqlDataReader` object. You must use the `NpgsqlDataReader` object to cycle through the records returned in the result set.

The `NpgsqlDataReader` object is an array value. The array is automatically created and sized based on the returned result set. Each value in the array is a column in the returned record, with zero being the first column returned in the result set, one being the second column in the result set, and so on until the last column. Each record in the returned result set is read individually using the `NpgsqlDataReader` object. After a record's values are read, you can advance to the next record in the result set. You are only able to advance forward through the result set using the `NpgsqlDataReader` object. You cannot go back to reread previous records.

The format for obtaining the result set from the `NpgsqlCommand` query looks like this:

```
NpgsqlDataReader data = comm.ExecuteReader();
```

The `NpgsqlDataReader` class contains several properties that can be used to analyze the result set returned. These are listed and described in Table 13-5.

Besides these properties, there are also several class methods available to use in the `NpgsqlDataReader` class, listed and described in Table 13-6.

The columns in each record in the result set are referenced by their index value. You can extract the record column values into variables using the `Getxxx` methods. You must know the column data type in the table, and extract the column data into the proper variable data type. Any mismatches are marked as errors when the program runs.

Property	Description
FieldCount	Indicates the number of columns in the record returned
HasRows	Indicates if the NpgsqlDataReader object has rows to be read
IsClosed	Indicates if the NpgsqlDataReader object is closed
Item	Gets the value of a column using the PostgreSQL data type
RecordsAffected	Indicates the number of rows changed, inserted, or deleted by the SQL command

Table 13-5. NpgsqlDataReader Properties

Method	Description
Close()	Closes the NpgsqlDataReader object
GetBoolean(*int*)	Gets the value of column *int* as a Boolean data type
GetDataTypeName(*int*)	Gets the data type name of column *int*
GetDateTime(*int*)	Gets the value of column *int* as a DateTime data type
GetDecimal(*int*)	Gets the value of column *int* as a Decimal data type
GetDouble(*int*)	Gets the value of column *int* as a Double data type
GetFloat(*int*)	Gets the value of column *int* as a Float data type
GetInt16(*int*)	Gets the value of column *int* as an int16 data type
GetInt32(*int*)	Gets the value of column *int* as an int32 data type
GetName(*int*)	Gets the column name of column *int*
GetString(*int*)	Gets the value of column *int* as a String data type
NextResult()	Gets the next result set when multiple result sets are returned
Read()	Reads the next record in the result set

Table 13-6. The NpgsqlDataReader Methods

The `getitemswon.cs` program demonstrates how to extract record data from a query result set:

```
using System;
using System.Data;
using Npgsql;

public class GetItemsWon
{
    public static void Main(String[] args)
    {
        String constring;
        NpgsqlConnection conn;
        NpgsqlCommand comm;
        NpgsqlDataReader data;

        constring = "Server=127.0.0.1;Port=5432;SSL=True;User ID=carl;";
        constring = constring + "Password=auction;Database=test;";
        conn = new NpgsqlConnection(constring);

        try
        {
            conn.Open();
            comm = new NpgsqlCommand("select * from auction.itemswon", conn);

            data = comm.ExecuteReader();
            if (data.HasRows)
            {
                while(data.Read())
                {
                    String itemkey = data.GetString(0);
                    String lastname = data.GetString(1);
                    String firstname = data.GetString(2);
                    float finalbid = data.GetFloat(3);
                    Console.WriteLine("{0} - {1},{2}\t${3}", itemkey, lastname,
                                firstname, finalbid);
                }
            } else
                Console.WriteLine("There were no rows in the result");
        } catch (NpgsqlException e)
        {
            Console.WriteLine("Problem: {0}", e.Message);
        } finally
        {
            conn.Close();
        }
    }
}
```

In the getitemswon.cs program, the SQL command performs a SELECT query on the itemswon view created in Chapter 12. When executing the ExecuteReader() method for the NpgsqlCommand class, the results are assigned to an NpgsqlDataReader object (data). The HasRows property is used to determine if any records were returned in the result set. If so, the Read() method is used to step through each record in the result set.

For each record, the individual column data values are extracted using the appropriate data type variables and column index value. When the view was defined in Chapter 12, the first column was a varchar data type representing the item key, the second column was a varchar data type representing the bidder's last name, and the third column was a varchar data type representing the bidder's first name. The data from each of these columns can be stored in a String variable. The fourth column contains the final bid value, which is a Double data type, and stored as a Double variable.

The values are displayed for each record returned in the result set:

```
C:\>getitemswon
SC001   - Blum,Barbara    $450
SC002   - Blum,Rich       $240
TR001   - Blum,Barbara    $575

C:\>
```

The Prepare() Method

In the NpgsqlCommand class examples shown so far, the SQL command is sent to the PostgreSQL server as it is executed. There is also a Prepare() method that allows you to send a SQL command to the PostgreSQL server before it is executed.

The benefit of using the Prepare() method before using one of the Executexxx methods is to give the PostgreSQL server advanced warning before executing the command. When the PostgreSQL server knows the SQL command that will be executed before execution time, it can process the prepare plan ahead of time. This reduces the amount of time it takes to execute the SQL command.

The Prepare() method can be used any time after the CommandText property is set, and before the Executexxx method is called:

```
NpgsqlCommand comm = new NpgsqlCommand();
comm.Connection = conn;
comm.CommandText = "Select * from auction.bidder where bidderkey > 100";
comm.Prepare();
try
{
   NpgsqlDataReader data = comm.ExecuteReader();
   if (data.HasRows)
     ...
```

The Prepare() method allows the PostgreSQL server to determine the optimal way to execute the query before the ExecuteReader() method is executed.

The NpgsqlParameterCollection Class

All of the SQL commands used so far have been built before being used in the Npg-sqlCommand object. This does not provide much flexibility. If you need to run a command again using different values (such as query using different WHERE parameters), you would have to rewrite the entire SQL command and place it in the NpgsqlCommand object. This can become tedious in larger applications.

To help solve this problem, the Npgsql library contains the NpgsqlParameters-Collection class, which holds parameters that are used as placeholders in Npg-sqlCommand objects. These parameters can easily be changed while using the same NpgsqlCommand object. This feature allows you to quickly and easily change SQL command values within your application.

The Parameters property of the NpgsqlCommand defines an NpgsqlParameter-Collection object that is used to contain the parameters used in the SQL command. If this is starting to sound confusing, sometimes it can be. The best way to demonstrate this concept is to use an example.

First, a parameter must be defined in an NpgsqlCommand CommandText object. A colon is used to identify a parameter in the CommandText object:

```
comm.CommandText = "SELECT * from auction.bidder where bidderkey = :bidder";
```

The :bidder identifier is a parameter placeholder that can be replaced with a value when the SQL command is executed. The next step is to add the parameter to the Npg-sqlParameterCollection object defined in the NpgsqlCommand object:

```
comm.Parameters.Add(new NpgsqlParameter("bidder", NpgsqlDbType.Int32));
```

The Add() method adds a new NplgsqlParameter object to the NpgsqlParameter-Collection object. The parameter name and data type are defined in the constructor.

You can add as many parameters as necessary. Each parameter added is referenced by its index value in the collection. To assign a value to the parameter, reference the Value property of the appropriate indexed Parameters property:

```
comm.Parameters[0].Value = 100;
```

The paramtest.vb program is a more complicated example of using the parameter feature:

```
Imports System
Imports System.Data
Imports Npgsql

Public Class ParamTest
   Public Shared Sub Main()

      Dim conn As NpgsqlConnection
      Dim comm as NpgsqlCommand
      Dim data as NpgsqlDataReader
      Dim connstring as String
      Dim comstring as String
```

```
        Dim bidder as String
        Dim bidderval as Integer
        Dim bidderkey as String
        Dim lastname as String
        Dim firstname as String

        connstring = "Server=127.0.0.1;Port=5432;SSL=True;User Id=earl;"
        connstring = connstring & "Password=auction;Database=test;"
        conn = New NpgsqlConnection(connstring)
        Try
            conn.Open()
        Catch e as NpgsqlException
            Console.WriteLine("Problem opening session: {0}", e.Message)
            Exit Sub
        End Try

        comm = New NpgsqlCommand()
        comm.Connection = conn
        comstring = "Select * from auction.bidder where bidderkey = :bidder"
        comm.Commandtext = comstring
        comm.Parameters.Add(new NpgsqlParameter("bidder", DbType.Int32))

        While(True)
            Console.Write("Enter bidder: ")
            bidder = Console.ReadLine()
            bidderval = Convert.ToInt32(bidder)
            If (bidderval = 0)
                Exit While
            End If

            Try
                comm.Parameters(0).Value = bidderval
                data = comm.ExecuteReader()
                If (data.HasRows)
                    While(data.Read())
                        bidderkey = data.GetInt32(0)
                        lastname = data.GetString(1)
                        firstname = data.GetString(2)
                        Console.WriteLine("{0} - {1},{2}", bidderkey,lastname,firstname)
                    End While
                Else
                    Console.WriteLine("   No bidder found")
                End If
            Catch e2 as NpgsqlException
                Console.WriteLine("Problem: {0}", e2.Message)
                Exit While
            End Try
        End While

        conn.Close()

    End Sub

End Class
```

The first part of the `paramtest.vb` program should look familiar. A connection is established with the PostgreSQL server, and an `NpgsqlCommand` object is created, using a parameter placeholder in the query. The parameter is defined using the `Add()` method, and set as an Int32 data type.

Next, a `WHILE` loop is started. In the `WHILE` loop a value is retrieved from the user input, converted to an int32 data type, then assigned to the parameter `Value` property. After the value is assigned, the `ExecuteReader()` method is executed and the result set is stored in the `NpgsqlDataReader` object. The values are extracted using the `Getxxx` methods, and the record is displayed. The output of the program should look something like this:

```
C:\>paramtest
Enter bidder: 110
   No bidder found
Enter bidder: 100
   100 - Blum,Rich
Enter bidder: 103
   103 - Blum,Jessica
Enter bidder: 150
   150 - Test,Ima
Enter bidder: 0

C:\>
```

SUMMARY

The Microsoft .NET technology has become a popular programming platform for both Microsoft Windows and web development. The Npgsql library allows .NET programmers to create applications that can access a PostgreSQL server. The Npgsql library can be downloaded and installed in a standard .NET development environment using either the Visual Studio suite or the .NET Framework SDK package.

The Npgsql library provides several classes for working with a PostgreSQL server. The `NpgsqlConnection` class allows you to establish a connection to a local or remote PostgreSQL server, using a Login Role and a database name. The `NpgsqlCommand` class allows you to specify a SQL command to send to the server. There are several methods contained in the `NpgsqlCommand` class for processing the returned result set.

The next chapter discusses how to interface your non-.NET C++ applications with a PostgreSQL server. The libqxx library is used to connect a Win32 C++ application to the PostgreSQL server, send SQL commands, and process the result sets.

CHAPTER 14

Visual C++

C hapter 13 demonstrated how to use the Npgsql library to incorporate a PostgreSQL database into your Microsoft .NET applications. However, not all applications for the Microsoft world are written using .NET technology. Many programmers still prefer to use the older Win32 programming platform. The workhorse of the Win32 programming platform is the Microsoft Visual C++ programming language, commonly used by professional application programmers. Fortunately, there is a library package that can be used to support PostgreSQL databases in Visual C++ applications. This chapter describes the libpq library package. This library package enables Visual C++ programmers to utilize C function calls to access PostgreSQL databases in their applications, without having to upgrade to the .NET technology.

THE VISUAL C++ PROGRAMMING ENVIRONMENT

For many years, the flagship of Microsoft development has been the Visual C++ programming language. Many programmers, starting from the Windows 3.0 days, have created and deployed professional applications using Visual C++. The Visual C++ language combines the industry-standard C++ programming language with the Microsoft Win32 application programming interface (API) to produce a single development environment for creating standard Windows application programs.

With the popularity of the new .NET technology, Microsoft has updated the Visual C++ programming environment. Now, Visual C++ supports not only direct Win32 API programming (also called native mode) but also the .NET CLR API (see Chapter 13).

For programmers who are creating Visual C++ programs that run in the CLR environment, the classes provided by the Npgsql library (see Chapter 13) work just fine, allowing those programmers to use the Npgsql .NET classes to connect to a PostgreSQL database and process data. However, many programmers (especially those using Visual C++) still prefer to program using Win32 API programming, and not utilize the CLR API. These programmers cannot use the Npgsql classes, but instead must use another library package that interfaces directly with the Win32 API.

Currently, the most popular C library available for PostgreSQL is the libpq library package. It provides simple C functions to interact with a PostgreSQL server, access tables, and process data.

The following sections describe how to set up a Visual C++ development environment and utilize the libpq library to access a PostgreSQL server from your Visual C++ applications.

Visual C++ Express Edition

The flagship development environment for Microsoft is the Visual Studio integrated development environment (IDE). The Visual Studio IDE uses a graphical editing environment for creating, compiling, debugging, and running programs written in Visual Basic .NET, C#, J#, and Visual C++.

The downside to the Visual Studio platform is cost. For hobbyists and programming students looking for low-cost ways of programming, there is an alternative choice. Microsoft has recently released the Visual Studio Express Editions of each of its compiler lines. Instead of purchasing the expensive Visual Studio package that includes all of the compilers in one package, Microsoft has produced separate free versions of the individual compiler packages. The Visual C++ Express Edition package is a free download that can be used to create C++ applications.

Of course, there are some limitations to the Express Edition packages. They do not incorporate all of the libraries and advanced features that are included in the Visual Studio package, but they do contain much of the same functionality.

To augment the Visual C++ Express Edition package, Microsoft also provides the Windows Platform Software Development Kit (SDK). This SDK contains C++ libraries for many commonly used Windows Win32 functions, such as creating Window Forms and using network connectivity. The Platform SDK can also be downloaded for free and incorporated into the Visual C++ Express Edition installation. This SDK and some creative configuring allow you to create regular Win32 Windows applications using the Visual C++ Express Edition software.

Downloading and Installing Visual C++ Express Edition

Before you can begin working with Visual C++ Express Edition, you must first download and install the Microsoft .NET redistributable package and Framework SDK. These packages are required to install the .NET CLR environment used by Visual C++. Chapter 13 describes in detail how to download and install these packages. If you have not already done that, you must first go back to Chapter 13 and install them.

After installing the .NET environment, you can begin work on installing the Visual C++ Express Edition package. This package can be obtained as a free download from the Microsoft Developer's Network web site (msdn2.microsoft.com). The main web page contains a link for Visual C++. Clicking this link takes you to the Visual C++ Developer Center web page. The Visual C++ Developer Center provides lots of resources for Visual C++ programmers, including articles on features, tutorials, and, of course, downloads.

At the time of this writing, there is a specific link are for downloading Visual C++ 2005 Express Edition. Clicking this link takes you to the Visual C++ Express Edition web page, which contains a large Download Now icon. Clicking this icon takes you to the Download web page, where you can choose between three types of downloads:

▼ An interactive network installation

■ An .img CD image file

▲ An .iso CD image file

If you click the Download link on the web page, you are directed to the interactive network installation. If you are installing Visual C++ Express Edition on a system with a high-speed Internet connection and want to install the package in real time, select the

Interactive network installation option. This option downloads the installation components as needed across the Internet during the installation. When the installation is finished, the installation files are removed from your system.

If you prefer to burn a CD that can be used any time for installation, click the Manual installation instructions link under the Download link. This link takes you to a web page where you can manually create an installation CD from either an .img or .iso CD image file downloaded from the web site. You must still manually download the image file to your system, so a high-speed Internet connection is required for these options as well. However, once you download the appropriate image file for your CD-burning software, you can use the created CD to install as many copies of Visual C++ Express Edition as you want.

After creating the installation CD, you are ready to install Visual C++ Express Edition. The installation CD automatically starts to the installation program, and you see the Welcome to Setup screen, shown in Figure 14-1.

To continue the installation, click Next. The next window displays the license agreement. If you agree to its terms, accept the agreement and click Next. The following window is the Installations Options window, shown in Figure 14-2.

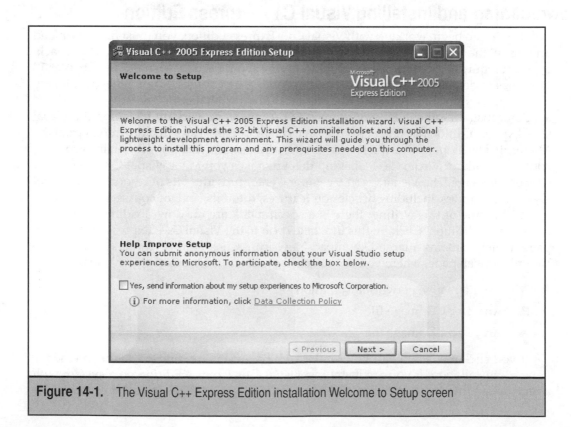

Figure 14-1. The Visual C++ Express Edition installation Welcome to Setup screen

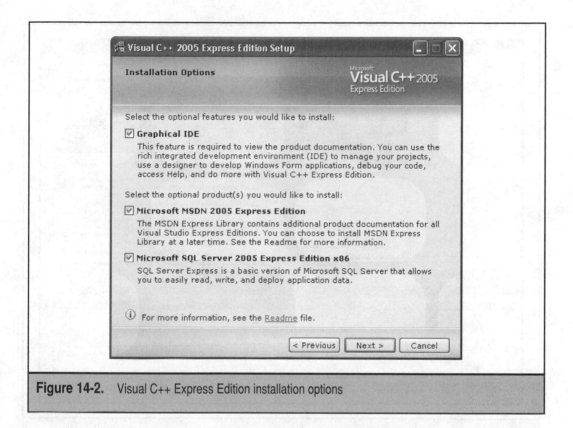

Figure 14-2.   Visual C++ Express Edition installation options

The installation package also allows you to install the Microsoft MSDN Express Edition library, which includes documentation for the Express Edition products. If you desire, you can also elect to install Microsoft SQL Server 2005 Express Edition. This is the free version of the popular Microsoft SQL Server 2005 database package (as described in Chapter 1). If you plan to use only PostgreSQL, you do not need to install the Microsoft SQL Server package.

After selecting the packages to install, click Next. Continue clicking Next until the Install button appears. Clicking this button starts the software installation. After a long process of installing files, the installation program completes.

After completing the installation, start the Visual C++ Express Edition graphical IDE by choosing Start | All Programs | Visual C++ 2005 Express Edition | Microsoft Visual C++ 2005 Express Edition. The main Visual C++ window appears, shown in Figure 14-3.

From this window you can start a new project, or select an existing project from the list in the window. The Visual C++ Express Edition installation also provides a command prompt compiler environment. You can use the command prompt compiler to quickly compile and run applications. There is a special link created that starts a command

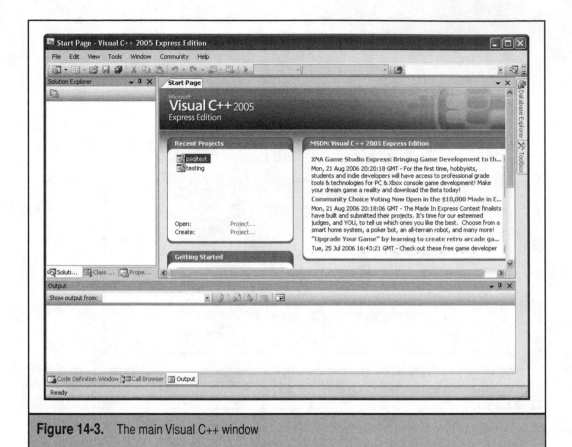

Figure 14-3.   The main Visual C++ window

prompt with the proper environment variables set for compiling applications. Choose Start | All Programs | Visual C++ Express Edition | Visual Studio Tools | Visual Studio 2005 Command Prompt. In the command prompt window, you can type **cl** (the compiler program) to see if it is available:

```
C:\Program Files\Microsoft Visual Studio 8\VC>cl
Microsoft (R) 32-bit C/C++ Optimizing Compiler Version 14.00.50727.42 for 80x86
Copyright (C) Microsoft Corporation.  All rights reserved.

usage: cl [ option... ] filename... [ /link linkoption... ]

C:\Program Files\Microsoft Visual Studio 8\VC>
```

The `cl` command started the compiler, which complained that there were not any files to compile. You are now ready for the next step in the installation process.

Installing the Microsoft Platform SDK

With the Visual C++ Express Edition package installed, you can now customize it to create standard Win32 Windows applications. This is done by downloading and installing the Microsoft Windows Platform SDK. As with the other development packages, you can either order the installation package as a CD from Microsoft or, if you have a high-speed Internet connection, download it from the msdn2.microsoft.com web site. The Visual C++ Development Center web page, described in the previous section, also contains a link to the Windows Platform SDK (it is currently located under Step 4 of the Download page). Click this link to go to the Windows Platform SDK area.

There are three ways to download and install the Platform SDK. Microsoft provides a minimal download file (about 1.2MB) that launches the Installation program and retrieves the necessary installation files directly from the Microsoft MSDN web site. You can also download the Platform SDK Installation program as a series of 25 packages that must be combined to create the installation package. Finally, you can download the Platform SDK Installation program as a single `.img` CD image file that can be burned onto a CD and used on multiple systems.

After downloading the Platform SDK package using the method of your choice, start the installation and follow the directions for installing the files.

After installing the Platform SDK package, you must take the following steps to make Visual C++ Express Edition recognize the SDK libraries installed and to allow you to create Win32 Windows applications:

1. Modify the Visual C++ Express Edition search directories.
2. Modify the Visual C++ Express Edition library dependencies.
3. Edit the Visual C++ Express Edition build restrictions.

The following sections describe how to perform each of these steps.

Modify the Visual C++ Search Directories

The first step is to tell Visual C++ where the executable files, include files, and library files are located in the Platform SDK install. You do this from the Visual C++ Express Edition Options window. Choose Tools | Options to open the Options window, shown in Figure 14-4.

Expand the Projects and Solutions item in the left frame and select VC++ Directories. This section lists the executable, include, and library directories used when compiling C++ programs using the graphical Visual C++ IDE. The Show Directories For drop-down list box at the top allows you to select the directory type.

Select Include Files and click the New Folder icon (the second icon from the left). A new entry line appears, allowing you to type a new directory location. Enter the location for the Platform SDK include files:

```
C:\Program Files\Microsoft Platform SDK for Windows Server 2003 R2\include
```

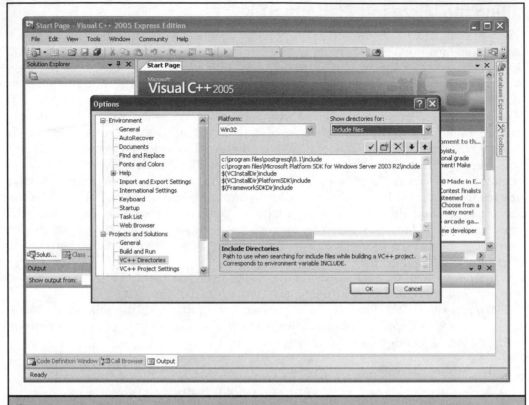

Figure 14-4. The Visual C++ Options window

Next, select the Library Files option in the Show Directories For drop-down list and click the New Folder icon. Enter the location for the Platform SDK library files:

```
C:\Program Files\Microsoft Platform SDK for Windows Server 2003 R2\Lib
```

After entering the new library location, click OK to return to the main window. You are now ready for the next step in the process.

Modify the Visual C++ Library Dependencies

Now that Visual C++ knows where to locate the Platform SDK files, you must tell it what library files need to be included when compiling Windows applications. Unfortunately, this is done by manually editing a configuration file in Visual C++. This file is `corewin_express.vsprops` and is located in the following folder:

```
C:\Program Files\Microsoft Visual Studio 8\VC\VCProjectDefaults
```

You can edit this file using the standard Notepad application. Look for the following line in the file:

```
AdditionalDependencies="kernel32.lib"
```

Change this line to the following:

```
AdditionalDependencies="kernel32.lib user32.lib gdi32.lib winspool.lib
comdlg32.lib advapi32.lib shell32.lib ole32.lib oleaut32.lib uuid.lib"
```

The actual line in the file should be a single line, with no carriage returns. After modifying the line, save the file under the same filename. Just one more step to go!

Remove Visual C++ Express Edition Build Restrictions

By default, Visual C++ Express Edition is restricted from building Win32 Windows applications. This is controlled within a configuration file that must be changed to allow Win32 Windows applications. The file is AppSettings.htm and is located in the following folder:

```
C:\Program Files\Microsoft Visual Studio 8\
 VC\VCWizards\AppWiz\Generic\Application\html\1033
```

Again, you can use the standard Notepad editor to edit this file.

The lines to change are line numbers 441 through 444. If you are using the Notepad application to edit this file, choose Edit | Go To and then enter the line number (441). These lines must be commented out by placing two forward slashes (//) at the front of the line like so:

```
// WIN_APP.disabled = true;
// WIN_APP_LABEL.disabled = true;
// DLL_APP.disabled = true;
// DLL_APP_LABEL.disabled = true;
```

This comments out the configuration files. After commenting out the lines, save the file using the same filename.

Now you should be able to create Win32 Windows applications using your Visual C++ Express Edition installation. To start a new project, choose File | New | Project. Under the Visual C++ section, there are three options, CLR, Win32, and General. In the Win32 section, you will still not see an option for creating Win32 Windows applications. However, if you select to create a new Win32 Console application, the Win32 Application Wizard now gives you the option to create a Win32 Windows application (after assigning a project name), as shown in Figure 14-5.

Your Visual C++ development environment is almost complete. All that is left is to configure the libpq library package. This is demonstrated in the next section.

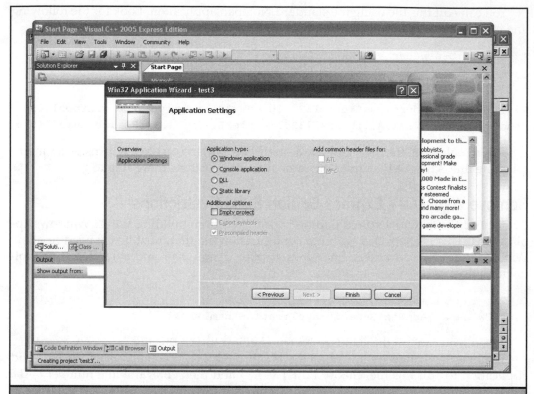

Figure 14-5. Visual C++ new Win32 Application Wizard

THE LIBPQ LIBRARY

The libpq library is part of the PostgreSQL project and provides basic connectivity and functionality for C applications. Because most C++ compilers (Visual C++ included) can also use C functions, the libpq library can also be used with most C++ compilers.

There are three components to the libpq library package:

▼ The libpq library file for compiling programs

■ The libpq include files for defining libpq functions

▲ The libpq DLL file for running libpq applications

The libpq.dll file is precompiled for Microsoft Visual C++ applications. It contains the libpq functions that are used by Visual C++ applications to access the PostgreSQL server. This file is installed in the PostgreSQL Windows installation.

The libpq include files are used to define the libpq functions for C and C++ programs. They are referenced in a Visual C++ program by using the `#include` directive to reference the lead header file, `libpq-fe.h`:

```
#include "libpq-fe.h"
```

This header file references all other libpq header files necessary to compile the programs. Likewise, the libpq library file provides the function code used to compile C and C++ programs that utilize the libpq functions. The library file must also be included when compiling the programs that use these functions.

The libpq include and library files must be installed as part of the PostgreSQL package installation (see Chapter 2). During the Installation Options section, the Development options allow you to install the include files and library files. You can check if you have already installed them by looking in the `c:\program files\postgresql\8.2\lib` folder. There should be an `ms` folder containing the library files.

If you did not install these options when you originally installed your PostgreSQL software, you can rerun the installation program and modify the installation to include them. Just click the X in the Development box and select the option to enable the installation. This is shown in Figure 14-6.

After your Visual C++ environment is ready and you have libpq installed on your system, you can start creating C++ programs that access your PostgreSQL database server. There are a few things you need to remember when creating libpq Visual C++ programs.

First, if you are developing new applications using the Visual C++ IDE, you need to include the PostgreSQL include and library directories in the IDE search path. This is the same procedure as performed earlier when configuring the Platform SDK features. Choose Tools | Options, expand the Projects and Solutions section, and then select

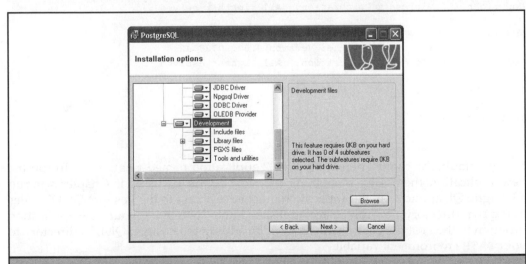

Figure 14-6. The PostgreSQL Development installation options

VC++ Directories. In the Show Directories For drop-down list box, select Include Files and then add the PostgreSQL include directory:

```
c:\program files\postgresql\8.2\include
```

Next, select Library Files and then add the PostgreSQL library directory:

```
c:\program files\postgresql\8.2\lib\ms
```

When you build a new Visual C++ project in the IDE, you must include the libpq .lib file in the files referenced in the project. To do that, right-click the project name in the left window frame, choose Add | Existing Item, and then find the libpq.lib file in the c:\program files\postgresql\8.2\lib\ms directory. The libpq.lib file appears as a resource file in the project file listing.

If you are adventurous and build Visual C++ applications from the command prompt, you must use the cl.exe command prompt compiler program. To do this, you must have the proper environment variables set for compiling. This is already done for you if you open a command prompt window by using choosing Start | All Programs | Visual C++ 2005 Express Edition | Visual Studio Tools | Visual Studio 2005 Command Prompt.

At the command-prompt line, you must use the /I parameter to manually specify the location of the include files, and include the libpq.lib file on the command line. The compiler must be able to locate the libpq.lib file. The easiest way to do this is to copy the libpq.lib file from the c:\program files\postgresql\8.2\lib\ms directory to the directory where you maintain your source code. A complete compile command should look like this:

```
C:\>cl /I"c:\program files\postgresql\8.2\include" test.c libpq.lib
Microsoft (R) 32-bit C/C++ Optimizing Compiler Version 14.00.50727.42 for 80x86
Copyright (C) Microsoft Corporation.  All rights reserved.

test.c
Microsoft (R) Incremental Linker Version 8.00.50727.42
Copyright (C) Microsoft Corporation.  All rights reserved.

/out:test.exe
test.obj
libpq.lib

C:\>
```

By default, the compiler creates a Win32 application named test.exe. To run the new application, there is one more thing you must do. As discussed in Chapter 3, to run a PostgreSQL application, the application must have access to the PostgreSQL DLL files in the bin directory. This can be accomplished either by moving your new application program to the PostgreSQL bin directory or by adding the PostgreSQL bin directory to your PATH environment variable.

Now your PostgreSQL Visual C++ development environment is complete. It is time to start looking at how to produce some programs. The following sections describe the libpq functions and demonstrate how to use them in Visual C++ applications.

THE LIBPQ FUNCTIONS

The libpq library provides many different types of functions to help you interact with your PostgreSQL server. This section groups the functions by the actions they perform. Along with the function, a simple example program is shown to demonstrate how to use the function in a real-life situation.

Opening and Closing Sessions

The libpq library provides five functions that are used for starting and stopping a connection to a PostgreSQL server. These functions are listed and described in Table 14-1.

The `PQconnectbd()` function is used to establish a new connection to a PostgreSQL server. The format of the `PQconnectdb()` function is

```
PGconn *PQconnectdb(const char *conninfo)
```

The `PQconnectdb()` function returns a pointer to a `PGconn` data type. This value is used in all subsequent functions that send commands to the server using this connection.

The `conninfo` constant character pointer defines the values used to connect to the PostgreSQL server. These values are not much different from what you are already used to for connecting to a PostgreSQL server. As expected, there are several standard parameters that can be used to define the connection. These are listed and described in Table 14-2.

Function	Description
PQconnectdb(const char *conninfo)	Start a connection to a PostgreSQL server using parameters in *conninfo* and wait for an answer.
PQconnectStart(const char *conninfo)	Start a connection to a PostgreSQL server in nonblocking mode using parameters in *conninfo*.
PQconnectPoll(PGconn *conn)	Check the status of a pending nonblocking connection attempt *conn*.
PQfinish(PGconn *conn)	Close (end) an established PostgreSQL server session *conn*.
PQreset(PGconn *conn)	Reset a PostgreSQL server session by closing a previous session *conn* and starting a new session using the same parameters. This command waits for an answer from the server.

Table 14-1.   libpq Connection Functions

Connection Parameter	Description
host	The DNS hostname or numeric IP address of the PostgreSQL server.
hostaddr	The numeric IP address of the PostgreSQL server.
port	The TCP port of the PostgreSQL server.
dbname	The database the session connects to.
user	The Login Role to use to log into the server.
password	The password of the Login Role.
connect_timeout	Maximum time (in seconds) to wait for the connection to establish. Use zero to wait indefinitely.
options	Command-line options to send to the server.
sslmode	Sets SSL preference: disable for no SSL, allow to try SSL first, permit to negotiate with server, and require for only SSL.
service	Sets a service name to specify parameters in a pg_service.conf configuration file.

Table 14-2.   PQconnectdb() Connection Parameters

When listing multiple parameters in the character string, each parameter pair must be separated by one or more spaces. Following is an example of creating a new connection:

```
const char *conninfo;
Pconn *conn;
conninfo = "host = 127.0.0.1 dbname = test user = earl password = auction";
conn = PQconnectdb(conninfo);
```

This example connects to the PostgreSQL server running on the local system using the loopback address (127.0.0.1). It attempts to establish the session with the database test using the earl Login Role.

The PQconnectdb() function is a *blocking* function. A blocking function stops (blocks) execution of the program until the function completes. If the PostgreSQL server specified in the connection string is unavailable, you will have to wait for connect_ timeout seconds before control will return to your program. For Windows applications that are event-driven, sometimes this can cause problems. While the program is blocking on a connection, it is not responding to events, such as mouse clicks or keyboard entries.

To solve this problem, you can use the nonblocking connection function. The PQconnectStart() function uses the same connection string information as PQconnectdb() and attempts the same type of connection to the specified PostgreSQL server. However, PQconnectStart() does not wait for the connection to either establish or fail.

Program execution continues immediately after the PQconnectStart() function is executed. To determine if the connection succeeded (or failed), you must call the PQconnectPoll() function. This function returns the status of the connection attempt. The PQconnectPoll() function can return one of several status values:

▼ CONNECTION_STARTED   Waiting for the connection to be established

■ CONNECTION_AWAITING_RESPONSE   Waiting for a response from the PostgreSQL server

■ CONNECTION_SSL_STARTUP   Negotiating SSL encryption scheme

■ CONNECTION_AUTH_OK   Authentication succeeded, waiting for server to finish the connection

■ CONNECTION_SETENV   Negotiating session parameters

▲ CONNECTION_MADE   Connection established, waiting for commands

If the connection has not succeeded or failed, you must poll the connection again. This should continue until either the connection is established or has ultimately failed.

After you have established a connection to a PostgreSQL server, there are several functions you can use that allow you to check on the status of the connection, as well as the connection parameters used to establish the connection. These are listed and described in Table 14-3.

All of the status functions use the PGconn data value returned by the PQconnectdb() function to identify the connection. Most of the status functions return a pointer to a string that contains the status information. An example of this is

```
char *user;
user = PQuser(conn);
```

The user character pointer points to the Login Role value used to establish the connection. The exception is the PQstatus() function. This function returns a ConnStatusType data type, which has two defined values:

▼ CONNECTION_OK for good connections

▲ CONNECTION_BAD for failed connections

Function	Description
PQdb(PGconn *conn)	Returns the database name of the connection
PQuser(PGconn *conn)	Returns the Login Role used for the connection
PQpass(PGconn *conn)	Returns the password of the Login Role used for the connection
PQhost(PGconn *conn)	Returns the server hostname of the connection
PQport(PGconn *conn)	Returns the TCP port of the connection
PQoptions(PGconn *conn)	Returns any command-line options used to establish the connection
PQstatus(PGconn *conn)	Returns the status of the server connection
PQtransactionStatus(PGconn *conn)	Returns the transaction status of the server
PQparameterStatus(PGconn *conn, const char *param)	Returns the current setting of a parameter *param* on the server
PQprotocolVersion(PGconn *conn)	Returns the PostgreSQL backend protocol version
PQserverVersion(PGconn *conn)	Returns the server version as an integer value
PQerrorMessage(PGconn *conn)	Returns the most recently generated server error message
PQsocket(PGconn *conn)	Returns the server file descriptor of the socket connection
PQbackendPID(PGconn *conn)	Returns the server process ID (PID) of the PostgreSQL process
PQgetssl(PGconn *conn)	Returns NULL if SSL is not used, or an SSL structure if it is used for the connection

Table 14-3.   libpq Connection Status Functions

The version.c program demonstrates connecting to a database, checking the status of the connection, and extracting the PostgreSQL server version:

```c
#include <stdio.h>
#include <stdlib.h>
#include "libpq-fe.h"

int main(int argc, char **argv)
{
    const char *conninfo;
    const char *serverversion;
    PGconn *conn;
    const char *paramtext = "server_version";

    conninfo = "hostaddr = 127.0.0.1 dbname = test user = earl password = auction";

    conn = PQconnectdb(conninfo);
    if (PQstatus(conn) != CONNECTION_OK)
    {
        printf("Unable to establish connection: %s",
                    PQerrorMessage(conn));
        return 1;
    } else
    {
        printf("Connection established!\n");
        serverversion = PQparameterStatus(conn, paramtext);
        printf("Server Version: %s\n", serverversion);
    }
    PQfinish(conn);
    return 0;
}
```

This small example demonstrates all the basics of connecting to and interacting with a PostgreSQL server in Visual C++. It connects to the test database on the localhost using the earl Login Role created in Chapter 12. If you have not created these database objects, you will have to use other values for these parameters on your system.

After attempting the connection, the PQstatus() function is used to test the status of the connection. If the connection is OK, the PQparameterStatus() function is used to obtain the value of the server_version parameter from the PostgreSQL server.

If you are compiling the program on the command prompt, the command should look like:

```
cl /I"c:\program files\postgresql\8.2\include" version.c libpq.lib
```

Remember the libpq.lib file must be available in the same directory as the version.c file. After compiling the application, the program version.exe is generated (assuming you do not have any typographical errors in your code). However, if you try to run this program, you may have a problem. You may get a Windows error message that a component necessary to run the application was not found.

In order for libpq programs to run, they must have access to the PostgreSQL DLL files, normally located in the bin directory of the PostgreSQL installation. To solve this problem, you must either include the PostgreSQL bin directory in your PATH environment variable or copy your applications to the PostgreSQL bin directory along with the other PostgreSQL applications.

After solving the DLL problem, the application should run with no trouble:

```
C:\Program Files\PostgreSQL\8.2\bin>version
Connection established!
Server Version: 8.2.0

C:\Program Files\PostgreSQL\8.2\bin>
```

The program worked as expected. The next section moves on to show more advanced functions that can be executed on the server.

Executing SQL Commands

After establishing a connection with the PostgreSQL server, you will most likely want to execute SQL commands on the PostgreSQL server. The libpq command execution functions are listed and described in Table 14-4.

The PQexec() function is the basic function used for executing SQL commands on the PostgreSQL server from C++ programs. Unlike the Npgsql library described in Chapter 13, the libpq library uses a single function to execute both query and nonquery SQL commands. The result of all the commands is returned into the same PGresult data type object:

```
PGresult *PQexec(PGconn *conn, const char *command)
```

The PQexec() function requires two parameters. The first parameter is the PGconn object created when connecting to the server. The second parameter is a character string that contains the SQL command to execute on the server.

When the PQexec() function is executed in the program, the command is sent to the server and the program waits for a response. The response is placed in an PGresult data object. Since there are many types of output associated with different SQL commands, this data object must be capable of handling lots of possibilities.

This data object must first be checked using the PQresultStatus() function to determine the status of the command and the type of output available from the command. The result status can be

▼ PGRES_COMMAND_OK   Command processed okay but with no result set returned

■ PGRES_TUPLES_OK   Command processed okay and returned a result set (even an empty result set)

Function	Description
PQexec(PGconn *conn, const char *command)	Submits a string *command* to the server and wait for the result.
PQexecParams(PGconn *conn, const char *command, int *nParams*, const Oid *paramTypes*, const char *paramValues*, const int *paramLengths*, const int *paramFormats*, int *resultFormat*)	Submits a command that includes parameters to the server and wait for the result. The parameters are defined, along with lengths and formats, in the other parameters. This command also specifies the result format (0 for text or 1 for binary).
PQprepare(PGconn *conn, const char *name*, const char *query*, int *nParams*, const Oid *paramTypes*)	Submits a command *query* to be prepared on the server using connection *conn*. The command may use parameters, defined in the PQexecPrepared() function. The prepared statement is referenced by *name*.
PQexecPrepared(Pgconn *conn, const char *name, int nParms, const char *paramValues, const int paramLengths, const int paramFormats, int *resultFormat*)	Submits a request to execute a previously prepared statement *name*. You may specify parameters and the result format (0 for text or 1 for binary).
PQresultStatus(Pgresult *result*)	Returns the result status of an executed command.
PQresStatus(ExecStatuwsType *status*)	Returns a string result *status* given a PQresultStatus value.
PQresultErrorMessage(PGresult *result*)	Returns an error message string from an executed command, or a NULL value if no error occurred.
PQclear(PGresult *result*)	Clears (frees) the storage memory of result status *result*.

Table 14-4. libpq Command Execution Functions

- PGRES_EMPTY_QUERY The command sent was empty
- PGRES_BAD_RESPONSE The response from the server could not be understood
- PGRES_NONFATAL_ERROR The server generated a notice or a warning
- ▲ PGRES_FATAL_ERROR The server generated a fatal error message

These values are defined in the libpq library and can be directly checked in your code:

```
PGresult *result;
result = PQexec(conn, "SELECT lastname from auction.bidder");
if (PQresultStatus(result) != PGRES_TUPLES_OK)
{
    ...
```

If the result returned by the command is a result set, there are several "helper" functions that can be used to determine what the returned data looks like, and how to handle it. These functions are listed and described in Table 14-5.

These functions are invaluable in sorting through the result set data returned within the PGresult object. The way your program handles the result set data depends on what type of data (if any) is returned. The following sections demonstrate how to handle different types of data returned from executing SQL commands in libpq.

Function	Description
PQntuples(PGresult *res)	Returns the number of records (tuples) in a result set res.
PQnfields(PGresult *res)	Returns the number of columns (fields) in a result set res.
PQfname(PGresult *res, int column)	Returns a column name given a result set res and a column number column.
PQfnumber(PGresult *res, const char *colname)	Returns a column number given a result set res and a column name colname.
PQftable(PGresult *res, int column)	Returns the OID of the table a given column column was fetched from.
PQgetvalue(PGresult *res, int rec, int column)	Returns the value of column column of a single record rec in result set res.
PQgetisnull(PGresult *res, int rec, int column)	Tests if a value in column column of record rec in result set res is NULL. Returns 1 if the value is NULL, and 0 if it is not.
PQgetlength(PGresult *res, int rec, int column)	Returns the length (bytes) of a value in column column in record rec in a result set res.

Table 14-5. libpq Command Result Information Functions

Commands Returning No Data

SQL commands such as INSERT, UPDATE, and DELETE do not return data, but rather return a status code indicating whether or not the command succeeded. In these situations, you must check for the PGRES_COMMAND_OK status in the result, since there are no tuples (records) returned. The update.c program demonstrates this principle:

```c
#include <stdio.h>
#include <stdlib.h>
#include "libpq-fe.h"

int main(int argc, char **argv)
{
   const char *conninfo;
   PGconn *conn;
   PGresult *result;
   char *insertcomm;

   conninfo = "hostaddr = 127.0.0.1 dbname = test user = earl password = auction";
   conn = PQconnectdb(conninfo);
   if (PQstatus(conn) != CONNECTION_OK)
   {
      printf("Unable to establish connection: %s",
               PQerrorMessage(conn));
      return 1;
   } else
   {
      insertcomm = "INSERT into auction.bidder values (125, 'Test', 'Another',
NULL, NULL, NULL, NULL, '555-2121')";
      result = PQexec(conn, insertcomm);
      if (PQresultStatus(result) != PGRES_COMMAND_OK)
      {
         printf("Problem with command: %s\n", PQerrorMessage(conn));
         PQclear(result);
         PQfinish(conn);
         return 1;
      }
      PQclear(result);
   }
   PQfinish(conn);
   return 0;
}
```

The update.c program establishes a connection to the test database on the PostgreSQL server running on the local system, using the earl Login Role. After the connection is established, a simple INSERT SQL command is executed on the server using the PQexec() function.

The status of the command is checked using the PQresultStatus() function and the PGRES_COMMAND_OK value. If the status is not OK, the PQerrorMessage() function is used to display the error message generated by the server. Finally, the

PQclear() function is used to clear the memory used by the PGresult object. It is always a good idea to clear this memory, especially if you reuse the PGresult object for another command.

After compiling the update.c program, execute it on your PostgreSQL system. If the INSERT command succeeds, nothing should display (not too exciting). You can then look at the auction.bidders table and see the newly added record. If you run the program a second time, you should get an error message, indicating that the Bidder table key value already exists:

```
C:\Program Files\PostgreSQL\8.2\bin>update
Problem with command: ERROR:  duplicate key violates unique
 constraint "bidder_pkey"

C:\Program Files\PostgreSQL\8.2\bin>
```

Commands Returning Data

For SQL commands that return data, you must use the PQgetvalue() function to retrieve the returned information. The PQgetvalue() function retrieves the data values as a character string data type, no matter what the actual data type of the table column data. For integer or floating-point values, you can convert the character string value into the appropriate data type using standard C functions, such as atoi() for integers or atof() for floating-point values.

The PQgetvalue() function allows you to retrieve data from the result set in any order. You are not limited in walking forward through each record in the result set. The format of the PQgetvalue() function is

```
char *PQgetvalue(PGresult *result, int record, int column)
```

In the function, you must specify the result set *result,* the desired record number *record* within the result set, and also the column number *column* within the record to retrieve a value from. Records and column numbers both start at 0. For commands that produce only one record, that is always record 0.

The getvals.c program demonstrates how to retrieve and convert data from a result set of a SQL function:

```c
#include <stdio.h>
#include <stdlib.h>
#include "libpq-fe.h"

int main(int argc, char **argv)
{
    const char *conninfo;
    PGconn *conn;
    PGresult *result;
    char *time, *pi;
    float fpi;
```

```
conninfo = "hostaddr = 127.0.0.1 dbname = test user = earl password = auction";
conn = PQconnectdb(conninfo);
if (PQstatus(conn) != CONNECTION_OK)
{
    printf("Unable to establish connection: %s",
             PQerrorMessage(conn));
    return 1;
} else
{
    result = PQexec(conn, "SELECT timeofday()");
    if (PQresultStatus(result) != PGRES_TUPLES_OK)
    {
        printf("Problem with command1: %s\n", PQerrorMessage(conn));
        PQclear(result);
        return 1;
    }
    time = PQgetvalue(result, 0, 0);
    printf("Time of day: %s\n", time);
    PQclear(result);

    result = PQexec(conn, "Select pi()");
    if (PQresultStatus(result) != PGRES_TUPLES_OK)
    {
        printf("Problem with command: %s\n", PQerrorMessage(conn));
        PQclear(result);
        return 1;
    }
    pi = PQgetvalue(result, 0, 0);
    fpi = atof(pi);
    printf("The value of pi is: %lf\n", fpi);
    PQclear(result);
}

PQfinish(conn);
return 0;
}
```

After establishing the connection, the PQexec() function is used to send a standard SELECT SQL command to the server. Notice that to check the status of the result set, you must use the PGRES_TUPLES_OK value, since the query returns a result set. The PQgetvalue() function is used to retrieve the result set, using record 0 and column 0 since there is only one data value returned. In the first instance, the timeofday() PostgreSQL function returns a string value, which can be directly placed in a character string variable.

After using the PQclear() function to reset the PGresult value, another query is made with the PQexec() function. Again, the PQgetvalue() function is used to retrieve the text result set from the query. This time, since the desired data type is a floating-point value, the atof() C function is used to convert the string value to a floating point variable.

Running the program produces the following results:

```
C:\Program Files\PostgreSQL\8.2\bin>getvals
Time of day: Sun Oct 01 16:37:29.092000 2006 EDT
The value of pi is: 3.141593

C:\Program Files\PostgreSQL\8.2\bin>
```

Handling Column Data

The getvals.c program was trivial in that we knew there was only one column of data in the result set. For more complicated result sets, you must determine the number of records returned and the order of the data columns in the result set. If there are multiple records in the result set, you must loop through the result set, reading all of the data records until you have read the last one.

To determine the number of records and columns in a result set, you can use the PQntuples() and PQnfields() functions, respectively:

```
int recs;
int cols;
result = PQexec(conn, "SELECT * from auction.items");
recs = PQntuples(result);
cols = PQnfields(result);
```

Once you know the number of records and columns in a result set, it is a snap to loop through the result set, extracting individual data items:

```
for (i = 0; i < recs; i++)
{
    ...
```

There is one thing you must be careful about, though, when extracting the column data. Remember, the PQexec() function returns all data items in text format. This means that if you intend to use the table data within your application program as another data type, you must use standard C functions to convert the string to the appropriate data type:

▼ atoi()   For converting to an integer value

▲ atof()   For converting to a floating-point value

The getitemswon.c program demonstrates how to extract individual column data elements from a result set:

```
#include <stdio.h>
#include <stdlib.h>
#include "libpq-fe.h"
```

```
int main(int argc, char **argv)
{
    const char *conninfo;
    PGconn *conn;
    PGresult *result;
    char *itemkey, *lastname, *firstname, *finalbid;
    float floatbid;
    int i;

    conninfo = "hostaddr = 127.0.0.1 dbname = test user = earl password = auction";

    conn = PQconnectdb(conninfo);
    if (PQstatus(conn) != CONNECTION_OK)
    {
        printf("Unable to establish connection: %s",
                PQerrorMessage(conn));
        return 1;
    } else
    {
        result = PQexec(conn, "Select * from auction.itemswon");
        if (PQresultStatus(result) != PGRES_TUPLES_OK)
        {
            printf("Problem with query: %s",
                    PQerrorMessage(conn));
            return 1;
        } else
        {
            printf("Item      Won by     Final Bid\n");
            printf("---------------------------\n");
            for(i = 0; i < PQntuples(result); i++)
            {
                itemkey = PQgetvalue(result, i, 0);
                lastname = PQgetvalue(result, i, 1);
                firstname = PQgetvalue(result, i, 2);
                finalbid = PQgetvalue(result, i, 3);
                floatbid = atof(finalbid);
                printf("%s - %s,%s    $%.2lf\n", itemkey, lastname,
                        firstname, floatbid);
            }
            PQclear(result);
        }
    }
    PQfinish(conn);
    return 0;
}
```

The getitemswon.c program starts off as usual, connecting to the sample database and using the PQexec() function to send a simple query. The number of records in the result set is obtained using the PQntuples() function, and a for loop is started to loop through the result set records.

Within the `for` loop, each iteration is a separate record in the result set. For each record, the individual column data values are extracted using the `PQgetvalue()` function. The function references the result set, the record number (controlled by the `for` loop value), and the individual column number for each data element.

Of course, this requires that you know what columns are produced by the query, and in what order. If you do not know this information, you can use the `PQfname()` function to find out which column number is which column name.

Each individual column data value is assigned to a character string variable, since `PQexec()` returns only string values. Since the `finalbid` column value is a floating-point data type, the `atof()` C function is used to convert the string representation to a floating-point value:

```
C:\Program Files\PostgreSQL\8.2\bin>getitemswon
SC001  - Blum,Katie    $120.00
TR001  - Blum,Rich     $3400.00
RR003  - Blum,Rich     $10.00
CC023  - Blum,Barbara  $15.00

C:\Program Files\PostgreSQL\8.2\bin>
```

Using Parameters

In many cases, it is necessary to perform multiple queries using the same SQL command but different data elements. Instead of having to rewrite each `PQexec()` command, you can use the `PQexecParams()` function and use a feature called *parameters*. Parameters allow you to use variables in the place of normal data values in the SQL command. Each variable is preceded by a dollar sign ($) and numbered (1 for the first variable, 2 for the second, and so on). An example of using parameters is

```
SELECT * from auction.bidder where lastname = $1 and firstname = $2
```

Variables can only be used for data values. You cannot use a variable for the table or column names. The format of the complete `PQexecParams()` function is

```
PGresult *PQexecParams(Pgconn *conn, const char *command,
                    int nparams,
                    const Oid *paramTypes,
                    const char * const *paramValues,
                    const int *paramLengths,
                    const int *paramFormats,
                    int resultFormat)
```

As expected, you must declare the values used in the variables within the function. After specifying the connection to use and the string command to send, you must define the variable values. The first value is `nparams`, which specifies the number of variables used. After that is the `paramTypes` value. This value is an array containing the OID of each variable type. You can also assign this value a NULL value. This value forces the PostgreSQL server to use the default data type for the column the data value is used for.

The next three values specify the variable values *(paramValues)*, their lengths *(paramLengths)*, and the format the variable is specified in *(paramFormats)*. Each of these values is an array. The first element in the array references variable $1, the second variable $2, and so on.

The format value of each variable can be either text mode (0) or binary mode (1). If the value is NULL, PostgreSQL assumes all of the variables are in text mode. If the format of the variable is text mode, PostgreSQL assumes the variable is specified as a text (or character) data type and converts the variable value to the data type required for the SQL command specified.

Thus, you can specify an integer or floating-point value as a text string and set the format value to 0, and PostgreSQL automatically does the conversion for you. If you use text mode for variables, you can also set the length value to NULL, as PostgreSQL automatically determines the length of the text string variable.

Alternatively, if you set the value format type to binary mode (1), you must specify the variable values using the appropriate data type (such as float or int) and specify the length as the byte length of the value.

The result format value *(resultFormat)* is also interesting. It allows you to set the data type of the result value. It can be either text mode (0) or binary mode (1). In text mode, the result set is returned as text values, just as with the PQexec() function. The appropriate data type conversion must be performed for binary values. In binary mode, the result set data is returned in the appropriate binary format, either integer or floating point. At this time, the result format value can only be one or the other; you cannot mix and match text and binary mode data elements.

Setting the PQexecParams() function can be confusing. For beginners, the easiest thing to do is set both the input and output formats as text mode. This cuts down on the amount of information you must collect and pass to the function.

The bidderresult.c program demonstrates using parameters with text mode for both input and output data values:

```c
#include <stdio.h>
#include <stdlib.h>
#include <sys/types.h>
#include "libpq-fe.h"

int main(int argc, char **argv)
{
    const char *conninfo;
    PGconn *conn;
    PGresult *result;
    char *paramValues[1];
    const char *query;
    char bidder[4];
    char *item, *desc, *strbid;
    float bid, totalbid;
    int i;
```

```
conninfo = "hostaddr = 127.0.0.1 dbname = test user = earl password = auction";

conn = PQconnectdb(conninfo);
if (PQstatus(conn) != CONNECTION_OK)
{
   printf("Unable to establish connection: %s",
            PQerrorMessage(conn));
   return 1;
} else
{
   query = "SELECT * from auction.item where bidderkey = $1";
   while(1)
   {
      totalbid = 0;
      printf("\nEnter bidder: ");
      scanf_s("%3s", &bidder, 4);
      if (!strcmp(bidder,"0"))
         return 0;

      paramValues[0] = (char *)bidder;
      result = PQexecParams(conn, query, 1, NULL, paramValues, NULL, NULL, 0);
      if (PQresultStatus(result) != PGRES_TUPLES_OK)
      {
         printf("Problem: %s", PQerrorMessage(conn));
         PQclear(result);
         PQfinish(conn);
         return 1;
      } else
      {
         printf("Item Won     Description     Final Bid\n");
         printf("---------------------------------------\n");
         for (i = 0; i < PQntuples(result); i++)
         {
            item = PQgetvalue(result, i, 0);
            desc = PQgetvalue(result, i, 1);
            strbid = PQgetvalue(result, i, 4);
            bid = atof(strbid);
            totalbid += bid;

            printf("%s   %s        $%.2lf\n", item, desc, bid);
         }
         printf("---------------------------------------\n");
         printf("Total bids: $%.2lf\n", totalbid);
         PQclear(result);
      }
   }
}

PQfinish(conn);
return 0;
}
```

The paramValues pointer is declared as an array. Since there is only one parameter used in the SQL command, there needs to be only one value in the array. The string used for the query is declared, using a parameter variable $1 for the data element in the WHERE clause.

Next, an endless While loop is used to continually loop through values until a stopping value is entered by the user. The C scanf_s function is used to allow the user to enter a bidder value to look up in the database. The scanf_s function is buffer-overflow safe, to prevent the user from trying any buffer-overflow exploits with the character buffer bidder.

After the desired variable value is entered, it is assigned to the paramValues array, and the PQexecParams() function is declared. Since the input value is in text mode, the paramLengths and paramFormats values can be set to NULL. Also, the result-Format value is set to 0, indicating that we want the output result set data in text mode as well.

After the PQexecParams() function is executed, the data in the result set is extracted within the for loop. Since the output data format is set to text, the finabid value must be converted to floating point using the C atof() function.

After compiling the program, you can run it to see the winning bids for a specific bidder. A value of 0 should be entered to stop the program:

```
C:\Program Files\PostgreSQL\8.2\bin>bidderresult

Enter bidder: 100
Item Won      Description        Final Bid
----------------------------------------
TR001    Trip to Tahiti       $3400.00
RR003    Gift certificate      $10.00
----------------------------------------
Total bids: $3410.00
Enter bidder: 101
Item Won      Description        Final Bid
----------------------------------------
CC023    Creative Basket       $15.00
----------------------------------------
Total bids: $15.00
Enter bidder: 102
Item Won      Description        Final Bid
----------------------------------------
SC001    Autographed baseball     $120.00
----------------------------------------
Total bids: $120.00

Enter bidder: 0

C:\Program Files\PostgreSQL\8.2\bin>
```

SUMMARY

The libpq library provides functions for C and C++ programs to access a PostgreSQL server. The most popular C++ development environment in the Windows world is Microsoft Visual C++. This development environment can be created using either the Visual Studio software suite or the free Visual C++ Express Edition. To create Windows applications in Visual C++ Express Edition, you must also download and install the Microsoft Platform SDK package.

The libpq package can be installed from the standard PostgreSQL installation program. The libpq package includes the library files, C header files, and DLL run-time files necessary for C and C++ applications. After installing these components, they must be configured in the Visual Studio or Visual C++ Express Edition development environment.

The libpq library contains functions to connect to a PostgreSQL server, send SQL commands, and retrieve the result set of the commands. Once the result set is retrieved, you can extract individual column data elements.

The last chapter in this book addresses yet another popular Windows development environment. The Java programming language has taken the world by storm. Many programmers program portable database applications using Java. Just as with .NET and Win32, PostgreSQL also includes a development package for Java programmers. The next chapter demonstrates how to use a PostgreSQL server from a Java development environment.

CHAPTER 15

Java

The Java programming language has quickly become the favorite of programmers who must create applications for multiple platforms. A Java application can run on Windows, Unix, and Linux operating system platforms without having to recompile new executables. Because of this feature, many programmers are learning Java and converting their applications to the Java environment. PostgreSQL supports the Java programming environment by providing a driver for the Java Database Connectivity (JDBC) programming interface. This chapter describes the Java development environment, JDBC, and how to use the PostgreSQL JDBC driver to create Java applications that can access data on a PostgreSQL server.

THE JAVA DEVELOPMENT ENVIRONMENT

The Java programming language has become a popular tool for developers who need to make applications work in environments that support multiple operating system platforms. Instead of having to have multiple versions of an application for each operating system platform, Java programs can be created and compiled on one platform, and then run on a totally different platform with (usually) no modifications or problems.

While the Java technology is relatively new to the programming world, it has already matured into a full-blown programming environment. There are three types of Java programming platforms to choose from:

▼ **J2SE**   Java version 2 Standard Edition, for developing workstation and server applications

■ **J2EE**   Java version 2 Enterprise Edition, for developing server-side web applications

▲ **J2ME**   Java version 2 Micro Edition, for developing mobile device applications

The Java Runtime Edition (JRE) package is not a development platform, but must be loaded on a system for Java applications to execute. It provides the Java Virtual Machine (JVM) core libraries required for Java applications (both desktop and web based) to execute. There are different versions of the JRE for each operating system platform. Once a Java application is compiled, it can run on any JVM on any operating system platform without having to be recompiled for the operating system.

You cannot develop new applications with just the JRE, though. To develop Java applications, you must have the J2SE, J2EE, or J2ME environment installed. All three of these environments include the Java compiler for creating Java applications, along with the standard Java library files for their specific programming environments. All of these development environments support JDBC for connecting to database servers.

JDBC is the Java layer that allows Java applications to connect and interact with databases. JDBC is a standard interface for all Java applications. Database vendors must supply a compatible JDBC library file for Java applications to interface with their individual database products. Java programmers can write code that interfaces with JDBC.

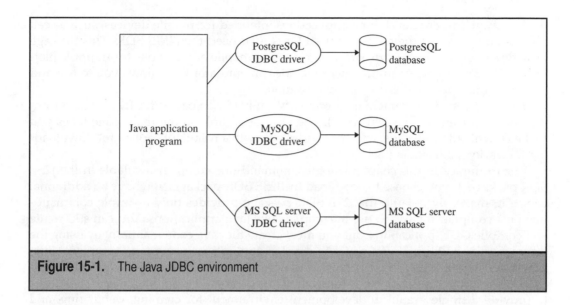

Figure 15-1.   The Java JDBC environment

This code can then be used to access any database that provides a JDBC driver. This is demonstrated in Figure 15-1.

After connecting to the database using JDBC, the Java application can access tables and data using standard JDBC methods and properties. These methods and properties remain consistent for all databases using the JDBC driver.

To develop Java applications for PostgreSQL, you must have a Java development environment and the PostgreSQL JDBC driver. The following sections describe how to download and install a Java development environment to start your Java programming. Following that, the PostgreSQL JDBC driver is discussed.

Downloading the Java SDK

As mentioned in the previous section, there are three different Java development environments available. Which development environment you should select depends on the type of applications you need to develop.

If you are creating standard desktop applications for workstations, you need the J2SE Software Developer Kit (SDK). This package allows you to create both command-line and GUI applications that can run on any operating system workstation or server.

If you are creating web-based applications, you need the J2EE SDK. This package allows you to create both command-line and GUI applications like the J2SE, but also provides a development environment for creating Java beans and web services. Java beans are small routines that are called by web applications to perform specific functions or tasks. These features are used in web servers to provide an application interface that allows clients to use standard web browsers to run applications.

Finally, if you are developing applications intended for mobile devices, such as cell phones and personal digital assistants (PDAs), you need the J2ME SDK. This package provides a development environment for creating mobile applications for multiple platforms. The development environment includes an emulator that allows you to test and debug mobile applications on your workstation.

Each of these development environments can be downloaded for free directly from the Sun Java web site (java.sun.com). The Download link on the main page takes you to the Downloads web page, which provides you with a wealth of choices for downloading the various developer packages.

The examples in this chapter use the command-line compiler available in the J2SE SDK package. If you choose to download the J2SE SDK package, you have an additional choice to make. By default, the J2SE SDK package provides only a simple command-line Java compiler for you to use to compile your Java applications. You can still create and compile GUI applications, but you must create the Java code manually by using the command-line utilities. If you prefer to develop applications using fancy graphical integrated development environment (IDE) packages, then the NetBeans program is for you.

The NetBeans application is a free IDE that is combined with the J2SE SDK package to provide a single graphical development environment for creating, debugging, and running Java applications. The graphical environment allows you to create Java GUI applications by dragging and dropping windows controls into a work area that resembles the completed window form. This allows you to visually see what you are creating.

The NetBeans package can be downloaded as a single bundle with the J2SE SDK. At the time of this writing, the current production version of this bundle includes the J2SE SDK version 5.0 Update 9 package and the NetBeans 5.0 package in a single download file from the Sun Java web site. There are different versions of the download package for different operating system platforms. The Windows development version is in the following file:

```
jdk-1_5_0_09-nb-5_0-win-ml.exe
```

This file is a self-extracting installation package. There is no need to extract the component files into a temporary directory before starting the installation. After downloading the package, run it to start the installation.

Installing the Java SDK

The J2SE SDK and NetBeans installation begins with a simple welcome screen, showing the version of the packages included in the installation, as shown in Figure 15-2.

Clicking the Next button takes you through the installation windows. You must accept the license agreement to continue the installation process. After accepting the license, you may alter the installation directories used for the Java applications. Both the J2SE SDK and NetBeans packages are installed in separate directories. When the installation completes, a window appears (see Figure 15-3) showing the location of the NetBeans IDE program and how to uninstall the individual components of the installation.

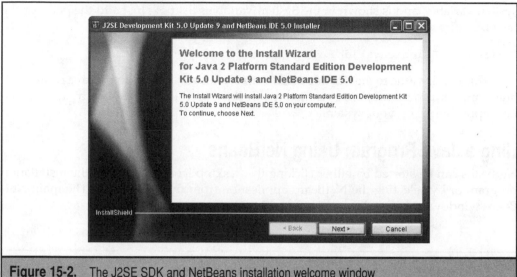

Figure 15-2.   The J2SE SDK and NetBeans installation welcome window

After installing the J2SE SDK, you should include the Java bin directory in your Windows PATH environment variable. This allows you to compile Java applications from any directory on the system. To access the PATH environment variable, right-click My Computer, select Properties, and then click the Advanced tab. Clicking the Environment Variables button takes you to the Environment Variables editor. The PATH variable is a

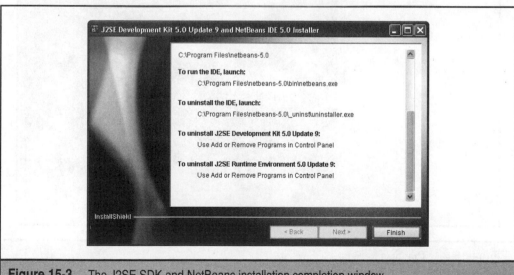

Figure 15-3.   The J2SE SDK and NetBeans installation completion window

system variable, and is shown in the System Variables list box. Just add the path for the Java `bin` directory to the end of the existing value (after a semicolon):

```
C:\Program Files\Java\jdk1.5.0_09\bin
```

Adding this value to the existing `PATH` variable allows you to run the Java command-line compiler program (`javac`) from any directory on the system. You can now create Java applications on your system.

Building a Java Program Using NetBeans

NetBeans can be started by either clicking the desktop icon installed by the installation program or by selecting the NetBeans application from the Start menu. The main Net-Beans window appears, shown in Figure 15-4.

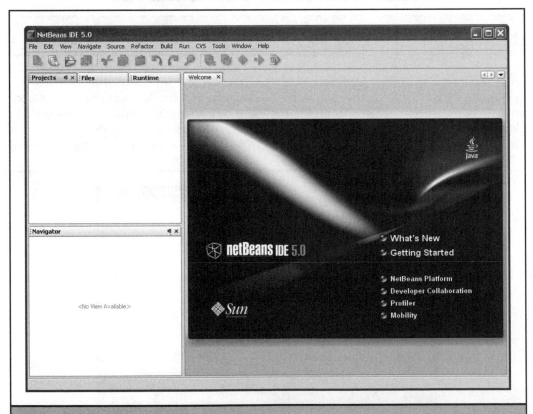

Figure 15-4. The main NetBeans IDE window

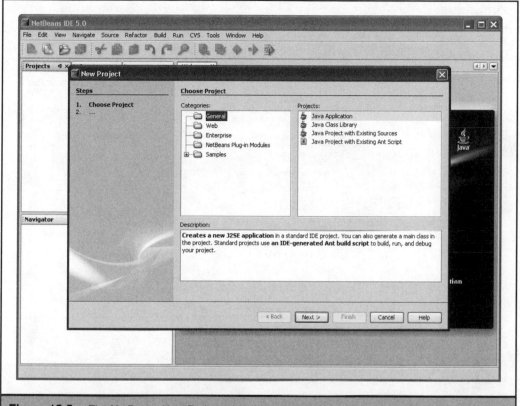

Figure 15-5. The NetBeans New Project wizard

To start a new programming project, click File | New Project. The New Project wizard starts, shown in Figure 15-5.

The New Project wizard walks you through selecting the type of Java application to build, the location of the project files, and the name of the main Java class in the application.

After you enter the desired values, the graphical development environment starts. The right-side window contains the code for the application, shown in Figure 15-6.

The New Project wizard creates a blank class template for your application. By default, the blank template creates a Java namespace using the project name, and a `Main` class that is used to contain the application code. You are now ready to start building your new Java application.

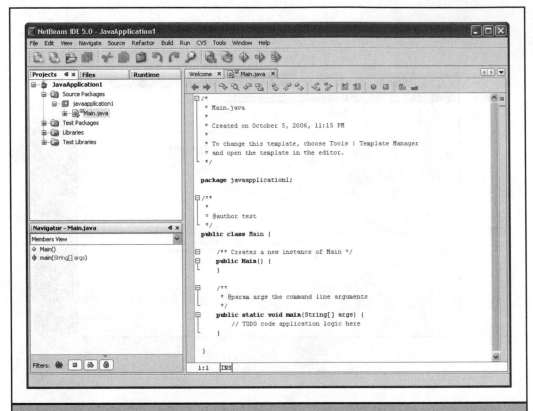

Figure 15-6. A new Java application template

POSTGRESQL JDBC DRIVER

To access a PostgreSQL server from a Java application you must include the PostgreSQL JDBC driver with the application. There are two ways to obtain the PostgreSQL JDBC driver:

▼ From the PostgreSQL server installation

▲ From the PostgreSQL JDBC web site

The standard PostgreSQL server installation provides an option to install the JDBC driver files in the Database Drivers section of the Install Options window, shown in Figure 15-7.

When choosing to install the PostgreSQL JDBC drivers from the server installation, they are placed in the `jdbc` directory under the standard PostgreSQL install directory (see Chapter 3).

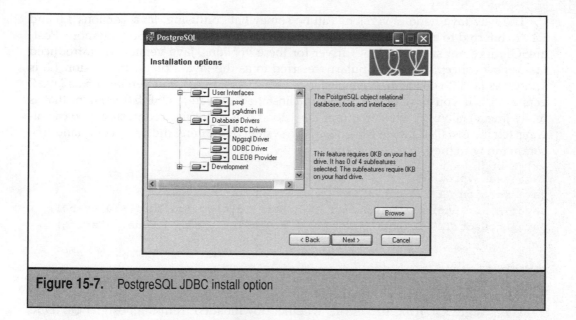

Figure 15-7. PostgreSQL JDBC install option

The other way to install the PostgreSQL JDBC drivers is to download them separately. The jdbc.postgresql.org web site provides the latest PostgreSQL JDBC drivers for download. Click the Download link on the left side of the main web page to go to the Download web page. You can download either precompiled binary versions of the driver or the complete Java source code to compile your own.

Since Java applications run on any operating system, there are no separate downloads for separate operating systems. You may notice, however, that there are still three different JDBC drivers to download, jdbc2, jdbc2ee, and jdbc3.

The different drivers relate to different versions of the Java environment. You must download the driver associated with the Java JVM version you are using. Different Java versions use different JDBC versions. Table 15-1 lists the JDBC driver versions and the Java versions they are used for.

JDBC File	Java Version
jdbc2	J2SE 1.2 and 1.3
jdbc2ee	J2SE 1.3 and J2EE
jdbc3	J2SE 1.4 and 1.5

Table 15-1. PostgreSQL JDBC Driver Versions

The way Java handles versions can be somewhat confusing. Java versions 1.0 and 1.1 are referred to as the Java 1 platform, which is not supported by Sun anymore. PostgreSQL does not supply a JDBC driver for these versions. Java version 1.2 introduced many new concepts and is popularly referred to as the Java 2 platform. Version 1.3 is known as Java 2 version 3.0, version 1.4 as Java 2 version 4.0, and version 1.5 as Java 2 version 5.0. If you have downloaded and installed the latest J2SE 5.0 version, that is really Java version 1.5, which requires the `jdbc3` driver. If this is confusing, you can always tell the installed Java JVM version on a system by running the `java` command-line command with the `-version` option:

```
C:\>java -version
java version "1.5.0_09"
Java(TM) 2 Runtime Environment, Standard Edition (build 1.5.0_09-b01)
Java HotSpot(TM) Client VM (build 1.5.0_09-b01, mixed mode, sharing)

C:\>
```

This system shows that it is using version `1.5.0_09`, which is the J2SE 5.0. The `_09` part shows that it is update (or patch) 9.

The PostgreSQL JDBC driver file, whether downloaded from the PostgreSQL JDBC web site or installed from the PostgreSQL server installation, uses a specific filename format to delineate which version it is. The format of the PostgreSQL JDBC filename is

```
postgresql-version.format.jar
```

where *version* is the driver version, and *format* is the JDBC type. At the time of this writing, the latest PostgreSQL JDBC driver version is 8.1-407. Thus, the JDBC driver to use for the J2SE 5.0 SDK is `postgresql-8.1-407.jdbc3.jar`. Note that the version available on the PostgreSQL JDBC web site is often newer than the JDBC drivers supplied in the PostgreSQL server installation package. You can still use the version supplied with your server installation package, but there may be bugs that have been fixed in the later releases.

The PostgreSQL JDBC drivers are created as a Java `.jar` file. A `.jar` file is a collection of Java classes that are grouped together into a single Java namespace and can be referenced by Java applications. Because the classes in the `.jar` file are called directly by Java applications, the `.jar` file must be present when the application executes, and the application must know where to find it. Because of this, you must distribute the appropriate PostgreSQL JDBC `.jar` file with your PostgreSQL Java application (or require your customers to download the PostgreSQL JDBC driver themselves). The following sections describe how to include the JDBC driver file in your application.

Using JDBC in a NetBeans Application

The NetBeans IDE creates a single `.jar` file that contains the application class files contained in a project. This `.jar` file should be distributed as your application and run directly in the Java JVM. When you build your application, NetBeans provides the created .jar file information, showing you the Java command to use to execute the application.

The NetBeans IDE also allows you to include library files within the project. The library files can include any .jar files required for the application to run. When your project is opened in the IDE, the Projects tab in the left window lists the files associated with the project. The Libraries section should include any .jar files that are required by the application. By default, the Libraries section includes just the standard JDK 1.5 libraries.

To include the PostgreSQL JDBC driver file, right-click the Libraries heading and select Add JAR/folder. From the window, select the appropriate PostgreSQL JDBC driver file required for your Java environment, either from the PostgreSQL jdbc folder or from the download from the jdbc.postgresql.org web site.

Adding the PostgreSQL JDBC driver file to the project library creates a copy of the driver file in the project's lib folder. If you distribute the application's .jar files to customers, the lib folder (and the PostgreSQL JDBC driver in it) is automatically included in the application .jar file. You do not need to include a separate copy of the PostgreSQL JDBC driver with your application.

Using JDBC in a Java Command-Line Application

Running a Java application from the command line requires that you manually reference the PostgreSQL JDBC driver file. The Java command-line runtime engine (java) references directories and libraries that contain Java classes using the CLASSPATH variable. This means that you not only must reference any directories that contain your Java application files, but must also directly reference any .jar library files in the CLASSPATH. There are two ways to do this.

The first way is to define the Windows CLASSPATH environment variable that references the required directories and libraries:

```
C:\javatest> SET CLASSPATH=C:\javatest\
C:\javatest> java JavaTest
Hello World!

C:\javatest>
```

The Java runtime engine uses the CLASSPATH environment variable to find the JavaTest.class class file necessary to run the application. If the application requires a .jar file (such as the PostgreSQL driver file), you must specifically add it to the CLASSPATH variable, even if it is in a directory already referenced:

```
SET CLASSPATH=C:\javatest;C:\javatest\postgresql-8.1-405.jdbc3.jar
```

The downside to using this method is that if you have multiple Java applications on your system, you would have to either place them all into the same directory or add each application's directory and libraries to the CLASSPATH environment variable.

To solve this problem, you can use the -classpath parameter in the Java command-line run-time engine:

```
C:\javatest> SET CLASSPATH=C:\nonsense
C:\javatest> java JavaTest
Exception in thread "main" java.lang.NoClassDefFoundError: JavaTest

C:\javatest> java -classpath c:\javatest JavaTest
Hello World!

C:\javatest>
```

In this example, the CLASSPATH environment variable is set to a different directory. When the Java application is run, the Java run-time engine cannot find the JavaTest .class class file and produces an error. The second time the application is run, the -classpath parameter is added to tell the run-time engine where the class file is located, and things work just fine. Just as with the CLASSPATH environment variable, .jar library files must be included separately in the -classpath parameter, even if the directory is already included.

JAVA DATABASE CONNECTIVITY

Now that you have your PostgreSQL JDBC development environment complete, you can start building programs that access your PostgreSQL server. This section walks through the pieces needed to get your Java applications talking to your PostgreSQL server.

Starting a Connection

Before you can send SQL commands to the PostgreSQL server, you must establish a connection. In JDBC, this is a two-step process.

First, you must declare the JDBC driver your application will be using. This is done using the Class.forName() method. Each JDBC driver has a different driver name that is used in this method. For PostgreSQL, the driver name is opt.postgresql .Driver. You should also place this command within a try-catch block to catch any Java exceptions that might be thrown if an error occurs:

```
try {
    Class.forName("org.postgresql.Driver");
} catch (Exception e) {
    System.out.println("problem with driver: " + e.getMessage());
    System.exit(1);
}
```

After defining the JDBC driver used, you can establish the connection. A JDBC database connection is handled by a Connection object. The Connection object is then referenced by other JDBC classes to send SQL commands to the server.

The connection is defined using a `DriverManager` class object. This is a standard JDBC class that manages connections to the JDBC driver. The `getConnection()` method is used to define the connection parameters. The format of the `getConnection()` method is

```
Connection conn = DriverManager.getConnection(url, user, passwd);
```

The `getConnection()` method takes three string parameters. The first parameter, *url*, specifies the protocol to use, the location of the database server, and what database to connect to. The format of the parameter is

```
jdbc:protocol://host/database
```

For a PostgreSQL server, *protocol* is set to `postgresql`. The *host* value is either the hostname or numeric IP address of the PostgreSQL server (it can be `localhost` if the application is running on the same system as the server). The *database* value is the name of the PostgreSQL database you are connecting to.

A complete example of connecting to a PostgreSQL database is shown in the `Connect.java` program:

```java
import java.sql.*;

public class Connect {
    public static void main(String[] args) {
        String URL = "jdbc:postgresql://127.0.0.1/test";
        String user = "earl";
        String passwd = "auction";
        Connection sqlcon = null;
        try {
            Class.forName("org.postgresql.Driver");
            sqlcon = DriverManager.getConnection(URL, user, passwd);
            System.out.println("connected to database");
            DatabaseMetaData dmd = sqlcon.getMetaData();
            String version = dmd.getDatabaseProductVersion();
            System.out.println("version: " + version);
            sqlcon.close();
        } catch (Exception e) {
            System.out.println("Problem: " + e.getMessage());
        }
    }
}
```

The `Connect.java` program uses the Java `import` statement to include the `java.sql` namespace, which includes all of the necessary JDBC classes to interact with the database. The program then defines the strings necessary to connect to the sample `test` database on the local host, using the sample `earl` Login Role and password.

If the connection fails, the `getConnection()` method throws an exception, which should be caught by your program. If the connection succeeds, you are ready to start sending SQL commands.

The `getMetaData()` method in the `Connection` class is used to retrieve information about the database you are connected to. This data is stored in a `DatabaseMetaData` object. One method available is `getDatabaseProductVersion()`, which returns a `String` value showing the database server version.

Remember, to run this application you must have the PostgreSQL JDBC driver in your classpath. Here is an example of compiling the application from the Java command-line compiler and then running it using the command-line run-time engine:

```
C:\test> javac Connect.java
C:\test> java -classpath c:\test;c:\test\postgresql-8.1-405.jdbc3.jar Connect
connected to database
version: 8.1.4

C:\test>
```

You do not need to include the JDBC driver file when compiling the application, only when running it. If there are no errors, the compiler creates the Java class file `Connect` `.class`. To run a Java application, you must use the JVM run-time engine and use the `-classpath` parameter to define the location of both the `Connect.class` file and the PostgreSQL JDBC driver `.jar` file.

To run the example in NetBeans, create a console application and place the code in the `main()` section into the `main()` section of the project class template (do not copy the `main()` or `class` lines into the template; those are already created for you by Net-Beans). You must also include the `import` statement in the class template before the `Main` class constructor. This is shown in Figure 15-8.

Remember to include the PostgreSQL JDBC driver in the Libraries section of the project. When you are finished, click the Build icon. The application should build with no errors. If so, click the Run icon to start the application. The output should appear in the output window, as shown in Figure 15-8.

Sending SQL Commands

SQL commands are contained in a `Statement` class object. They are created using the `createStatement()` method from the `Connection` object:

```
Connection conn = DriverManager.getConnection(url, user, passwd);
Statement stmt = conn.createStatement();
```

Once the `Statement` class object is created, you can use it to send SQL commands to the server. There are two methods that are used to do this:

▼ executeUpdate()

▲ executeQuery()

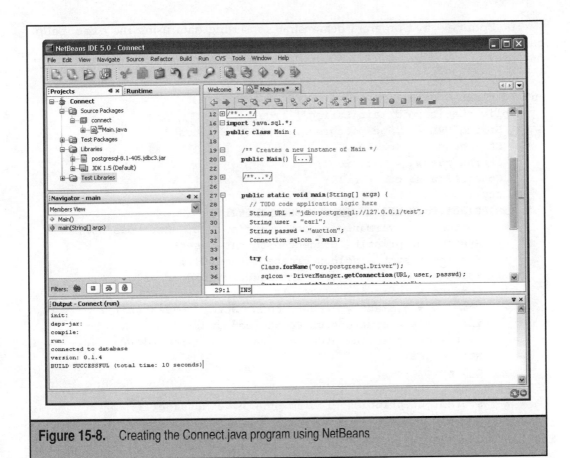

Figure 15-8. Creating the Connect.java program using NetBeans

The executeUpdate() method is used to send nonqueries, such as INSERT, DELETE, and UPDATE SQL commands, to the server. The executeQuery() method is used to send queries using the SELECT SQL command to the server. The following sections demonstrate both of these methods.

Processing Nonqueries

Performing SQL commands that do not return a result set (such as INSERT, DELETE, and UPDATE) requires using the executeUpdate() method of the Statement class. The executeUpdate() method has one parameter, the SQL command as a String value, and returns an integer value indicating the number of records affected by the command:

```
int result = stmt.executeUpdate("INSERT into auction.bidder values(...
```

If an error occurs in the SQL command processing, the executeUpdate() method throws a Java Exception, which should be caught by the program.

The `Update.java` program demonstrates inserting data using the `executeUp-date()` method:

```
import java.sql.*;

public class Update {
    public static void main(String[] args) {
        String URL = "jdbc:postgresql://127.0.0.1/test";
        String user = "earl";
        String passwd = "auction";
        Connection sqlcon = null;
        try {
            Class.forName("org.postgresql.Driver");
            sqlcon = DriverManager.getConnection(URL, user, passwd);
            System.out.println("connected to database");
            Statement stmt = sqlcon.createStatement();
            String command = "INSERT into auction.bidder values ";
            command = command + "(126, 'Pierce', 'Alex', NULL,";
            command = command + " NULL, NULL, NULL, '555-5392')";
            int result = stmt.executeUpdate(command);
            System.out.println("added " + result + " record");
            stmt.close();
            sqlcon.close();
        } catch (Exception e) {
            System.out.println("Problem: " + e.getMessage());
        }
    }
}
```

The `Update.java` program uses the standard JDBC methods to load the driver and connect to the database. Next, a `Statement` object is created and the `executeUp-date()` method is used with a normal `String` value that contains a SQL `INSERT` command. Compiling and running the program produces the following results:

```
C:\test> javac Update.java
C:\test> java -classpath C:\test;C:\test\postgresql-8.1-405.jdbc3.jar Update
connected to database
added 1 records

C:\test> java -classpath C:\test;C:\test\postgresql-8.1-405.jdbc3.jar Update
connected to database
Problem: ERROR: duplicate key violates unique constraint "bidder_pkey"

C:\test>
```

The first time the `Update.java` program is run, the record is added successfully. You can use the standard pgAdmin III program to check the inserted value. If you try to run the program again to perform the same INSERT command, a Java exception will be thrown. The error message produced specifies the cause of the exception. As expected, the new record was rejected because the primary key value already existed in the table.

Processing Queries

Performing SQL commands that return either a single data value (such as functions) or a multirecord result set (such as SELECT queries) requires that you use the execute-Query() method of the Statement class. In both situations, the method returns data in a ResultSet object:

```
Statement stmt = sqlcon.createStatement();
ResultSet rset = stmt.executeQuery("SELECT * from auction.bidder");
```

The ResultSet object contains the result set data retrieved from the executed SQL command. You can move back and forth between records in the result set using the next() method to go forward and the previous() method to go backward in the ResultSet object. You can also read a specific record in the result set using the absolute() method.

One oddity of the ResultSet object is that when it returns with result set data, it does not point to the first record in the result set, even if there is only one record in the result set. Instead it points to "just before" the first record. When the result set returns, you must perform a next() method to point to the first record in the result set. This is demonstrated in the GetVals.java program:

```
import java.sql.*;

public class GetVals {
    public static void main(String[] args) {
        String URL = "jdbc:postgresql://127.0.0.1/test";
        String user = "earl";
        String passwd = "auction";
        Connection sqlcon = null;
        Statement stmt = null;
        ResultSet rset = null;

        try {
            Class.forName("org.postgresql.Driver");
            sqlcon = DriverManager.getConnection(URL, user, passwd);
            System.out.println("connected to database");
            stmt = sqlcon.createStatement();
            rset = stmt.executeQuery("SELECT timeofday()");
            rset.next();
            String day = rset.getString(1);
            System.out.println("time: " + day);
```

```
        rset = stmt.executeQuery("SELECT pi() AS output");
        rset.next();
        float pival = rset.getFloat("output");
        System.out.println("pi: " + pival);

        rset.close();
        stmt.close();
        sqlcon.close();
    } catch (Exception e) {
        System.out.println("Problem: " + e.getMessage());
    }
  }
}
```

After successfully establishing a connection to the database, the GetVals.java program sends a query using the PostgreSQL timeofday() function. The result is retrieved using a ResultSet object. As mentioned earlier, you must first perform a next() method to get to the first record in the result set. If you attempt to retrieve data from the result set before doing this, you will get a Java exception.

After getting to the first record, you can read the data using the JDBC getxxx() methods. The getxxx() methods allow you to extract data from the result set record using either the integer column number (which starts at 1 for the first column) or the column name (as a case-insensitive String value). The GetVals.java program demonstrates using both methods. Note that for a function, unless the SELECT AS keyword is used, you can only reference the column by number.

The JDBC allows you to extract any PostgreSQL data type as a String value using the getString() method, and will automatically convert the PostgreSQL data type to a string. For advanced data processing, you can match the appropriate Java data type to the PostgreSQL data type (such as getInt(), getFloat(), or getDate()). This allows you to directly handle data retrieved from the result set in equations.

Compiling and running the program produces the following results:

```
C:\test>javac GetVals.java
C:\test>java -classpath c:\test;c:\test\postgresql-8.1-405.jdbc3.jar GetVals
connected to database
time: Tue Oct 10 19:12:53.992000 2006 EDT
pi: 3.1415927

C:\test>
```

Processing Multirecord Result Sets

When using a ResultSet object to process result sets that contain multiple records, you must loop through the result set records using the next() method. The next() method will return a TRUE Boolean value while there is another record to retrieve. If you are at the end of the result set, the next () method will return a FALSE value. The easiest way to loop through result set data is to use a while () loop:

```
while(rset.next())
{
    ...
}
```

When the last record has been processed, the while () loop exits. This is demonstrated in the GetBidders.java program:

```java
import java.sql.*;
public class GetBidders {
    private String URL = "jdbc:postgresql://127.0.0.1/test";
    private String user = "earl";
    private String passwd = "auction";

    private Connection sqlcon = null;
    private Statement sqlstmt = null;
    private ResultSet sqlrset = null;

    public GetBidders() {
        String output, lastname, firstname;
        int bidderid;

        try {
            Class.forName("org.postgresql.Driver");
            sqlcon = DriverManager.getConnection(URL, user, passwd);
        } catch (Exception e) {
            System.out.println("Problem: " + e.getMessage());
            System.exit(1);
        }

        try {
            sqlstmt = sqlcon.createStatement();
            sqlrset = sqlstmt.executeQuery("Select * from auction.bidder");

            while (sqlrset.next())
            {
                bidderid = sqlrset.getInt("bidderkey");
                lastname = sqlrset.getString("lastname");
                firstname = sqlrset.getString("firstname");

                output = bidderid + " - " + lastname + "," + firstname;
                System.out.println(output);
            }
            sqlstmt.close();
```

```
        } catch (Exception e) {
            System.out.println("Problem: " + e.getMessage());
        }
    }

    public static void main(String[] args) {
        GetBidders tst = new GetBidders();
    }
}
```

The GetBidders.java program also demonstrates an alternative way of creating a Java application. The program code is defined in a class constructor:

```
public GetBidders {
...
}
```

Since the program is in the class constructor, the main() method (which is automatically run by the JVM by default) must create an instance of the class:

```
public static void main(String[] args) {
    GetBidders tst = new GetBidders();
}
```

When the new instance is created, the program code in the constructor is executed. The program uses the standard methods for loading the JDBC driver and connecting to the PostgreSQL server. Next, the SELECT query is sent using the executeQuery() method. Data in the ResultSet object is processed within the while() loop. For each record, the bidderkey, lastname, and firstname columns are extracted, based on their column names.

Using Parameters and Prepared Statements

The JDBC programming interface also allows for using parameters within prepared SQL statements. The PreparedStatement class allows you to create a SQL command that is sent to the PostgreSQL server to be prepared ahead of execution.

The PreparedStatement class can save execution time when you must execute the same SQL command multiple times. Even better, the statement can contain variables that are replaced at execution time. This allows you to create a single generic SQL command, send it to the PostgreSQL server as a PreparedStatement object, then execute the command multiple times with different data.

The variables used in the PreparedStatement object are replaced with question marks:

```
PreparedStatement ps = null;
String command = "UPDATE auction.item set bidderkey = ?, finalbid = ? WHERE";
command = command + "itemkey = ?";
ps = sqlcon.prepareStatement("SELECT * from auction.bidder where bidderkey = ?");
```

The three variables are each represented using question marks as placeholders. The actual variables are defined using the setxxx() methods of the PreparedStatement class.

Each variable must be set using the proper data type format of the setxxx() method:

▼ setInt() for integer data types

■ setFloat() for float data types

▲ setString() for String data types

The setxxx() methods take two parameters:

```
ps.setInt(1, biddervalue);
```

The first parameter is an integer representing the order in which the variable appears in the PreparedStatement, starting at 1. The second parameter is the value that is assigned to the variable. This value must be in the same data type as the setxxx() method.

The UpdateItem.java program demonstrates using a PreparedStatement object with variables to update the Items table with the winning bidder and final bid values:

```
import java.io.*;
import java.sql.*;

public class UpdateItem {

public static void main(String[] args) {
    String URL = "jdbc:postgresql://127.0.0.1/test";
    String user = "earl";
    String passwd = "auction";
    Connection sqlcon = null;
    PreparedStatement ps = null;
    String command = "UPDATE auction.item set bidderkey = ?, finalbid = ? WHERE
itemkey = ?";
    DataInput in = new DataInputStream(System.in);
    String itemkey, input;
    int bidderkey, result;
    float finalbid;

    try {
        Class.forName("org.postgresql.Driver");
        sqlcon = DriverManager.getConnection(URL, user, passwd);
        System.out.println("connected to database");
        ps = sqlcon.prepareStatement(command);

        while (true)
        {
            System.out.print("Enter item key: ");
            itemkey = in.readLine();
            if (itemkey.equals("exit"))
                break;
```

```
            System.out.print("Enter winning bidder: ");
            input = in.readLine();
            bidderkey = Integer.parseInt(input);
            System.out.print("Enter winning bid: ");
            input = in.readLine();
            finalbid = Float.parseFloat(input);
            ps.setInt(1, bidderkey);
            ps.setFloat(2, finalbid);
            ps.setString(3, itemkey);

            result = ps.executeUpdate();
            System.out.println("updated " + result + " record");
         }
      ps.close();
      sqlcon.close();
      } catch (Exception e) {
         System.out.println("Problem: " + e.getMessage());
      }
   }
}
```

By now you should recognize most of the UpdateItem.java program. After the usual connectivity stuff, a PreparedStatement object is created. The SQL command contains three variables: one to identify the updated bidderkey column value, one to identify the updated finalbid column value, and one to be used to search for the proper itemkey value in the table so that the proper record is updated.

After the PreparedStatement object is created, a while() loop is used to continually ask the user to enter new information. If the user enters the word exit for the itemkey value, the while() loop is exited and the program stops.

After retrieving the values input by the user, the program converts the values to the appropriate data types for insertion into the Item table, assigns them to the appropriate variables for the PreparedStatement object, then executes the PreparedStatement object using the executeUpdate() method.

Similar to a normal Statement object, the PreparedStatement object contains both the executeUpdate() and executeQuery() methods. Since this SQL command is an UPDATE command, the executeUpdate() method is used.

After compiling the program, enter some data into the Item table using the pgAdmin III data editor (see Chapter 4). Be sure to leave empty the winning bidder and final bid column values. Run the UpdateItem program and enter a few values. After entering a few valid values, try entering values for an invalid itemkey. To end the program, enter exit as the next itemkey:

```
C:\test>java -classpath c:\test;c:\test\postgresql-8.1-405.jdbc3.jar UpdateItem
connected to database
Enter item key: SC002
Enter winning bidder: 100
Enter winning bid: 240.00
updated 1 record
```

```
Enter item key: TR001
Enter winning bidder: 101
Enter winning bid: 575
updated 1 record
Enter item key: SC010
Enter winning bidder: 100
Enter winning bid: 10.00
updated 0 record
Enter item key: exit

C:\test>
```

As the program executes, enter the appropriate Item `itemkey` value, the winning bidder `bidderkey` value, then the winning bid `finalbid` value. As seen in the example, if the `itemkey` value is valid, the output indicates that the record was updated. If the `itemkey` value is invalid, no records are updated. After entering data for a few items, type **exit** to quit the program. You can use the pgAdmin III program to view the data in the table to ensure that the proper data was updated.

SUMMARY

The JDBC library provides a standard set of classes for Java applications to access databases. PostgreSQL provides the necessary JDBC driver for Java applications to access a PostgreSQL server.

The PostgreSQL JDBC driver comes in three versions, one for older Java 2 Standard Edition environments (versions 1.2 and 1.3), one for newer Java 2 Standard Edition environments (versions 1.4 and 1.5), and one for the Java 2 Enterprise Edition environment. All of these JDBC drivers can be downloaded from the PostgreSQL JDBC web site or installed with the PostgreSQL server installation package.

Once the PostgreSQL JDBC driver is included with a Java application, you can use standard JDBC database classes to connect to the PostgreSQL server, insert, update, or delete data, or retrieve query information. Query information can be read as a single result set returned from the server. Individual columns can be accessed from each result set record using either the column name or the column index value. SQL commands can also be sent to the PostgreSQL server as prepared statements. The server will prepare an execution plan for the statement before the statement is actually executed. This can greatly increase the performance of applications. This feature also allows you to create SQL commands with variables that can be replaced at run time as the program is executed.

At this point you should be comfortable installing, configuring, and programming a PostgreSQL server in a Microsoft Windows environment. Many different topics have been discussed in the last 15 chapters, but there is always more to learn. The Open Source database world in general, and PostgreSQL in particular, is constantly evolving. New features are being added with each new update and version. I strongly encourage you to frequently visit the PostgreSQL web site (www.postgresql.org) and actively participate in the many user forums available.

INDEX

B

D

O

▼ P

Q

R

S

U

V

W

X

Z